African American Southerners in
Slavery, Civil War and Reconstruction

African American Southerners in Slavery, Civil War and Reconstruction

by

CLAUDE H. NOLEN

McFarland & Company, Inc., Publishers

Jefferson, North Carolina, and London

Library of Congress cataloguing data are available

Nolen, Claude H.
African American southerners in slavery,
Civil War, and Reconstruction /
by Claude H. Nolen.
p.   cm.
Includes bibliographical references and index.
ISBN 0-7864-0967-3 (illustrated case binding : 50# alkaline paper) ∞
1. African Americans—Southern States—History—19th century.
2. African Americans—Southern States—Social conditions—19th century.
3. Slaves—Southern States—History—19th century.
4. Slaves—Southern States—Social conditions—19th century.
5. Slavery—Southern States—History—19th century.
6. United States—History—Civil War, 1861–1865—African Americans.
7. Southern States—History—1775–1865.
8. Reconstruction.
9. Southern States—Social conditions—19th century.
10. Southern States—Race relations.
I. Title.
E185.6.N83   2001
975'.00496073—dc21   2001030568

British Library cataloguing data are available

On the cover: "Croppers" picked cotton by hand until replaced by mechanical
pickers in the twentieth century. Julian A.C. Chandler and others, editors,
The History of the Southern States: The South in the Building of the Nation,
12 Vols. (Richmond, VA, 1909, Vol. III, 429.

Manufactured in the United States of America

*McFarland & Company, Inc., Publishers
Box 611, Jefferson, North Carolina 28640
www.mcfarlandpub.com*

For Jeanne
and Cosette, Andrée, Denise, Adrienne, Hunter, and Lisa

Contents

Acknowledgments

I am grateful to my wife Jeanne for her many contributions in the making of this book. Denise and John Sommer helped me get and use a computer and provided assistance in other ways. Adriana Martinez, Monique Sommer, Andy Coles and Kelly Smoot helped with the bibliography. Cosette Coles, Adrienne Sudolsky and Hunter Nolen helped with the index. Eileen Shocket, librarian, and her associates, made the resources of St. Edward's University Library readily accessible. Melondy West typed the final draft. The American Philosophical Society awarded me a grant from its Penrose Fund for a summer's research and St. Edward's University provided a semester off.

Introduction

In the seventeenth century the American colonists created a society with a thrust toward freedom, yet entangled with slavery. In the eighteenth century they made progress toward a more perfect freedom by founding a new nation on the proposition that all men are created equal. Although slavery was abolished in the northern states during the era of the American Revolution, it was left intact in the South, where it was more deeply entrenched. A strong movement to eradicate bondage from the entire nation soon gained momentum and at last provoked slaveholders, except those in the border states of Missouri, Kentucky, Maryland, and Delaware, into founding the Confederacy. Defenders of the Union then went to war against the Confederacy, opening the way for antislavery people, especially slaves themselves, to demand the complete abolition of slavery. Without the support of Southern blacks it is doubtful that the Union could have defeated the Confederacy. In consequence, Unionists were led to change their aim from preserving the old Union to establishing a new Union free at last from slavery.

Southern blacks were great agents of the advancement of freedom during the critical era of Civil War and Reconstruction. In the 1840s and 1850s they maintained their dignity and a measure of independence within the tyranny of slavery and struggled and prayed for freedom. During the cataclysm of war they helped, as collaborators and soldiers, to transform the Union Army into the Army of Liberation. As freedmen in the years of Reconstruction they endeavored to gain the rights of citizens and consolidate their strength for future crusades against remaining vestiges of slavery.

PART ONE

LAST DECADES OF SLAVERY

1

Cabins and Quarters; Food and Clothing

In the final years of slavery, as in the preceding two centuries, slaves endured hardship and oppression and where possible humanized their condition, including building communities in the quarters and expressing themselves in everything they touched.

Slave cabins clustered in a square, rectangle, semicircle, or scattered here and there, made up the "quarters," the slaves' plantation neighborhood. On a Simpson County, Mississippi, plantation the cabins hugged the manor house, except for the stockmen's, which were close to the barn. On another Mississippi plantation the cabins formed a semicircle a hundred yards from the big house but still in full view of the master in his chair on the front gallery, from where he surveyed his domain. Cabins on a third place were out of sight of the big house, but the cook's cabin was placed up close, in the master's backyard. Streets separated rows of cabins. On a short street of a modest place a few cabins might house a couple with small children, a grandmother, and an aunt or two. On a big place cabins would be strung along both sides of a mile-long street.[1] Some quarters would hardly make a village but row upon row of cabins along wagon-wide streets on a South Carolina plantation practically made a town. A big place near Shreveport, Louis-iana, had, besides 50 cabins in five rows of 10 cabins each, a spinning house, smoke-house, blacksmith shop, nursery for slave children, numerous sheds, and the master's house.[2]

However rude their quarters, slaves could create, within the limits of thrall-dom, relatively pleasant communities in them. In one such community slaves would gather after a hard day's work to refresh themselves: rest under trees, hum and sing to the tune of an old guitar, tell stories. Late in the evening while strolling along a street in her quarters young Harriet Payne enjoyed the aroma of good things cooking coming from the open doors of the cabins. Such everyday activities, as well as the great events of marriage, birth, and death, endowed the quarters with dignity.[3]

Most cabins were one-room log structures, no more than 20 feet by 20 feet, with a door and window; a plank, log-slab, or dirt floor; a wood-shingle roof; and a stick-and-mud fireplace. A rough-hewn plank door, suspended on wooden or leather hinges, was barred from within. The one window, without glass pane or screen, was protected by a wooden shutter. In winter, with shutter and door closed, the fireplace was the source of fluctuating heat and flickering light. Chink and daub filled cracks between the logs. The logs

5

Quarters such as these on a Louisiana sugar plantation provided the setting for the plantation slave community. *Harper's New Monthly Magazine*, Vol. VII, No. XLII (November 1853), 753.

years, from first cabin to last, to fit all the cabins on a Texas plantation with slab floors.[4]

The shell of a cabin could be built from ground up at a "house raising," with the cabin to be completed sometime later. Logs would have been cut, dragged by mules or oxen to the building site, and hewed on two sides with a broad-ax, with the other two sides left unfinished. At the house raising ax-men would notch the logs to make them fit together securely, and eight or ten men, with lively accompaniment of shouts and song, would hoist the logs into place, laying them along the sides of a square, until the cabin's walls were raised. Openings would be cut for the door, window, and fireplace. Finally, topped with shingles or thatch,

themselves were split or hewed and notched on ends, one resting upon another to build up the four walls. Pole rafters supported a roof of wood shingles or thatch.

When a plantation was first established slaves cut, split, and hewed logs for the manor house, cabins, barns, and sheds. Meanwhile they cleared woodlands for fields, built fences, dug wells, and planted crops. With so much to be done earthen floors served until the men found time, if they ever did find time, to cover the dirt floors with puncheon slabs. It required two chinked and daubed, and fitted with a door, window shutter, fireplace, and dirt or slab floor, the cabin was ready for occupancy. Celebration with food, music, and dancing might compensate the workmen and honor their achievement.

An important adjunct to a cabin was the fireplace. Approximately eight feet wide, it provided heat and light. Live coals were banked in it summer and winter for new fires. Pots and pans hung on hooks, ready at hand, and a portable oven, poker, and tongs stood in their places. Roaring fires could warm the cabin and light it "bright as sunshine," as Vinnie Busby remembered, but could ignite straw and sticks in the chimney. If a chimney caught fire, it was pushed down and away with poles to save the cabin. Bricks rather than flammable sticks, straw, and mud were sometimes used in fireplace-chimney construction, as in Jasper Battle's cabin on a Georgia plantation.[5]

There were variations from the usual log cabin. On a James River plantation slaves had stable-like apartments, six of them for families, and one each for single men and single women. Monroe Brackins lived in a "little, old picket house" on a Hondo River ranch in Texas, and Gabriel Gilbert's New Iberia, Louisiana, cabin had walls of upright posts connected with pickets sheathed with mud. On a Harrison County, Mississippi, plantation slave houses were solid, brick structures. A place near Sparta, Georgia, like other regions of abundant pine forests and sawmills, had cabins of frame lumber. A Kentucky master provided ten stone huts served by water piped several hundred yards from a spring to barrels in front of the huts, but he locked his slaves in each night with iron bars slipped through rungs on doors and windows.[6]

On some plantations slave dwellings were kept in good repair. Mand Morrow lived in a stout cabin near Georgetown, Texas, that had regular windows, a good wood floor, and hand-made chairs; her grandfather was an enterprising carpenter. Thrifty slaves, not the indolent, kept up their houses, said the Reverend Squire Dowd, himself an ex-slave. Thoughtful slaveholders would cooperate with thrifty slaves. Elvie Herrin's master provided her with a cabin that was good and warm, "a heap better than the houses" she occupied when free.[7]

Many cabins were rundown. Masters were negligent and slaves could see no bright future in the quarters, and their labor was demanded not in cabin upkeep but in planting, tilling, and harvesting cotton and corn. For whatever reason, Marion Johnson's cabin was so dilapidated that while lying on her bed she could count the stars through gaps in the logs. Henry Daniels could, he said, throw a dog "by the heels" through "de cracks" in his house. Frederick Law Olmsted visited a plantation in North Mississippi where the cabins were dilapidated and dingy and without "windows which, indeed, would have been a superfluous luxury, for there were spaces of several inches between the logs, through which there was unobstructed vision."[8]

Families, large or small, often cooked, ate, and slept in one room. Dave Walker's family lived in one big room; the children rolled on the floor before the fire and slept under the adults' bed. Eighteen men, 10 women, seven children, and two half-grown boys lived in four houses on the Polk plantation in Mississippi. George Patterson, his parents, and his 17 brothers and sisters occupied a one-room cabin, with a dirt floor, on a South Carolina plantation. Wash Anderson recalled that two or three families sometimes lived in a single cabin of one room on a Texas place. In the Bayou Boeuf Country of Louisiana John Tibeats put Solomon, Eliza, and Bristol in the same cabin with Lawson and his wife Mary.[9]

The cramped and flimsy cabin sheltered unstable but for the most part cherished family life. *Harper's*, Vol. VII, No. XLII (November 1853), 754.

Lucky families had two- or three-room houses. A plantation near Montgomery, Alabama, had row houses two stories high. Georgia Baker's family lived in a three-room house on a Georgia plantation. The children slept in one room and their parents in another, with a kitchen separating the bedrooms. Hannah Plummer's plank house in North Carolina had three rooms and a porch, and James Tubbs's two-room log cabin in Arkansas was equipped with a double fireplace in which, he said, were baked the most delicious ash cakes. James V. Deane's Maryland cabin had a large room, a room above that, and windows in both rooms. On a Mississippi plantation families were housed in good cabins with two rooms and a loft, and a gallery in front. Near each cabin were a chicken house and a pig sty.[10]

In the city masters and slaves usually lived close together on relatively small lots. The slaves' house was likely to be in the backyard and, designed to emphasize bondage, was long and narrow, facing the back, without windows opening on the street, and with living quarters above a bottom floor of stables and storerooms. Three rooms of 10 by 15 feet would, perhaps, be joined by a balcony. Furniture was scarce. The whole compound would be enclosed by walls. Urban slaves hired out by their owners or permitted to hire themselves out lived in sheds, basements, attics, single rooms, even alleys and warehouses. Shabby as these places might be they offered escape from jail-like compounds.[11]

Cabins were furnished with make-do beds, chairs, and tables. Bed frames might be nailed to walls on one side and supported by one or two legs on the other side. Homemade ropes laced through the frame would support a tick filled with cotton, cornshucks, straw, or moss. Sometimes a mat of oak splits was placed between tick and cords. A piece of canvass attached to a wall on one side and to a couple of legs on the other served Louis Davis, and Harriet Barrett had a deerskin stretched over posts and covered with moss for a bed. Others slept on boards supported by braces and connected to a wall, with a sack stuffed with grass for a mattress. A Texas family drove forked saplings into their dirt floor to support high bunks for the children and low ones for the adults. Some children slept in half-lofts, others on the floor on pallets or in trundle beds. Charlie Meadow slept on a tick filled with straw in summer and feathers in winter, but Lizzie Williams had only a quilt spread on the dirt floor. Other children lay on pallets in winter but in summer slept wherever they dropped-in the grass, under trees, in a barn or shuckhouse. "It didn't make no difference to nobody where I happened to drop off to sleep," Sylvia Floyd said. Sena Moore slept on the floor and fought off chinches, fleas, and mosquitoes. Quilts were common but pillows were scarce. "Pillows! Dem days us never knowed what pillows was," Georgia Baker exclaimed.[12]

Benches, boxes, and blocks of wood served for tables and chairs, although a skillful father, such as Molly Ammonds's father, might make a sturdy table, and chairs with cane bottoms for his family. Nap Mc-

Queen's family possessed a set of chairs with white oak bottoms. Frank Patterson's family sat at their homemade table on a plank bench for adults and blocks of wood for children. George Green's chair was a box, and Richard Carruthers's was a chunk of cordwood.[13]

Boxes and chests served for storage as well as for tables and chairs. Clothes not packed in such containers were hung from pegs on the wall. Plates and trays and utensils were made from tin or sawed and carved from wood, preferably from oak and cypress. Baskets were woven from white oak splits. Dirt floors were swept with brooms made with sage or other brush at hand; wood floors were scrubbed with shuck mops, sand, and water. Candles, pine knot torches, and fireplaces gave light. Augustus Robinson used candles, but Laura Montgomery supposed candles were reserved for whites. Children gathered pine knots to make torches by which their mothers would spin and sew.[14]

Wooden buckets and barrels, baskets, and gourds held water, molasses, and other goods. Dippers were made from small round gourds with long necks. A hole of about three inches in diameter was cut in such a gourd when mature but still green, seeds and pulp removed, and the dipper hung up to dry. Dried, then scalded and scoured, it was ready for use. Water from a gourd tasted good and sweet, said Laura Ford, "de water sparkles from de round rough bowl makin' it seem lak yo' is a drinkin' from a mossy spring right out ob de ground." A large round gourd could hold several gallons of water, or be used to store quantities of food. Grease was saved in "fat gourds." Besides making dippers, torches, soap, mops, brooms, and buckets for household use, slave families also carved wash tubs from logs and tree stumps.[15]

In contrast to the cabin, the manor house, usually designed to emphasize the distinction between master and servant, ranged from grand to simple, from mansion to shanty. A big house on a Mississippi River plantation in Louisiana might rival George Washington's Mount Vernon and Thomas Jefferson's Monticello, but a typical manor house, though substantial for its day, was not very grand. Such a house would be, perhaps, 60 feet long and 20 feet wide, of hewn logs sheathed in plank siding. A wide hall would be flanked on each side by several rooms; a gallery would stretch the length of the building; and a brick chimney would stand at each end of the house. The kitchen would be detached. An avenue bordered by oaks would lead to the house.

Vinnie Busby's master had a fine two story house kept "jes so" by a corps of house servants and gardeners. Nathan Best's master's house was white, two storied, with a long hall, big dining room, and columns ornamenting the front. But James Reeves's mistress lived in a simple log house of four rooms and a hall, and Tom Holland's master's house of two rooms and a hall had deer skins tacked over the doorway to keep out wind and rain. A slaveholder in Mississippi occupied a cabin just like the cabins in the quarters.[16]

Slaves needed plenty of good food to maintain health and energy in a discipline of hard labor. But they were likely to be provided with monotonous, and sometimes short rations. Planters distributed basic salt pork, cornmeal, and molasses, and perhaps supplements of fruit and vegetables, usually at weekly intervals. Slaves made up what was lacking in their rations with produce from their gardens, nuts and berries, fish and game, and, for some, whatever they could "take."

On a Mississippi plantation the head of each family drew weekly for each member of the family three pounds of pork, one peck of meal, and, from January to July, one quart of molasses. Monthly, he received one pound of tobacco and four pints of salt.

No drink was provided except to ditchers working in water, who were given a glass of whiskey daily. Families on this place had gardens from which they ate and made money and some chickens and a few hogs, from which they also ate and sold. These slaves were able to buy from their master a barrel of flour once a year, and, illicitly, some liquor and small luxuries from neighboring poor whites. They also trapped a good amount of game.[17]

On a plantation near Ashby Gap, Virginia, each family received ten pounds of cornmeal, a quart of blackstrap molasses, six pounds of fatback, three pounds of flour, and a quantity of vegetables — all produced on the place. Game and fish, vegetables raised in each family's garden, and chicken and eggs from each family's small flock made up the balance of the diet. Frank Patterson's family received, in addition to its usual weekly rations of meat, meal, and molasses, a few pounds of flour or wheat shorts on Sundays. Dicey Thomas's family was issued an additional supply of sweet potatoes, while Della Briscoe's family received supplements of milk. Celeste Avery's rations of cornmeal, meat, and vegetables included a little fruit at Christmas. Ebenezer Brown's master handed out each Saturday a "lil'l flour, rice, peas, meat, an' meal" and "iffen de rashuns giv out 'fore next Saturday — well, dat wus too bad, fur yo' had ter do wid out."[18] George Taylor's master allotted seven pounds of meat per week for a man, six pounds for a woman, and five pounds for a child. Prince Smith's master distributed six quarts of corn per grown man and four quarts for young men. Although Henry Walker had plenty to eat, he winced at the indignity his people suffered when the master called them up by horn and dished out their rations.[19]

Provident masters raised a variety of food crops and herds of cattle and hogs to feed their slaves. Vinnie Busby recalled that on their place, "wid all de wuk and hardships deir wuz alwas plenty some 'en to eat."[20] To supply meat for his people one planter slaughtered from 300 to 400 hogs each fall and winter. Some of the men killed the animals, others scalded and scraped the carcasses, still others cut the meat and rendered the lard. Children kept hickory chips smoldering to make smoke for curing the meat. The slaves were given chitterlings, backbones, spareribs, shoulders, ears, pickled feet, and sidemeat. If pork ran out, turkey and deer were hunted or a goat or steer butchered. On the Ebenezer plantation in North Carolina slaves were issued a wide variety of vegetables, fruits, and meats to maintain health and energy, and sugar and coffee and other small luxuries to lift the spirit.[21] Slaves who had the same food as their masters doubtless ate best. On some plantations the cook prepared, except on special occasions, identical meals for both master and servants. On other places house servants would sit at table after their masters had dined and, despite this sign of their inferior status, enjoy the better meals of the manor house.[22]

Some masters let their slaves go hungry. When rations ran out, Mattie Gilmore "jus' went lank."[23] Field hands had better eat whatever they got, however unappetizing, said Tines Kendricks, because they would not get anything more from their stingy master and mistress. Sarah Gudger was worked so hard and fed so little that when all were asleep she would walk barefoot, even in the snow, to her grandmother's house two miles away for a piece of corn pone, a slice of meat, and some milk. Other ill-fed slaves would sneak at night to neighboring places to beg from their more fortunate friends.[24]

Some slaves resorted to theft to get what they had to have and were cheated out of. Charlie Crump's master, who sought to grow richer by keeping his slaves on spare rations, and who said that "empty niggers am good niggers an' dat full niggers has

got de debil in dem," was paid back when his starved slaves retaliated by "taking" a chicken, a pig, or a calf.[25] Annie Row's family, never given enough to eat, also felt obliged to "steal" to make up for rations unjustly held back. Whenever Lula Jackson became burned out on the rations her "awful master" doled out, she would steal one of his pigs. Julius Jones's father took food for his hungry children and hid them under the bed to eat it. A Tennessee family would share a pig, a mess of potatoes, or whatever it managed to get hold of, with their hungry neighbors. When poorly fed slaves failed to work well, they were whipped, and when caught stealing food necessary for hard work they were whipped again. Thus Sarah Ashby's family stored in a box hidden under the fireplace food they felt forced to steal. Wes Brady's women-folk slipped "flour siftin's from Missy's kitchen," and Mary Raines "took" but did not "steal" jams, biscuits, and butter.[26]

On some plantations slaves obtained their vegetables from one big garden for all. In one such garden slave boys were joined by the master's sons in pulling the plow, because the skittish horse trampled the growing plants. Although families received allotments from the plantation garden, they might raise additional vegetables on their own. Usually, families tended gardens next to their cabins, or in their allotted plots in the "nigger field" set aside for gardens; the "nigger field" might also contain land for a money crop for the slaves. Prince Smith's people had a separate garden, along with a place for chickens, and Sam Mitchell's folks were allotted a piece of land in the field and a place for one pig.[27] Families raised " a heap of stuff" in their fence-corner gardens and did better, Henry Lee believed, than they did years later when they "got figured clean out" by the sharecrop system. On many places the slaves' garden produce kept their tables full until the hard days of the Civil War. They cultivated their vegetable, "tater," melon, and goober patches at odd times, even in moonlight.[28]

Although a daily round of salt pork, greens, corn bread, and molasses could become, to say the least, unexciting, slight variations in diet might stimulate dulled tastes. "Ash roasted 'taters and groundpeas was de best somepin t'eat," according to one slave, while others relished sweet potato pudding, molasses corn bread, and "tater" biscuits. Still others loved biscuits baked in a three-legged skillet with live coals on the lid, and cracklin' bread, "de sweet savor of life." Some looked forward to fresh meat when neighboring planters slaughtered in their turn hogs, sheep, or beeves and sent around portions, some of which fell to the slaves.[29]

The most delicious meals were prepared for Sundays and holidays. Workers might anticipate all week good biscuits on Sunday mornings. Charity Jones remembered biscuits baked in a community oven in the yard: "Dey pulled de fire out'n de oven an' den put big pans of biscuits and bread in dere an' when dey came out dey tasted like cake."[30] Christmas dinner would be the best of the year. On that day a master might slip the people some liquor to go with turkey, fish, ham, baked yams, apple pie, pound cake, raisins, coffee, and popcorn. The plainest fare on some places would include, from hogs slaughtered around Christmas, hogshead, lights, chitterlings, and pigfeet, along with flour, sugar, and coffee. At least a big fat hen, hogshead, game, bread, pastries, coffee, and other treats would grace all but the meanest table.[31]

Families regularly cooked their food in fireplaces, using a long-handled iron skillet with three legs and a tight-fitting lid, and pots hanging from a crane over the fire. Cleaned and shined, the pots "sho was pretty hangin' dar in dat big old fireplace," thought Georgia Baker.[32] Much of the food was boiled, baked, or fried. Greens and

sweet potatoes were boiled. Meat was most often boiled or fried. Bread and potatoes were baked in fireplace ovens, or, for the whole plantation community, outdoors in large clay or brick ovens. Betty Powers's mother, a field worker, cooked for her family of 14 in the cabin in winter and outdoors in summer. She fixed breakfast before daylight and supper, after a day in the field, by the light of a pine torch.[33]

On one South Carolina plantation meals for the quarters were cooked in a large, round clay oven in the yard on Wednesdays and Saturdays. However, a "taken" chicken could be baked surreptitiously in the field. It would be cleaned, wrapped in clay with feathers unplucked, put in a hole in the ground, and covered with hot coals. When done, the feathers fell away when the clay shell was broken.[34]

On some places food was kept cool in containers partially immersed in spring water. A big place might have an ice house constructed of two layers of brick separated by charcoal insulation. A door at the top would reduce the loss of cold air. Ice was cut in winter from frozen lakes and ponds, stored in the ice house, and covered with cotton seed or sawdust. Precious ice in summer was reserved for the white folks, except when needed to cool the fever-stricken of all ranks.[35]

The central kitchen was a focus of work and art, of sustenance and pleasure. It had a fragrance of good things to eat, cakes, ham and chicken, greens, sweet potatoes, and corn bread. Minnie Davis's mother, an accomplished cook, practiced her art in the great kitchen on the John Crawford plantation, Greene County, Georgia, where she made "beautiful biscuits" and cakes, and baked the "most delicious fish."[36]

Many slave women were resourceful cooks. They made tasty ash cakes as standard fare from a batter of cornmeal, water (or milk, if they had any), salt, and baking powder (made from corn cobs). They shaped the batter into cakes of about nine inches in diameter and one inch thick and wrapped the cakes in collard leaves or left them bare and placed them on a swept, hot spot in the fireplace. If bare they were allowed to become firm and dry, so that ashes would not stick to them, before being covered with hot ashes. When done, and the ashes brushed off, they were "sho fitten to eat." Tilda Johnson pleased her master with ash cakes made with meal, sour milk, and sorghum molasses and served with butter and cold buttermilk.[37]

Tilda's plain dinners consisted of boiled meat, greens, corn bread, milk, and perhaps fish or game. But when the master had guests she often roasted a pig and served the roast pig with an apple in its mouth and surrounded by red pigs' feet jelly. Tilda not only prepared fine dishes, she chopped the wood needed for cooking, gathered chips and pine cones to brighten the fire, and carried water up the hill, one pail on her head and another in each hand. Mary Joiner was proud of her fried chicken and Millie Young recommended her persimmon loaf.[38] Granny Lee made, she said, a great squirrel pie, and Ellen Gooden boasted that she was the best "coon cooker" there was.[39] Della Buckley knew how to turn a 'possum, baked with sweet potatoes, into a good meal for her eager family. William Wheeler's persimmon beer with corn bread crumbled in it, was, he said, something extra special.[40]

When Millie Boyd loaded the table in the big house with good things to eat prepared by the accomplished cook and served in dishes from "across the water," she wore a polka-dot dress, a white apron, and a white turban. Standing by were a boy to fan away the flies and a girl to fill the glasses from a side table with wine and mint julep. Millie served six kinds of meat pies; sauces, relishes, and pickles; and cakes of every kind.[41]

A hungry slave would relish a well-cooked meal, though it might be quite plain:

> When horn blows for dinner
> I goes up on de meatskins
> I comes down on de pone —
> I hits de corn pone fifty licks,
> and makes dat butter moan.[42]

Cooks often had multiple duties. Isom Weathersby's mother not only was the head cook, she was responsible also for the young children while their mothers worked in the fields. She could, said Isom, easily manage a gang of children, and when she took a child in her lap and sang a lullaby the child would just naturally go to sleep.[43]

Many slaves who took their meals in their cabins on weekends were fed from the central kitchen on workdays. They would perhaps assemble in a mess hall or in a room in the big house. On pretty days they would eat at long tables under the trees. On a South Carolina plantation the main meal was prepared out in the fields so the workers would lose little time at the noon break. On many places breakfast was brought to the fields on carts after sunup to hands who had been at work since daylight. Pails distributed from the carts and hung on fences until a food break contained corn bread, greens, cow peas, meat, molasses, and such like. Sometimes the pails held little more than collards in collard time and potatoes in potato time. Slaves called in from the fields to dine at the big house, as Liza Strickland's people were, could expect good food carefully prepared by skilled cooks, such as house servants usually enjoyed. Town slaves, working at home or abroad, were generally better fed than country slaves.[44]

Children too young for field work were fed together, except on weekends and holidays when they joined their families at mealtime. These children were supervised by an older woman helped by bigger children.

A skilled cook was prized by the plantation community. *Harper's*, Vol. XLIX, No. CCXCII (September 1874), 465.

They were relatively well fed in terms of quantity. One master would come along at meals and ask the children, "Has everybody got 'nuf t'eat 'cause I don't want nobody to go hungry at my house."[45] Some children were left by their mothers with the old nurse before daylight. The mothers worked in the fields until dark and then, bone weary, picked up their children and fixed them supper before putting them to bed. Nursing mothers would come out of the fields at midmorning, noon, and midafternoon to nurse their babies, or have the babies brought to them. An old nurse, retired perhaps from the big house or the fields, ran the day-care center. Some mothers took their babies to the fields and kept them on blankets in a fence corner or in cradles suspended from a tree limb, and watched by older children. When the babies cried their mothers would take a break to nurse or comfort them.[46]

The children's diet consisted of variations of corn bread, vegetables, meat, milk, and molasses. Squire Irvin had mush and milk; greens, pot liquor, and corn bread; and rabbit, 'coon, 'possum, and fish. Mary Jane Mooreman had in a steady round buttermilk, corn bread, and fat meat. Israel Jackson remembered greens and milk but no meat. Benny Dillard was given meat when he was big enough to work in the fields. Harriet Miller ate corn bread and pot liquor at noon, and clabber sweetened with molasses in the evening; John Belcher had grits for breakfast, pot liquor and bread for dinner, and nothing, unless a piece of bread, for supper. But an old nurse saw that Ned Chaney had peas, greens, potatoes, and dumplings. Alex Montgomery punched a hole in his bread and filled it with molasses to make it like cake. Lewis Jefferson, in with the cook, got a treat of sweet potato cooked with 'possum before the 'possum made it out of the kitchen. On one place little ones wore a piece of bacon tied on a string around their necks to serve as a pacifier.[47]

Some children ate their milk-soaked corn bread from wooden bowls, with mussel shells for spoons. Others joined small groups around a big tray. Still others used tin plates. Many children ate from troughs filled with bread and milk or bread and pot liquor. On one plantation girls lined up on one side of a feed trough and boys on the other. A nurse with a long stick kept them

in order. A negligent nurse on another place allowed those who ate the fastest to get the most. On a place where dogs competed with the children, the children shoveled in the food, said Lizzie Williams, "'cause de dogs would get it all if we didn't."[48]

More fortunate children were given bowls and spoons, and could sit and eat where they pleased. One of these children, Mahalia Shores, said, "We had all the meat we could eat and all the milk we could drink."[49] On Sunday mornings Mary Anderson's master required the slave children, bathed and dressed, to take breakfast at his house so that he could evaluate their health and prescribe for the sickly. These children enjoyed plenty of fruit from the plantation's large orchard.[50]

Shoemakers often processed the leather they used. A common way they tanned leather was to soak a fresh hide in a trough of water and ashes to loosen the hair for scraping. The scraped hide would be further soaked in water and red oak bark, and hung on poles to dry. The dry hide would be beaten until flexible, and perhaps further softened with a mixture of alum and eggs. The pliable, tanned hide would then be ready to cut into patterns for shoes or other leather goods. Shoe cord was made of horsehair or strands of thread twisted together with beeswax. Tacks to fasten soles to uppers likely were made from maple and sumac wood. If made of wood the soles could outlast several sets of leather uppers.[51]

Tom Huntley's rust-colored, brass-toed shoes could be, he said, outgrown but never worn out. Such shoes were likely to come in three sizes, large, medium, and small, and were designed to fit either foot. Nevertheless, Frances Willis felt quite dressed up in new brass-toed brogans rather than in cast-off white folks' shoes.[52] Some shoemakers made superior boots and shoes for the outside market, and good money for their masters. Planters without shoemakers depended on neighboring slave craftsmen or on shoe companies in the North. A North Carolinian, in 1852, ordered 87 pairs of shoes, sizes 7 to 13, for his slaves. Larnce Holt helped his father, a man of note on his plantation, make white folks' shoes as well as colored folks' shoes, and dye them black with soot. Similarly, women on an Alabama place blackened their red russet shoes for Sunday wear with a mixture of hog gristle and chimney soot.[53]

Many slaves went barefoot to save their shoes for Sundays and cold weather. Others would rather endure stubbed toes and thorn-pierced heels than ill-fitting brogans. People who wore out their shoes early went barefoot until the next issue of shoes. "I's been to de field many a frosty mornin'," said Lizzie Williams, "with rags tied 'round my feet."[54] But Monroe Brackens could not do without shoes and rawhide leggings when punching cows in the thorn-brush country along the Hondo River in Texas. Children often went barefoot, even when their feet cracked raw in winter. Thus Susan Snow thought shoes were for grownups. Frank Patterson got his first pair of shoes when he was sent to the fields at age 12, and July Ann Halfeen was not given shoes until in her teens. Tom Holland was married barefoot.[55]

Many slave women spun and wove cotton, wool, and flax and made clothing for all on the plantation. Some worked with "boughten" bolts of cloth. Others were provided with ready made clothing. Slaves purchased dress-up clothes for Sundays, if they had money.

It was the usual thing for slave women to spend rainy days and slack days of lay-by season and winter in the loom room and attend their spinning machines in the evenings in the cabins. The loom room could be a place of work, song, and visiting. On a large Mississippi plantation regular workers of the loom room were the

handicapped and decrepit, men and women with physical and mental disabilities or unfitted by age for field work. The sole duty of a group of clothiers on a North Carolina plantation was to make women's dresses, men's shirts and pants, cotton and linen sheets, pillow cases, blankets, and other articles of cloth needed on the place. On a small plantation in North Mississippi women whose obligations were many also made in their cabins the everyday clothing for all on the place, and the bed clothes, towels, curtains, and like articles. Here, as on some other places, slaves were allowed to buy Sunday clothes with money they made from the small crops they raised on plots allocated to them.[56]

Makers of cloth and clothing often were mighty workers, or workers driven to extremity. Rachel Bradley could weave eight yards of plain cloth and four yards of jeans, and knit socks, all in a day. Georgia Baker's Aunt Betsy and Aunt Tinney, helped by the older children, labored until 10 at night turning out bolt after bolt of cloth. Sarah Gudger carded and spun until 10 each evening and got up at four the next morning for the day's work in the fields. "I had to plow in de fiels in de day," Lucindy Shaw said, "an den at night when I was so tired I cu'dn't hardly stan' I had to spin my cut of cotton befo' I cu'd go to sleep."[57]

Women dyed their cloth with dyes made from indigo plants, bark of trees, leaves, husks, roots, and berries. Along with blue from indigo, beech bark made a slate color; hickory bark and bay leaves, yellow; gum bark and pine straw, purple; red oak bark, brown; walnut hulls, black; and bamboo or sumac, red. Blends produced other colors. Mammy Rachel, of North Carolina, knew just about everything concerning making dyes from materials at hand, according to Tempie Herndon Durham. She knew every root, bark, leaf, or berry that gives color. She boiled her dyestuff in water, strained the mixture, added vinegar and salt to set the colors, and turned out cloth of every color of the rainbow. Despite the skills of such Rachels a drabness prevailed on some places. Ellen Polk, of Texas, exclaimed, "O Lawd, all de slaves wore de same color clothes."[58]

Women would labor for many hours making a quilt when working alone, but could enhance their production and enjoy one another's company at a quilting party. Similarly, women made blankets, counterpanes, and carpets singly and in groups. They might gather at each other's cabin in turn until all in the party had bed covering for the winter. Women from neighboring plantations sometimes were allowed to come together for quilting parties. Much bed covering was required for the plantations; when a "passel" of women worked together they could meet the demand.[59]

Cloth from the loom room went to make coarse clothing for people of the quarters, principally. But Hannah Austin made clothes for both her master's and her own family, and Mistress Marguerite sewed her slave Mollie's clothes, after Mollie was orphaned. Hannah Hancock's grandmother, too old for fieldwork, was assigned the task of making plain dresses for the women of the plantation. The mistress of the plantation sometimes supervised the sewing of her assembled slave women.[60]

In summertime women often wore uncolored or dark homespun cotton dresses with a full skirt gathered into a tight fitting waist, with a white apron. They went bare legged and barefoot. In winter they wore linsey-woolsey dresses, heavy underclothes, knitted stockings or leggings, and brogans. A long woolen cloth wound around the lower legs served as leggings. Minnie Davis's winter dress was checked linsey over balmoral petticoat and osnaburg drawers; Jane Morgan had a woolen underskirt and a woolen jacket dyed yellow with laurel leaves. But Calline Brown's

"white trash" master kept his few slaves ragged and barefoot, winter and summer.[61]

Everyday outfits for women often included a yarn hood, shawl, a one piece dress, and pantalets (knit stockings from shoetop to knee). Some women had linsey or gingham dresses, but Delia Garlic "never had nothin' but a shimmy an' a slip for a dress, an' it was made out'en de cheapes' cloth dat could be bought; unbleached cloth, coarse, but made to las'."[62] Adeline Marshall wore a plain cotton slip with a string around the neck, every day the year round. Julia Frances Daniels had a one piece garment made from sacking, and no underwear.[63]

On Sundays slave women wore their best dresses, often striped or plaid. The stripes and plaids had the "prettiest colors you ever seed," said Callie Washington, and Lizzie Norfleet thought alternating dark and bright stripes made dresses beautiful. On a Bayou Teche plantation near Opelousas, Louisiana, the women were issued a bolt of blue cloth and white tape to make fancy Sunday dresses: "Us all have de fine drawers down to de ankle, buttoned with pretty white buttons on de bottom."[64] Blue and white beads added style. Some women had dress shoes which they wore on Sundays, never on weekdays. Women carefully packed their fine clothes in a trunk, but hung everyday clothes on wall pegs.[65] On a North Carolina plantation each woman was issued one store-bought dress a year. An Alabama master bought Sunday clothes for his slaves twice a year in Mobile, in July and at Christmastime. Annie Cole, of Mississippi, bought her own dress-up clothes by working at night and on weekends raising a little cotton on a set-aside plot.[66]

Straw hats and bonnets to shield women from the harsh summer sun were made from plaited grasses, wheat straw, or corn shucks, and from cloth. Bull rush grass made good winter bonnets, as did cloth. Some women wore handkerchiefs wrapped around their heads instead of bonnets. Women also wore shawls for warmth and fashion. "A purty young gal dressed in dem sort of clothes" looked "mighty sweet" to Jasper Battle.[67] Some women had combs. Others made do with a corncob or a wire-toothed carding comb. According to Jane Morgan, women carded their hair "caze we never had no combs."[68]

Men wore homespun shirts, dyed trousers, usually jeans, knitted socks, if they had any, a straw or wool hat, and brogans. They also wore overalls, a "round-about" coat, old clothes of their masters, and perhaps their own store-bought clothes. The Reverend Silas Jackson recalled that in summer men wore overalls, muslin shirts, brogans, and straw hats; in winter, home-made woolens. On the Perry plantation in Texas, June 1st was known as straw hat day. Women such as Alice Houston made jeans dyed with copperas and sumac berries for the men. When waiting on his master, Gabe Emmanuel donned his master's old dress suit.[69]

Runaway men in the Mid-South around the middle of the nineteenth century were described as wearing sack or blanket coats, occasionally frock coats; jeans, cotton, or linsey pants; straw, wool, fur, or silk hats; and brogans or boots. When last seen in November, 1847, Lige had on a fur hat, a striped cotton coat, black cloth pants, and boots. Next year, in January, 1848, Dock left wearing a light sack coat, "reddish" pants, and a white wool hat. In February, 1851, Jurden ran off in a blue sack coat, a black cloth cap, and white twill pants. Of three men who escaped in March, 1851, Henry wore a green blanket coat and an old silk hat; Birl had on a gray blanket coat, cloth cap, and black linsey pants; and Bowler was dressed in blue cotton shirt, cloth cap, and black linsey pants. In June, 1851, Jerry had on a round-topped white wool hat, bluejean pants, and brown jean coat. In October, 1851, Tom wore striped linen pants, dark sack coat, and a black hat. In May, 1852, Milton sported a black Kossuth hat, black frock coat, and light kip shoes. In January, 1853, Ned was described as wearing a blue silk plush cap and carrying an umbrella. And in June, 1853, Washington and Wesley were last seen in coat and pants made of bed ticking.[70]

Infants and small children wore dresses. At about age five boys were taken out of dresses and put in shirts that reached to mid-calf; and girls were given one-piece slip-over dresses. At age 12 to 14, boys and girls graduated to adult clothes. The shirt and shift of their childhood were of osnaburg, lowell, linsey-woolsey, or jeans. Some boys were given pants for winter; others were simply put in a second shirt. Most boys and girls had underclothes for winter, but some were skimpily clad only in an outer garment of cotton in summer and of wool in winter. Mattie Curtis went about naked year round until she was 14, she said. Robert Weathersby was provided with pants when he was 14, but only to wear to church on Sundays. Albert Cox got his first pair of pants at fifteen. Some boys, such as Charlie Rigges, were able to put away their long shirts for shirt and pants only when they "got to courting," and Virginia Harris was sixteen before she was given a dress in place of "shirt tails."[71]

2

Religion, Education, Medicine, and Recreation

White clergymen ministering to slaves suppressed the fullness of Christian belief and practice in deference to slaveholders who generally distrusted the effects of religion on slaves and reluctantly permitted the clergy to care for the souls of their bondsmen. Some of the clergy sought to ameliorate the condition and lift the spirit of their charges while others, some of them slaveholders themselves, preached little more than, "Servants, obey your masters!" However distorted, enough of the Christian message got through to affirm the dignity of the slaves and give them hope.

In biracial meetings masters stressed the inferior social status of slaves by relegating them to the back of the church or to the gallery. However, when masters and slaves participated in the same religious service, heard the same Scripture texts and sermons, and were portrayed as people for whom Christ died, social distance maintained by segregated seating could weaken but not nullify the unifying effects of common worship. To make it easier to tailor Christian doctrine to uphold slave society, some masters gathered their slaves in separate meetings to hear homilies exhorting them to be contented with their bondage. Others allowed slaves to govern their own worship, but with a monitor present to

check subversion. Still other masters tolerated unsupervised religious meetings in cabins or brush arbors. A few slaveholders obstructed even very limited religious practice of their slaves. Whether in biracial churches or in praise-and-shout meetings of their own, slaves gained some hope for a better life in this world as well as in the next.

A South Carolina church reserved front pews for local aristocrats, middle pews for common whites, and rear pews, painted blue, for slaves. Arrie Binns and fellow slaves were required to sit in the gallery of the neighborhood white church without looking to the right or to the left. In a Mississippi church blacks and whites were separated by a partition. A slave member of another Mississippi church said, "Dey had us a co'ner fixed to our se'ves."[1] Bondsmen in Abbeville, Louisiana, occupied segregated pews while assisting at Mass. In St. Martin's Church, St. Martinsville, Louisiana, white parishioners received Holy Communion first, free people of color followed, and slaves came last in line. Jane Sutton's master made his slaves accompany his family to the Strong River Baptist Church, but had the white clergyman baptize the slaves apart from whites in the plantation mill creek. Churchgoing slaves usually bathed on

Saturday and wore "preaching clothes," clean, starched, and ironed, to Sunday services. Some slaves attended church in their capacity as servants, to wait on the white folks and "to see 'bout de horses an' buggies an' take 'em water an' keep de fires a gwine if it wuz cole weather."[2]

In some churches attended by both blacks and whites, blacks were segregated at a different service, as on a Mississippi plantation when the white clergyman presided at 11:00 A.M. for whites and at 3:00 P.M. for blacks. On another Mississippi plantation a Methodist circuit rider came occasionally to preach to the whites, then afterwards to the blacks. In one Baptist area masters assembled slaves from various plantations who had "got religion" to be baptized together at Big Creek on the Tombigbee River. Louis Fowler's master built a log church for his slaves and permitted them a black "preacherman." Andrew Goodman's master also built his slaves a church and allowed Kenneth Lyons, a slave on a plantation nearby, to preside at worship and to baptize the converted at a waterhole on the property.[3]

Some masters opposed their slaves practicing any religion, even closely regulated religion. One group of slaves ready to go to church was forced by its master into the fields, in their go-to-meeting clothes, to work all that Sunday. Gus Clark's master, who practiced no faith himself, whipped any slave discovered praying. Charlie Moses's master prevented his wife from reading Scripture to the slaves on the ground that slaves did not need religion. Frances Willis said their white folks never taught them anything about the Savior but rather treated them like work animals. Betsy Holmes was whipped time and again for talking about religion and singing hymns.[4]

Some Catholic masters did little to provide catechetical instruction for their slaves, forbade slaves to leave the planta-

tion to attend Mass, and prevented priests from blessing slave unions, for the Catholic Church taught that the marriage bond was inviolable. Irregular marriages, they supposed, need not be protected against the demands of the slave trade.[5]

The institution of slavery tended against the sacredness of the person, thus slaves had to struggle to pay proper respect to their dead. As in Sunday worship, a distinction between free white and servile black was made at funerals, although dignified ceremony accompanied the slave to the grave on some places. Willis Cofer remembered that the same oxcart carried both black and white dead to the graveyard, but whites were honored by a sermon while relatives and friends of blacks had to wait for a slack season, like lay-by time, for memorial services. Some slaves were buried without a ceremony of any kind and their graves marked by nothing but a wood post.[6] On Lizzie Norfleet's plantation a slave's body was taken in a wagon to the grave but "there wasn't no song, no prayer, no nothing, over the dead."[7] When "Little Mose" died, Uncle Billy Jordan led the black plantation community in "moanin' an' singin' an' prayin'" until the master galloped up and threatened that if they did not "shut up dat singin' an' carryin' on, he gwine lash every one of dem."[8]

Many slaves did, however, manage to bury their dead with decency. On one place mourners would sit up with the deceased and "mo'n, an' shout, an' sing all de night long, while de co'pse laid out on de coolin' board." Next day, with the master's family in attendance the deceased was buried in the plantation cemetery.[9] On an Orange, Texas, plantation, slaves from all around sat up with the dead, and at the graveyard Uncle Bob led in prayer and song. Hamp Kennedy recalled that the blacks clapped and stomped, chanted and hummed "Walking Egypt" all night until the dead was "funeralized." On one place women made shrouds for the dead of both races, the carpenter made the same type coffin for black and white, and members of both races were buried in the fenced-in plantation cemetery. On another plantation whites were buried inside the graveyard fence and blacks outside.[10]

White clergy officiated at some slave funerals. Blacks themselves held brush-arbor memorial services in lay-by time in August for all who had died during the year.[11] Mourners might sing:

> Dark was de night
> And cold was de groun'
> Whar my Master was laid
> De drops of sweat
> Lak blood run down
> In agony He prayed.[12]

Masters generally supervised the content of religious instructions so that, as Hannah Austin said, "We seldom heard a true sermon, but were constantly preached the doctrine of obedience to our masters and mistresses."[13] One old slave had "no better sense" than to shout an "Obey yo Missus an' yo Master," complained Lizzie Williams.[14] Crozier Moore, also incensed at selective instruction, declared, "Dey ought to have been hung" for preaching fake doctrine.[15] Dempsey Pitts, however, remembered one white clergyman who promised that the slaves would be free one day; when reprimanded the clergyman declared that he did not care, for he meant to preach the Bible. A scattering of slaveholders permitted freer religious instruction than was commonly allowed. "A good old Christian woman" held a prayer meeting each night for her slaves who, in consequence, would "go the length for her." Olivier Blanchard's mistress saw that the slave children were baptized, and made their first communion. And Mary Smith's young master, later killed in the War, used to come to the quarters to read the Bible to

his people. Others brought the slaves to the big house for Bible study. Gabe Emanuel's mistress not only gave Bible lessons on Sunday, she taught house servants and some of the field hands to read and write. Rachel Hawkins's master taught his slaves the Bible and hymns; and Manda Boggan's master would walk along with the field hands at work reading the Scriptures to them, and singing and praying with them. Pauline Johnson and Felice Boudreaux's master would send for a priest to minister to dying slaves. 16

Lucy, a houseservant of the Reverend C.C. Jones, a distinguished Georgia planter and author of *Catechism for Colored Persons* (1834), wrote to her master expressing appreciation for his religious instruction: "How thankful I am for the feelings which now occupy my heart in regard to my Savior. Often have I thought of your sermons filled with warning and admonition and your beautiful hymns with great pleasure and interest."[17] Frederick Law Olmsted saw kneeling black and white women in St. Louis Cathedral, New Orleans, "bowed in equality before their common Father."[18] Slaves and free blacks joined whites in Our Lady of the Gulf Church, Bay St. Louis, Mississippi. There Louis Joseph Piernas was baptized, made his first communion, and was married.[19]

Charles Coles of Maryland had, he said, an exemplary master and mistress who did not overwork, beat, or sell slaves, but rather instructed them in the plantation chapel, and welcomed priests to say Mass for blacks and whites on Sundays and Holy Days and to baptize, witness marriages, and conduct funerals for black or white in the presence of the entire plantation community. Similarly, on a plantation in Lafayette Parish, Louisiana, slaves attended Mass with the master's family and the priest baptized them and presided at their marriages. At Grand Coteau, Louisiana, also in Lafayette Parish, Jesuits, with the educational cooperation of the nearby Religious of the Sacred Heart, ministered to the large population of Catholic slaves of the area. Also in Louisiana, Donaville Broussard and fellow slaves were taught catechism by their master's sister, and a priest came 15 to 20 miles from his parish church to say Mass for them. The priest required the master to have recorded in the presence of the justice of the peace the names of those who had "jumped the broom" in a marriage ceremony.[20]

Slaves often saw their master's behavior as reflecting little of their professed Christianity. Susan Boggs, for example, roundly denounced a clergyman who, after he had finished his sermon, whipped a slave tied up for that purpose. Isaac Throgmorton was disillusioned by a clergyman who married into the slaveholding class and drove his slaves hard.[21]

Slaves sometimes accompanied their masters to camp meetings, when crops were laid by in late summer. Camp meetings would last through the weekend or longer, with plentiful preaching, singing, and baptizing. Men would sleep on hay in the wagons; women and children on feather ticks in cabins. Tables were loaded with barbecued beef, pork, lamb, and chicken; vegetables; pies and cakes. Clergy delivered their sermons from pavilions, such as one covered with sweet gum branches and carpeted with sawdust. Black and white children who frolicked during religious ceremonies were threatened with a brushing "to help them get sho' 'nough 'ligion," Benny Dillard said.[22] One old slave at a camp meeting who had promised that he would not again interrupt the preacher, let enthusiasm get the better of him and jumped to his feet and began shouting "when the preacher 'gan to tell about heaven en fare-ye-well to this worl'." On November 11, 1854, Lucy Skipwith informed her master that there had been a great revival among blacks and whites at

the Baptist church in Greensboro, Alabama, and that she hoped the revival would continue until the "whole country" was saved.[23]

Separate revivals for slaves were sometimes held. A Baptist clergyman would come to a plantation near Blackstock, South Carolina, in August after the crops had been laid by, and invite clergy of the area to join him in a revival for the slaves round about. Many would be converted and baptized. One slave who "got religion" at a camp meeting shouted and sang for three days and spread the word that she was born again and that she wanted all not yet saved to join her on her way to paradise.[24]

The slave clergy had limited learning and opportunity to practice their calling, to say the least, but they earned respect and gratitude in helping their flocks express their spiritual lives in relative freedom from the master's domination. Slave clergy were chosen, apart from any divine calling they may have had, by themselves and their plantation communities.

Colored folk "jes kinder raised em up a colored preacher," said Simon Hare.[25] When a slave wanted to preach, Robert Weathersby said, "He wuz give a try out, by gitting up an' trying to preach a time or two an' if he suited de folks an' dey thought he could preach, dey would say fer him to preach an' if he didn't suit 'em dey would say fer him not to."[26] Jeptha Choice said that his people "just put an old Prince Albert coat on some good nigger and made a preacher out of him."[27] According to Harrison Beckett almost every plantation had a black man "learning to preach."[28] When a white clergyman confirmed their choice by "laying hands" on their black preacher, all the slaves on a plantation in Harrison County, Texas, responded with "hollerin' and shoutin' and prayin'."[29]

Some of the slave clergy received permission from their master to minister to the people, while others carried on their calling in secret. When a slave would "claim he done been called to preach," said James Bolton, "and effen he kin git his master's cawnsent he kin preach 'round under trees and in cabins when t'aint wuk time."[30] A clergyman in Mississippi earned general permission to preach as a reward for bringing the master's son to profess Christianity.[31]

Master-approved clergy had to be careful what they said lest they lose their license to preach. Thus Robert Lofton never heard a clergyman say "anything the white folks did not like." A Texas clergyman sometimes obtained permission from his master to preach but he had to be on guard lest his enthusiasm lose him his privilege. Virginia slave James Smith was flogged and sold south to Georgia for making his flock discontented. When Uncle Lew preached that black and white were equal his master demoted him to plain field hand. Uncle Ben, a Texas slave who had learned to read and expound on the Scriptures, had his Bible taken away on the ground that it filled his mind with bad ideas, but he got another Bible which he kept well hidden.[32]

Some of the clergy learned to read the Scriptures with assistance of members of the master's family or by "stealing" literacy. Washington Allen was taught to read by the sons and daughters of his master and Charlotte Stephens's father, educated by his master, who was also his father, became a minister. But the only learning any slave clergyman or layman secured on another place was "stolen" learning. Mark Oliver's master bought some house servants who had earlier "stolen" a little learning which, in their new home, they secretly passed on to others. Richard Parker learned to read with secret help from a white boy, who took his pay in marbles, and from his master's daughter, whom he led to Christian belief.[33]

Clergy unable to read relied on strong memory native wit to expand on what they had heard. Mary Watson's father had Scripture read to him before he rose to exhort the people.[34] Clara Young liked best a minister who "neber larned no real readin' an writin' but he sho' knowed his Bible" and he could "preach de purt'est preachin' you ever heard."[35] On a Maryland plantation Sandy Jasper, also coachman, conducted services in one of the larger cabins on Sundays. Neither he nor any other slave on the place could read the Bible.[36]

Some black clergymen went openly or secretly about the neighborhood to serve their flocks. Ellen Claiborne's grandfather who had been freed by "Old Master" but whose children were owned by "Young Master," rode through the countryside dressed in beaver hat and frock coat with tails bringing spiritual succour to the slaves of the area. Richard Macks, a Central Mississippi slave, walked as far as 50 miles to officiate at funerals. Charlie Meadow's favorite clergyman, a "big black African" named Williams, would show up to preach now and then. Another "Ole African," in Mississippi, would come from a nearby plantation "en wud preach ter us under de trees."[37]

In cities blacks, slave and free, often worshipped in churches under their practical control, even though slaveholders feared separate churches fostered discontent. Omnipresent stimuli to literacy helped urban blacks gain the capacity to manage church and other affairs and enjoy some prestige, even among whites.[38] Commenting on "I Have Fought the Good Fight," a sermon of a black clergyman in New Orleans, Olmsted noted, "Much of the language was highly metaphorical; the figures long, strange, and complicated, yet sometimes...beautiful."[39]

Although slaves learned Scripture, theology and forms of worship in the "white" church — they made up a substantial proportion of membership in Methodist, Baptist, and Presbyterian churches in Amite County, Mississippi, in the 1850s — most of them worshipped unfettered in the fields and other out-of-the-way places, because "out der we could turn loose in our own way. We could sing, shout, an' pray," said Laura Ford, when the overseer was not present.[40] Field workers sometimes crouched in low places to pray, or gathered in a fence corner, because they "feared for anybody to see 'em." Whites might preach to blacks in public, said Lizzie Hughes, but, when unobserved, blacks "preached to theyselves."[41] When worshippers secretly met in a cabin they were likely to turn a kettle or pot upside down in expectation that that would muffle the sound and keep the master unaware.[42] Blacks escaped from master-controlled religion because "something inside jes told us about God and that there was a better place hereafter." That is why they could not be stopped by beatings by the slave patrol when caught slipping away to prayer meetings in a brush-arbor church in the woods.[43]

A brush arbor would have a roof of tree branches supported by posts, benches of saplings nailed to stumps, and "a place fer de preacher to stand." Maggie Woods and Lucy Donald were among those who stole off to the woods to pray and sing.[44] "The only chu'ch I knowed 'bout," recalled Stearlin Arnwine, "was when we'd get together in de night and have prayer meetin' and singin'. We use' to go way out in de woods so de white folks wouldn't hear nothin'. Sometimes we'd stay nearly all night on Saturday, 'cause we didn't have to work Sunday."[45] Silvia King remembered that down in the bottoms when the black folks gathered to shout and sing and pray, "Dey gits in de ring dance. It am jes' a kind of shuffle, den it git faster and faster and dey gits warmed up and moans and shouts and claps and dances. Some gits 'xhausted and drops out and de ring gits closer. Sometimes dey sings and shouts all night."[46] At meetings under the trees, John Macy said, "De spirit jes' come down out de sky and you forgits all you troubles."[47] In the fields a leader would call out a line which the group would repeat, and so they all would advance through a hymn. Some of the group would hum in the background.[48]

With or without permission slaves often met on Sundays in a cabin "as us didn't hab no churches," said Steve Weathersby. "De slaves did like ter git tergether an' praise de Lord. Dey would set fer hours on straight oncomfo'table benches an' planks, while some would be seated on de ground or standing. Dey would hum deep and low in long mournful tones swayin' to an' fro. Uders would pray and sing soft while de Broder Preacher wuz a deliverin' de humble message. De songs wuz old Negro spirituals sung in de deep rich voice of our race. We didn't hab no song books nor couldn't read, if we had 'em. We sorter made em up 'long as we went."[49]

When the slaves held their own services their songs would "come a-gushin' up from the heart."[50] Jacob Branch said they got their spirituals through visions.[51] Anderson and Minerva Edwards believed that the "Lord done give us our songs," one of which, sung in a whisper so the master could not hear, was:

> My knee bones am aching,
> My body's rackin' with pain,
> I 'lieve I'm a chile of God,
> And this ain't my house,
> 'Cause Heaven's my aim.[52]

James Green's people were fond of:

> I goes to church in early morn,
> De birds just a-sittin' on de tree —
> Sometime my clothes gits very much worn —
> 'Cause I wear 'em out at de knee.
>
> I sings and shouts with all my might,
> to drive away de cold-
> And de bells keep ringin' in gospel light,
> till de story of de Lamb am told.[53]

One good-hearted master permitted his slaves to build a brush-arbor church in a pecan grove for their Sunday worship.[54] Another allowed his slaves to worship unhindered in their own prayer house. The slaves assembled there every Saturday night, recalled Lina Anne Pendergrass:

> Dey sot on benches, and den dey would git down on dere knees and pray. I was a little gal, and me and de other gals would fetch water for dem to drink. Us toted pine when it was cole, and us'd take coal 'round fer de ole folks to light dere pipes wid. Atter while, dey git to singin' and shoutin'. Den de Spirit done come down and tuck hole of dem. Dat would be when everybody would get happy. De ole rafters creak and shake as de Spirit of de Laud sunk deeper and deeper in de hearts of de prayin' folks. Tate Sanders, de preacher from Lowryville, would come in 'bout dat time and raise his hands 'bove de congregation and plead wid de Lawd to open de hearts of de wicked so dat de Holy Spirit would come in.[55]

Those experiencing conversion in such a meeting would look "plum sanctified." Sometimes it would take "pretty nigh all night to make a sinner come through."[56] In one church the converted knelt while all sang:

> Rassal Jacob, rassal as you did in the days of old,
> Gonna rassal all night till broad day light
> And ask God to bless my soul.[57]

At baptisms the converted would perhaps sing as they went down into the water, "Dar's a Love Feast in Heb'en Today."[58] They might shout and roll about in their joy, and have to be restrained.[59] At her baptism Easter Lockhart wore a long, white gown gathered at the shoulders with big sleeves, a white cap, and no shoes. She sang and jumped and walked "real light." Back in church she shouted until she could shout no more.[60]

Alone, and with their families, mothers prayed and sang in worship and petition. One woman, who had been sold away from her mother, sang to her children:

> I wished I wuz in de Heaven,
> To see my mother when she enter;
> To see her try on de long white robe;
> P-r-a-y — let mother be de one![61]

And Sarah Thomas's mother sang:

You're selling me to Georgy,
But you can not sell my soul,
Thank God Almighty, God will
fix it for us some day!

I hope my ole gran'mother
will meet poor John some day,
I knows I won' know him, when I meets him,
'Cause he was so young when dey sold him
away.[62]

Mothers prayed for freedom for their families as well as for reunion with members sold away. A mother would shut the door and window, put a tub upside-down, or filled with water, in the center of the room to muffle sound, and pray for her family's freedom.[63] Remembering how his mother would kneel with her children by her side and pray for freedom, Tom Robinson said: "It's come to me lots of times since. There she was a' praying, and on other plantations women was a' praying. All over the country the same prayer was being prayed. Guess the Lord done heered the prayer and answered it."[64] Mary Colbert agreed: "Abraham Lincoln was an instrument of God sent to set us free, for it was God's will that we should be freed."[65] In 1859 Harriet Tubman said, "When I think of all the groans and tears and prayers I've heard on the plantations, and remember that God is a prayer-hearing God, I feel that his time is drawing near."[66] Fannie Moore's mother, who had been praying every night for freedom, one day began "singin' an' a shoutin', and a whoopin', an' a hollerin'" because, she said, "de Lawd done tell me I's saved" and that she and her children would be freed, so, she said, "I ain't gwine a grieve no more."[67]

Many mothers had "prayer grounds" in cane breaks, bushes, and groves. Andrew Moss's mother would go into an old muscadine growth to pray for the deliverance of the slaves. But when Annie Row's mother prayed "powerful loud" at her hiding place in the woods, she was heard, and whipped. In her secret place, W.L. Bost's mother petitioned the Lord for freedom and offered thanks that she and her children had not been separated and that their master was not so mean as others.[68]

Their prayer life enabled mothers to endure their hard life while waiting for freedom. One among them said that she could not have borne whippings, overwork, and sexual abuse "widout Master Jesus. He's held me up. I'd 'er died long ago widout him."[69] Another, Delia Garlic, "jest prayed for strength to endure."[70]

Henriette DeLille, daughter of a white man of New Orleans and his black mistress, rejected her mother's encouragement to form a like alliance and instead dedicated herself to religious life. She founded the Congregation of the Sisters of the Holy Family in 1842 through which she and her Sisters ministered to both the slave and the free. Her Congregation continues her mission in the United States, Central America, and Africa.[71] Another religious community of black women, The Oblate Sisters of Providence, was established in Baltimore, in 1828.[72]

Some slaves had visions and other mystical experiences and were alert to signs and portents of real significance or mere superstition. Some employed tricks aimed to manipulate the supernatural. When the "stars fell" in 1833 it "sho would hab been a purty sight," said Isaac Wilson, had not "dey say hit wuz de sign of all kinds of dreadful troubles."[73] One day

some women washing clothes at a creek saw "guns and swords streaking across de sky," and when war came a few days later they saw real guns like those they had seen in the vision.[74] Malinda Edwards, worried about her salvation, was about to drink from a bucket when, she said, the water cried, "Unworthy, unworthy!" Later, at her praying ground in the woods a rattlesnake crawled between her feet without striking. Warned — and grateful — she joined a Baptist Church.[75]

Death's approach was thought to be marked by signs such as an owl hooting in the yard or screeching in daylight, a bird flying in the house, cows lowing, and dogs howling.[76] Shortly before her death Mary Jane Hardrige's sister said, "Sis, do you hear that peckerwood? He's driving a nail in my coffin."[77] People born with a "veil" over the face could, some claimed, see spirits and "hants." One ghost, so it was said, was that of a young mistress accidentally killed by a hunter, who afterwards was seen riding through the night, with her white robe trailing behind. Mary Williams's father claimed that he had a tug-of-war with a "hant" over a bag of potatoes.[78]

Various rituals and objects could, the superstitious claimed, ward off otherwise imminent trouble. When one hears a screech owl, he should, Hamp Kennedy said, throw salt in the fireplace and put a broom across the door to forestall some tragic event. For good luck Minnie Ross recommended throwing a teaspoon of sulphur on the fire at 12 noon; wearing a dime tied on the leg; and carrying a bone of a black cat that would float upstream. And William Adams favored wearing coins, sprinkling powders, and carrying a lodestone to ward off evil. A "conjure man" was supposed to be able to cast or take off a "spell." One such "voodoo doctor" was said to have stuck pins in the back of a little mud doll to cause his mean master to get down in the back. Rosanna Frazier thought a "conjure man" made her blind by sprinkling rattlesnake dust in her hair.[79]

Hamp Santee complained that slaves had "signs fer dis and signs fer dat" but they had little else. Manus Brown thought that among the slaves religion and superstition were much entangled,[80] but Martha Colquitt's grandmother and mother taught their children that "voodoo wuz a no 'count doin' of de devil, and Christians wuz never to pay it no 'tention."[81]

Well founded fear that literacy would make their slaves discontented and rebellious led slaveholders to try to keep their slaves ignorant. They proclaimed themselves public benefactors, and friends of the blacks, in depriving their servants of rudimentary reading and writing. In response to pressure from abolitionists, apologists for slavery abandoned the notion of an earlier era that bondage was a necessary but temporary evil and asserted instead that it was a positive and permanent good. Before this shift in opinion had become entrenched, the South tolerated some plans and projects for freeing slaves, and deporting them as missionaries to their brethren abroad. The African Colonization Society championed such a policy. Similarly, Nashoba, a school of freedom for slaves, and an example of gradual emancipation, was established in 1825 on the Wolf River, outside Memphis, Tennessee, by the renowned feminist Frances Wright, with the Revolutionary hero the Marquis de Lafayette and the utopian reformer Robert Dale Owens as members of her board of trustees. By 1831 Wright had abandoned her experiment and had colonized the Nashoba blacks, as freedmen, in Haiti.[82]

By the 1830s the South had become hostile to all abolitionists, even the gradualists among them, and all their projects. One proslavery publicist argued that any assault upon slavery was a dastardly attack upon the body politic, a positively good body politic. To admit that slavery was an evil would "delight the attacking cohorts of abolition," and oblige the South to find ways to get rid of the evil. The correct ground for the South to take, therefore, was that slavery was not evil but a "blessing beneficial alike to master and servant." Such propagandists maintained that there was a "radical and irrevocable distinction" between the "superior" white race and the "inferior" black race. They opposed any action that would reject this claimed distinction, such as the diplomatic recognition of Liberia, "based as it must be upon the assumption of the social and political equality of the negro with the white man."[83]

A "rotten" policy of teaching slaves to read, said pro-slavery men, would be practical abolition, for an "enlightened man can never be a contented slave." Literate slaves would read abolitionist literature and disseminate their incendiary ideas throughout the slave population, "morally poisoning the otherwise happy Negro, and disturbing the security of society." Moreover, such a course would promote equality and amalgamation of the races. Teaching blacks to read Scripture, as some naively proposed, would open to them all fields of knowledge and have momentous consequences for both blacks and "for those who were born to command them and are stamped with the seal of power by the God of the Universe."

Depriving slaves of literacy was not an injury to them, propagandists argued, for Southern slaves "were the happiest class of laborers on whom the sun has ever shone, who in the beneficent providence of the Almighty have been removed from a land of the darkest barbarism, where not a ray of light illumined their hearts and minds, where not a spark of religious intelligence relieved the gloom of their desolate condition, and they were scarcely elevated above the beasts which roamed through their forests. They have been spared the horrors of that barbarism, and have been placed where the truths of Christianity, without the aid of any *literary* education, may be revealed to them." As laborers "their tasks are lighter, they are better clothed and better fed" than any similar class "in the North or in any other part of the world," and "while enjoying all these advantages, they are relieved from a thousand cares, and are attended by their masters in sickness as in health, in helpless age as in active and vigorous youth." They are better off than free blacks. They are slaves by the law of Nature and should receive the education of slaves, "and not that of their masters." Let religious instruction that they are slaves by the will of God be given them "ORALLY and in no other way." Slaves were to be cut off from emancipation and treated as children, never to grow up.[84]

The proper education for slaves, advocates of slavery believed, was in work and obedience. As Laura Ford said, they were not taught "book learnin' but how to wuk, to cook, sew, knit, an' de lak ob dat. Den us wuz teached how to be polite an' how to treat white folks."[85] Most masters were vigilant in preventing slaves from learning to read: "I declar' you bettuh not git kotch wid a papah in you han'," said Cecelia Chappel.[86] When Milton Marshall's master spotted him playing with letter blocks he leaped off his horse and thrashed delinquent Milton. Sam McCallum was whipped for studying a reader, because, his master asserted, Sam did not need to know anything but to feed the mules the right number of ears of corn.[87] If Frances Willis's mistress caught a slave "wid a piece o' paper up next to his eyes she'd talk 'bout bustin' his brains out."[88]

Some slaves who learned to read and write proved their master's vigilance apt by using their skills to undermine slavery. Although Minnie Davis's master ordered his children to cease teaching Minnie how to read, by then Minnie had learned enough to read newspapers surreptitiously and pass along her knowledge to her fellow slaves. A young boy who somehow learned to read gave uncensored Bible lessons to other slaves as they worked in the fields. Literate slaves might forge passes for themselves and friends to go and come in the neighborhood, as Anderson Williams's father did, or to escape to Canada, as C.H. Hall did. Frederick Douglass's master warned his wife that if she taught Frederick to read he would want to write, and that accomplished, "he'll be running away with himself." Douglass did learn these skills and used them to escape from Maryland to New York.[89]

Despite opposition, some slaves managed to snatch a degree of literacy and keep their accomplishment secret from their hard masters. Tom McAlpine, for example, acquired a little learning from the books he carried to school for his master's children without being found out.[90]

The master and mistress, as lord and lady in their dominions, could ignore the law and teach certain slaves to read. Thus James Singleton "stole" an education, with the help of his mistress. "Uncle Tom," instructed by his master, became an excellent reader. In consequence he got into trouble with neighboring slaveholders who wanted no contrary example to interfere with their purpose to keep their slaves in ignorance. Jimmie Johnson's mistress taught him to read, and his physician-master helped him with difficult words as they traveled in a buggy together on the doctor's rounds. With her master's permission Lucy Skipwith conducted school for slave children on Philip St. George Cocke's Alabama plantation. Her Sabbath school enjoyed some success, but she could not keep work-weary children's "eyes open no time" in the night school.[91]

Mary McFarland, of Tyler, Texas, taught her own children and the slave children together. So did Mrs. Isaac Van Zandt, of Marshall, Texas. Olmsted visited a North Mississippi plantation where slaves taught one another and bought their own books, with the indulgence of their master who was impressed by their enterprise and intelligence. Although Harre Quarls's mistress humanely taught him to read, his master, he said, treated him no better than if he were a good mule. Lafayette Price's master taught him to read and write for the practical reason that he could then better handle the duties of slave driver.[92]

Adora Rienshaw's mistress taught slave children "on the sly," and a governess of white children also taught James C. James. W. Solomon Debham played and dined and learned to read and write with his young master. Secretly instructed and slipped books by his young master, Robert Glenn became, he boasted, the best educated slave of the area, but he kept his achievement hidden from the white folks. Because of greater opportunity city slaves were more likely to be literate than country slaves.[93]

Joseph Davis, brother of Confederate President Jefferson Davis, taught Isaiah Montgomery to read and write and opened his extensive private library to him. Isaac advanced in knowledge and skills to such a degree that Joseph employed him as private secretary. Later Isaiah confirmed slaveholders' opposition to educating slaves: he gave aid to both General Ulysses Grant and Admiral David Porter in their capture of strategic Vicksburg, the Confederacy's last great stronghold on the Mississippi River.[94]

Even though some slaves gained a measure of the dignity and power of literacy, slaveholders were generally successful in keeping their bondsmen illiterate. Thus the only slave who could read and write that Louis Davis knew was a carriage driver who picked up a bit of learning as he waited to conduct his young masters to and from school.[95]

When slaves got sick home remedies of poultices and teas most often were tried. If folk medicine failed a physician would be called in. The doctor would ride horseback or in his buggy to visit his patients, in response to a crisis or on a regular schedule. Dr. Crawford Long, for example, had charge of the health of the slaves of Georgia politician-planter R.R. Cobb.[96] When cholera carried away 16 or 17 slaves on a plantation in Eastern Arkansas, in May, 1852, the planter brought his remaining slaves out of the mosquito-infested lowlands to Memphis where they responded well under a physician's care. Memphis itself was, however, none too safe. During the week June 12 to June 19, 1852, cholera and typhoid fever killed four Memphis slaves, ages 13 to 40.[97] A levee contractor in Mississippi in March, 1853, urged planters not to fear to bring their slaves to clear and settle on hitherto flooded and unhealthful lands, because, he said, a doctor's fees for guarding the health of 50 slaves for a year was a mere trifle.[98] A Nashville physician advertised to prescribe for slaves by correspondence: "All communications from persons at a distance, post paid, enclosing five dollars, will be promptly attended to." Doctors dosed patients, set broken bones, delivered babies, performed surgery, then filled their own prescriptions for calomel, castor oil, aspirin, quinine, paregoric, salts, whiskey, and a variety of other remedies.[99]

Some planters did without a doctor's services, as much and as long as they could. They relied on a "doctor's book," a prescription manual and a well-stocked medicine chest. The overseer of a large Mississippi plantation, with the help of a slave "nurse," regularly treated the sick. He almost never called a physician.[100] The mistress of a plantation was expected to take a special interest in the health of her slaves, especially that of the children. She might bring the sick to the big house for close attention, or visit them in their cabins, as did Lindsey Faucette's mistress, who carried out to the ailing chicken soup and wine. One mistress had the old slave nurse march the children up to the big house for a regular dose of worm medicine before sending them off to their bread and milk. Mistresses of plantations lined up the children each spring to be dosed with garlic and rum, sassafras tea, or some other spring elixir.[101]

Slave midwives delivered both black and white babies. Among them, Clara Walker, trained for midwifery by a physician, brought many babies into the world without losing a single one. She called in the doctor when a problem got beyond her. In January, 1855, Sucky earned $6 for her mistress for attending Elyn, Ann and Tempy on a neighboring place. A physician's fee then was $25 a delivery.[102]

Minerva Wells thought that slaves seldom got sick, "For dey went barefooted, an' wore jes' a few clo'se, slept in open airy cabins, an' et a plenty ob common sense cooking, an' drunk good water out ob de hills from springs an' dug wells."[103] The low country was, however, infested with fever carrying mosquitoes. If the master's family went to the hill country until frost, the slaves, except for a few house servants, likely had to stay behind to work the land, and take loads of quinine to contend against fevers.[104]

For minor aches and pains poultices and teas, oils and charms, were resorted to, especially by the old mammies. "Mammy Mary" prepared boneset tea for colds; red oak bark tea, with alum, for sore throat; and scurvy grass tea to clean out the system in springtime.[105] Besides common medicines such as castor oil, calomel, and salts, there were poultices of peach tree leaves, clay, and vinegar, and numerous teas. A lye tea for colds was made by pouring hot water over a bag of ashes, and splinter tea for pneumonia was produced by straining boiling water through lightwood splinters. "Bitters tea" from bark of wild cherry, black haw, and elm, and dried mullen leaves, was said to be a sovereign remedy for innumerable ailments. Samson's snake root, fever grass, holly bush, and parched corn made other medicinal teas. So did sassafras root and bark, St. John weed, Jerusalem oak, and smartweed. Hickory bark tea was given for cough; and red oak bark tea for chills and fever and diarrhea. Horehound tea, sweetgum bud tea, and cowfoot oil were recommended for a range of ailments. A poultice made with okra leaves, a dirt dauber's nest, and vinegar was prescribed for sprains. Elderberry tea, Jerusalem oak candy, pine-top tea, and mullen tea combatted colds, fevers, and parasites. One folk doctor favored a mixture of charcoal, honey, and onions for sick babies, and prescribed cactus root tea for colicky infants. On a Texas plantation sick slaves could expect to be dosed with a concoction of whiskey, cherry bark, and rust from old nails.[106]

Practioners of folk medicine, combining the roles of midwife, healer, and conjurer, might slide into employing fantastic and superstitious prescriptions to preserve health or effect a cure. Rena Clark, a midwife and herb doctor, had a bag of tricks to treat sick babies: a mole's right foot on a string around a baby's neck to ward off illness; a mole's foot and six small white buttons on a string to ease the pain of teething; soot from the tenth chimney brick sweetened with sugar to stop colic; and a bag of asafetida on a string around the neck to drive away measles, mumps, and whooping cough. Henrietta Collins, who learned doctoring from a native African and an American Indian, prescribed horse-radish poultice on the forehead and nutmeg on a string around the neck for headache. More understandably, Mary Kincheon chewed slippery elm bark for "bad feelings, or jes' to be chewin'."[107]

Occasionally a folk doctor succeeded when a medical doctor failed. Josephine Cox was carried to the big house desperately sick, and given up for lost by a doctor, but a slave nurse stepped in, made Josephine comfortable on a sheepskin pallet, with a saddle for a pillow, and nursed her back to health. Dread diseases could prove difficult for any doctor. On a South Carolina place smallpox victims were isolated in a makeshift shelter at the edge of a swamp. There they were provided with food but with next to nothing else. Most of them died. Some plantations, such as the Parlange plantation in Louisiana, maintained good slave hospitals.[108]

Slaves found occasions for recreation in simple joys of rural life, during holidays, even at work. Clara Davis, for example, delighted in moonlight shining through the willow trees and the feel of cool grass under her bare feet as she chased after lightning bugs. She enjoyed the music of hounds on the trail of a 'possum and the perfume of new-mown hay. She liked the swaying of a wagon and the groaning of its wheels as it lumbered down a country road. She smacked her lips at the thought of fresh-baked ash cakes dripping with sorghum molasses. She contemplated the passing up and down of boats on the Alabama River, and responded with joy to laborers singing at their work. She marveled at dawn breaking over a dark ridge and at twilight enveloping the environment with a golden hue. She loved "to walk de paths th'ew de woods an' see de rabbits an' watch de birds an' listen to frogs at night."[109]

At Christmas children received small gifts, such as fruit and candy, and the adults, dress clothes, extra and better food, perhaps some alcoholic beverage, and, not least, permission to give and attend parties. Although a few masters begrudged their slaves anything more than a day of rest at Christmas, most allowed celebrations with other slaves of the neighborhood, and provided holiday food and drink in abundance. A master likely would furnish a cow, a hog, or a goat for barbecue, as well as time off work as long as the Yule Log, soaked in the creek and placed at the back of a fire, burned. The standard time off was from Christmas Eve through New Year's Day.[110]

James Quattlebaum recalled with pleasure that his mistress handed out presents from under a big Christmas tree as each person's name was called, and distributed to everyone candy, fruit, and nuts. She then led the assembled people in prayer. Afterwards the happy people went their way singing and laughing. On a Texas place on Christmas Eve the mistress hung up stockings for all the children, black and white, and they all got something. On Christmas morning a keg of cider or wine was tapped. Then a big dinner and supper were served, followed by a dance, with guitars, banjos, and fiddles making merry, and the caller singing out, "Heads lead off, sashay to de right, do-si-do, swing you partners." When the Virginia reel wound up the gaiety the revelers returned to their cabins and rested all next day. Planters along Bayou Boeuf in Louisiana took turns entertaining slaves of the neighborhood at Christmastime. From 300 to 500 slaves would assemble for a feast and dance.[111]

Annie Stanton's master gave the women a new dress and handkerchief, and the men a hat, knife, and bottle of whiskey at Christmas. Few slaves drank to excess during the holidays, thought John Smith, but Molly Ammond complained that "no 'counts" got drunk. With religious ceremonies, feasts, and parties, fireworks marked the Christmas season. On a plantation near Atlanta, children would blow up hog bladders, saved from hog-killing time, tie them to sticks and hold them over a fire until they exploded. Some slaves made money at Christmastime, as on a Texas place where in addition to giving a present to each person and a hog for every four families, the master bought baskets and cornshuck horse collars the people had made. Some slave communities erected a Christmas tree and made sure that when presents were exchanged "nobody wan't lef' out, big or little." Although most slaves received at least sugar plums, nuts, and egg-nog, those whose master "gave no Christmas" visited their neighbors for a share of holiday cheer.[112]

Besides Christmas, slaves enjoyed other holidays. Despite their rejection of the Declaration of Independence, that all men are created equal, many planters celebrated Independence Day and threw big barbecues for their slaves. On one plantation Old Sam and Old Levi barbecued a beef over a pit covered with green poles which would not catch fire. They painted the great piece of meat with barbecue sauce and turned it with a pitchfork. Meanwhile, Old Viney baked the bread in ovens under the trees. While the food was being prepared the people danced and patted their feet and sang songs, such as:

Cum 'long boys an' let's go huntin'
Cum 'long boys an' let's go huntin'
Cum 'long boys an' let's go huntin'
Heard de dogs bark an' kno'ed dey treed
     sum'in.[113]

Many slaves greatly enjoyed the incongruous Fourth of July "dances wid fiddlin' music an' singin' wid old guitars." As they sang and danced and courted, often in the presence of white spectators, blacks strengthened their unity and elaborated their culture in their own way.[114]

Slaves celebrated also when the crops were laid by (cultivated for the last time before harvest), when the cotton was picked, on Washington's Birthday, at Easter, and on other occasions. Children perhaps would have an egg hunt on Easter Sunday. James Boyd enjoyed especially "dem times when us fish all de hot day or hunts or jus' lazed 'round when de crops am laid by."[115]

For young people to go to a dance on a neighboring plantation they had to get permission not from their parents but from their masters, because, Sarah Fitzpatrick noted, "We b'long to de white folks not to our mamas and papas."[116] It was, however, acknowledged that they had a limited right to attend neighborhood frolics, where they did much of their romancing. A North Carolina planter permitted all who had earned passes by good behavior to attend such dances. Those denied passes could sneak away to a party and take their chances with the patrol. At a dance in Arkansas given by some Indians who welcomed slaves to their affairs, a patrol surprised about 50 slaves without passes. The party goers ran in all directions and, frustrating the patrol, made it safely back to their own quarters.[117]

Dancers did the back step, the pigeon-toe, the buck dance, and square dances, reels, and ring dances. Many were agile and graceful. A Texas dancer would balance a glass of water on his head while making snaredrum-like music with his feet. Hannah Crasson's aunt "sho could tote herself" as she danced all over the place with a glass of water on her head, not spilling a drop. Another great performer could dance with a bucket of water on his head. Lucy Lewis was proud of being a "right smart dancin' gal," and Ellen Betts "cut de pigeon wing and cut de buck" and danced every kind of dance. At one Christmastime dance on Bayou Boeuf in Louisiana Sam's feet flew with great speed, Pete leaped and shuffled, and Lively, "the fastest gal" on the Bayou, whirled like a top, outdancing everyone. Solomon Northup played the violin. The people also made music "patting," alternately striking their hands on their knees, then on their shoulders, keeping time with their feet, and singing.[118]

White folks sometimes came down from the big house on Saturday night to watch dancers in the quarters strut their stuff and express their exuberance in accompanying song:

Yo go down de new cut road
I'll go down de lane
If yo' git deir befo' I does
Kiss Miss Liza Jane."[119]

Juba this and Juba that,
Juba killed a yaller cat.
Juba this and Juba that,
Hold you partner where you at.[120]

It's gittin mighty late when de Guinea hen
  squall,
and you better dance now if you gwine dance
  a-tall-
If you don't watch out, you'll sing nother tune,
For de stars gettin' paler and de old gray coon,
Is settin' in de grapevine a watchin' de moon.[121]

At dances and on other occasions slave musicians played the fiddle, the guitar, the banjo, the Jew's harp, and the accordion. They made music, also, with a hoe, an axe, or a saw. They clapped their hands, stomped their feet, and snapped their fingers. They rattled bones, blew on quills, drummed on rawhide stretched over a barrel top. They coaxed music from a tin can, a pan and a washtub. They got music from a stick fiddle arched with a taut string and sawed on with a bow stick hair from a horse's tail, and from a willow stick flute, made by slipping off the bark, slitting the shaft, and replacing the bark with spaced holes cut in it.[122]

Musicians sprang from every slave community. One such natural musician learned to play on a long gourd fixed with horsehair strings. Later he bought a fiddle for $1.80, and at last got a "fiddle sure enough." An accomplished musician and also carriage driver played the violin at both black folks' dances and white folks'

dances. John Drayton, a violinist and rail-splitter, could make such music that even the preacher was set to dancing. At some dances the chief fiddler was himself the preacher. Bill Crump's father regularly played the violin at the Cross Roads dances in North Carolina, and Mance McQueen made the fiddle sing at neighborhood dances in Smith County, Texas.[123]

At festive gatherings, besides dancing, there might be candy pullings, watermelon slicings, party games, and athletic contests. In the "well game" a boy or girl, sitting in a chair and pretending to be stuck in a well, would call out the name of a desired rescuer. The rescuer would be rewarded with a kiss. After a party there were opportunities for practical jokes, such as "tick tack." The joker would tie a long rawhide string to a loose board on a cabin and, while hiding in a tree or behind a bush, make a "tick tack" sound in the cabin by jerking on the string. Unable to account for such a tick tack, Tom and Mandy one night fled their cabin and slept outdoors.[124]

Athletes might wrestle or box, high jump or vault, and race over hurdles. In a "free for all" as many as 30 contestants would flail away at one another with 10-pound bags of cotton or improvised boxing gloves until one last man was left standing, and victorious.[125] In a game of nines, a form of baseball, catching a hit ball on the first bounce made an "out." Pitchers threw slow, drop balls. No one wore a mask or glove. Games could last half a day, with the winners scoring 40 or more runs. "De aim was," according to Ben Leitner, "to see how far a batter could knock de ball, how fast a fellow could run, and how many tallies a side could make."[126]

Families enjoyed good times in the privacy of their cabins. Charlie Davenport's mother made dewberry and persimmon wine for the adults, and the children gathered nuts, for pleasant evenings at

Untutored artists coaxed beauty from simple homemade instruments. *Harper's*, Vol. LVII, No. CC-CXLII (November 1878), 861.

home. When the work was finished, "We'd set around de dyin embers en eat a pan of cracked walnuts pickin de meat out wid horseshoe nails," Davenport said. "Den mammy would pour herself en he ole man a cup ob wine."[127] In summer after a day's work and when it was still too hot to sleep families might tell stories and sing well known spirituals and songs made up on the spot. On Sundays Ann Drake's people "jes sot 'round de cabin doors an' talk an' wrap hair, an' sumtimes dey wud sing."[128] Charity More's father told stories about the rabbit and the fox, the squirrel and brer terrapin, before these tales were collected in books. One of his Bible stories had black Adam turning white after eating the forbidden fruit.[129] Most slaves could not read or write but they could entertain one another with stories, and express their sense of humor, as did an old woman who responded to a query as to where she was going with: "Lawd, chile I ain't gwine nowhere. I'se done been where I was gwine."[130]

Men and boys enjoyed hunting and fishing as a sport and as a means to bring home fish and game to vary the usual salt pork fare. 'Possum, 'coon, rabbit, and squirrel were plentiful around plantations and deer, bear, and wild hogs roamed the backwoods. Wild duck and geese in season, and quail and wild turkey, offered good hunting. Fishermen caught bass, perch, carp, and catfish in lakes and streams; and saltwater fish, crab, and shrimp in coastal inlets and bays.

A rabbit had next to no chance to escape James Bolton with his master's hounds. Gus Clark hunted rabbits barefoot in the snow; in summer he might bring home rattlesnakes to be fried and served like chicken.[131] Virginia Newman's people, who ate "mos everything what run or crawl or fly outdoors," also liked rattlesnake. They would skin, dice, and "stew him slow with lots of brown gravy."[132]

Some fathers were able to supply their families with a good amount of game and fish, bringing home from time to time a fat 'possum or a fine string of crappie. During the Christmas holidays men often bagged extra game and caught a surplus of fish to be preserved for leaner days. Privileged slaves, such as Zeb Crowder's father, were allowed to hunt with a gun and dog. Sam Polite also hunted 'possum and 'coon with dogs, and caught shrimp with a net on St. Helena Island, South Carolina. In new plantation country just a little easy hunting would be enough to fill empty stomachs. When a plantation was first established in the game-rich area of Belton, Texas, the best shooters, guided by an old Indian, who was paid with calico cloth and a hatchet, were sent out to bag game for the entire plantation community.[133]

A hunter without a gun could perhaps still take deer. He might fix sharpened stakes on deer trails to impale the deer when they jumped a fence. One stock tender who spent much time in the woods looking after the cattle and knew all the deer trails would lash a sythe blade or butcher's knife to the end of a pole to make a deer lance. He would fix the lance at a fence crossing or behind a log on the trail to spear deer that leaped the obstacle. Men could hunt even while they worked by setting traps for wild animals and fowl. At the end of the day they would run their trap lines and harvest the catch. In Edgefield County, South Carolina, when not hunting 'possum, squirrel, turkey, and dove, slaves trapped game such as partridge and rabbit. In bird blinding in North Carolina nighttime hunters would strike down with a branch of a thorn bush birds which they blinded by torch light when flushed from bushes and brush piles.[134]

Slaves near Beaufort, South Carolina, took mullet, crab, oysters, and clams from the river nearby with line, net, or seine. Seafood, rather than meat, was standard in their diet. In the Bayou Country of Louisiana slaves snared alligator, eel, crawfish, a variety of fish, and waterfowl, which they often cooked in gumbos.[135]

Women sometimes joined in the hunting and fishing for sport and food. Susan Kelly liked to go hunting with the boys for 'possum, in the autumn.[136] They would likely find "Mr. Possum settin' in the 'simmon tree just helpin' hisself to them good old ripe juicy 'simmons."[137] Israel Jackson's mother would scour the woods at night for 'possum to feed her hungry children.[138] Harriet Jones's family enjoyed hunting, and singing about the hunt:

> Possum up de gum stump,
> Raccoon in de hollow —
> Git him down and twist him out,
> And I'll give you a dollar.[139]

Lizzie Hughes also celebrated hunting in song:

I went to the barn with a shinin' bright moon,
I went to the woods a-huntin' a coon.
The coon spied me from a sugar maple tree,
Down went my gun and up the tree went me.

Nigger and coon came tumblin' down,
Give the hide to master to take off to town,
That coon was full of good old fat,
And master brung me a new beaver hat.[140]

Slaves often had fun while they worked, telling stories, singing, and courting. Isaac Wilson enjoyed hoeing or picking up one row and down another with a "heap" of people "a singin' an' a hollerin'."[141] Song and story helped keep up the spirits of workers in fields that seemed to stretch from horizon to horizon and promise everlasting monotony:

Old cotton, old corn, see you every morn,
Old cotton, old corn, see you since I's born.[142]

This ain't Christmas mornin', just a long
  summer day,

Hurry up, yellow boy and don't run 'way,
Grass in the cotton, and weeds in the corn,
Get in the field, 'cause it soon be morn.[143]

If you liker me
Like I liker you
We both liker the same.[144]

Watch de sun; see how she run;
Never let her ketch yo' wid yer wuk undun.[145]

Since there was no use to complain about being tired, workers kept right on, said Ambus Gray, "singin' and whistlin'." John Patterson's people sang as they worked from about four in the afternoon until quitting time at dark; they worked hard but they enjoyed one another's company, the singing, and the courting. Stories of all kinds, including ghost stories; stories of signs, omens, and conjuring; and stories of Br'er Rabbit and Br'er Fox gave pleasure and lightened the burdens of the day.[146]

Observing and doing good work were themselves sources of joy. It was a pleasure to Philip Johnson to watch cradlers cutting wheat, others raking it, and still others binding it into bundles.[147] Susan Kelly enjoyed skillfully managing her team of oxen, singing and shouting all the day, "Gee thar Buck, whoa thar Peter, git off dat air co'n, what's de matter wid yo' Buck, can't yo' heer."[148]

When just 10 Edwin Walker liked working in the fields with the adults, listening to their stories and songs. The spirituals, he said, "Sho' wuz purty."[149] Ebenezer Brown enjoyed hearing during the heat of the day:

Howdy, my brethern, Howdy yo' do,
Since I bin in de lan'
I do mi'ty well, an' I thank de Lord, too.

And,

See my brudder down de hill; fall down on
  he knees;
Send up your prayers. I'll send up mine; de
  good
Lord to please.[150]

Seasonal activities such as corn shucking, hog killing, and log rolling, when neighbors came to help, were occasions for feasts and frolics. Sometime in November, usually, a group of workers, men and women and older children, would tackle a mountain of several hundred bushels of corn, aiming to shuck every ear before the day was done. Captains of competing teams would mount the stack and whoop it up to spur their shuckers on to win the prize, perhaps some money. They would pace back and forth shouting encouraging lines of a corn-shucking song, their team members answering back, until the task was finished. Then a jug of whiskey would be passed around and a big dinner for all would be served, followed by sporting events, and a dance.[151]

In an area of South Carolina near the North Carolina border it was a practice after the corn had been shucked for the workers to carry the planter on their shoulders, and then, singing and laughing, gather for the promised feast. One South Carolina planter passed around a jug of whiskey to the corn shuckers so often, himself taking a swig each round, that master and slaves ended up intoxicated. Children enjoyed the contests and celebrations but were called in when the hour grew late or the frolicking rowdy.[152]

Log rolling and hog butchering were, like corn shucking, occasions to focus the labor of the neighborhood on intense and short-lived seasonal activity. Slaves shared in the work and in the celebration that marked completion of the task. Men enjoyed testing their strength in the festive and communal activity of log rolling, in lifting and carrying logs, and in stacking them high to the accompaniment of singing and shouting. "Us would throw dem logs ober to de time ob a tune," said Manus Robinson, "All de time us wuz a thinkin' ob de big dinner a waitin' for us.

Hit was spread on long tables in de shade o' de trees."[153] While men hoisted the logs women prepared the meal and made ready a party. After the big dinner all relaxed, told stories, and visited with one another until musicians struck up a tune and dancing into the night began.[154]

Hog butchering once or twice a year also called for gathering slaves of the neighborhood for concentrated work of strength and skill. A hundred hogs perhaps would be slaughtered, the hides scalded and scraped and the carcasses cut up. Finally the meat would be salted or placed in smoke houses for curing. Upon completion of the demanding tasks, the workers would be rewarded, as at corn shucking and log rolling times, with a dinner-on-the-ground, including fresh pork and other good things to eat, and a dance. Henry Cheatam thought these days the greatest days of the year. House-raising, quilting, wood cutting, and other activities also drew slaves together for work and recreation. In a neighborhood near Lafayette, Louisiana, slaves gathered to make hundreds of candles and to celebrate afterwards.[155]

Slave children played together in the yard of the big house, in streets of the quarters, and in fields, woods, and streams. They played marbles, made from clay, and shot missiles with bows, slingshots, and blowguns. They jumped rope and swung on vines. Girls made rag dolls with a scrap of cloth, a roll of cotton, and a piece of string, and outfitted their dolls in dresses and hats of grass and leaves and pieces of cloth. They swept and decorated their playhouses secluded under trees and bushes.[156]

Children played the usual games of prison base, blind man's bluff, tag, and hide-and-seek. Isaac Johnson enjoyed "roun tree," a version of baseball; Charlie Barbour favored fishing, and hunting with "Ole Uncle Jeems" and his hounds; and

Gatherings of seasonal workers like these Delaware peach pickers offered occasions for exuberant recreation. *Harper's*, Vol. XLI, No. CCXLIV (September 1870), 517.

Jane Arrington loved ring games, especially the one where children ran in a circle holding hands and singing "Little Gal remember me."[157]

Boys and girls slid down haystacks, rode stick horses, climbed trees, and splashed in the swimming hole. These children of nature caught crawdads in a stream, and picked and ate berries in the spring and nuts in autumn. They climbed saplings, rode them to the ground, and let them snap back upright for another ride.

A dog, a fishing pole, and nearby woods and streams beat latter day roller skates, picture shows, and swimming pools, Tony Cox asserted.[158] Emily Dixon saw the hickory tree as a gift of God to children: "Deir's de shade ter play under, de tree ter climb, de big limbs ter hang swings from, de leaves ter pin tergether wid pine straw ter make dresses and hats, de nuts ter eat an' throw at each uder…. Den yo' can hide 'hind de trunk in playin' hide an' seek, or hab hit for de base."[159]

Fernandina, Florida, street performers. *Harper's*, Vol. LVII, No. CCCXLII (November 1878), 847.

Slaves in cities had, as one would expect, greater opportunity for varied recreation than did country slaves. In New Orleans along Baronne Street between Perdido and Poydras Streets there were for blacks a church, an ice cream parlor, a restaurant, coffee houses, and a barber shop with a rear connection to a saloon. Passes given by indulgent masters and forged passes held by slaves of strict masters permitted drinking, carousing, and gambling.[160] Militia musters with their parades, martial music, drinks, and fights, and other public spectacles, brought out crowds of urban blacks and whites.[161]

3

Marriage and the Family; Slave Trade and the Family

The institution of slavery required that marriage and the family be radically limited by the intrusive authority of slaveholders. Husbands and fathers could not protect their wives and children. Although mothers were, so much as their masters indulged them, practical centers of their families, they could be torn from their children, as from their husbands, at their masters' pleasure. Courtship, marriage, and the entire life of the family were subject to slaveholders' arbitrary control.

Marriageable slaves courted at church meetings, at festive gatherings, and on the home plantation. Virginia Sims's master allowed her "to get out and cote," but not before she was 19.[1] But slave girls on a North Mississippi plantation married at 14, at 16, and 18.[2]

Choice of spouses was strictly limited. Ephom Banks's father was "put in a house" with a woman he did not want. At first opportunity he left her for Ephom's mother. A favorite might, on the other hand, persuade his master to give him an unwilling wife, "whether or no, willy-nilly."[3] "Patience, I brung yo' er husband," said one master as he introduced his newly purchased man to Patience.[4] Andy Marion complained that if you did not find a suitable girl on the plantation, "What could you do?" You could not "grab a mule and

ride to de next plantation widout a written pass." And then the "gal," her parents, and the masters concerned had to give their consent.[5]

Some men persuaded their masters to buy a pretty girl for them at a slave sale. Sometimes a master would heed the pleas of a slave to buy a wife or husband hitherto separated on a different plantation. It also happened, that a master would purchase a woman for one of his slaves even "if she were somebody else's wife." Such forced marriages could be beyond enduring. Thus John Matthews's mother left her husband for another man as soon as freedom came. Imposed marriages sometimes turned out well, as did that of Nelson Dickerson's parents who, put together without their leave, grew contented and happy with one another.[6]

Weddings ranged from a simple announcement to a formal ceremony, and a grand party. Often a wedding ceremony was nothing more than a couple jumping a broom with the master declaring, "Jacob, I brung you a good woman, take her an' live wid her," or "Jim and Nancy, you go live together."[7] At a typical wedding of a couple who had been "walking together" the groom likely would be dressed in patched jeans and the bride in cast-off clothes of her mistress. The wedding would be celebrated with a feast and a frolic, unless it was during busy season, "den dey jes went on wid out de frolicking part."[8]

Since marriages could be broken by sale or gift, not so much was made of them. Still an occasional wedding was a great affair with a clergyman officiating and celebration following. One favored bride wore a fine new dress provided by her mistress. The wedding party processed to the bride's white folks' church. Afterwards all returned for "good eatings" at the manor house.[9] At a wedding dinner in East Texas a long slab table was set under a tree with plates and spoons, wooden dishes, china bowls, and knives and forks of bone handles. On a North Carolina plantation slave weddings were held in the flower-decorated dining room of the big house, with a clergyman brought in and neighbors invited. After the wedding supper, a dance with banjos and fiddles was given. When Mom Agnes James got married she wore a white dress trimmed in blue, Preacher Charles Reynolds presided, and a dinner of rice, cake, custard, and a yearling pig with an apple in its mouth was served.[10]

Many slave marriages were of couples belonging to different masters of the neighborhood. A partial solution to this disorder was the practice of allowing husbands to visit their wives on weekends. On a plantation near Winnsboro, South Carolina, there were eight women, said Charlie Robinson, "dat men come from other places to see and marry them and have children. I doesn't 'member nary one of de women havin' a husband livin' wid her every night."[11] Tempie Herndon's husband had to return to his plantation the day after the wedding, but afterwards was allowed to visit Tempie weekly from Saturday night until Sunday night. He and Tempie had 11 children, nine before freedom. Susan Snow's father, like Virginia Jackson's father, was allowed to visit Wednesday

nights and Saturday nights, but Jane Sutton's father, who visited Saturday nights only, was such a stranger to Jane that she called him "dat man."[12]

Some masters allowed husbands small gifts to take to their wives. Men, such as Parke Johnson's father, who hired out and made more money than they had to turn over to their masters, were able to buy gifts for their wives and children, including delicacies for the family table.[13] But other husbands were forced to sneak off to see their families, and take a beating if caught, as Vinnie Busby's father did.[14] Manda Walker's father once overstayed his pass because of high water, and was seized by the patrol. The patrol would not accept his excuse and instead "tied him up, pulled down his britches, and whipped him right befo' mammy and us chillen."[15]

Husbands and wives often were separated by removal or sale. Warren Taylor's parents were separated when his mother was moved far away by her master, leaving his father stranded with his own master. When Sena Moore cried when her husband was sold away her master urged her to take up with another man, which she did, but her second husband turned out "no 'count."[16] The temporary nature of marriage required by slavery made it easy for some husbands to abandon their wives. The probability that their marriage would be broken up at some time anyhow offered a ready excuse. Thus a master told a suitor from a nearby plantation that he could have the woman he asked for, but that "he mustn't knock or cuff her 'bout when he didn't want her no more, but to turn her loose."[17]

Among the fruits of slave unions, however unstable they might have been, were millions of descendants. One mighty progenitor of these millions was Lydia Stewart, born about 1832, who left at her death March 21, 1935, 491 living descendants—11 children, 96 grandchildren, 248 great grandchildren, and 136 great, great grandchildren. Another prolific mother of the race was Adeline Crump, who gave birth to 21 children, including five sets of twins.[18]

The integrity of black families often was assaulted by overseers and masters who abused their power over black women. In calling the roll of a plantation community Jim Allen included a family, some of whose children were fathered by the overseer. Casper Rumple's father was an Edgefield County, South Carolina, overseer. Viney Foster's mother became a victim of her overseer when she was 14, thus Viney was, as she said, a product of the "cotton house."[19]

"Young" and "old" masters fathered children of mixed race. Mary Estes Peters was conceived, she said, when the three sons of her mistress raped her mother. Lizzie Hawkens' mother, who was as "white as white folks," was her master's daughter. One unconventional planter raised his black children and his white children together in the big house. Nanny Madden's mother had three children by her master; and Dora Franks was daughter of her young master. Black women who "made a fuss" about being taken advantage of by white men risked being whipped or sold. Sella Martin's mother was forced to be a concubine to her mistress's brother and was rewarded with a special cabin, nominal duties, and food from her mistress's table. Even so, she and her children were sold from their North Carolina home down to Georgia.[20]

Mary Reynolds said her master had a "passel" of children by a "yaller gal" he bought as a seamstress in Baton Rouge. Hattie Rogers's master had, she said, 11 children by his slave Lucy. Donaville Broussard said his mother was daughter of one of the Carmouche boys of Louisiana. Elvira Boles was, she said, daughter of her first master and mother of a son by her sec-

ond master, because "effen dey had a pretty girl dey would take em." Gabriel Gilbert, born and raised near New Iberia, Louisiana, said his master's boys ran after black girls and had children by them but went on to marry white women, though "dey allus treat dey chillen by de slave women good." A planter told Frederick Law Olmsted that race mixing was universal, that every good looking black girl in the state was the concubine of a white man.[21]

"Colored women had to go through a plenty," said Fanny Berry.[22] W.L. Bost said many colored women had white men's children against their will. "If the missus find out she raise revolution," Bost said. "But she hardly find out. The white men not going to tell and the nigger women were always afraid to. So they jes go on hopin' that things won't be that way always."[23] Martha Allen's young master hit her grandmother over the head with a stick of wood when she refused him. Martha Bradley, however, knocked down with her hoe an overseer who made advances toward her, and her master approved her spirited defense of her honor.[24] Mattie Curtis said her cruel master made available "yaller gals" to men of his family, and to friends. "Dem yaller wimmen wus highfalutin' too," and thought "dey wus better dan de black ones."[25]

White wives sometimes retaliated against their disloyal husbands by mistreating their black rivals. One jealous wife shaved the head of her husband's black mistress. Betrayed wives often made life miserable, also, for their husband's half-black children. A philandering clergyman, when found out, felt compelled to sell at once his black mistress and their mixed-race children. Augustus Robinson's father, also his master, sold him to a kind clergyman to get him away from his wife's beating, kicking, and knocking him about. The betrayed white wife, like the coerced black mistress, was disgraced, humiliated, and hurt. It nearly killed Chaney Spell's mistress when she discovered her husband's weakness for "pretty yaller gals." Patsy, a "queen of the field," who picked the most cotton and rode the wildest horse, was lashed often, because she was slave of a licentious master and a jealous wife, a "victim of lust and hate."[26]

Many slaves were of mixed African-Indian descent, living as Africans did next to large numbers of Southern Indians. Mary Gaines's grandfather was "pure African" and her mother Indian. Tom Stanhouse's father was half "Black Creek," his mother half "Red Indian." Robert Solomon's father was African and his mother Cherokee. Eugenia Weatherall's father was a Choctaw Indian. Commenting on his parents being of African, Indian, and Caucasian descent, J.N. Gillespie said "three fourths of me is something else." Becky Hawkins's grandfather was simply Indian; Elizabeth Hines's father was half-Indian; and Matthew Allen's grandmother was all Cherokee. Many slaves claimed to be, and were as much as they were of any other race, Indian. The Seminole Chief Oceola's grandmother was African.[27]

Considerable miscegenation occurred in cities. In New Orleans, particularly, white men and their black mistresses had long-term relationships. Around 50 percent of the city's blacks were, it was said, of mixed race. Beautiful girls of mixed race might even be sent to Paris to become educated and accomplished. They met their paramours at "quadroon balls" and made arrangements, approved by their mothers, whereby they and the children they might have would be provided for. The arrangements usually terminated at the white partner's marriage to a white wife, though the mistress would receive some compensation and, sometimes, continued support in a second household.[28]

Children of mixed race were less often children of white mothers than of black mothers, but Adora Rienshaw's father was the son of a black man and a white woman. In consequence, he was bound out until 21, then freed. Millie Markham was daughter of her young white mistress; her father was a son of a white man and black woman. The master sold Millie's father, but the young mistress ran away, bought her lover and married him, pretending that she was herself of mixed race to conform to the law forbidding mixed marriages. This couple had 15 children. George Patterson's free white mother from Ireland lived with her slave husband and their 18 children in a one-room cabin on a South Carolina plantation.[29]

Mixed-race children were favored sometimes, beaten sometimes, often rejected. Ervin Smith's white grandmother was, he thought, his best friend, though he remained a slave. Adaline Johnson said her master whipped children "black as me" but not his half-white nephew. Andrew Moss said his master had five children by Andrew's grandmother, and, when he died willed them a house, land, and money. James C. James's master, his father, gave James and his mother special food, clothing, housing, and other privileges. Other slave children derided Dora Franks as "Ole Yellow Nigger."[30] Alexander Robertson expressed the pain of being forced to associate with one side, while related to the other side, and being rejected by both. Neither side liked the color of his skin. Alexander hoped "dat dere'll be no sich thing as a color line in hebben."[31] Jack Johnson declared, "You see me right here, de sin of one? My master was my father."[32] Cato Carter said it no longer mattered that he was of mixed parentage now that he was near the end of his days.[33] One ex-slave hated his white father for allowing him to remain a slave, ignorant and neglected. He concluded that although there were some good white folks, there were "mighty few" of them.[34]

Michael Morris Healy, a planter near Macon, Georgia, had 10 children by his slave mistress Mary Eliza. Three of the sons, James Augustine, Patrick Francis, and Alexander Sherwood, were among the first African American priests in the United States. James Augustine Healy became Bishop of Portland, Maine, in 1875, and Patrick Francis Healy was president of Georgetown University, 1874–1882. Three of Healy's daughters, Martha, Josephine, and Eliza, became nuns.[35]

Slave traders separated wives from husbands, children from parents, and sisters from brothers. They criss-crossed the countryside dealing with planters, buying and selling at auction, and carrying on their trading through a network of markets in Richmond, Memphis, New Orleans, and other Southern cities.

Slaveholders cooperated with traders in breaking apart families to meet demands of the market. Though they might claim moral superiority over the traders and doubtless were more concerned about the welfare of their bondsmen, they bought and sold youths 10 to mid-teen, mothers with young offspring, females in early womanhood, and adult men in their prime. Both slaveholders and slave traders excused themselves for their complicity in destroying slave families by declaring that blacks were naturally deficient in family attachments.[36]

Although some masters were reluctant to separate husbands and wives, economic exigency could force them to sell spouses apart, to say nothing about heirs and creditors breaking up families in slave sales. When Foster Weathersby's parents met again six years after they had been sold apart, "Dey didn't know how to ack or what to say; dey seemed kinda let down lak. You see, he had married ag'in an' my mother had too."[37] Sarah Wells's father was bought, then sold away, as a carriage driver. Julia Brown's uncle, who visited his wife on Wednesdays and Saturdays, one day arrived for his visitation to find his wife gone, sold to "speculators."[38] Clay Bobbit was married "by de broom stick ceremony" but, "shucks," he said, "dey sold away my wife 'fore we'd been married a year."[39] Virginia Bell's father was sold from his wife and five children in Virginia and given a young wife, Virginia's mother, in Louisiana. Another Virginia couple was purchased together and brought to Mississippi but there sold apart, to the great sorrow of the wife who wept night after night for the husband she would not again see in this world.[40]

Like husbands and wives, children were taken from parents and from one another. Harriet Hill was sold from "dear old Mammy" when she was three. Rose Holman's mother, sold away, would slip back at night with gifts for her children. When six, James Singleton was sold, with his brother John and sister Harriet, from his parents. Carolyn Stout, sold when age five, never again saw her mother. When sold as a boy Robert Glenn was not allowed to tell his mother and father goodbye. When Laura Clark was sold with nine other children, and Old Julie as guardian, Laura's mother urged Old Julie, "Iffen I never sees her no mo' raise her for God." Laura's grandmother prayed that they all would be reunited in heaven.[41]

Children, as one would expect, scattered like quail when a "speculator" appeared.[42] Mary Ferguson remembered that, when she was about 13, in 1860, two strange men came into the house and said, "Get your clothes, Mary; We has bought you." Mary vainly appealed to her master. As she was being driven past the field where her mother and all her folks were at work, her farewell cries went unheard. The slave dealers thrust her down into the buggy out of sight and drowned out her voice with their singing. "I ain't never seed nor heared tell o'my Ma an' Paw an bruthers, an' sisters from dat day to dis," Mary said. And she expressed her sorrow and resignation with the song:

> Must Jesus bear the cross alone
>   and all the world go free?
> No, there is a cross for every one:
>   there's a cross for me;
> This consecrated cross I shall bear til
>   death shall set me free,
> And then go home, my crown to wear;
>   there is a crown for me.[43]

Separation of brothers and sisters by sale also grievously wounded slave families, such as when two sisters and two brothers of Jane Williams were, she said, "Took plumb off some wheres. Us never did see 'em no more."[44] Elmira Hill, herself put on the auction block in Richmond, grieved that she never again saw her two brothers, sold away to New Orleans. Although raised with her white father's family, Martha Johnson was sold by her half brother at their father's death.[45]

Black families were scattered by gift and inheritance too. When the master's children came of age they were, likely, given a portion of the family slaves to start them off as full-fledged members of the slaveholding class. At the death of the old master and mistress their slaves would be "drawn" for by the heirs, or sold and the proceeds distributed among the heirs. Anna King and her grandmother were "drawn" by their young mistress. George Williamson was traded in a land deal, then disposed of as part payment for a gristmill, and finally awarded to his young mistress as part of her share of the estate. Mattie McLain and his sister were sold to different buyers, and Martha Wheeler was sold at auction, in consequence of estate settlements.[46] "Old Mistress" made a wedding gift of Julia Casey and mother, sister Violet, and brothers Andrew and Alfred to her daughter. Bill Homer and 49 other slaves were given to Miss Nancy when she married. Adeline Jackson's master did not sell slaves but he readily swapped them to relatives. Although Jane Harrington's master did not believe in selling slaves, his slaves fell into the hands of slave-dealers at his death. Jonathan Thomas ran away before his turn came when he saw that his young master was selling his recently inherited slaves one by one. Slaves kept alert to conditions in families they belonged to that could force on them new masters—a prospect about which they could not be indifferent.[47]

Families sometimes lost members to thieves. Kidnappers grabbed Abram Harris and his sister Delia while the men of the place were cutting timber down on the river. The thieves yoked Abram and Delia to other boys and girls they had stolen along the way, and marched them to Georgia, where they were sold.[48]

Resistance within the master's family occasionally stopped a proposed sale. One woman rescued from the auction block a favorite slave by threatening to quit her husband if he went ahead with the sale. Slaves themselves sometimes mounted extraordinary resistance to being sold. One woman chopped off her hand, it was said, and defiantly threw it in her master's face. Traders were forced to chain, beat, and closely guard their chattel property. Cleve and Lissa tied up their master and killed him by pouring boiling water down his throat, when he would not promise to keep them together. Mary James's grandmother drowned herself in the James River when her husband was sold.[49]

Some slaves would resist being sold but in time resign themselves to their fate. Tom Holland said, "It took me most a year to git over it, but there I was 'longin' to nother man."[50] Others were anxious to try a new master, hoping that he would turn out better than the one they had. Clara Jones was glad to be sold by a master who beat her to Rufus Jones who worked her less hard, fed her better, and allowed her to attend dances and prayer meetings. Andy Anderson was happy that he had been sold by his hard old master until he discovered that "hell am too good" for his new master.[51] Because slaves generally dreaded to be uprooted from their families and communities masters threatened to sell or did sell unruly slaves for disciplinary reasons. Some slaves conformed to the rules of the plantation, simply because they knew that otherwise their masters would "put them in their pocket," that is, sell them. Millie Simpkins was separated from her husband and sent away in traders' chains in punishment for "stubborness." When slapped, James V. Deane's aunt struck her mistress back, and, in consequence was sold south. Slaves were, of course, sometimes sold for presumed misbehavior, as a maid was, when food she served was mistakenly believed to be poisoned.[52]

Although there was little direct breeding for the slave trade, such as lower animals were bred for the market, there was indirect manipulation of the birth rate of slaves; a mother and child would bring a higher price than a barren woman of comparable skill and vigor. With the closing of the overseas slave trade, except for rare smuggling, the domestic slave population was expected to be self recruiting. And the slave population of the Upper South needed to supply a "surplus" of people for the expanding plantation economy of the Lower South. A stable plantation in Virginia with a full complement of workers having a birth rate mirroring that of the contemporary White South could keep its ranks filled and also be able to export surplus slaves to a new plantation in, say, Texas. Thus the interregional slave trade flowed south and west, from old to new plantation country.

A master could stimulate growth in his workforce by buying young, fertile women and providing them with mates.

He would have to relieve these women of hard labor during the late stages of pregnancy and on through a recovery period after childbirth. He would have to provide mothers and children sufficient food, shelter, and medical attention to maintain health and vitality.

Most slave children were born into slave families; few were sired by "studs," bought or hired. Masters and traders never spoke of stud farms, but they did show enthusiasm for natural increase and so valued youths for their capacity for labor and reproduction. Slaves too, though subject to tyranny, had their say about reproduction. They could resist being made into breeders.[53] Some slaves certainly believed that there were masters who bred slaves, as they bred livestock. They spoke of "studs" or stock men used for that purpose. Others heard about deliberate breeding on other plantations, not on their own. Still others said masters generally did not coerce slaves into having children, but were partial to women who did give birth to many children.

Maggie Stanhouse was one who thought masters bought or rented "studs" to get young women on their places pregnant. Ida Blackshear Hutchinson claimed that her grandfather, Luke Blackshear, sired 56 children as a "stock negro." Lewis Jones was told by his mother that his father was used to breed slaves, that he fathered 12 children by Lewis's mother, 12 by Mary, 10 by Lisa, eight by Mandy, six by Betty, and one or two by several other women. Some women were bred, it was said, not by stock men but by husbands provided them, or forced on them, specifically for that purpose. One master who had four male slaves, and one old woman, joined with a relative, it was claimed, to buy a young couple to get a "start of darkies," which the two owners would share.[54] Rose Williams was forced to live with a bully by her master, who declared: "Woman, I's pay big money for you and I's done dat for de cause I wants you to raise me chillens. I's put you to live with Rufus for dat purpose. Now, if you doesn't want whippin' at de stake, you do what I wants." Rose had two children by Rufus, but she drove him away the moment freedom came.[55]

Women who had many children, "breeding women," were prized. Mary Jane Jones was, she said, in the last "litter" of her mother's 16 children. Her mother had been a wedding gift to "breed slaves," she said, thus her new master promptly bought her a husband to get on with the breeding. Annie Coley's mother "foun' a heap of children," one every other year. Mary Barbour's mother had 16 children, 12 of whom were sold, she said, when very young; the last four were saved by the coming of the war. Martha Jackson said that her aunt, "a breeding woman," had a child every year, and because of that, was never whipped or worked hard.[56]

Allowing women to rest during late stages of pregnancy and after childbirth indirectly increased the birthrate and decreased mortality for both mother and child. Eustace Hodges's mother was provided a doctor at childbirth and permitted to remain in bed for several days. Betty Simmons's mother was given light labor for a month after delivering a baby. Like West Indian planters who learned that improved conditions could lead to a self-recruiting slave population, when the African slave trade was prohibited, Southern planters promoted increase of their slave population by ameliorating conditions, especially for fertile women.[57]

Since masters recruited the next generation of slaves from the ranks of children, it seemed only right to call masters breeders of slaves, so thought Mandy McCullough Cosby, who said her master "raised niggahs to sell." She said that on her plantation little black children played until sundown then were fed buttermilk and corn bread from a trough. When full some of them dropped to the ground asleep. The old "nurse" who looked after them would carry them to a pallet in the big children's room. "Dey git good care," Mandy said, " fo' de master expects dey will bring good money." When they were sold their mistress "cried, but then master jes laugh an' go on."[58] Raised in such a way, David Blount remarked, "As one ole 'oman raised all of de chilluns me an' my brother Johnnie ain't neber knowed who our folkses wuz."[59]

Traders bought and sold people along the road, in small towns, and in busy city markets. One New Orleans market was enclosed by a high, prison-like wall. Inside, a brick building held those for sale. Out in the yard bidders gathered around the auction block. As purchased slaves were led away new lots were driven in to take their place. Swedish traveler Fredrika Bremer was shocked to see at a New Orleans slave market in December, 1850, a buyer take a pretty girl by the chin and open her mouth to inspect her teeth, with no more consideration than if she had been a horse.[60]

Slaves whose turn it was to be sold were aroused early to be spruced up and sorted into groups according to age, strength, and skill. At this point still intact families were broken asunder. All were made to exercise, dance, and act spirited, encouraged by small presents or a broad whip that would sting but not scar. The unsold were sent to bed at 10 in the evening.[61] Olmsted saw at a New Orleans market a group of young men in blue suits and black hats, "silent and sober" and perhaps gratified by the admiration of onlookers, one of whom estimated that these prime specimens must cost at least $1200 each.[62] Prices for assorted slaves in the Memphis market in 1852 were, according to J.M. Keating: carpenters, $2500; a hammerer for a blacksmith, $1114; painters, $1005; field hands, $750–$1000; boys about

12 years of age, $700; girls, 12 to 18 years of age, $600–$800.[63] Prices fluctuated according to place and time, of course. At an estate sale in Columbia, South Carolina, in 1853, young men 15 to 25 sold for $900–$1000; young women, for $750–$850.[64]

The St. Louis market collected "surplus" slaves from its hinterland to be sent down the Mississippi to cotton and sugar-cane country. When traders there encountered heckling from outraged citizens along their route to the river wharf they changed their loading time to four in the morning, before the city began to stir. In Memphis, too, slaves were put on river boats for distribution in the expanding plantation country to the south and southwest. Among these was Betty Simmons, who was loaded on a river boat with about 200 others and shipped to New Orleans where she was sold, and then taken on to the Red River Country of Texas.[65]

Traders also transported their human cargo by sea from the Chesapeake to Gulf ports, particularly New Orleans. During their voyage bondsmen were locked in the hold at night and allowed exercise on deck during the day. Before they reached their new masters some slaves would have traveled by rail, sea, river, and over country roads, from Virginia to Texas.

Slaves going overland were driven in coffles, or droves of up to 300 bondsmen; the usual number was 30 to 40. A drove making around 20 miles a day might be on the road up to a month. Charlotte Willis's grandfather walked with such a group from Virginia to Mississippi. The traders rode horses. The coffle camped at night, and every now and then stopped for some slaves to be "cried off" and others to be bought.[66] Minerva Wells traveled in a caravan where the men walked and the women and children rode in covered wagons. When the caravan made camp the horses were fed, wood cut for the camp fire, food cooked, and places to sleep found. "Dey wuz alwas' so tired from de day's hard journey dat dey et an' turnt in to res' an' sleep. Dey alwas' stopped at all de trading places to buy, sell, an' trade slaves. In dis way mos' any ob 'em wuz liable to be sold any whars long de way."[67] Taverns in Bryantown, Maryland, supplied lockups, with downstairs cells for men and rooms above for women. Next day the coffle would be driven on, or sold.[68] John Smith saw a drove "wid nothin' on but a rag twixt dere legs bein' galloped roun' fore de buyers." Among them a mother, sold apart from her baby and driven chained to 20 or 30 others, fell out of line and died.[69]

W.L. Bost saw slaves chained together without clothes enough to "keep a cat warm." The women in this drove wore dresses with ice clinging to the hems, "as they ran along, jes like sheep in a pasture 'fore they are sheared. They never wore any shoes." The "speculators" rode horses and stayed in hotels while the slaves were locked in quarters and watched by an armed guard. "All through the night I could hear them mournin' and prayin'."[70] Sella Martin observed a coffle set in motion. First marched a row of about 30 men, chained together. Next came the "quiet slaves," followed by women without children. Children able to walk were next in line, and then came mothers with children in arms. Children too old to be carried and too young to walk rode in wagons.[71] James Brown watched speculators bring droves of slaves to Waco, Texas, and vicinity and trade at sheds on the edge of the towns. When parted from family, "Dey has to drag 'em away," he said.[72] Green Cumby, of Henderson County, Texas, observed traders on horses drive big bunches of slaves past his place. "De women would be carryin' l'il ones in dere arms and at night dey bed 'em down jus' like cattle right on de ground 'side of de road."[73]

Slaves of a coffle being sold along the way were displayed for inspection; perhaps stripped naked to reveal flaws or whip scars that could signal rebelliousness, and made to run and jump to test strength and stamina. The auctioneer would, perhaps, as Cato Carter remembered, keep the buyers laughing and in a good mood. A mighty worker would bring a good price, but a worn-out field hand would go for next to nothing.[74] Henry Warfield remembered, when he was sold at age 12, the auctioneer crying, "What do I hear you bid fur this slave? A strong well built slave, clean white teeth, shoulders like a good ox, healthy, clean habits, a bargain, ladies and gentlemen? A fine slave going fur what, sixty dollars? Who will say seventy? Seventy five?"[75]

Slave traders in Memphis during the 1850s brought slaves by water and rail from the Upper South, where they were a surplus in the labor force, for sale to planters in the expanding cotton country of the Southwest. At the beginning of the decade Bolton, Dickens & Co. was the great slave dealing concern in Memphis with agents and branches all over the South. By the end of the decade Nathan Bedford Forrest, later a famous Confederate general, had become the leading slave trader of the city. In 1855 Forrest claimed to have a slave pen, comfortable, clean, and secure, with a capacity of 300. He once expressed surprise that Nat Mayson, carpenter, barber, and fiddler, had run away, "without cause," from his well run establishment.[76]

Other traders in Memphis included M.A. & A.S. Levy, G.B. Locke, Moran & Co., and J.E. Phillips. On February 27, 1852, Locke advertised: "I will sell, in front of my office, on Madison street, 10 likely negroes—consisting of men, women, boys and girls. These negroes are acclimated—sold for no fault, and will be fully guaranteed as to title, health and habits." On May 27, 1852, Locke offered "boy Tom, 14 years old; woman Nancy, 40 years old; woman Nelly, 38 years old; man Jerry, 40 years old; woman Alice, 22 years old; woman Esther, 38 years old. Terms: cash. Also woman Nancy, 20 years old, and her child, 5 months old. Terms. Note satisfactorily endorsed, payable in Bank at 4 months."[77]

On June 15, 1852, Bolton, Dickens & Co. promised to have a large lot of Virginia blacks in the fall for the Southwest trade. The following autumn, Forrest advertised to buy 500 blacks, also for the Southwest trade.[78] Blakey & McAfee, of 93 Olive St., St. Louis, informed the Memphis dealers that it could send Missouri slaves to Memphis at good prices, for the Southwest trade: "Our agents in all parts of the state are continually buying and shipping to us. With our facilities, we feel assured that we can sell Negroes at prices $100 to $150 below Southern rates."[79] Advertisements in the Memphis *Daily Appeal* of slaves for sale were accompanied by a logo of a man carrying on his shoulder a bag tied to a stick and a woman carrying a bag, both ready to travel to some new master's place.[80]

Traders advertised slaves with special skills: "a first rate Cook, Washer and Ironer, and her husband a good Gardener;" Sally Ann, 24, a "No. 1 cook, washer, ironer, general servant;" Sam, 28, "a house and body servant"; Jerry, "a first rate Steward and Manager," and Joanna, "a superior house servant"; a 14-year-old girl, "a good house servant"; a woman, 22 years old, "a good cook, washer and ironer, and a first rate house servant;" an 18 year old boy, "a good waiter, stout and healthy;" a 23 year old girl, a "splendid meat and pastry cook;" "a No. 1 Blacksmith and wife and child." But they were also ready to sell young children. Locke offered "likely boys" seven and nine years of age, and a "very smart" 11-year-old girl.[81]

Slaves were sold also through judicial process to satisfy debt and settle estates. By virtue of a decree of the Chancery

Court, Memphis, three slaves and 100 acres of land of the late Joshua C. Lundy were to be sold at auction, January 18, 1851. Similarly, on January 31, 1851, slaves of the deceased William S. Abernathy were to be sold to the highest bidder: Jack, about 40; Sam, about 28; Martha, about 30; and Rosa, about 30. To satisfy debt the following were offered at auction in front of the Commercial Hotel, Memphis, May 24, 1851: "John and his wife Harriet, both about the age of 25 years, Charlotte, about the age of 25 years and her three children: Tom 6 years old, Maria 4 years old, and infant child." The administrator of an estate just south of Memphis offered, December 29, 1852, 25 "valuable slaves, men, women, boys and girls," Virginia blacks acclimated three years. In consequence of the death of their master 15 to 20 blacks "under good discipline and easily managed" were offered for sale, January 17, 1853. So it went: slave families and communities were broken up and scattered because of indebtedness or death of their owners. Slaves also suffered the further indignity of being sold with livestock, feed, and farm implements, as at a sale near Memphis, December 20, 1853, of 24 blacks, and furniture together with farm implements, mules, horses, steers, cows, hogs, corn, a buggy, and a Pratt's cotton gin.[82]

Money to be made in selling slaves tempted some particularly shady dealers to trade in stolen slaves. The business of stealing blacks was, the Memphis *Daily Appeal* declared, February 9, 1852, carried on to an alarming extent in Arkansas, West Tennessee, and North Mississippi, and slave stealers were reported prowling around Memphis. One of the kidnapped, Anne Eliza Webster, a free woman, was seized in Pennsylvania, where she was raised, and sold as a slave in Louisville. Brought to Memphis, she made her freedom known and her pretended owner was forced to flee. About the same time another slave stealer was sentenced to three years in jail for attempting to run off with a slave of a Colonel Thornton. Earlier in the year a kidnapper was foiled in an attempt to seize a "very valuable negro man" who managed to break loose and make good his escape. In this connection slaveholders were warned that many suspicious characters were lurking about Memphis.[83] Solomon Northup was kidnapped in Washington, D.C., carried to the Bayou Country of Louisiana, and kept in slavery for 12 years, until he managed to get news of his predicament to former owners of his family in the North.[84]

4

Runaways; Crimes and Punishment

Slaves ran away to gain freedom, to be reunited with loved ones, to enjoy a little leisure, and for sundry other reasons, although many never attempted to flee because the vigilance of the slaveocracy made success unlikely and punishment for failure practically certain. Would–be fugitives often held back because they could not bear to leave behind family and friends.

When one master went on a journey and his overseer, who was "nothing nohow but poor white trash," took advantage of his absence to play the bully, some of the abused slaves hid out until their master returned. From time to time slaves ran off to nearby woods in the hope of avoiding an expected whipping. If promised leniency they often promptly returned. One woman came back when she was allowed to hire herself out and thus get out of the reach of her cruel mistress. Another fugitive returned in exchange for the privilege of hiring herself out to escape the sexual demands of the overseer.[1]

Some slaves chose life in the woods over drudgery of the work gang. Whenever Ellis Jefson's runaway father was caught, for example, he stoically took his punishment and at first opportunity headed again for a spell of freedom in the woods. Friends and relatives gave aid and comfort to such

fugitives by carrying them "somethin' to eat along." An "African king," who, it was said, could not be owned, was supported in his hideaway cave by people he believed were bound to serve his majesty's needs.[2]

In many cases slaves ran away to see relatives from whom they had been separated. Lizzie McCloud often went off, without anybody's leave, to visit her mother who lived some miles away, despite the whipping she invariably suffered when caught.[3] Unwillingness to leave families behind kept many slaves, especially females, at home. Men recently from Africa with remembrance of lost freedom and few family ties in their new land of bondage were, said Cinte Lewis, "ones what mostly runs away to de woods."[4]

Abram Harris's father would hide in the cane thickets but come in close at night for food the women would slip him. When it was cold he would sleep under the corn crib with the dogs. Masters usually could count on hunger to bring runaways in, for "when they got starved out they'd come outen the woods." An overseer on a great Central Mississippi plantation would pressure the slaves to withold food and other aid from runaways by requiring all to work on Sundays and by depriving them of other privileges until the runaways returned.[5]

Caroline Hammond's father smuggled his family from Maryland to Pennsylvania with the help of the Underground Railroad; Jim Taylor found refuge at Allen's Mission in Philadelphia, an African-American church that actively helped runaway slaves; and Joe Nick escaped from Maryland by riding the rails west. William and Ellen Craft, with Ellen masquerading as the master and William as her slave, escaped from Georgia to Boston. After the enactment of the Fugitive Slave Law in 1850, which made runaway slaves anywhere in the North liable to be sent back South, the Crafts fled to Liverpool, England.[6] Slaves from Texas who fled to Mexico happily discovered that Mexicans were untroubled about their color.[7]

Harriet Tubman escaped from slavery in Maryland but often risked her freedom by returning to Maryland to lead relatives and friends out of bondage. In forays into slave country she was courageous and prudent, imaginative and practical. She went in winter when nights were long and few people abroad, and started back northward on Saturday night so that her followers would not be missed until work call on Monday morning. She led her charges across streams on railroad bridges; reckoned time by the stars, and would not allow anyone to turn back. She prayed fervently for divine assistance and was confident her prayers were heard. She believed that God's good time of freedom for all her people was approaching.[8]

Although the great characters Harriet Tubman and Frederick Douglass, and many others, escaped from the South, most fugitives hid in nearby woods and swamps until caught or until they voluntarily returned to their plantations. Runaways were likely to be tracked down within a week, whipped hard, and put back to work. But some fugitives held out for long periods, keeping ahead of hounds and patrols and living on Old Master's hogs and chickens and food provided by friends and relatives in the quarters. Nancy resourcefully remained hidden in the woods for three long years. Charlotte kept out of sight for several months in basements of a county court house and the Baptist Church, where she was secreted food by other slaves and from where she would come out at night for dances and entertainments. A seamstress whose hiding place was a hollow tree remained free for much of one winter but lost her legs because of frost bite. Thereafter she hopped about swinging her padded knees between her arms. One house servant, it was said, ran to the woods to escape a whipping and remained there three years sheltered in a cave, where she bore three children and where she and her children kept hidden until freedom came. Edinbur Randall lived for several months on berries and various wild plants, barely protected by briar-shredded clothes.[9] The woods were full of runaways, said Gill Ruffin of Harrison County, Texas, "I heered them houn's a runnin' 'em like deer many a time, and heered dat whip when they's caught."[10]

Many masters would not wait for hunger and loneliness to force fugitives to return but would set dogs on their tracks at once. It seemed to Louis Johnson that rich planters kept poor whites with hounds in the neighborhood just to run down fugitive slaves. If there were no poor whites available the sheriff would bring along his own dogs. "Mars Billy" would borrow hounds from a neighbor, hunt down the runaway — and "make him pay." One tracker who kept 16 hounds charged 10 dollars for each fugitive captured. An Alabama slave catcher with bloodhounds charged 10 to 20 dollars for a two-or three-day chase. Tracker A.G. Neal, of Shelby County, Tennessee, advertised that he held in readiness six "Negro dogs" to recover runaway blacks.[11]

If not restrained dogs would maul a cornered runaway. As Evie Herrin reported, "Them dogs went right straight to the ditch where my mother was hid, and before the men could get to them, they had torn most of her clothes off her, and had bitten her all over. When they brought her in, she was a sight to see, all covered with blood and dirt."[12] Tom Wilson was caught and cut up viciously by hounds; but in a second attempt succeeded in eluding the hounds and making his way to freedom.[13] Runaways tried various devices to confuse the hounds and throw them off the trail. They greased their feet with lard and snuff and covered their shoes with pepper. They ran in streams and through pig sties. They sprinkled soil from a newly dug grave behind them as they ran and they turned on pursuing dogs with any weapon available. One runaway attacked pursuing dogs with a scythe, scattered them, and got away.[14]

One master would leniently punish a captured runaway lest severity make him run again; another would react with vengeance. A seemingly incorrigible female runaway was at last threatened with the fodder block, a machine that crushed feed for livestock. Faced with the prospect of torture and perhaps death she promised never to run away again and, according to Eugenia Weatherall, never did. Tom Wilson's father, caught by hounds, was tied over a barrel, and whipped, off and on, from sunup to sundown. Some runaways were yoked and belled; others were shackled with ball and chain.[15] Jack Flowers's master allowed the dogs to rip Jack's flesh, then shackled him in irons and flogged him every day, until Jack escaped for good. Frequent runaway Lavima Bell was branded, her ears cropped, and one finger cut off, so that her master could readily identify her if she fled again. She did flee again but as usual was caught. Another captured runaway had a wooden frame with a bell fastened over his shoulders, like a steer in a yoke, and was kept in this contraption for about a year. A Raleigh, Tennessee, slaveholder laid on the lash hundreds of times and cut off both ears of a fugitive. Incensed neighbors did chase this brutal slaveholder out of their country with a warrant for his arrest.[16]

Incorrigible runaways were more likely to be sold "down river" than punished barbarously. William Jackson was caught, put on bread and water, then sold. His master avowed that he would never keep a slave that would run off. Inveterate runaway Jack was sold from the Polk plantation near Coffeyville, Mississippi, because neighboring planters judged him a bad example for their slaves. "Old Joe," like many another, quit his running away when threatened with being auctioned on the block. J.W.C. Pennington was restrained from attempting escape by love for his family and fear that he would be severely punished and sold South if he failed. But the hour came when he must risk everything, and, after much hardship and danger, he reached the North and freedom.[17]

In seaports traffic with distant places offered routes of escape. River cities, especially Mississippi River cities, also provided fugitives various opportunities to reach the Free States. In border towns the proximity of free territory constantly lured the enslaved. Ships, steamboats, and North-South railroads, even rafts and canoes, and wagons and drays, could carry runaways on their journey to freedom.[18]

Runaways, urban and rural, hoped to and often did lose themselves in the crowds of the city. Bob, for example, described as copper colored, about 29, about five feet eight inches tall and weighing around 155 pounds, "sprightly and quick," a stammerer, fast walker, fond of music and a banjo player, probably with whip marks on his back, fled in March,

1851, from Hemstead County, Arkansas, to a city, his master believed. In May, 1851, John, 25 to 30 years old, was thought to be "lurking" about Memphis. Also somewhere in Memphis, in October, 1852, Marshall, about 19, a "bright mulatto," and "quite sensible," was supposed to be in hiding. In September, 1853, Caroline, about 25, copper colored, with straight hair and a small scar on her forehead, was believed to be on her way to New Orleans, or up river.[19]

Public notices, such as in the Memphis *Daily Appeal* in the late 1840s and early 1850s, reveal something of the purposes of runaways. Some of them, as we have seen, hoped for reunion with relatives and friends from whom they had been torn by the exigencies of slavery. For example, Adam, about 30, approximately five feet seven inches tall, and "yellow" in complexion, ran away in September, 1848, from Will Polk, of Walnut Bend, Arkansas, and was, his master surmised, "lurking" around the plantation of Isaac Burgett, his former master. In February, 1851, Jurden, about 30, six feet four, and black, also was thought to be "lurking" near the place of Osa Pool, owner of Jurden's wife. Next month, in March, 1851, John, around 30, approximately five feet eight, and weighing about 180 pounds, compactly built, black, frank and open in countenance, "likely and sensible," was believed to be in his wife's neighborhood, near Covington, Tennessee, or trying to get to a free state. In October, 1851, Tom, 25, weighing 155 pounds, left his new master in Tippah County, Mississippi, and, it appeared, was heading for his former home in Overton County, Tennessee. In late November, 1851, Jim, six feet tall, with a burn scar under his chin and a gap between his teeth, was, his master thought, trying to get from Lake Providence, Louisiana, to Wayne County, Missouri, from where he had been sold. Sam, about 33, five feet eight, about

140 pounds was thought headed for Weekly County, Tennessee, where he had been bought. In January, 1853, Ned, about 40, six feet and weighing 170 pounds, dark brown, worked well in wood and could stock a plow, was believed to be trying to get to Texas, where his wife had been taken, or to a free state. Ned, his master thought, probably had a pass. In April, 1853, Isaac, 25 to 30, 150 pounds, and yellow, was on his way to his former home in Bourbon County, Kentucky, his Jefferson County, Mississippi, master thought.[20]

Other fugitives most likely trying to get from the Mid-South to the free states during the 1850s included, among an indeterminate number, Henry, who could read and write and probably had a pass; Billy, knock-kneed, with one big toe cut off, vowing never to acknowledge his master's name; and Rueb, whose name was branded on his forehead. Although many fugitives struck out on their own, some left in twos and threes, as did Guy and his wife Caroline, and Henry, Birl, and Bowles.[21] Some Abolitionists, black and white, notably those of the Underground Railroad, actively helped runaway slaves gain freedom in the North and in Canada. Clashes between these activists and slave-catchers escalated as war approached, and riots broke out in various places. It took federal troops to remand fugitive Anthony Burns from Boston to Virginia in 1854.[22]

Southern States developed a system of patrols to discipline slaves off their plantations and to prevent them from fleeing or engaging in subversion. For their part slaves did slip away from their prison-camp plantations, even rise in bloody but futile rebellion, as in the Nat Turner Rebellion in Virginia in 1831 and in scattered uprisings elsewhere. Like military police on the lookout for soldiers absent without leave or behaving in a forbidden manner, patrols halted slaves and inspected their passes. Those absent without permission were whipped and taken back to their plantation. Members of patrols often acted the tyrant, but their abuse of authority could be checked by the big planters, principal rulers of the community, whose word was law.

Patrols of six or eight and more mounted men took their turn scouring their militia districts on the lookout for trouble from roaming blacks. Their chief aims were to keep slaves from "runnin' 'round at night an' from runnin' away."[23] Everywhere slaves went or assembled they found patrols keeping an eye on them. "Dere was no jail for us," said Isiah Jefferies, "de Patterollers kept us straight."[24] But Manda Walker said "classy white bukra men" never patrolled, just "some low down white men, dat never owned a nigger in deir life, doin' de patarollin' and a strippin' de clothes off men, lak pappy, right befo' de wives and chillern and beatin' de blood out of him."[25] Lewis Clark claimed that the meanest men of the district were selected for the patrol. Such men entered slave cabins at night, he said, and did what they wanted with wives and daughters. In Walker County, Texas, this sort would, Harriet Barrett said, go through the quarters and "walk right over us when us sleeps." Some masters would not, however, permit the patrol to come on their places and bully their slaves.[26]

The main reason slave men slipped out at night, according to Henry Green, was on account of their courting some girl on another place. At a dance the patrol might rush in, grab the men, and take those without a pass to the woods for whipping. They did not bother the women so much. A man with a pass might have such a merry time at a dance that he would over stay his pass and become fair game for the patrol.[27]

There were many men willing to test the vigilance of the patrol. Tom Holland, among them, liked to visit young people on neighboring places. Though sometimes caught and whipped he was not deterred from slipping away to see his friends, especially on moonlit nights when he could see to travel and yet avoid the patrol. Other daring men managed to hide from, outrun, or outfox the patrol. Women hid suitors, or visiting spouses, perhaps under a loose board in the floor.[28] A widely told story was that a band of men would tie a strong grapevine to trees and across a road and then at night lure a patrol in hot pursuit to be ignominiously thrown from their horses when they hit the taut vine. Another popular story told of pursued slaves pitching shovels full of ashes in the faces of patrollers as they broke through the cabin door, then dashing to safety while the disabled patrollers struggled to a creek to wash out their eyes.[29]

The ordinary way to escape the patrol was to run fast, dodge trees, and jump fences. As a variation of a well known song had it:

> Run, nigger run
> The pateroles'll get you
> That nigger run
> That nigger flew
> That nigger bust
> His Sunday shoe
> Run, nigger, run
> The pateroles'll get you[30]

Patrollers whipped those caught without passes within limits prescribed by slaveholders and permitted by their own humanity. Sam Broach knew patrollers who lightly brushed "em to make 'em stay home." Hattie Suggs reported, on the other hand, that a patrol forced her aunt to pull her clothes down to her waist, whipped her, and proclaimed: "We came to whip you niggers pass or no pass." More common perhaps was the behavior of a patrol which Adrianna Kerns saw run a slave down, drag him from under a bed, and give him a regular thrashing.[31]

The patrol was, the slaves knew, effective in apprehending runaways and in general surveillance; they experienced its power. In her vicinity, "Nobody ever studied about running off to the North or to anywhere else for that matter,"remarked Sally Dixon. "We knowed well and good them patrollers would catch us if we ever started. We would hear about such as that going on once in a while from some of the folks what would come into our dances." An inventory of slaves on a large Louisiana plantation in 1849 designated 10 of the men but none of the women as having at some time run away. From time to time, Jack, Ben, Hardy, Gilbert, Harbart, Charles, and Addison would run from the Polk plantation in Mississippi and when caught would take their whipping and wait an opportunity to flee again. Their punishment did not make them accept the life of the slave.[32]

Slavery was not maintained by the violence of the lash alone. It was supported also by the education of slaves in a sense of inferiority and of whites in a spirit of arrogance. Differences between the races were emphasized in all areas of life, and whites exercised constant surveillance over blacks to enforce these differences. However, when the inferior-superior relation between the races was challenged whites resorted to the police power of the state, which meant, in practical terms, to the whip.

Since slaves would not willingly endure bondage and attendant exploitation, they had to be coerced into doing their master's will. A generally enlightened planter of Central Mississippi, who believed that God would bring an end to slavery one day, thought that it was necessary to use the lash occasionally because slaves "never really felt under any moral obligation to obey their masters," that " they were obedient just so far as they saw that they must be to avoid punishment."[33]

Slaves were whipped for leaving the plantation without permission, "sassing" a white person, fighting in the quarters; lying, stealing, slacking; running away; doing careless work; failing to meet a work quota; violating plantation rules, such as keeping a light in the cabin after hours. Masters were likely to use the whip, also, to punish offenses which in a free society would be punished by fines and incarceration. The whip kept some people out of the pen, admitted Gabe Butler.[34]

On some plantations the whip was wielded gently and seldom used; privileges would be withdrawn instead, or extra work assigned. On one of these places only light "brushings" were permitted; on another delinquents were confined in a plantation jail on weekends. A Georgia planter would make a show of whipping by taking a delinquent into the barn and have him cry out as if he were suffering blows, to impress the others. Emily Dixon's mistress whipped her only once-and then with a straw. Harrison Beckett's master, it was said, never whipped without cause; then he used only a switch to sting but never to cut and bruise. A modest whipping, Willis Cozart thought, "wuz thirty-nine or forty lashes an' a real whippin' wuz a even hundred," too many for most people to stand.[35]

On a plantation near Madisonville, Texas, one got 50 licks for a first offense and 75 for a second offense. The practice on a North Carolina place was for the master, or overseer, to strip the offender, beat him with a paddle with holes to raise blisters, break the blisters with a cat o' nine tails, and wash the wounds with salt water. An Alabama overseer would strip the slave, lock his feet in a block, bend him over a log, and lash him with a leather strap with holes. A pregnant woman usually was whipped face down, with her protruding belly in a hole dug in the ground, to protect her unborn baby.[36]

Besides the whip, chains, stockades, and other instruments of punishment were used. A blacksmith might be ordered to fasten heavy irons to a recalcitrant's legs or an iron collar, with prongs, around his neck. Some hard-to-manage slaves were chained to a tree for a spell. A slacker might be shamed by being required to wear a barrel, a "Louisiana shirt," said C.B. McCray. Difficult slaves might be put in plantation jails. One jail, constructed like an ice house, without windows and dark, was "sho' bad to git locked up in." Pauline Grice's master did not whip troublesome slaves but confined them in his jail, without food, until they promised to "do right." A deep, well-like hole served one planter as a jail. Ordinarily slaves being disciplined by jail were confined at night or on weekends so that their daily labor would not be lost.[37]

Failure to meet a work quota usually resulted in punishment. When a cotton picker weighed in at the end of the day with too few pounds picked, he might there and then be whipped, with his head fastened between two fence rails. James Morgan's mother used to slip some of her cotton to slower pickers to save them a whipping.[38]

Quotas were assigned according to age and ability. Prime workers might be expected to pick 300 or more pounds of cotton but the less able might get by with as little as 100 pounds. A hard taskmaster would drive his people long hours, feed them by torchlight morning and evening, and lash them if they failed to meet their quotas. Prince Smith had to finish his week's work or get 15 to 25 lashes and extra tasks on Sunday. Many had reason to sing: "Watch de sun, see how she run; never let her ketch yo' wid yer wurk undun." Morning and evening chores also had to be done. One who neglected to feed the horses or milk the cows could expect to be punished.[39]

Enforcing a certain pace as the standard of satisfactory work, the master or his overseer would ride along the ranks of workers cracking his whip at anyone lagging. Mary Tabon's mother bore a scar of the lash on her shoulder made by her master as she hoed cotton at a rate that displeased him.[40] The old and young were seldom pushed so hard. "Gran'pa Berry wuz too old to wuk in de field so he stayed roun' de house an' piddled," said Alec Bostwick. "He cut up wood, tended to de gyardens an' yard, an' bottomed chairs."[41]

Lapses in the house, as in the field, brought punishment, sometimes severe punishment. One cook was staked to the ground and whipped for burning waffles. Annie Row was whipped when still a child for stumbling and breaking a plate. Elizabeth Finley's mistress lashed the house servants with a cowhide whip whenever they did not "do to suit her."[42]

Slaves who displeased their master by word or demeanor, the "sassy," "rude," or "stubborn," were likely to get stung by the whip. The "sassy" ones, according to William Gant, were the ones most frequently whipped. Other delinquencies, such as fighting, brought punishment, but slaves had so much work to do that for the most part they had, thought Reuben Fox, little time or energy for "devilment." Some slaves believed that they deserved the whippings they got for, say, lying. Others could not be corrected, or conquered, by lashes. One great worker was whipped so often to no avail that her master gave up and "turned her loose."[43]

Some favored persons were exempt from whippings. No one was allowed to lay a hand on Uncle Arch, a carriage driver. Also protected from the lash were Jack Green's father, a house servant; Uncle Julius, foreman of the plow hands; and Uncle Edwards, foreman of the hoe hands. Martha Jackson was never whipped, because she, a "breeding woman," bore a child year after year.[44] What Mary Reynolds, not among the favored, hated most "was when they'd beat me and I didn't know what they beat me for, and I hated them strippin' me naked as the day I was born."[45]

Arbitrary masters found excuses to whip their slaves for being late, turning in trashy cotton, being saucy, breaking a tool, for any reason. One master would whip his workers "for half doin' the plowin' or hoein' but if they done it right he'd find something else to whip them for."[46] Some masters whipped slaves not to get work done or to maintain discipline but to give vent to their violence. When drunk, with his passions unleashed, Austin Parnell's master would grab any slave, force him to strip, and give him a beating. The spirit of violence often spread throughout the master's household. When the grownups were not whipping her, Rachel Harris said, their children were.[47]

Brutal whippings left Maggie Wesmoland scarred "all over." Her master would, she said, "strip me stark naked and tie my hands crossed and whoop me till the blood ooze out and drip on the ground when I walked. The flies blowed me time and again. Miss Betty catch him gone, would grease my places and put turpentine on them."[48] A Georgia master when angry would, it was said, lock a slave, head, hands, and feet, in the stocks for several days, and whip him each day. Even the cows and horses flinched when Charlie Moses's master approached. He would whip a slave near to death, Charlie said, then kick him. When a small boy Charlie Hunter could do nothing but stand by and cry when his mother was chained to a log and mercilessly whipped for little or no reason. Charles Crawley learned to hate white people, he said, when he watched an overseer string up his mother, and beat her till the blood ran down to her heels, as she dangled above the ground.[49] Delia Garlic

said "dem days was hell," when they could "tie you up to a tree, wid yo' face to de tree an' yo' arms fastened tight aroun' it," and with a long, curling whip bring blood with every blow, and "folks a mile away could hear dem awful whippings."[50] A South Carolina master sometimes would lock a slave in a cramped sweat box, or tie him on the floor with a heavy weight on his chest, or put him on a high scaffold on which he hardly had room to stand. Victoria Perry was as afraid of her master as of a mad dog. If he became angry at one slave, he was apt to whip them all. Hector Smith saw his master whip his grandmother "like he didn't have no soul to save."[51] An ex-slave reflecting on the cruelty of slavery remarked, "I ain't never seen how God can forgive those mean white folks for what they done to niggers way back yonder."[52]

Cruelty unbounded resulted in the deaths of some slaves. W.L. Bost saw a rebellious slave tied to a post and cut up with a whip, washed with salt water, and beaten again until he died. Frank Menefee knew a person who was slashed so severely he died from his injuries a few days later. Pasa Barnwell said an old blacksmith was, because he quit work at nine at night with his work unfinished, beaten so cruelly that he died the next day. Mary Armstrong said her mistress whipped Mary's nine-month old sister to death, for crying. Henry Walton claimed that his mother was whipped to death. Leah Garret said her master beat the cook to death. Vinnie Busby said her master beat to death a slave he hitched to a plow like a horse. Lucindy Shaw saw an overseer beat a pregnant woman and cause the death of both mother and child, born prematurely because of the beating. A rebellious slave who refused to take off his shirt to be whipped was, Thomas Jones said, shot dead.[53] Hilliard Johnson said, "I did see 'em kill old Collins, but dey done dat wid a shot gun jes' ca'se dey couldn't control him."[54]

Slaves usually submitted to whippings rather than face even harsher punishment. One slave who resisted an overseer was kept in chains during the day and in a jail at night. A rebel on another plantation was put on the auction block.[55] Regardless of the consequences an occasional slave would openly rebel against his master.

After suffering one hard whipping, Sylvia, when threatened with another, struck the overseer with a fence rail. Frederick Douglass revived his almost conquered spirit by fighting a "negro beater" who had whipped him over and over again. To avenge his mother's being whipped Warren McKinney threw rocks at his master. Mother Anne Clark's father, who had never been whipped, was shot dead for refusing to take a whipping. Lucy, who had slipped away to a dance, drowned herself rather than be whipped by the patrol. J.L. Smith's Uncle Lewis had to be whipped by his master's mother, for he would strike back, except at a woman. One man would not permit his wife to be whipped but would himself accept her punishment, an exchange the master allowed for there was nothing else he could do but kill the stalwart husband, who was a good worker. Eugenia Weatherall's father was, she said, never whipped by an overseer because everyone knew what a crack shot he was. Ervin Smith's Uncle Saul was executed for killing a man who had whipped him, and Ervin's Uncle George, who also killed a man for the same reason, was saved by being spirited away by his white sister.[56]

Anna Huggins said that her mother killed an overseer who was beating her. A group of women jumped an overseer who had caused one of them to have a miscarriage and threatened to burn him in a brush pile but were quieted by the master who sent the overseer away. Anna Williamson's mother tore the clothes off an overseer who whipped her, and forced him

off the place. Dianah Watson's aunt seized the whip of an overseer who was whipping her and, in turn, thrashed him until he was unable to stand. Fellow slaves then threw the disabled overseer over a cliff, which broke his neck and killed him.[57]

It was difficult to maintain control over urban slaves. They often were away from their owners, many of them hired out, going about the city doing their work. They associated with other slaves from all over the city, with free blacks, and also with whites, perhaps in a grog shop or in a church. Grocers, saloon keepers, clergy, especially those with connections to black churches, and employers of hired slaves, objected to rigid restrictions on their clients. Still, slavery did exist in the city, and, because slaves were away from their masters so much, public authorities exercised considerable control over them.[58]

Urban slaves found that at any time the police could drag them before a judge for real or trumped-up violations of the city's elaborate slave ordinances. Before the judge they had next to no chance to defend themselves, and then masters did not usually appear in court to help them. Punishment might be time in the workhouse, but most often it was a whipping. Sometimes the master was fined for his slave's dereliction.[59]

Ordinances closely regulating assemblies were hard to bear since slaves assembled for games, to visit with family and friends, to view spectacles, and for other purposes of social intercourse. But slaves might also gather to conspire against their masters, so their assemblies were carefully regulated. An 1856 Memphis ordinance prohibited night meetings of slaves without written permission of the mayor, and supervision by the police. Slaves were also required to go to their homes at "nine taps of the bell in Court Square."[60] In the early 1850s Memphis slaves were most often punished by public authorities for stealing, fighting among themselves and with whites, drunkeness, insolence, gambling, driving carts and drays recklessly, hiring themselves without their master's permission, and gathering at disorderly houses. Whites were fined for forbidden dealings with slaves, such as selling them liquor. Sometimes masters were fined to encourage them to govern their delinquent slaves with a tighter rein.

Memphis police hauled slaves charged with various offenses before city judges who sentenced them, as a rule, to 10 to 39 lashes at the whipping post. Among these unfortunates Ben was given 25 lashes for insolence, but Francis, also convicted of insolence, was punished with only 10 lashes because of his youth. In response to complaints about growing insolence among the slave population, authorities would round up considerable numbers of the sassy to learn proper deference at the whipping post, and to serve as examples to the rest.[61]

Rather than be sent to jail Albert had to endure 39 stripes of the whip for stealing a watch; Aleck, 36 for stealing wood; Sarah, a "light" whipping, on account of her youth, for stealing six or seven dollars. Amey was merely admonished by the judge for theft, because the "delicate state of her health prevented the usual penalty." Wallace bore 25 lashes, also for petty theft, and his master was charged with court costs. Giles, Cyrus, Moses, and Peter were sentenced to 25 lashes each for gambling. Charles also had to take a whipping for gambling. Five other gamblers were fined three dollars each, their masters paying their fines. But Spencer, Jacob, Danger, Anderson, Stephen, and Chester had to take their turn at the whipping post.[62]

Complaints about "black rascals" driving drays and carts at a furious speed to the peril of women and children prompted the Memphis police to bring some of the culprits before the judge. One speeding driver resisted arrest and was given a "sound beating" by the police officer. Another, Ephriam, was dragged before the court for "fast trotting." Harassed by strict enforcement of an ordinance against reckless driving, a long line of draymen and cartmen responded by proceeding down the street so close together and at such a leisurely pace that pedestrians were kept waiting while the drivers "looked on with perfect indifference."[63]

Slaves were publicly flogged for fighting among themselves and with whites, the number of lashes given varying, with some sentences following the "law of Moses—forty save one." Other delinquencies brought similar punishment. Davis had 25 blows of the whip laid on him for being abroad in the city after nine at night, without a pass. Others were disciplined for assembling on street corners and "offending the ears and propriety of passers-ladies as well as gentlemen-by their coarse and profane language." John, George, and Isaac received stripes for drunkenness. Jim was whipped for disorderly conduct while taking his "gal for a Sunday drive on the Plank Road." Lewis had to endure 25 lashes for threatening a policeman with an axe, while drunk.[64]

Murder committed by a slave on a white was punished severely but murder of a slave by a slave or of a slave by a white person was leniently dealt with. Two males who confessed to killing their master, in DeSoto County, Mississippi, in January, 1852, were at once hung from a tree near the scene of the crime by "citizens" administering "summary justice." Their pregnant confederate was not, however, lynched. Grundy, convicted of murdering a fellow slave, Si, was sentenced by a Memphis court to receive 150 lashes, given in portions at different times, and to be jailed for three months. In October, 1852, George was sentenced to 39 lashes and removal from the state for killing Jim because of an affair involving George's wife. In March, 1852, a Memphis white boy was, on the other hand, acquitted of murder for killing a black man who used abusive and threatening language to his mother.[65]

Occasionally masters saved their slaves from public flogging by paying fines. Newton Mitchell paid one dollar and costs to save his slave from being whipped for fast driving. A mistress whose slave hired herself out without permission nevertheless paid the fine to protect her. Harriet also was saved from the whip for "rambling away" from her master's residence; her master paying five dollars and costs. Candace's master too paid five dollars and costs to satisfy for Candace strolling about and living away from her master's residence.[66]

Whites were fined for selling liquor to slaves, trading with them without their masters' consent, even for providing certain forms of entertainment for a fee. During 1852–1853 certain whites who contributed to slaves' "demoralization" and "insubordination" by selling them liquor were ordered to pay assorted fines. A Memphis employer of a large number of slaves complained when one afternoon nearly all his workers showed up intoxicated. Other whites were brought before the court for trading with slaves in various ways. And Charles Lenehart traded in entertainment by giving a "Grand Fancy Ball" in consideration of which his black guests were thrashed and he was fined $20. These fines amounted to little or nothing compared to the 15 years in prison a Louisville court sentenced the Reverend Calvin Fairbank for "enticing a slave to run off."[67]

5

Slave Labor and Labor Management

Slave carpenters, bricklayers, masons, lathers, plasterers, and other craftsmen built on their home plantations and were often hired out as well. One carpenter superintended his master's grist mill and was hired out as a carpenter to the neighborhood. Carpenters were in such demand that in the Memphis slave market in 1852 they brought $2500 compared to $1000 for field hands. Some bricklayers, plasterers, and other tradesmen, who did a great deal of building in Wilmington, North Carolina, negotiated their own wages and sent a portion to their masters. One stonecutter hired his time, paid his mistress her share, and with the rest of his earnings kept his wife and children with him.[1]

Slaves owned or hired by business concerns worked in textile mills and tobacco factories, in iron works and sugar refineries. They helped build railroads and turnpikes and operate canals and riverboat lines. Those hired could be rented with year-long or short-term contracts to meet fluctuating demand or hired by businesses or individuals for special projects.[2] In February, 1848, J. Delafield, Jr., notified slaveholders in and around Memphis that he wanted to hire three stout slave wood choppers. Another Memphian wished to rent out his "good washer and cooker" on moderate terms. In August, 1851, Thomas

Peters and Byrd Hill advertised for 50–100 strong men until Christmas to work on the Hernando Plank Road in Mississippi. Masters were assured that the road went through "healthy country" and that their men would be well provided for. In February, 1852, Jacob, 12 years old, and Sam, 11, were offered for hire by the month or year to "good masters." In March, 1852, 50 black men were wanted for hire by the Memphis and Charleston Railroad. Thomas, rented by James Campbell to J.M. Fletcher, ran away in the fall, 1847, but was captured and jailed in Tipton County, Tennessee, pending his master's arrival, with jailor's costs, to take him back to slavery in Memphis.[3]

Hired out slaves could make some money for themselves. J.W. Fairley was "tasked" for one dollar a day but earned two dollars, one dollar for his master and one dollar for himself. Prince Johnson's grandmother earned enough beyond her master's take to buy two feather beds. Parke Johnston, a carpenter in the Richmond, Virginia, area, made enough above his hire to buy gifts for his wife and children. Other hired-out slaves made some money for themselves and their masters in towns and cities as bakers, barbers, cooks, seamstresses, washerwomen, warehousemen, painters, and shipyard workers. An occasional hired-out slave was able to buy his freedom and, more rarely, freedom for his family too.[4]

Slave craftsmen who contracted their time encountered resistance from white artisans who refused to work alongside them and who sought to monopolize the skilled trades for themselves. In New Orleans only Irish and German craftsmen would, according to Frederick Law Olmsted, work with slave craftsmen. In Memphis in 1852 the cost of hiring slave laborers per month varied from $10 to $12, while white workers earned $12 to $15 per month. The resulting competition led to strikes, such as that of journeymen bricklayers of Memphis in the spring of 1852, which aimed to check the hiring of slaves in the crafts. On the other side of the coin, masters feared that their artisan slaves would see themselves as equals of white craftsmen and demand like freedom.[5]

Slaves also operated mills, gins, and stills. On the Walker place near Pine Bluff, Arkansas, Ben Moon drove an eight-mule team that powered the cotton gin. A few slaves of Edgefield County, Georgia, ground the grain for the people of the vicinity. Slaves also operated numerous mills that processed cane into sorghum molasses, and stills that turned out brandy and whiskey.[6]

When a planter moved to virgin land he was likely to send pioneers on ahead to erect a complex of houses, barns, and sheds. These men also made furniture for the houses and implements, such as metal-tipped wooden plows and harrows with teeth of sharpened pegs, for the farm. A Texas plantation community of master and slaves migrated with their cattle, sheep, hogs, and chickens and ducks, six weeks on the road from Washington County to new land near Belton. The builders of the group set about constructing the master's house of logs, with two large rooms and a hall; a kitchen; an office for the master; log cabins for the hands; and chairs, beds, and tables for everybody. All the while they and the rest of the workers made ready the land, planted the crops, and tended the animals. Other builders-woodsmen cleared land, split rails, cut timber for sawmills and firewood for home or sale, and hewed railroad cross-ties.[7]

In the 1850s planters bought for 50 to 75 cents an acre swamp lands and sent in slaves to transform thousands of acres into productive cotton country. In the summer of 1853 the St. Francis River Valley of Arkansas was being rapidly opened and the nearby White River region already required four to five steamers to carry out its cotton. Wooodsmen humanized the hard labor of clearing the bottom land with their work songs.[8]

Like house servants, artisans belonged to the slave elite. Among the artisans, indispensable blacksmiths made and repaired wagons, buggies, and carriages; agricultural implements; and all kinds of hardware. When caught up, they took on jobs of neighboring farms lacking resident smiths, engaged in allied trades, or helped in the fields when crops were "pushing." Some blacksmiths made money for their masters by manufacturing goods for sale: wagons; plows; hoes; and knives, forks, and spoons. "Old Mike" earned more than $100 a month for his master in building wagons and buggies for white folks in his part of Mississippi.[9]

A Georgia smith made iron bars for fire places and metal points for plows, and kept all the tools in repair. An Alabama smith fashioned everything from chains and buckets to wagon wheels, and a North Carolinian shaped wood and metal into shovels, rakes, pitchforks, hoes, and picks, and fastened metal bands to the soles of wood shoes. A Mississippi smith made lanterns for Saturday night dances and plaited wicks and extracted oil from lard for the fuel.[10] Smiths often were jacks of

The cotton gin harnessed slaves to industrial processes. *Harper's*, Vol. VIII, No. XLVI (March 1854), 459.

all trades. One served as foreman of field workers; another combined machine manufacturing with house building. Luke Blackshear worked in iron, leather, and wood, and trained his son in smithing, shoemaking, woodworking, and carpentering. Another versatile smith was a horseman, plowman, gardener, carpenter, and anything else wanted.[11]

A few smiths, and other artisans, earned enough money to buy their freedom and that of their families. With his portion of the profit he made for his master, James Holmes's father bought himself, his wife, and his children, except for James, who had been given as a wedding present to the young mistress. Others, try as they might, could not accumulate enough to purchase freedom for anybody.[12]

Carriage drivers, and the less elegant wagoneers, got to go places and see things. Jerry Eubanks served at table, and, outfitted in a fancy suit and a high beaver hat, drove the master's family round about the country. A rich planter's driver might cut a smart figure: "Dat was a fine lookin' turn-out of Marse Joe's—dat rock-a-way car'iage wid bead fringe all round de canopy, a pair of spankin' black hosses hitched to it, and my brother David settin' so proud lak up on the high seat," said Elisha Doc Garey. One driver boasted that his master had "a $2500 carriage, a $1500 pair of horses, and a $5000 coachman." Another high-priced coachman wore a high hat, blue uniform decorated with brass buttons, and shined black boots as he maneuvered six horses pulling a fine coach.[13] Drivers kept informed about community affairs, including things not intended for their ears. "I used to hear lots of things from behin' me," one coachman said, "while drivin' de folks and saying nothin'."[14] Some smuggled goods in their vehicles for clandestine sale while their masters dealt and visited about town.[15]

Large numbers of wagoneers, such as Barney Alford's father, hauled cotton to market and supplies back to the plantations. In the fall roads leading to market towns were crowded with wagons. Eight bales of cotton per wagon was a heavy load, but one huge wagon carried in October, 1853, 16 bales of cotton, of about 500 pounds per bale, to Memphis from the R.S. Manning plantation, De Soto County, Mississippi. Five hundred teams and wagons might be seen at the waterfront in Memphis in the busy season. Slave boatmen, like carriage drivers and wagoneers, transported men and material. They plied the great Mississippi to New Orleans and other major river ports, and lesser rivers to varied markets, as the Broad River to Columbia, South Carolina.[16]

There were other workers of many skills from jockeys who raced their masters' horses to factory hands who steamed, rolled, and packed tobacco. Isaiah T. Montgomery acted as secretary to Joseph Davis, brother of Confederate President Jefferson Davis; and Daniel Phillips, a cowboy near San Marcos, Texas, rounded up wild horses. Slaves could always be found to practice the arts needed by the plantation and ranching and manufacturing South.[17]

The slave work force varied by age, sex, skill, and duties. For example, on a plantation near Liberty, Mississippi, there were Viney, the cook; Zias, carriage driver and field hand; Irwin, horseman; Jim who "beat rice" every Friday; Sara, field hand; Ria, field hand and milker, crippled in her frost-bitten bare feet; Peggy, field hand and milker; Patience, field hand and milker; Monday, field hand "bad about running away;" and children who helped in the field. A plantation in Grenada County, Mississippi, of 1400 acres, was worked by 15 men, a number of teen-age boys, and women and children. A North Carolina work force included Mac, Curley, William,

Woodsmen felled timber, cleared land, and supplied material for construction. *Harper's*, Vol. XIII, No. LXXV (August 1856), 316.

Wagoneers enjoyed some prestige and a measure of liberty in hauling crops to market and supplies to the plantation. *Harper's*, Vol. X, No. LVII (February 1855), 300.

Sanford, Lewis, Henry, Ed, Sylvester, Hamp, and Jake; and Nellie, the two Lucys, Martha, Nervie, Jane Laura, Fannie, Lizzie, Cassie, Tensie, Lindy, and Mary Jane.[18] On a large South Carolina plantation slaves were arranged in a social and occupational hierarchy. At the top were the house servants, butler, maids, nurses, chambermaids, and cooks. Next came carriage drivers, gardeners, and stable men, then carpenters, blacksmiths, wheelwrights, waggoners, and foremen, and, at the bottom of this group, cowmen and dog handlers. These upper division workers had relatively good houses, moderate work, and exemption from beatings by the overseers of the field hands. Leading the ordinary workers were cradlers, threshers, and mill and gin hands. Common field laborers came last in the procession. Female house servants were discouraged from taking husbands from the common field crew. Opportunity to avoid close management, chance to make money, and service to other blacks affected status within the black community.[19]

Because so much was manufactured for home use by the village-like plantation community a variety of skills were required. Shoemakers tanned the hides

Much cotton was hauled to river landings and then shipped to Memphis, New Orleans, and other river ports. *Harper's*, Vol. VIII, No. XLVI (March 1854), 460.

Top: A procession of slaves tote cotton from the fields. *Harper's,* Vol. VIII, No. XLVI (March 1854), 457. *Bottom:* Blacks manned the rice plantations of the Sea Islands. *Harper's,* Vol. LVII, No. CCCXLII (November 1878), 853.

they made into brogans; blacksmiths fashioned and repaired farm implements, vehicles, and all sorts of metal objects; spinners, weavers, and seamstresses made clothes; and candlemakers, carpenters, cooks, and other workers exercised their special skills. On a large plantation near Natchez, Mississippi, among 135 slaves there were a blacksmith, a carpenter, and a wheelwright; two seamstresses; two cooks; one stable servant; one cattle tender and one hog tender; one teamster; and one midwife and nurse. There was also a driver of the hoe-gang of 30 or 40 hands, and a foreman of the 30 or so plowmen. Two young water toters attended the work gangs.[20]

The corps of field workers, the largest group in the plantation community, made the crops, laboring from "sun to sun." They were roused out of bed at about four in the morning by horn, conch, or bell, and. after chores and breakfast, took their places in the fields ready for work at daylight. At twilight, after a hard day's work, they trudged back to their cabins for chores, supper, and rest for the next day's tasks. On a Mississippi plantation

> De fiel hands went out early in de morning after de horn had blowed an' dey had all et breakfas' at Marse's house. When dey reached de fiels dey went to plowing, strewing fertilize, planting an' hoeing. At twelve o'clock a cowhorn wuz blowed an' dey would go to dinner, den dey would go back an' wuk till nite. In gathering time fiels full ob 'em would cut, rake, bind, an' stack. Wagons would be coming an' gwine stacked high wid grain an' stuff dey had growed. Acres an' acres o'snowy white cotton would be dotted here an' deir wid bunches.[21]

Lizzie Norfleet's people stopped picking before dark but the lanterns might have to be lit before all the cotton had been weighed. Phillis Hicks's mother would be so tired after a hard day in the fields that she would fall asleep while nursing the baby and not wake until time for the next day's work. Jennie Webb, born "twixt de fiel's an' de cabins," never saw her parents going to or coming from the fields in daylight, for "it was wuk, wuk, all de time."[22] Henrietta Evelina Smith said her people had to work from "can to can't," and that "Reb time" was like the penitentiary. "It never got too cold nor too hot to work. And there wasn't any pay."[23]

Marriah Hines's master, called by his white neighbors a "nigger lover," did not send his hands out very early or keep them at work late. On cold or rainy days he gave them odd jobs under shelter. David Blount's master did not mind when his slaves took a break, even a brief swim, on a hot day. And Charles Coles's master set a "short" workday of from seven in the morning until six in the evening. However, Wes Brady, a Texas slave, claimed they sometimes were roused at three in the morning, weighed their cotton by candlelight, and allowed only 15 minutes to eat dinner from their dinner buckets.[24]

When cotton had to be got in and the moon was bright pickers might be kept at their task until quite late. Then it was work, eat, sleep, and work again. At such times men would work all day Saturday, but women would knock off to do their washing and other household duties. When caught up by laboring moonlit nights pickers might be sent to help neighbors who had fallen behind. The extra hours were compensated for by a chance to be with friends and neighbors, maybe even by the side of a sweetheart or a spouse.[25] In some areas completion of tasks assigned, rather than daylight or moonlit hours, determined the length of the work day. A prime laborer would have to complete a whole task; women with nursing infants,

Picking cotton was hard labor but also an occasion for lively social interaction. *Harper's*, Vol. VIII, No. XLVI (March 1854), 456.

and the old and the young, some fraction of a task. Although tasks could be completed early, and leave time for rest or play, they generally required a typical worker to remain at his task from daylight until five or six in the evening.[26] But when the work was really "pushing," plowhands might fix lanterns to their plows; pickers struggle to fill the wagons with cotton to be ready for ginning at daybreak, next morning; and hoehands assemble in place waiting for daylight in order to begin thinning and weeding the growing plants.[27]

In the grinding, or harvest, season on sugar plantations, from October to December, every man and woman worked 18 hours a day, resting six hours in relays so that three quarters of them were constantly laboring. Some slaves were glad when this season of extra hard work began, because they expected better food and drink and more freedom. From January to March, planting and sugar manufacturing season, these slaves worked very hard also. On one place families were given a bonus of a dollar for each hogshead of sugar produced.[28]

Sugar cane culture demanded intensive labor. *Harper's* Vol. VII, No. XLII (November 1853), 760.

Work during long hours also had to be done at an acceptable pace, a minimum quantity and quality, and in a seasonal cycle. Field hands had to plow, hoe, pick cotton, pull corn, drive the mule at the gin, clear land, split fence rails, and so on. A round of work could include clearing new ground; plowing; and planting — corn first, then cotton; chopping, or thin-ning the stand; hoeing and tilling; and pulling corn. Then it was lay-by time, and perhaps a camp meeting. Afterwards, all took to the fields to pick their several hundred pounds of cotton a day, until cold weather. Then it was time to split rails and build fences, kill hogs, erect and repair buildings, and do other fall and winter work.[29]

On many plantations agricultural activity came to a focus at cotton picking time. Men were expected to pick 200–300 pounds per day; women, 150 pounds; and children lesser amounts. Fast pickers often would slip some of their cotton to slower ones to save them from being punished for coming up short. Tildy, a champion picker on the Walden place, near Lexington, Mississippi, left everybody behind as she picked 600–700 pounds a day, crawling between rows filling two long sacks slung from her shoulders. She snatched cotton from prickly bolls, barely pausing to drop full sacks and shoulder empty ones. However, it was more prudent to maintain an easy and steady pace: it made the work tolerable and kept the quota within reasonable limits. Thus groups of pickers would make their way through the snowy fields steadily filling their long, snake-like sacks, but not so quickly as the master or overseer might wish. Prizes were sometimes offered to hurry the workers. Mary Kincheon won a dress and a pair of shoes for outpicking the rest of the crew.[30]

Pulling worms from tobacco plants was quite unpleasant. Rather than giving prizes a Virginia overseer with the eyes of a hawk would make workers bite in two overlooked worms, or take three lashes on their backs. The lashes were "wusser dan bittin' de worms," said Susan Kelly, "fer yo' could bite right smart quick, and dat wuz all dat dar wuz ter it; but dem lashes done last a pow'full long time."[31]

Before crops could be planted plowhands had to break and harrow the soil. During spring plowing on a big place 10 to 15 plow hands would work 20 to 30 horses or mules readying the ground for seed. Women were more likely to be put in the hoe gang than the plow gang, but some women did heavy and dangerous work usually reserved for men, such as splitting rails and clearing new ground. One mother of 14 children who weighed just 95 pounds

plowed like a man. Another woman, it was said, would plow all day and milk 20 cows in the evening. Women sometimes wielded the ax and saw and cut and rolled logs and split rails. In the "Big Cane Break" on the Red River in Louisiana large and stout girls Charlotte, Fanny, Cresia, and Nelly chopped down trees, piled logs and kept up with the men clearing land. Henrietta McCullers had to plow, dig ditches, and clear new ground, because her master was puny and the only male slave on the place was old and feeble. Clara Jones was forced to do every kind of work, she said, because her master squeezed as much work out of his 50 slaves as if they were 150. Still, when women took on men's work their quota was lighter, as when Henry Essex's mother was expected to split 350 rails a day while the men were required to split 500. Women doing men's work ran special risks. In one incident a plow struck a root and its handle snapped back and hit the plowwoman in the stomach, causing her to miscarry.[32]

In addition to working from daylight to dark slaves had chores to do before going to the fields and after returning in the evening: feeding livestock, milking, spinning and weaving, and like activities. Adam Singleton's father fed the stock and his mother milked the cows before they reported for the usual day's field labor. Georgianna Foster's mother after a day in the fields turned to housework "while de white folks hardly done a han's turn of work." Sarah Gudger had to card and spin at night until 10 and rise next morning at four to get ready for a day in the field. On a Marshall, Texas, plantation the slaves had some night tasks after a day's work: to spin, weave, knit socks, make baskets and bottom chairs.[33]

When plowing, growing, and gathering seasons were over, and during bad weather or at night, laborers turned to hog killing, molasses making, cutting firewood, clearing land, and a host of other

Hands cultivated tobacco in the upper South for a great international market. *Harper's*, Vol. XI, No. LXI (June 1855), 8.

activities of farm life. As Liza Strickland noted, there was always plenty to do:

Deir wuz a heap o'wuk 'sides de field wuk, depending on de time an' season. Deir wuz hog killin's. Dey would kill 'em by de dozens and der meat ter be dried by hickory smokes in de smoke house, sausage ter be made an' lard. Eber thing us used had ter be made at home; de soap, candles, cloth had ter be spun an' wove an' made inter clo'se fer Mar's family and all de slaves, den quiltin' fer civer fer us all, wood had ter be cut, hauled and stacked an' cannin' wus to be done while other things had ter be banked fer winter sich as sweet taters ter eat an' cane fer seed, water had to be drawed an' toted to de house an' cabins. Lasses makin' time would las' a week or mo'. I could jest keep on namin' things mos' all day sich as de big wash an' all de ironin' an' scrubbin' an' cleanin' up all 'round. De place wuz kept alive wid slaves gwine in an' out busy wid deir duties wid big fires a burnin' an' chickens a cacklin' and cows a lowin' an' pots an' pots ob good food a cookin'. Hit wuz wuk, but good ole days too.[34]

Ebenezer Brown recalled that besides cultivating the big crops, slaves cared for the horses and mules, hogs, sheep, chickens, geese, and pigeons. They cut and stacked fodder, threshed and winnowed rice and peas, sheared the sheep, ginned and pressed the cotton, and made candles, soap, and cloth.[35]

Women, aided by children, did their washing on Saturdays. They would draw water from the well or tote it from the spring to fill hewed-out logs or tubs; soak the clothes in the water, with lye soap; and with paddles beat out the dirt, on hickory blocks. Instead of carrying water up the hill they might haul the clothes down to the spring or stream. Once on Bayou Teche, Louisiana, an alligator bit off a washerwoman's arm. Washed clothes were hung on fences and bushes to dry. The white folks' white and ruffled things were, however, starched and ironed.[36] The drudgery of wash day was lightened by social interaction, as Jasper Battle of Georgia remembered:

> Dere was a long bench full of old wood tubs, and a great big iron pot for bilin' de clothes, and de batten block and stick. Chillen beat de clothes wid de batten stick and kept up de fire 'round de pot whilst de 'omans leaned over de tubs washin' and a-singin' dem old songs. You could hear 'em most a mile away. Now and den one of de 'omans would stop sin-gin' long enough to yell at de chillen to git more wood on dat fire 'fore I lash de skin offen your back.[37]

Slave women practiced many arts in domestic manufacturing. In addition to meals and clothes, they made candles, brooms, dyes, soap, lard, baskets, canned goods, cheese, and many other things needed by the plantation community. They made tallow candles when the first yearling steer was killed, and beeswax when the bees were robbed. They made beer from persimmons, preserves from berries and fruit, butter from cream, brooms from sage brush, dippers from gourds, soap from grease and lye, and dyes from trees and shrubs. Besides all this they washed, cleaned, and looked after the children.[38]

Women could do almost everything, but they sometimes took turns at various tasks and specialized to some degree, although in their cabins they remained generalists. On one plantation Phiney washed, Easter milked, Lisa served, Judy looked after the children, Sarah tended the cows, and Clarissa raised chickens, ducks and geese, and turkeys, and churned. On another place Patience ran the loom, Cynthia and Starrah and Tenna made the clothes, and Phoebe took charge of the dairy and fed the children. Some women who worked in the big house joined the field crew when needed. When cotton had to be picked in a rush, all the women but a skeletal staff of house servants would be sent into the fields. During holidays, when the white folks had a "passel" of guests, field women were called to the big house to lend a hand.[39]

Slave women in the big house usually could avoid the heat and fatigue of the open field, but they had plenty to do under the close supervision of the white folks. Cooks, maids, and nurses of children were kept busy from morning until night. Ella Wilson, for example, rose early, made coffee at five, set the table and served breakfast, cleaned house, tended the white children, served dinner and supper, and so worked her way through the long day. One servant scrubbed the floors bright and clean with sand, water, and a shuck mop. Another, in good clothes though barefoot, met visitors, ushered them into the parlor, and fetched those asked for, and stood behind her mistress ready for orders. If any of her fellow slaves would have suggested that she ought to work in the fields, she would have, she said, "slapped 'em in the face." Other servants complained that their masters and mistresses never did a thing for themselves but insisted that their servants stand ever ready to wait on them. Still other servants stayed busy cooking, washing, cleaning, looking after children, and doing the never-ending work of a big household. On a Marion, South Carolina placc, Yaneyki waited on the mistress, Becky served as house girl, Hannah did the cooking and Dicey the cleaning, while Mom Genia Woodberry cared for the white children.[40]

"Mammies," who in many cases practically raised the white children, exercised considerable influence in the big house. They bathed and dressed and fed the children, went to church with them, and governed them in many ways.[41] In consequence, they became quite close to the children. Dinah Hayes said her white children called her "Mammie," and "I was. I loved those children like they be mine. I scolded and whipped them, too, when they needed it. I planned and cooked their meals, mended their clothes, took them to the park, bathed them and put them to bed, told them bedtime stories, and settled their disputes between themselves, and they would tell me all their troubles. It was my white children that taught me how to read and write and how to speak. We taught each other things."[42]

House servants were likely to have better food, clothing, and housing than field hands. Their houses were sometimes situated close to the big house to mark their distinction. On a Georgia plantation women servants were outfitted in dresses made from checks and plaids from an Augusta factory while women of the field wore homespun woven on the master's own loom. Rebecca Phillips was proud that members of her family were house servants, not common laborers. Her mother served as maid, her brother drove the carriage, and she, too, worked in the big house. Her father, though occupied in the field, was, she said, a driver, not an ordinary hand.[43]

For all their privileges house servants were, nevertheless, members of the slave community, with many common interests with the field workers. This was notably the case when spouses of the women house servants were field hands. On a North Carolina plantation two washerwomen, a cook and helpers, two serving women, a house girl, and the full-time spinners and weavers had men who were field laborers.[44]

When too young to be integrated into the work force little children were left in the care of an older woman from early morning until after dark, often half asleep when dropped off and picked up. One nurse who cared for the "chaps" lived to be 115.[45] Another who watched the children while their parents labored in the fields was Peg, who "wuz old and cripple; she walked wid one crutch, and she smoked a pipe an' tied up her head wid a red rag." "She wud knock us round," said Hattie Jefferson, "wid her crutch an' make us mind," and not wake the babies.[46]

When old enough, children were given chores to start them learning their duties as slaves. A child would drive the cattle to pasture, sweep the yard, feed the chickens, and chase crows from the corn. In the big house a slave child would tote

House servants enjoyed certain prerogatives and privileges but were subject to omnipresent scrutiny and gratuitous discipline. *Harper's*, Vol. XV, No. LXXXVIII (September 1857), 440.

"Mammies" exhibited dignity. *Harper's*, Vol. XIII, No. LXXV (August 1856), 309.

firewood and water, shine shoes, polish silverware, and run errands.[47] Jenny Proctor helped clean house until, when she was 10, her master ordered, "Git dis yere nigger to dat cotton patch."[48]

Eight-or 10-year-old children not selected for house duty were sent to the fields to be gradually integrated into the work gangs. Mary Island washed dishes when four, helped cook at six, grubbed sprouts in the field at seven, and at eight picked 100 pounds of cotton a day. Henry Waldon and his sister made "one hand" and were given a row together. John Gregory hoed with his mother for a year then was assigned a row to himself. Adrianna Kerns also advanced from hoeing a row with her mother to taking charge of her own row. Eliza Scantling started training as a field worker by scaring birds from a rice field and finished as a full-fledged plowhand.[49]

Slaves judged their masters, overseers, and drivers as ranging from relatively good to thoroughly bad. Joseph Davis and his brother Jefferson Davis, President of the Confederacy, were about as good as masters could be. Joseph encouraged Benjamin and Benjamin's son Isaiah to learn to read, accumulate a library, and participate modestly in intellectual, technical, and mercantile affairs in the Davis family.[50] According to John Williams, Jefferson Davis told his slaves: "'Dar is de mules and tools to work wid–go out dere and work and make something so's we'll all hab plenty to eat.' An everybody worked and we did have plenty to eat an' wear."[51] Slaves of Alexander Stephens, vice-president of the Confederacy, enjoyed being called "Stephens' free Negroes." One of these "free Negroes," Georgia Baker, never heard of anyone getting a beating on the Stephens's place. One rich family judged as good enjoyed a life of leisure: the men knocked about on horseback and the ladies rode in style in a fine carriage driven by a coachman. Charlie Davenport was proud that he belonged not to "white trash" but to a rich and generous family, the mistress of which was from the "out fightinist, out cussinist, fastest ridin', hardest drinkin' folks" around.[52]

Walter Long's mistress "was so kind and gentle, she moved 'mong us as a livin' benediction. Many was de blessings dat fell from her hands for de sick and 'flicted." She taught her slaves to read, write, and figure.[53] John Sneed's master, a physician who practiced in rural areas south of Austin, Texas, saw to it that each child's birthday was celebrated with cake and a gift, and in other ways demonstrated respect for his slaves. Another Texan was addressed as "Papa Day," for he rejected the title "master" and told his slaves that they were born free even though other slaveholders would not say so. Hagar Lewis's master not only gave extra food to neglected slaves from other plantations, with his shotgun he forced a brutal neighbor to stop beating a slave.[54]

Some masters were kind when not angry or drunk. Lewis Wallace's master was, for example, a good man when not in a "whiskey fit." Then he would drag "old Missus" up and down the gallery and run his slaves ragged. Emma Johnson's mistress similarly was kind–when in good humor.[55] One master was judged "purty good, because he treated his slaves, jus' 'bout like you would a good mule." When "mean drunk" Edwin Epps would sneak about the quarters stinging surprised slaves with a flick of his whip; when "merry drunk" he would force the slaves to dance to exhaustion, and, next morning drive them to the fields worn out.[56]

In contrast to the fair-to-middling masters were the heartless ones. One of the cruel ones was said to have been unable to rest if he had not whipped a slave before sundown. Another fastened an iron frame with a bell to the shoulders of his slave-son,

Children were trained for slavery at an early age. *Harper's*, Vol. XIII, No. LXXV (August 1856), 10.

forcing the harnessed son to sleep upright in a chair-for no reason, thought the son, than that he had been born. One degraded master fed his slaves uncooked meat, worked them in the fields naked, and branded them. When he caught his wife slipping food and clothes to them, he whipped her too. He himself was at last hanged as a horse thief. Annie Griegg's master stomped on her hand and broke it; Josephine Howell's master stripped her naked and thrashed her in the presence of the field hands, and "forced motherhood" on her. One slaveholder of "poor quality" treated his slaves like dogs, often worked them Sundays and nights, fed them little, clothed them scantily, and beat, knocked, and kicked them.[57] Tines Kendricks's mistress, cursing, drove her slaves to the field while her son handed out grub, threatening: "Take a sop of dat grease on your hoecake an' move erlong fast 'fore I lashes you."[58] Soured by harsh treatment, Barbara Haywood said, "None of de white folks wuz good ter none of de niggers,"[59] and Thomas Hall thought that whites were, had been, and always would be against blacks.[60]

A humane mistress could moderate her husband's severity. Miss Emmaline was able to protect the house servants but her efforts to control her husband's temper in his dealings with the field hands were futile. Her mistress allowed no one to whip Rosa Lindsey. Henrietta Williams's old mistress fussed at old master so much for whipping Henrietta that he never again dared beat her. Charlie Rigger's master was, on the other hand, kind but his mistress was "a terrible piece of humanity," and Hattie Hill's mistress beat the slaves when her husband was away, as did Maria White's mistress.[61]

Big planters hired overseers to supervise plantation production. A typical overseer roused the slaves and, after breakfast and chores, led them into the fields to begin work at break of day — to plow, plant, hoe, or harvest. At noon, he called a halt for dinner and rest and at one o'clock ordered all back to work until dark. At harvest time workers cut grain and cane, pulled corn, dug potatoes and picked cotton. Wagons stacked high with the harvest lumbered back and fourth. Cotton pickers, dotting the white fields, filled their long sacks while the overseer rode up and down hurrying his charges on, perhaps getting "a holt" of laggards. He likely carried a pistol, a bowie knife, a whip, and was accompanied by dogs.[62]

The overseer sometimes belonged to the master's family, perhaps was his son, but more often came from a lower social class. One overseer-son was judged by his charges as being a man of quality, poor but learned, kind to all. Another, said to be a good "Christian man," would sometimes call a slave into his house for a hot biscuit and a sweet potato. Overseers from lower ranks might be said to be all right, not quality folk, but respectable, like Annie Coley's poor white overseer who was good to colored folks. Occasionally an overseer would rise to the local aristocracy, perhaps through marriage. In two generations his family would escape the "overseer's taint."[63]

Slaves often showed their contempt for overseers by ranking them as "white trash." One was said to be "nobody, nohow;" the average overseer was denounced as a "low down" man, lower than poor white trash, a brute really. Such a man would strip a woman to the waist and lash her. One surly overseer, said Abe McKlennan, knocked and cuffed "us 'roun like dawgs when we hain't done nuthin'."[64] A particularly arrogant overseer forced slaves to attend the funeral of the hound dog he had used to hunt them down when they ran away. Brutish overseers kept from masters their abuse of women and girls among the slaves.[65]

Overseers could be restrained, even driven off by the slaves. Slaves out to get an overseer might slow down their work and thus force their master to replace him in order to get good work done again. More often one of the slaves would report the overseer's misdeeds. Field women got James Lucas, a house servant, to inform Varina Howell Davis, wife of Jefferson Davis, about the wrong behavior of an overseer. Lucy Skipwith, chief housekeeper on an Alabama plantation, submitted written reports on plantation affairs to her absentee master and acted as counterweight to overseers, one of whom she got dismissed.[66] Amy Chapman's mistress fired an overseer when she learned he had chained Amy's brother like "Christ on de cross" and that Amy had stayed by him crying, "lack Mary an' dem done."[67] David Blount's master also drove away a "pesky varment."[68]

In the war between overseer and slaves, overseers went about armed, nevertheless they were from time to time stabbed and beaten and run off. Hard-driving, profit-making overseers in the 1850s made $1000 to $1500 per year rather than the usual $200 to $600, but planters who successfully bid for their services could learn that the health and morale of their slaves had been undermined and their plantations run down for short-term profit.[69]

A slave who acted as overseer had to manage affairs to suit his master, and, at the same time, keep the slaves satisfied in order to get acceptable work from them, or be demoted back to the ranks. On the other hand, when successful, his very success proved the master unjust for holding black men in bondage while claiming that they were by nature inferior beings. There were black overseers who managed plantation operations with the least possible insult and injury to their fellow slaves. John Gilstrap's granduncle ran things well without a whip, as did Major Nelson who directed the work of about 50 slaves. A black overseer on a Tennessee plantation stirred up complaints by area whites because he successfully ruled the slaves with too gentle a hand.[70]

Doubtless the average slave overseer precariously balanced the interests of both master and slave, sometimes leaning to one side, then to the other. Rita Sorrell noted that her master simply told Squire Holman and Sam Sorrell what he wanted and these joint overseers saw that it was done. Fannie Dunn said that her master listened to his black overseer; Richard Macks's father was in charge of a Maryland tobacco plantation; and Annie Young Henson stated that black overseer Peter Taylor's "orders were law." Georgia Baker's master did not need a white overseer, for her Uncle Joe handled the job so well. George Skipwith reported to his master John H. Cocke of Virginia and Alabama that he gave Frank, Isham, Evally, Dinah, Jenny, and Charlotte 10 lashes for plowing less than their quota; Evlyann eight or 10 licks for misplacing her hoe; and Robert a whipping for rebelliousness. He administered punishment in connection with managing the complex agricultural operations of the plantation, mediated disputes in the quarters, and brokered the slaves interests and the master's designs. But he fell from favor and was demoted to driver, then to hand.[71]

Some slave overseers succumbed to the temptation to trade their people's well being for a little power, prestige, and privilege, and in consequence ruled as petty tyrants. Ellen Claibourn's grandfather, freed by his master, served as overseer until, fearing he would lose his faith by unjustly compelling slaves to work, quit and went to preaching. But Jane Johnson said their strutting slave-overseer whipped other slaves unmercifully, and Anna Baker's mother ran away, abandoning her children, to escape a black overseer's sexual aggression.[72]

Black "drivers," or foremen, stood between overseers and workers. Like craftsmen and house servants, they were classed with the slave elite. They were used by their masters to exploit slave labor, although many of them did what they could to protect the ordinary laborers. Some drivers, afraid that leniency would cost them their posts, became hard taskmasters. Others, just and effective, were respected leaders in the fields and in the quarters.[73] Masters sought to win the support of their foremen-drivers with privileges: extra food, better housing, larger garden plots, and cash bonuses. And they withdrew their privileges, demoted, whipped, or sold them, for unsuccessful performance. Drivers Henry Bibb, William Wells Brown, and Josiah Henson rebelled against being used in managing the slave system by running away.[74] Rufus Dirt was, however, proud that as driver he did not have to work hard and that he could strut about in front of the other slaves. But Squire Irvin's master managed his plantation with the help of two drivers who used the lash only on slackers. Callie Washington's master would trust no overseer to treat his hands right, so, aided by a slave driver, he supervised the laborers himself. Rina Brown's father identified with those he "drove" by working by their side. Sarah Fitzpatrick's father carried a strap, with authority to use it, but managed the workers without violence.[75]

There were drivers who, freely or under coercion, harshly whipped their fellow slaves. A big and strong Mississippi driver helped "control de udder darkies" by "throwing" them for his master to whip. In exchange he was allowed to raise and sell for himself several bales of cotton a year and to act as if he were no slave at all. Other drivers who served as "whipping boss" were likely to be denounced as "mean" and "bad." A South Carolina driver "would strut 'round wid a leather strap on his shoulder and would whip de other slaves unmerciful."[76] If Prince Smith and fellow slaves failed to complete their week's quota, their black driver would lay on them 15 to 20 lashes and made them work on Sunday.[77] Josephine Howard knew cruel black drivers who "If dey done took de notion dey jes' lays it on you and you can't do nothin'."[78]

Black drivers roused slave workers in the morning and checked them in at night, assigned tasks, set the pace and enforced quotas of work, administered punishment, and generally acted as supervisory agents under the master and overseer. They also participated in the life of the quarters, often as leaders. They were both men of their masters and, at their best, defenders also of their fellow slaves. Many of them protected more than they drove their subordinates, but some were selfish, self-important, and heartless.[79]

PART TWO

CIVIL WAR

6

Experience of War

At the outset of the Civil War radical Abolitionists wanted the federal government to conduct a crusade against slavery root and branch, but moderate Northerners hoped for a quick restoration of the Union with little disruption of Southern society. They accepted slavery where it existed but opposed its extension into Western territories; and they looked for slavery to come to a peaceable end in some indeterminate future. In conformity with the moderates President Abraham Lincoln hoped to restore the Union with negotiation backed by limited armed force. He feared that a war to overthrow slavery would harden the South, divide the North, lose the slave-holding Border States, and end in the ruin of the Union.

Early in the War, therefore, the Administration discouraged slaves from fleeing to the Union Army's lines, and Lincoln countermanded proclamations granting freedom to slaves of disloyal masters made in the field by Generals John Fremont and David Hunter. However, invading Union armies soon secured the Border States but encountered hard fighting inside the Confederacy. When it became clear that the South would fight until subjugated, the federal government then sought to weaken the South by confiscating as contraband of war slaves employed by the Confederacy and putting these "contrabands" to work for the Union Army. Then

on January 1, 1863, Lincoln as commander-in-chief went further and emancipated as a war measure all slaves behind Confederate lines. He soon began to enlist freedmen in the armed forces to help the North overwhelm the South and destroy slavery. Enlistment of blacks in the Border States strengthened the advance of freedom in that region too.

For their part, slaves were eager at first opportunity to hurry on God's good time of freedom, and they forced the pace of the nation's groping toward freedom. When Union armies approached, able-bodied male slaves of loyal as well as disloyal slaveholders often fled the plantations, and in doing so undermined the Southern economy. As laborers, friends, informers, and soldiers they greatly strengthened the Union in its assault on Southern society when the Union at last gave up half-measures, as black and white Abolitionists had demanded, and focused on conquering the Confederacy and destroying slavery.

By the spring of 1863 the federal government had shifted its aim from the restoration of the old Union of free and slave states to the creation of a new Union unsullied by slavery. *Instructions for the Government of Armies of the United States in the Field*, approved by President Lincoln in April, 1863, justified destruction and appropriation of enemy property, even starvation of the Southern people, to hasten the subjugation of the Confederacy. And the *Instructions*, applying the Emancipation Proclamation of January 1, 1863, declared that captured or fugitive slaves were entitled to the rights and privileges of free men.[1] No longer were Union armies to be aimed principally at rebel armies; they were, also, to attack and destroy the entire social and economic structure of the slave South.

The devastating effect of the Union Army on plantation society is revealed in a report of Frank P. Blair on his operations in the Yazoo Valley of Mississippi during General U.S. Grant's Vicksburg campaign in the spring and summer of 1863. "I destroyed every grist-mill in the Valley," Blair wrote, "and have driven in to this place about 1000 head of cattle. I brought with me an army of negroes, nearly equal to the number of men in my command, and the cavalry and infantry have seized and brought in 200 or 300 head of mules and horses." Blair seized or destroyed 500,000 bushels of corn, immense quantities of pork, and all the cotton he could lay his hands on.[2]

Also in the Vicksburg campaign, Brigadier General Frederick Steele reported from Greenville, Mississippi, April 10, 1863, to Lieutenant General Grant that his men had "burned up everything there was to eat on the plantation," and that he needed instructions as to what should be done with the "poor creatures" who had followed his command.[3] Confederate Brigadier General Stephen D. Lee corroborated Steele in his own report to Lieutenant General J.C. Pemberton, April 9, 1863, from upper Deer Creek, near Greenville, that Union forces "did not leave a particle of anything for the planters to subsist on," and that the "Negroes are in a pretty bad condition."[4] Just six months earlier, in October, 1862, Union destruction in the general area had been more selective. In reprisal for guerrilla attacks on Union gunboats near Bledsoe's Land-

ing, fifty miles south of Memphis, the inhabitants were given "half an hour to remove necessary articles from the houses, when buildings and fields were laid in ashes."[5]

Toward the end of the War Brigadier General Benjamin H. Grierson led a raid, December 21, 1864 to January 5, 1865, from Memphis to Vicksburg seizing and destroying Confederate subsistence and demoralizing the people. Included in his powerful force were the Third U.S. Colored Cavalry and a pioneer corps of 50 blacks. One thousand blacks joined the column during its march. Grierson summed up his work as follows:

20,000 feet of bridges and trestle-work (cut down and burned); 20 miles of telegraph (poles cut down and wire destroyed); 4 serviceable locomotives and tenders and 10 in process of repair; 95 railroad cars; over 300 army wagons and 2 caissons; 30 warehouses filled with quartermaster, commissary, and ordinance stores; large cloth and shoe factories (employing 500 hands); several tanneries and machine shops; a steam pile-driver; 12 new forges; 7 depot buildings; 5,000 stand of new arms; 700 head of fat hogs; 500 bales of cotton (marked "C.S.A."); immense amounts of grain, leather, wool, and other government property, the value and quantity of which cannot be estimated.[6]

Union soldiers wrecked the Confederacy's economy by seizing and destroying plantation stores, burning rail fences, appropriating draft animals, recruiting slaves to directly oppose the Confederacy as laborers and soldiers and by undermining the planters' power and authority over slaves and freedmen who stayed on the plantations. Conquering soldiers could do whatever they wished on an occupied plantation and in doing so they humbled masters and their households in the presence of the slaves.

After taking whatever they wanted on one plantation soldiers burst into the big house, broke open the wardrobe and tore up the mistress's clothes. On another place they gave the mistress's silk dresses "to their slave gals." On an Arkansas place after federal soldiers slaughtered the farm animals and ripped apart things generally they drafted the mistress and her daughters to cook their dinner. On a Georgia plantation soldiers scattered clothes from the mistress's closet and decorated their horses with her earrings and bracelets. They urged blacks on a place near Bowling Green, Kentucky, to take whatever they wanted from the big house, including the silver plates and silk dresses; they burned down the home of an Arkansas woman who refused to cook them dinner. After grabbing the silver and other valuables, soldiers at a North Carolina plantation stripped from the mistress her rings, gold bracelets, earrings, and gold comb. In Mississippi Yankee cavalrymen turned "Miss Sallie's" fine blankets into saddle blankets and, adorned in her silk dresses, rode away whooping and hollering. On an Alabama plantation troops forced the white women to cook dinner for the slaves and wait on them at table. Out to humiliate a slave owner soldiers rode one young master to death on a fence rail. Another band of federals forced Ike McCoy's mistress to cook their dinner, then stand by to witness them whip her husband. Hitherto exalted masters impotently watched as their women were robbed and humbled. A slaveholder who ordered his slaves to go back to work in the fields or depart with the Yankees, was surprised to see them utterly reject him and walk away. On the march from Atlanta to Savannah, Sherman's troops shouted and sang, and their bands and

drum corps played exuberantly, to accentuate their humiliation of the slaveocracy. In many instances, as Northern troops approached, masters fled, as their slaves formerly had run from the patrols. At other times slave men went off with the soldiers, leaving their women and children to stay with old master to work the crops for subsistence. The collapse of their authority left some masters mean tempered, others psychologically crushed. Jane Morgan's mistress sat and cried while the Yankee invaders forced her slaves to cook all the food on the plantation for them to consume or carry away.[7]

The Union Army's destruction of property to weaken civilian support for Confederate military operations could easily degenerate into wantonness. Union soldier Rice Bull complained that some fellow troops did not "have any scruples or make any exceptions in their works of destruction." On a North Carolina plantation soldiers poured the molasses on the ground, killed the chickens, and shot the dog. On a Mississippi place they emptied the big house and set the furnishings on fire, poured molasses on the ground, fouled the well with gunpowder, and tore up the fences. On another place soldiers "done right smart of mischief" including killing sheep and destroying the carriage. Black soldiers took the horses from a Mississippi place and left the geese lying where they had been shot. At Joseph Davis's Hurricane Plantation troops burned the books, smashed the glassware, and set the house on fire. They also looted Jefferson Davis's place and set his house aflame, but the slaves put out the fire. A band of rampaging cavalry poured the syrup and milk on the ground, cut off the heads of the turkeys, and galloped back and forth, as in a tournament. They took quilts and counterpanes for saddle blankets, burned the gin and the cotton, broke open the corn crib and scattered the grain.[8] Soldiers who rifled a North Carolina plantation were, according to Charlie Barbour, "de darndest yo' eber seed, dey won't eat no hog meat 'cept hams an' shoulders an' dey goes ter de smoke house and gits 'em thout no permission."[9] Raiders sometimes were generous to the slaves-from the plantation's store houses. One slaughtered a shoat and gave John Bectom a ham for his mother.[10]

Federals sometimes assumed an easy familiarity with the slaves. One said to Talitha Lewis, "Dinah, hold my horse. You got anything buried? Is they good to you?"[11] A company took all the cattle from an Arkansas plantation, not for themselves but to feed fugitive slaves huddled in camp below Pine Bluff; and they left the milk cows and some corn for slaves who remained on the place.[12] Yankees marched into Brookhaven, Mississippi, smashed store windows and passed out to slave children all the pies and cakes they could eat. The children wished "de Yankees would come every day." Although Sherman's men burned much property in Milledgeville, Georgia, Rice Bull and friends conscientiously paid an old black woman $2 to cook them Thanksgiving dinner.[13]

Although they took everything in sight soldiers in blue were nice to colored people, Sarah Jane Patterson recalled. Thousands of Lincoln's men advancing through woods, across fields, and through swamps in South Carolina burned fences, shot farm animals, and took everything they could carry but in their mighty passage hurt no one, said Henry Pristell. Jerry Hinton, a North Carolinian, also remarked that Union soldiers did not kill or injure noncombatants, but they did enjoy tearing things down and killing and eating cattle, hogs, and barnyard fowl. When Sherman marched through South Carolina black troops of the 54th Massachusetts besieging Charleston adopted Sherman's tactics and gleefully burned down slaveholders' mansions. The 54th's Colonel Norwood

Hallowell justified the destruction, stating it was "South Carolina and it must be." A band of soldiers in Arkansas burned down the big house but entertained the slave children, riding them on their mules.[14]

Fannie Dunn's experience was that "One Yankee would come along an' give us sumptin' an another would come on behind him an' take it." Others saw federal soldiers steal indiscriminately from both masters and slaves. Lila Nichols was glad to see the Yankees come but was shocked when they "acted like a pack of robbers" as they seized and destroyed, knocking down doors, pulling pictures from the walls and smashing them, insulting black and white women alike, cursing, laughing, and drinking. Josie Martin, of Arkansas, thought the Yankees who forced the slaves on her place to barbecue the hogs were not so good to the blacks as they were to their own "feelings." Mandy Coverson complained that Yankees were "mean 'bout cussin'," but were no worse than Confederates. A federal soldier cut off the head of a slave's pet rooster with a swipe of his sword without a bother about the rooster's owner. A South Carolina black complained that Yankee soldiers, far from being "gentle folk," cut hams off half-killed shoats, leaving the mangled shoats quivering on the ground. Although Union fighting men deliberately attacked the plantation economy, Confederates also took what they wanted and, according to Lindsey Faucette of North Carolina, gave the slaves lice that took years to be rid of.[15]

Bushwhackers, deserters, draft dodgers, and fugitives of one kind or another also preyed upon people behind the lines, robbing, burning, and looting. Early in 1862 Union General H.W. Halleck denounced Kansas Jayhawkers, an irregular Union military force, for making life miserable for noncombatants in Missouri, and in June, 1863, Alabama Governor John Shorter sought troops to stop deserters and stragglers from the Confederacy's Army of Tennessee from plundering the people of the Valley of the Tennessee. Bands of fugitive slaves along the Tombigbee River lived on plunder from plantations of the region. A year earlier, in June, 1862, Union Captain John W. DeForest thought it woeful that the Lafourche Country of Louisiana was being laid waste by black fugitives and runaway soldiers foraging for provisions, plundering houses, and "destroying furniture, books and pictures in mere wantonness." In the spring of 1865 West Tennessee, along the Mississippi River, was overrun with fugitives, stragglers, and deserters, and in the Vicksburg district of Mississippi near the war's end "Yankee Negroes" on one side and Confederate outlaws on the other made life and property fearfully insecure. Whenever bushwhackers approached her plantation a stalwart Arkansas mistress locked the slave women and children in a secure place and confronted the lawless gang with her big gun ready to fire. Jane Lee found the woods in her area of North Carolina so full of runaway slaves and Confederate Army deserters that it was too dangerous to walk about.[16]

Some Confederate draft dodgers hid out near their plantation homes and were secretly supplied with necessities by loyal slaves. Others risked sneaking up to their houses at night to eat and sleep. One young Confederate soldier home on furlough who hid in a canebrake rather than return to bloody and hopeless fighting was caught by the authorities and shot.[17]

When Union soldiers showed up some slave children hid under the bed, behind the corn crib, in nearby woods, or behind the skirts of mother or mistress, fearing the soldiers had come to steal or harm them. Cornelia Ishmon's mistress told Cornelia that she had saved her from having her brains beaten out by the Yankees. Louise Prayer hid under the bed, and R.F. Parker under the corn crib, at the approach of Union soldiers. Frances Cobb and friends slipped into the bottoms to keep "blue coats" from running away with them.[18] When Lizzie McCloud ran from the soldiers, one called, "Dinah, we're fightin' to free you and get you out from under bondage." Still, Lizzie ran on to her mistress for protection from her liberators.[19]

When word spread that Union soldiers were approaching planters hurriedly stashed away valuables they had some chance of saving: food, silver, jewelry, money, and, crucial to plantation economy, horses and mules. It is not surprising that General N.P. Banks ordered, April 22, 1863, the commander of his advance brigade to mount fugitive slaves to drive in cattle and to offer cash for information as to the whereabouts of horses.[20] Earlier Brigadier General S.G. Burbridge had reported that planters were desperate to hold onto their stock, especially horses and mules, and in nearly every instance they attempted to hide them.[21] There was, of course, no way to hide slaves who wanted to be found other than to drive them out of the reach of federal troops.

Soldiers often located hidden treasure with the help of a slave. A Georgian, like many another planter, hid his money in a swamp only to see it found by soldiers guided by one of his young slaves. Tom, who had been "skulking" in an Alabama swamp, brought the horses and mules out of their hidden enclosure in the swamp, and then helped the soldiers find his master's jewelry and gold. Soldiers could worm information from children, as when Anna Baker, questioned, obediently and innocently revealed that her master had hidden the gold behind the mantle. A young Arkansas boy, Willie Wallace, similarly betrayed the whereabouts of the plantation stock. Others were forced to reveal the hiding places.[22]

While soldiers were threatening the life of a Mississippi planter to extort from him his valuables, his loyal slaves ran to the woods with the silver and hid it in a hollow log, but the soldiers found it, doubtless with the help of a rebellious slave. It is not surprising that "Miss Rosa" despairingly told her slave Andrew Jackson Gill that there was no use to hide her valuables because the Yankees would find them anyway.[23] Soldiers found the treasure of a South Carolina mistress that she had hidden in a well and in the woods by questioning the slaves one by one. "Must have been a Judas 'mongst us," said Henry Jenkins. "These valuables and hosses, sheep, cows, chickens, everything carried away by an army that seemed more interested in stealing than in liberating the slaves."[24]

Some slaves protected their masters' gold and silver, such as a slave who cited, "Thou shalt not steal" in explaining why he guarded his master's hidden wealth.[25] Soldiers who dragged a South Carolina mistress about by her hair in a vain attempt to force her to disclose the whereabouts of her treasure got no help from her slaves either. After they had helped themselves in the smokehouse and the big house, and had gone on their way, Martha Colquitt said, "Grandma 'gin to fuss: 'Now, dem sojers wus tellin' us what ain't so, 'cause ain't nobody got no right to take what belongs to Master and Mist'ess.' and Ma joined in: 'Sho' it ain't no truf in what dem Yankees wuz a-sayin' and us went right on livin' just like us always done 'til Marse Billie called us together and told us de war wuz over and us wuz free to go whar us wanted to go, and us could charge wages for our work."[26] Cyntha Jones, of Arkansas, also fumed at Yankee soldiers for taking things, because, she said, "I thought what was my white folks' things was mine too." Her father, in charge of the stock, chased after the soldiers to get the master's horse back, and got it somehow.[27] A gang of soldiers divided their loot with some Mississippi slaves and told them to have a feast, but after they had departed the slaves returned everything to their master.[28]

Some slaves actively helped their owners hide valuables and kept the hiding places secret. Rosa Thomas, as an example, saved her mistress's money by concealing it on her person. A group of slaves kept the secret that their master's money was buried in the graveyard and the silver stashed in a carriage hidden in the woods. An Arkansas slave helped his master bury a pot of gold and, after the war, dig it up. On a Mississippi place soldiers consumed everything edible and tore up what they did not want, but they never located the silver in a hollow tree near the big house. Reuben Jones joined his master in successfully hiding the mules in a cave and the meat and money in a hole in the ground. A group of Arkansas slaves dug holes, covered the bottoms with rocks and the rocks with planks. On the planks they placed iron and tin vessels containing money and silver, and piled on more rocks, and dirt, and covered the traces of their work with freshly planted grass. A young mistress in Mississippi saved her best dresses by hiding them in "Aunt Hettie's" cabin. On another Mississippi plantation Yankees found the mistress's fine jewelry, but Sam kept the rest of her valuables, and the cattle, safe in the woods.[29] Hidden but forgotten treasure occasionally was found by strangers after the War. Ex-slave Martha Richardson and her brothers found gold and silver worth $5700 on a farm they rented in South Carolina. Their family was then able to buy two houses, one to live in and one to rent, and have some cash left over. An Arkansas planter died before he could retrieve his buried treasure, but his nephew from California returned and found it.[30]

With the priceless bounty of freedom blacks experienced hardship and radical upheaval during the War: their plantation communities shaken to their foundation; food scarce; young men going off with the Yankees, leaving old men, women, and children behind on wrecked plantations; nerves frayed. "Dem was squally times and de folks up sot," said Minerva Wells. "Folks had to hide and slip 'bout. Foods an' close an' all de living stuff had to be hid out to keep de war mens from taking 'em."[31] Laura Ford said things were quiet until infantry and cavalry began rampaging through the country seizing and destroying. "De fust thing we knowed dis land ob ours dat wuz so purty wuz all tore up an' ruint."[32] Tony Cox remembered dark days "wid eber body riled up an' not knowin' what wuz a gwine ter happen or how things wuz a gwine ter turn out fer no body. At times us wouldn't hab half 'nough ter eat. De Yankees would come through an' destroy what us had made, an' take off de meat an' cl'ose an' tear up things gwine an' comin'."[33] Occasionally soldiers thought of the hardships blacks left behind faced, and gave back some of what they had seized.[34]

As a consequence of the assault on the plantations blacks and whites suffered together. When soldiers consumed and destroyed food supplies, burned fences for firewood, and made off with draft animals, those remaining on the disrupted plantations experienced extreme hardship, and seriously impaired means of producing foodstuffs, let alone a cash crop for market. After Sherman cut his wide swath through Georgia and the Carolinas sure-enough hard times set in. Jessie Rice's people had nothing but ash cake and persimmon beer for days on end. Their white folks had no more. Finally, garden vegetables came along. "Till den us nearly starved." When the new crop was made, he said, "we sho did fall in and save all us could for de next year. Every kind of seed and pod dat grow'd we saved and dried for next spring or fall planting."[35]

In Mississippi with draft animals driven off people were reduced to breaking ground with hoes, "so things was awful scarce." On a North Carolina place workers also had to prepare the soil with grubbing hoes, instead of plows, for the scarce seeds available. They were without chickens, ducks, or geese but they did have one fresh cow left. The proud "mistis" would not, however, bow her head, even when her daughter ran off with a Yankee soldier.[36] When soldiers wrecked an Arkansas plantation the people faced near starvation. "After that round," Mose King said, "we had no use for the Yankees."[37] Nettie Henry did not understand why federals put her people, who had not done anything to them, in such difficult straits. After the battle of Fisher's Hill General Philip Sheridan's men were so thoroughly destructive in the Shenandoah Valley that Union Officer John W. DeForest could not imagine how the people escaped starvation. DeForest wrote, "It was a woeful sight for civilized eyes; but as a warlike measure it was very effective."[38] Soldiers in blue carried off in wagons everything from his place, Henry Walker complained. "Colored folks," he said, "didn't like 'em taking all they had to eat and had stored up to live on. They didn't leave a hog nor a chicken, nor anything else they could find." Walker's resourceful Old Miss set all the children to gathering hickory nuts, chestnuts, walnuts, and chinquapins to eat and to sell. She sent them to the hills in search of ginseng to sell.[39]

Even though slaves resented being left without food, there was little they could do to protect necessities for themselves. As Tom Wilson reported, a soldier rode up, stuck a bayonet at him, and demanded, "Boy, whar de tater house? and I sho' did show him whar twas."[40] Maria Parham complained, "My mammy had two big fat hogs what she had raised to feed us children on through the winter when who

should come right to our house but some
Yankee men and all they left us of them
hogs was the skin and guts."[41] Yankees
took what blacks had partly because they
believed blacks had nothing of their own
but pretended to possess things they were
in fact keeping for their master. When soldiers took the gold earrings her master had
given her, Jane McLeod Wilburn burst into
tears. But her mother chided her, "Hush
up you fool, crying 'bout earrings when
you ought ter be crying 'bout this here
food they has stolen."[42]

People at stripped plantations scram-
bled for substitutes for certain necessities.
They dug up the dirt floor from the smokehouse, strained water through it, and
boiled the water to get salt. They made soda
from burned corn cobs, and something like
coffee from parched rye, corn, okra, or
potatoes. Raiding Union soldiers, on the
other hand, enjoyed "Lincoln coffee." In
place of buried or stolen silver, folks used
forks made from cane.[43] With vessels broken or taken cooks wrapped food in leaves
and baked it on the fireplace floor, covered
with ashes and live coals, and "hit would
come out jist as purty and sweet as yo'
please," thought Dave Walker.[44]

In early spring women and children
scoured the woods for pokeberry greens,
and picked berries in spring and summer
and gathered nuts in the fall. Slaves mostly
used in good times as well as bad the "long
sweetening" of molasses instead of the
more precious "short sweetening" of
sugar.[45] In some areas slaves had to desert
their plantations because there was nothing left to eat or to work with, "So de slaves
jiss had to scatter out and leave right now,"
said Wylie Nealy of Briscoe, Arkansas.[46]
Annie Coley remembered the Yankees
came riding over a hill, beating a drum,
telling the slaves they were free, and grabbing two of her mother's four hens, and
taking her father to their camp to clean
and cook the hens for their feast.[47]

Some young black men who deserted
their plantations soon found themselves
put to work and carried where they did not
want to go, forever away from their families. When Union cavalry rifled a North
Carolina place of food and horses a few
youths followed them away. And when
Union gunboats steamed up the James
River and made off with slaves, Richard
Slaughter ended up as a cook in the 19th
Regiment of Maryland, Company B. But
John Sparks was spared separation from his
wife and baby, by pretending to be lame
and unfit for military service. Runaway
slaves no longer feared the old slave
patrols, but many of them were carried
away by Yankee patrols to serve the Union
military as workers or soldiers.[48]

Others eagerly and voluntarily
departed from their places of bondage.
When soldiers came near, Gabe Butler's
father "stole missus finest horse en run way
en jined de Yankees, en pappy wus de missus favorite slave. He oughtern done that,"
Gabe thought.[49] Lots of black men in
Arkansas went off with Union troops to
fight for freedom and to earn, they hoped,
a farm and a mule.[50]

Some planters tried to hang on to
their slaves by "refugeeing" them away
from approaching Union armies, hoping
that at least a remnant of the collapsing
Confederacy would survive. Texas did
remain virtually free of Union military
forces except for the capture, and loss, of
Galveston, until after the surrender. Some
black men near Pine Bluff, Arkansas, rode
off on the plantation's horses to nearby
Yankees, provoking their alarmed ex-master to round up his remaining slaves and
drive them to Texas, where he had their
services until Juneteenth (June 19, 1865),
more than two years after the Emancipation Proclamation. Similarly, about one-
half the slaves on a Black River, Louisiana,
plantation left with a band of Union soldiers, and their ex-master hurriedly

Most of the men had gone to war from this plantation in Mississippi. Francis Trevelyan Miller, ed., *Photographic History of the Civil War*, 10 vols. (New York, 1911), Vol. IX, 183.

"refugeed" the rest to Navasota, Texas. An agent of several masters unable to leave themselves, collected 15 or so slave families in Arkansas and drove them to Texas.[51]

Some planters evacuated their entire slave corps while others carried away only their prize hands. Pete Newton's and Jane Oliver's masters ran all their slaves to Texas, but Mary Myhand's master fled with only two of his slaves, and Dinah Perry's master carried away the prime hands and abandoned the children and old folks at Pine Bluff, Arkansas. Betty Haskell, who was too little, and Betty's mother,

who was too sick, were left behind. John Wells's father, who was waiting an opportunity to join the Yankees, was spirited away as his master's personal servant, to the Confederate Army. John's mother died on a refugee march, and his Uncle Granville was forced to leave his wife behind on a neighboring plantation. John Wesley's master "smuggled" his slaves to Texas in the hope of selling them in that more secure environment.[52]

Adeline Hodges's master drove his slaves hither and yon in Alabama and Mississippi in an effort to keep them from federal troops–and freedom. Children were carried in wagons; adults walked. Men without wives to keep them attached to the group, and youths, were chained to trees and wagon wheels at night. Grownups "would rake up straw and throw a quilt ober hit and be dat way all night, while us children slep' in wagons."[53] Plantation work forces driven in flight before advancing Union armies resembled coffles in the slave trade. But fast-moving troops often caught up with them. A federal military force overtook a slaveholder at Dardanelle, Arkansas, depossessed him of his cattle, horses, and provisions, and took away his slaves and led them to freedom at Fort Smith. Parrish Washington's master was cut off in the Sabine River bottoms and forced to return his people to his Arkansas plantation, then being occupied by federals, and there to acknowledge their freedom.[54]

Clarice Jackson's master put his slaves in wagons and took them to Texas, "because it would be longer 'fore we found out we was free and they would git more work out of us."[55] When Minerva Lofton's master got his slaves to Texas he found that the Yankees had occupied Corpus Christi, so he abandoned his fruitless attempt to hang on to his slaves and marched them back to Camden, Arkansas. When the federals took Little Rock, Joe Golden was hauled away to Texas, where he remained until 1868, and Susie King was taken on a long journey to Sherman, Texas, with a great drove of "darkies and many horses."[56]

Other planters forced their slaves to run between the federal armies in the Southeast. Hattie Sugg's "old boss man" and his family rode in wagons with little black children while his drove of older slaves walked, heading for the Mississippi bottoms in a vain attempt to dodge the Yankees. Ernest Branon was taken from Mississippi to Georgia, but it did no good,

for the Yankees overran Georgia, too. Rebecca Brown Hill's two brothers were "refugeed" to Opelousas, Louisiana, but ended in the Union Army when the federals captured that town. A Mississippian refugeed his people to Alabama, hiding them in the woods on the banks of a stream at night. A few of the men escaped to the federals, and when Union forces closed in, the slaveholder at last gave up.[57]

The Union Army provided refuge for slaves thrown upon the road by the vast upheaval of war. A federal lieutenant loaded Molly Horn and the other children, and her mother, into a wagon and took them to a camp in Helena, Arkansas, where her mother cooked for the troops several months before taking the family back to the old place where she worked once again, now for wages for her erstwhile master.[58] When about 200 Union soldiers assembled by a roadside in Georgia and played drums and fife, "Lots of de Niggers followed 'em on off wid just what dey had on," observed Julia Bunch.[59] In Mississippi Yankee soldiers came by, said Sally Dixon, "put us all in wagons, and carried us up to Memphis." There they were settled in a camp and fed from the commissary. And Sally's father was turned into a soldier.[60]

Union gunboats scoured the Arkansas banks of the Mississippi River, called black people from the fields, and carried them out of Confederate General Hindman's reach to Helena. There soldiers of the garrison paid the fugitives to "wait on" them. In Virginia, federal gunboats steamed up the James River, fired on towns and plantations, ran the whites off, and carried the blacks down river to Union lines.[61]

Some slaveholders gave up everything in their haste to get away from Union forces. Port Royal, South Carolina, planters rushed to escape Samuel DuPont's fleet, and left their property to the mercy of rampaging blacks and Yankee soldiers and sailors. Rosa Lindsey's master ran away to Texas to elude the Yankees.[62] When Sherman's army slashed through South Carolina some masters ran to the woods and hid. The abandoned blacks laughed and sang:

White folks, have you seed Old Massa
Up de road, with he mustache on?
He pick up he hat and he leave real sudden
And I 'lieve he's up and gone

Old Massa run away
And us darkies stay at home.
It mus' be now dat Kingdom's comin'
And de year of Jubilee.

He look up de river and he seed dat smoke
Where de Lincoln gunboats lay.
He big 'nuff and he old 'nuff and he orter know
   better,
But he gone and run away.

Now dat overseer want to give trouble
And trot us 'round a spell.
But we lock him up in de smokehouse cellar,
With the key done throwed in de well.[63]

The overwhelming power of the federal army so humbled the formerly unassailable slaveholder such that, as Ann Drake remarked, her "Marse" rode to war on a fine horse but came home on a mule, and Rosa Simmons's master, who ignominously returned on a three-legged mule, was so stricken by fear that whenever a Yankee came near he ran into the house and hid under a feather tick.[64] The War gave slaves an opportunity to weaken the bonds of discipline, even when they remained on the old place. Restive blacks on Cape Fear River threatened rebellion and could be managed only by extra overseers and heightened vigilance. Radical loss of power by the master was often emphasized by soldiers breaking in on the plantation, doing whatever they wished to do, and encouraging the slaves to aggressively assert their freedom. On a Kentucky plantation federal soldiers urged the blacks to take anything they wanted. The slaves reported the soldiers' injunctions to their master, who, unnerved, ran away.[65] Some masters, knowing the war was all but lost, showed unexpected generosity. Adaline Johnson's master, home on furlough and predicting that he would never return from the war alive, and he did not, gave each of the men on the place $5 and every woman a sow. Since most men formerly in the patrol were in the Confederate Army, the patrol, which had sustained the master's power, was hardly a bother, and, in the vicinity of Union soldiers of no consequence at all. When there was a patrol, it was composed of old men and boys. Overseers, too, lost much of their power. That pretty much left the colored people free of abuse, noted J.M. Parker. Lula Coleman saw her master's power and authority vanish when he hid in the slave quarters while Yankee soldiers took everything they laid hands on, and burned the barn.[66] Frank Patterson witnessed Union troops take possession of the country and celebrate their triumph over slaveholders in song:

Here's my little gun
His name is number one
Four and five rebels
We'll slay 'em as they come
Join the ban'
The rebels understan'
Give up all the lan'
To my brother Abraham
Old Gen'l Lee
Who is he?
He's not such a man
As our Gen'l Grant.[67]

Where slaveholders were courageous they were, nevertheless, defeated, even killed, in battle. Tines Kendricks believed his master, wounded in Virginia, would die, for a flock of screech owls occupied a tree in front of the big house, and a mist enveloped the place. The mistress tried to avert impending tragedy by shooting at the owls to drive them away, but that failed, Tines said, for next day news came of the master's death.[68]

At a secret meeting in one of the cabins on a North Carolina place where the people were praying for freedom, one of the women, the cook, burst outdoors yelling, "Blue bellies come on, blue bellies come on." She had to be run down and spirited back into the meeting. During the War all the slave women prayed for freedom, according to Dora Franks. Annie Young's mother and grandmother confidently predicted that their prayers would be heard and that, "We'll be free after awhile." A gathering of Texas slaves told a Confederate clergyman that they wanted the South to win but at a prayer meeting that night down in the hollow they prayed for the Yankees. The Lord got into the Yankees' hearts, thought Elvie Lomack. When Mary Jones ran from the soldiers her mother called, "Don't run, them's the Yankees what freed you."[69]

A few slaves did not welcome the army of liberation. John Cameron remarked that, "When folks started a-comin' through talkin' 'bout a-freein' us an' a-givin' us lan' an' so on, it didn't take wid Master's slaves. Us didn't want nothin' to come 'long to take us away from him. Dem a tellin' de niggers dey would git lan' an' cattle an' de lak ob dat was all foolism no how. Us was a-livin' in plenty an' peace."[70] When Union soldiers destroyed everything and left them "on starvation" some blacks became disenchanted with their liberators, and, on one place when asked to accompany the soldiers to camp, hid in the cane brakes instead.[71]

As the War approached some blacks were troubled by signs and portents, ghostly armies in the sky, the elements blood red, the advent of a comet.[72] Temple Wilson recalled that "Everything wuz stirred up fer a long spell fo' de war to free us come on. It wuz talked an' threatened an' all kinds o' bad signs pinted to war, till at las' dey jes' knowed it wuz bound to come on."[73]

When the war did come blacks near the fighting front and along marching routes witnessed, as well as participated in, the terrible and fascinating drama of war. "Wid de Yankees a comin' through a tearin' up de whole face ob de earth," with the rumble of guns and flashing lights of battle, "dem wuz scary days," recalled Manda Boggan.[74] Even the animals around Vicksburg were upset "while they was bustin' all their big cannons." During fighting around Pine Bluff, Arkansas, slaves slept in their clothes ready for flight if battle threatened to engulf them. Turner Jacobs narrowly escaped being hit by a bullet that ripped into a scaffold on which he was perched while viewing a battle. John Jones watched awestruck as Union gunboats steamed unchecked up and down the Arkansas River.[75]

A slave girl dazzled by the young men marching by in their blue uniforms with brass buttons got a slap from her mistress when she remarked, "Ain't them men pretty?"[76] William Rose marveled at a train-load of Confederate soldiers going "down to die"; one picked a banjo, another played the fiddle, and they all whooped and hollered and sang. "And it seem to me dat is de most wonderful sight I ever see. All them soldier, laughing light, singing and shouting dat way, and all riding fast to battle."[77] Elijah Hopkins witnessed thousands and thousands of Sherman's troops marching through Atlanta and crowds of Confederates fleeing before them. William Porter was amazed by Confederate General J.B. Hood's men marching on to battle, day and night, for two days.[78]

Some slaves visited battlegrounds to bury the dead or view the carnage. George Ward, with others, was sent to bury in long trenches about 80 soldiers left dead in the wake of a raid by Confederate General N.B. Forrest at Troy, Mississippi. Jane Osbrook was shocked to see at Jenkins Ferry, Arkansas, the dead lying in shallow graves, row after row, still uncovered.[79] Edwin Walker "went to Vicksburg after dat awful battle an' dat wuz de worse sight I'se eber seed afore or since, everything tore up an' dead folks all over creation an' hit wuz de worse smell I is ever heard of, so much blood had been shed an' so many soldiers an' horses killed."[80]

All along the routes of armies slaves were kept on edge by the sounds of battle. Flashes of light and roar of artillery at the great siege of Vicksburg kept everyone in the area, slave and free, sleepless and trembling. A fight between armies of Confederate General Braxton Bragg and Union General Don Buell near Savannah, Tennessee, was a time of roaring and shaking, of fear and distress. When cannons boomed far off people stopped to "listen to the home-made thunder." Elmira Hill observed in the last battle in Pine Bluff, Arkansas, federals secured in the court house, protected by breastworks of cotton bales, check and then drive off attacking Confederates. Tom Wylie Neal was fascinated by the soldiers, wagons, beautiful horses, and booming guns at the Battle of Atlanta.[81]

Away from the strife, Julia Cox listened attentively to her young master's war stories, told on furlough, "how dey would fight, camp, and march. Now us set 'round an' took in eber word."[82] Sarah Anne Green was impressed by the charity her mistress showed a wounded Yankee soldier she hid on her place, binding his wounds and feeding him and, when he was strong enough, sending him to the Yankee camp. Mother of two sons in the Confederate Army, she treated the enemy soldier as one of her own. Similarly, James Gill's slave mother smuggled food and medicine from the Union camp at Helena, Arkansas, to Confederates hiding in the area.[83]

Slaves anxiously awaited news of the Union Army's advance. "Sometimes a sharp nigger would slip over on our place to tell us what he done heard," said James Brittian, "but we never knowed whether it was true or not."[84] But Minnie Davis's mother, who had learned to read from her master's children, read on the sly newspapers coming to the plantation, and kept the rest of the slaves posted on the course of the War. As news and rumors of the War spread from plantation to plantation, blacks prayed for freedom and gathered in little groups and whispered to one another, and slaveholders began to act "queer."[85]

7

The Military and the Slaves

At the beginning of the Civil War slaveholders in Missouri, a border state that remained in the Union, anxious that their ownership in slaves be protected, wanted to know whether it was the intention of the United States Government to interfere with or protect slavery in Missouri or in any slave state. General Wilham S. Harney, Commanding Military Department of the West replied, May 14, 1861, that he was astonished at such a question. He pointed out that since the commencement of the War slaves that had sought refuge in the camps of United States troops were returned to their owners and, he went on to say, his acquaintance with the statesmanlike views of President Lincoln made him confident that slavery was secure.[1] Only a few months later, on August 30, 1861, General John C. Fremont, now commanding the Western Department, declared martial law throughout the state of Missouri and proclaimed: "The property, real and personal, of all persons in the State of Missouri who shall take up arms against the United States, or who shall be directly proven to have taken an active part with the enemies in the field, is declared to be confiscated to the public use, and their slaves, if any they have, are hereby declared freemen."[2] Lincoln rescinded Fremont's order.

In neighboring Kentucky on October 1, 1861, Headquarters U.S. Forces, Paducah,

ordered that no slave be "set free by any military commander."[3] Then General William T. Sherman, Commanding, Louisville, Kentucky, informed a subordinate October 15, 1861, that laws of the United States and of Kentucky compelled the military to surrender runaway slaves to their owners and thus it was best to keep blacks out of camp.[4]

There were, however, stirrings of abolitionism in the military. Major C.W. Phifer reported to Confederate General T.C. Hindman, from Cave City, Kentucky, October 28, 1861, that "Black Republican" troops had carried away valuable Negroes from the Williams plantation.[5] By then the federal government had tentatively moved against slavery by harboring runaway slaves of rebels. But military authorities were wary lest runaways be the property of loyal slaveholders. In correspondence, in November, 1861, with General Sherman, General A. McD. McCook was troubled that in giving protection to fugitive slaves of rebel masters he might also be sheltering slaves of loyal masters and thereby weakening the Union cause in Kentucky. Although he had no desire to uphold slavery McCook feared rebels would "bolster themselves up by making the uninformed believe that this is a war upon African slavery." Sherman, also concerned about the loyalty of Unionists in Kentucky, replied that fugitives ought to be turned over to their masters or to the sheriffs.[6]

Confederates, very much aware of the essential character of the War, urged Kentuckians to join them, for, they warned, the federal government would free the slaves, arm them, and at last give them political and social equality with whites. "We saw these things in the beginning," wrote General F.K. Zollicoffer to the "People of Southeastern Kentucky," December 16, 1861. "The honor of your wives and daughters, your past renown, and the fair name of your posterity forbid that you should strike for Lincoln and the abolition of slavery against those struggling for the rights and independence of your kindred race."[7] Others, like W. Preston, of Bowling Green, tried to convince Kentuckians that the abolitionists would force the federal administration to free the slaves. They pleaded with Kentucky officers in the Union Army to recognize the drift of events, and come over to the Confederacy. The people of the State had been deceived by "promises that the War was conducted in no spirit of hostility to the institution of slavery," declared Preston, but "the mask is laid aside and the true character of the contest is revealed."[8]

The North moved slowly toward recognizing that the abolition of slavery, not simply the restoration of the old union, must be the great goal of the war, and that the army was the instrument to achieve that end. When General H. W. Halleck issued orders for the Department of Missouri in November, 1861, that fugitive slaves be excluded from the military's lines, he could not thereby stop slaves from seeking refuge with his army. By December 1861 Halleck had shifted his position and was giving employment to fugitives of disloyal masters.[9] As the Union advanced to the point of liberating slaves employed by Confederate authorities, designating them as "contrabands" subject to seizure, Confederates had to adopt extraordinary measures to prevent the slaves from escaping

to Union lines. Confederate General M. Jeff Thompson, for example, transferred slaves he was employing in Missouri across the wide and swift Mississippi to Tennessee each night in order to prevent their fleeing to the Union Army, strengthening that army while weakening his own forces.[10]

Union naval forces also were slow to harbor fugitive slaves as a means to advance freedom and win the war, and found it troublesome to distinguish between runaways of rebels and runaways of loyalists. Charles Ellet, commanding Ram Fleet off Memphis, informed Lieutenant Crandall of the *Lioness*, June 11, 1862, that there was no room in their fleet for runaway blacks nor time to adjudicate questions of rights of masters and slaves. Ellet ordered Crandall to put fugitives and their claimants on shore in Memphis and not again receive on board "any runaway negroes or any pursuer."[11] In July, 1862, General Samuel R. Curtis, now out of Border State Missouri and down the Mississippi at Helena, Arkansas, was giving free papers to fugitive slaves who had been impressed for military labor by Confederates. Slaves were throwing down their tools and rushing to his lines, he said, creating a general stampede. The fugitives were, Curtis reported, generally mutinous but not abusive of their masters. "Society is terribly mutilated," he continued, "and masters and slaves are afraid of famine."[12]

Fugitive slaves flocked to U.S. Grant's army too as he occupied West Tennessee in his drive down the Mississippi, and the slaveholders applying for permission to look for runaways got to be a problem. On February 26, 1862, Grant ordered his officers to keep the fugitives out. The incremental change in policy from accepting slavery to taking hesitant steps against the instituion can be seen, again, in Grant's order that only those slaves within Confederate lines at the capture of Fort

These "contrabands" served as teamsters with General Benjamin Butler at Bermuda Hundred, Virginia, in 1864. Miller, ed., *Photographic History of the Civil War*, Vol IX, 181.

Donelson, or used by the enemy in building fortifications, were not to be released to their masters but were to be employed in the quartermaster department for the benefit of the government.[13]

Grant's second-in-command W.T. Sherman wrote his brother Senator John Sherman from Memphis, September 3, 1862, that to make slaves "free and see that they are not converted into thieves, idlers or worse is a difficult problem and will require much machinery to carry out." Sherman was employing two thousand contrabands, one-eighth of his command, and had to provide for the women and children. Where were all the freed people "to get work? Who is to feed them, clothe them, and house them?" he asked. Sherman did not have enough tents for his soldiers, and, he added, "If we are to take along and feed the negroes who flee to us for refuge it will be an impossible task. You cannot solve this negro question in a day."[14] Lincoln himself expressed concern, September 13, 1862, that if slaves came over

in response to a proclamation of his, "*What should we do with them*? How can we feed and care for such a multitude?"[15]

Lincoln's decision to emancipate the slaves was doubtless influenced by the experience of his generals and by controversies such as that between Major General Benjamin Butler and Brigadier General J.W. Phelps in the spring and early summer of 1862, the documents of which were laid before him by Secretary of War E.M. Stanton. Late in April, 1862, Admiral David Farragut protected the landing at New Orleans of General Butler's occupying army. Nearby communities were thrown into turmoil. Many slaves broke out of bondage and sought refuge with the Union Army; young men among them offered to join the Army to fight for freedom. Butler excluded from his lines fugitives he did not employ, explaining, "What would be the state of things if I allowed all the slaves from the plantations to quit their employment and come within the lines is not to be conceived by the imagination."

Concerning black soldiers, he said that he could raise all the white troops he needed, that the war would be over before blacks could be trained sufficiently, and that blacks "had a horror of firearms." Anyhow, he noted, Lincoln had overruled General David Hunter's enlistment of blacks in South Carolina and Florida.

General Phelps at Camp Parapet, Louisiana, ignored Butler's order to exclude fugitives from his lines. He admitted men, women, and children, and the old and infirm to his lines. And he trained and equipped young black men as soldiers. He argued that blacks had begun an exodus and that it was time for the federal government to protect them. He asserted that the government should make the Declaration of Independence good, that the slaves' cry for justice could be answered by the "abolition of slavery, and by no other course." Neither the states nor Congress, Phelps thought, would abolish slavery, as the public good required. "But there is one principle which is fully recognized as a necessity in condition like ours, and that is that the public safety is the supreme law of the state, and that amidst the clash of arms the laws of peace are silent." "It is then for our President, the Commander-in-Chief of our armies, to declare the abolition of slavery, leaving it to the wisdom of Congress to adopt measures to meet the consequences." Phelps recommended an apprenticeship system to ease the transition from slavery to freedom. Anyhow, the labor system was falling apart as the result of the intrusion of Union military force. The sudden abolition of slavery would hasten the end of the war. If it would devastate the South that would be better than the present "disaffection and rebellion," the "buying and selling of human beings–a shameless act, which renders our country the disgrace of Christendom." Phelps was convinced that a proclamation freeing the slaves, "coupled with offers of protection,

would devastate every plantation," and raising black troops would do more than anything to end the war.

General Butler, restrained by unclear and undeveloped federal policy and by his duty to maintain order among a large civilian population, charged that Phelps was trying to mold the policy of the federal government. Both Phelps, who had the clarity of purpose of an uncompromising abolitionist, and his superior Butler, asked that their communications be presented to the president.[16]

Union generals, except radical abolitionists among them, were uncertain what to do about slaves they encountered, in part because their commander-in-chief was, early in the war, uncertain too. Lincoln believed that he could not save the Union if he alienated, and lost, the Border States. But when these precariously loyal states had been bound to the Union by federal military and political power, he appealed to them to initiate gradual, compensated emancipation, and asked Congress to provide monetary support for such a program. He hoped Confederates would give up, if they lost hope of bringing to their side these important states, with their population, resources, and strategic location.[17] But the Border States delayed emancipation, and Confederates continued formidable resistance. Concluding that stronger measures were necessary, Lincoln issued the Preliminary Emancipation Proclamation, September 22, 1862, giving Confederates three months to return to the Union, keeping possession of their slaves. Spurned by Rebels, Lincoln issued the Emancipation Proclamation, January 1, 1863, freeing the slaves within Confederate lines, an "act of justice warranted by the Constitution, upon military necessity," and invoking the "considerate judgement of mankind, and the gracious favor of Almighty God."[18]

On April 4, 1864, Lincoln explained that he did not employ emancipation earlier, as when he rescinded attempted military emancipation by Generals John Fremont and David Hunter, because he did not think it indispensable. But, "When in March, and May, and July, 1862 I made earnest, and successive appeals to the border states to favor compensated emancipation, I believed the indispensable necessity for military emancipation, and arming the blacks would come, unless averted by that measure." He added, "I claim not to have controlled events, but confess plainly that events have controlled me."[19] On August 10, 1864, he declared: "No human power can subdue the rebellion without using the Emancipation lever as I have done. Freedom has given us the control of 200,000 able bodied men, born and raised on southern soil. It will give us more yet. Just so much it has subtracted from the strength of our enemies."[20]

In his Second Inaugural Address, March 4, 1865, Lincoln saw the war and the end of slavery in the light of Providence:

> If we shall suppose that American Slavery is one of those offenses which, in the providence of God, must needs come, but which, having continued through His appointed time, He now wills to remove, and that he gives to both North and South, this terrible war, as the woe due to those by whom the offense came, shall we discern therein any departure from those divine attributes which the believers in a Living God always ascribe to Him? Fondly do we hope–fervently do we pray–that this mighty scourge of war may speedily pass away. Yet, if God wills that it continue, until all the wealth piled by the bondman's two hundred and fifty years of unrequited toil shall be sunk, and until every drop of blood drawn with the lash, shall be paid by another drawn with the sword, as was said three thousand years ago, so still it must be said, "the judgements of the Lord, are true and righteous altogether."[21]

Jefferson Davis denounced Lincoln's Emancipation Proclamation "by which several millions of human beings of an inferior race, peaceful and contented laborers in their sphere, are doomed to extermination, while at the same time they are encouraged to a general assassination of their masters by the insidious recommendation 'to abstain from violence unless in necessary self-defense.'"[22] The Confederate Congress threatened death to anyone, including Union officers, who incited slaves to rebel.[23]

Emancipation by Lincoln's proclamation had, as expected, great consequence. Cyrus Bussey, colonel commanding at Helena, Arkansas, wrote, January 13, 1863, that he was at a loss what to do with the "great many negro men, women, and children coming into our lines since the proclamation."[24] And General Samuel R. Curtis reported to Lincoln, January 31, 1863, that thousands of blacks were pouring into his lines. Curtis ordered General B.M. Prentiss, commanding, Eastern Arkansas, not to send fugitives on to Missouri but to deal with the problem himself rather than transfer it to Missouri.[25]

Black soldier George E. Stephens, of the 54th Massachusetts, complained that the Proclamation was a poor excuse for what should have been a sweeping abolition of slavery everywhere, but black teacher Charlotte Forten, in the Sea Islands of South Carolina, declared, "our hearts were filled with exceeding great gladness; for, although the government had left much undone, we knew that freedom was surely born in our land that day."[26] In Mississippi the Proclamation, together with the proximity of federal troops, made slaves, according to a Confederate report, "very insubordinate."[27] His proclamation and the arming of Negroes was the "bugbear in Mississippi," General S.A. Hurlbut reported to Lincoln, August 13, 1863.[28]

Congress prohibited, March 3, 1863, the military from returning fugitives, in support of the new policy to deplete the South's labor force and undermine slavery.[29] On March 31, 1863, General H.W. Halleck wrote General Grant that government policy was to withdraw from use by the Rebels all slaves possible and to employ them as laborers, even as fighting men, against the Rebels. The character of the War had changed; there was now no hope of reconciliation. There could be no peace but that "forced by the sword." Grant was to use his influence to remove prejudice against the subject and to carry out the policy "ordered by the Government."[30]

In turn Grant wrote Major General Frederick Steele, commander of the Eleventh Division, Army of Tennessee, April 11, 1863, from Milliken's Bend, Louisiana, that the rebellion had reached such a state that it could be terminated only by the "complete subjugation of the South or the overthrow of the Government. It is our duty, therefore, to use every means to weaken the enemy, by destroying their means of subsistence, withdrawing their means of cultivating their fields, and in every other way possible." He instructed Steele to encourage all blacks, particularly able-bodied "males, to come within our lines." By this time, Grant informed Steele, General Lorenzo Thomas had arrived with "authority to make ample provision for the negro."[31]

When Grant was stymied in operations up river from Vicksburg he decided to dig a canal to bypass the city to the westward and get around its guns. Such a work required enormous labor, so he collected all the suitable blacks he could. George W. Deitzler, colonel First Kansas, sent from Lake Providence, Louisiana, 100 blacks to work on the canal, and promised to send out a force to collect as many more as possible and forward them to Grant, but, he reported, planters were taking their slaves 12 to 15 miles away from the river to get them out of reach. While Grant was digging his canal, Confederates were working several thousand slaves in a salt mine at Raven's Lake, west of Monroe, Louisiana.[32] Grant found that large numbers of blacks could clog his army's movements. As a consequence he issued field orders that since he could not transport or provide for all that would come, "enticing of Negroes to leave their homes to come within the lines of the army is positively forbidden." Whenever the services of Negroes were required, "details will be made by Army Corps Commanders for the purpose of collecting them."[33] A few days later Grant reported to General Halleck that he was using several hundred "contrabands" on the canal but humanity dictated that he prohibit more from coming in. Planters, he noted, had taken away the able-bodied, leaving the old and the very young, and these would not have shelter when he left.[34] Grant was now leading not only an invading army but also an occupying army responsible for the general population of the area.

Still Grant needed diggers. He requested that General Stephen A. Hurlbut, commanding the 16th Corps at Memphis, send him at Young's Point, Louisiana, as many able-bodied black laborers he could spare from Memphis and vicinity for work on the canal.[35] But the question of the contrabands remained a troublesome one for Grant. He ordered General J.B. McPherson to use 300 men in a pioneer corps of each division but to send the rest to Memphis, when the Lake Providence post was abandoned.[36] He continued to employ thousands of men felling trees and grubbing up roots on the cut-off canal. C.A. Dana reported to Secretary of War E.M. Stanton, April 6, 1863, that the cut-off was half finished and that 3500 men were at work on it.[37]

Grant finally abandoned the canal project. Instead he marched his troops down the west bank of the Mississippi out of range of the Confederate guns, while the fleet raced down river through Confederate bombardment from Vicksburg to ferry Grant's men to the east bank at Bruinsburg, Mississippi. Grant and his men drove on in their great campaign to capture Jackson, and then, after a long and bloody siege, Vicksburg, July 4, 1863.

In the siege Grant employed black laborers, now freedmen, at $10 per month digging trenches to enable his men to close on the embattled Confederates. After his victory, Grant ordered that male blacks captured from the Confederates be organized into working parties for policing grounds, unloading steamers, and erecting fortifications. He even permitted black servants to accompany their paroled Confederate ex-masters out of the city, if they freely chose to go.[38] Like Grant, with whom he cooperated in the Vicksburg Campaign, Admiral David D. Porter found good use for blacks in his Mississippi squadrons. At Cairo, Illinois, he ordered that first-rate young male contrabands be put to work at $9 per month. Down river at Memphis, December 19, 1862, the admiral ordered Lieutenant Joshua Bishop, of the *U.S.S. General Bragg*, to furnish light draft vessels with 10 contrabands each and to fill out short-handed vessels with contrabands.[39]

When slaves sought freedom under the protective shield of the Union military, commanders were seldom sure how to respond. They could employ many able-bodied men as laborers and soldiers, but there were the women and children, the infirm and aged, and the problem of maintaining families. Courses of action gradually became clearer after the Emancipation Proclamation but were never altogether satisfactory.

On June 15, 1862, Major Frank Peck of the Twelfth Regiment of Connecticut Volunteers, at Camp Parapet, Louisiana, reported to General Phelps that blacks of "all ages and physical condition, a number of infants in arms, many young children, robust men and women, and a large number of lame, old, and infirm of both sexes" with boxes, bedding, and luggage were on the levee. They had nothing to eat but what the soldiers gave them from their own rations. Without changed regulations the fugitives would be reduced to "starvation in the very sight of the overflowing storehouses of the Government." The large numbers of blacks streaming into his camp was a matter of intense concern to General Phelps, who passionately hated slavery. He served rations to the fugitives, employed as many as he could, and, without authorization, as we have seen, set about enlisting their strong young men.[40]

On November 8, 1862, General Sherman, at Memphis, was willing to furnish 200 contrabands to Admiral Porter, but only if Porter would receive their families with them. But Porter wanted only single men; families, he said, would be no use to him.[41] A year and a half later, May 28, 1864, Captain Albert Brockman, at Macon, Missouri, wrote that, "Negroes of both sexes keep constantly coming in; they are crowding our camps. Think they ought not to be brought in so close contact with soldiers. Prostitution is worse than slavery."[42]

In the meantime, commanders continued to struggle with the problem of dealing with uprooted fugitives needing help and protection. In November, 1862, General Grant appointed Chaplain J. Eaton, Jr., of the Twenty Seventh Regiment Ohio Infantry Volunteers to take charge of fugitive slaves coming within his lines; establish a camp for them at Grand Junction, Tennessee; and organize them, and set them to work picking, ginning, and baling cotton. A regiment guarded them, physicians of the regiment treated their sick, and commissary officers issued them rations, substituting rye for the more luxurious coffee.[43]

It was at this point that, as Grant recalled in his *Memoirs*, the Freedmen's Bureau began to emerge. With thousands of blacks congregated at Grand Junction there was no authority to feed them unless they were employed by the Army, but only strong, young men were suited to serve as teamsters and pioneers. The plantations of the area were deserted, cotton needed to be brought in, and men, women, and children 10 and older could be employed to do that. Grant gave Eaton assistance, and military protection, to organize the work. He and Eaton fixed wages to be paid by the quartermaster, who shipped the gathered cotton north to be sold for the government's benefit. Planters who remained on their plantations could employ freedmen on the same terms. In consequence, the freedmen became self-supporting. However, Grant and Eaton collected and spent the wages, according to their judgment, for the freedmen's benefit. Later freedmen were set to cutting wood for sale to Mississippi River steamers. With the income a fund was created to feed and clothe the freedmen, and build cabins and hospitals and provide other benefits for them. This program sustained the freedmen and kept them from hampering Grant's military movements. It also marked a shift from the Army's destroying the plantation economy to its managing that economy, now with partially freed labor. Similar programs were developed in the Sea Islands of South Carolina where Union occupying forces early encountered a large population of slaves.[44]

But provision for fugitives remained a problem in Grant's department. In February, 1863, General S.A. Hurlbut, commanding in Memphis, wrote Grant that General McClernand had sent up the river to Memphis 200 women and children, "who were dropped upon the levee, not a humane treatment of them, and without any communication concerning them."[45]

Next month, March 27, 1863, Hurlbut wrote to President Lincoln concerning problems relating to blacks. There were about 5000 males and females of all ages maintained by the government, in addition to those employed as teamsters, cooks, and pioneers, and in other capacities. Most of these 5000 were women and children who were an encumbrance to the Army. Another 2000 or so blacks in Memphis, not supported by the Army, were crowded into houses and sheds, "living by begging or vice," and were victims and source of "contagion and pestilence," and petty crime. Hurlbut could see nothing before them but disease and death. But there was a way out of the gloomy prospect, he thought.

There were many farms and plantations within the Army's lines despoiled of fences, stripped of horses and mules, and deprived of customary labor, that could be made productive again. The owners were ready to cultivate, but had no labor. It was spring, the time to plant cotton, corn, and vegetables, "singularly beneficial to the health of an army." Many wanted to hire their former slaves. But Hurlbut had no power to enforce contracts, and there were no civil or criminal courts. He thought that the freedmen ought to be hired for wages, subsistence, or a part of the crop, but he was concerned that guerrillas would carry them off to areas not under Union control, or that their employers might treat them unfairly. Still, "if the fugitives now lurking about Memphis could return to their homes in the city and vicinity, and their former owners would receive them and treat them kindly until the final determination of their status, much of the misery and vice which infest the city and vicinity would be removed."

In Tennessee, Hurlbut remarked, it was not clear whether or not slavery existed. The laws of the state recognized it but the laws were in abeyance, for there were no courts to interpret and administer nor sheriffs to enforce the laws. But military authorities, from choice and under orders, ignored the condition of slavery. They allowed the blacks to come within their lines or leave, and this worked little difficulty in the field. But when the lines enclosed a large area of country or fenced in a city, such as Memphis, "this incursion of ungoverned persons, without employment and subject to no discipline, becomes vitally serious." The police and administration of justice were thrust upon the Army. The necessity for prompt action was paramount, both for reasons of humanity and to relieve the Army of this burden. Hurlbut requested President Lincoln to adopt a policy to deal with the problems he was wrestling with. Andrew Johnson's organization of a loyal government in Tennessee under Lincoln's executive authority, which abolished slavery, and the establishment of the Freedmen's Bureau (Bureau of Refugees, Freedmen, and Abandoned Lands) relieved in part Hurlbut's and other commanders' responsibilities for freedmen and civil society in the occupied South.[46]

Until a general program for dealing with the problems of the newly freed could be developed, the Union military established temporary camps for immediate relief and employment. Quartermaster General M.C. Meigs reported to the Secretary of War, November 3, 1864, that his department had employed persons of African descent as teamsters, grooms, dock workers, steamboat hands, and in all sorts of manual labor. He never had enough of these workers, because the generals needed all they could get. General N.P. Banks claimed that his department could not spare a single man, woman, or child. Meigs believed that the strong demand for the freedmen's labor eased the distress of the sudden change from slavery to freedom. Around Washington refugees were at first

gathered in camps and hovels. But in time deductions of $5 per month from wages of those in public service was used to support the women and children. Comfortable quarters were built; hospitals and schools founded; mortality checked; lands abandoned by rebels cultivated. Wives and children of men in service of the Army as soldiers or laborers were employed in homes or on farms. The people were clean, comfortable, and contented as much as possible amidst the great upheaval.[47]

Blacks who took advantage of Sherman's conquering army to assert their freedom included a North Carolinian who seized horses and wagon and escaped during the night with his wife and children. In New Bern he made a good living for his family by making boots for Union soldiers. George W. Harris also ran to Sherman's lines at New Bern and was put to work by the Army as cook, stable hand, and general laborer. Others, less fortunate, showed up in camps in rags, the women in cast-off coats and skirts made from bags, and men in jackets of carpet or blanket and pants held up with pieces of rope.[48] Troops urged blacks not already on the road to leave the plantations, and trainloads of them were hauled to New Bern, and dumped on bare ground in a camp. There they erected make-shift shelters. The provost-marshal issued them hard-tack, codfish, and left-over beef. Later, those who wanted to leave the unsettled conditions of the camps to go back to their old places were given train tickets. Nathan Best returned to his old master as a free laborer for $3.50 per month, shelter, and food.[49]

In Nashville, Tennessee, in September, 1863, Major G.I. Stearns, in connection with enlisting black troops, established a camp for women and children, put them in an abandoned chapel, provided them with rations, and hired them out. Stearns set up similar refugee camps in the area as a result of General

George H. Thomas being ordered, in December, 1863, to receive destitute women and children at Nashville. Hardship attended the collection of these refugees; on their way to Nashville a group of about 100 women and children and infirm men were put off at the Chattanooga depot and left for hours standing between the tracks. Superintendents of the camps around Nashville were selected from the officer corps of the 101st U. S. Colored Infantry.

Schools were established for children at the camps, as chaplains conducted schools in the colored regiments. The military cooperated with the Pennsylvania Freedmen's Aid Association to found other schools for blacks in Middle and East Tennessee. Stearns procured volunteer laborers in place of impressed laborers and had a hand in establishing a new general hospital for "colored people" to replace a makeshift contraband hospital where mortality was high. Doctor W. Clendenin, associated with Stearns in securing the hospital, saw that black nurses were paid for their services. Stearns believed that his program influenced public opinion in Tennessee to turn against slavery.[50]

Around Jacksonville, Florida, in the spring of 1864, able-bodied males were put into the army as soon as they came in, or were brought in by a raid into the plantation country. Females were sent to camps at Fernandina, Florida, or Hilton Head, South Carolina. They were a pitiful set, black Sergeant George E. Stephens observed, without shoes, barely clothed, the women without turbans, which the poorest slave women normally had, and halting in speech.[51]

Rather than encourage freedmen to gravitate to the Army or gather in temporary camps, Union commanders in secure possession of territory organized labor systems to keep the blacks on plantations, as free laborers under the protection of Union authorities. General Benjamin Butler reported to Secretary of War E.M. Stanton, November 14, 1862, that his experiment in free labor in Louisiana was succeeding. He had provided in General Orders No. 91, November 9, 1862, that rebel property west of the Mississippi in Louisiana in the La Fourche district be sequestered and unemployed workers put to work on the plantations, under a commission appointed by the general. The commission would run the plantations with "loyal or disloyal" planters who had remained quietly at home, and with the labor of blacks in the district who claimed the protection of the United States. The commissioners would furnish supplies to planters during the making of the crop, with their outlay being a lien on the crop. They would direct for the benefit of the United States plantations abandoned by their owners or held by disloyal owners. Persons who had not been in arms against the United States since the occupation of New Orleans, who remained peaceably on their plantations, or who returned to allegiance of the United States could be allowed to work their own plantations. The commission would recommend that those who proved their loyalty be granted amnesty and protection of their property.

Butler had a memorandum drawn up that regulated these matters in the parishes of St. Bernard and Plaquemines, stating that since many persons had left their masters and had come to New Orleans and to the camps of the Army of the Gulf claiming to be emancipated and these men and women were destitute, it was the duty of the United States to provide them with food and clothing and to employ them. It was also necessary that the crops then growing be saved, and levees repaired and strengthened. At the same time some planters claimed that these persons were still held to service, and that their crops and plantations would be ruined if deprived of such service. These conflicting claims could not be determined by tribunals then existing in Louisiana. In order to preserve the rights of all parties the United States would employ the blacks of St. Bernard and Plaquemines Parishes under the day-to-day supervision of the loyal masters, who still claimed their services; Lincoln had exempted occupied Louisiana and other areas from the effects of the Emancipation Proclamation. The military would furnish guards and patrols to preserve discipline. The planters were required to pay $10 per month to each able-bodied male, and provide food, housing, and medical attention, and care for the disabled members of the laborers' families. The work-day was set at 10 hours and the work-month at 26 days, except for a 20-day December. Corporal punishment was prohibited although the provost-marshal might punish the insubordinate and the slacker, even by imprisonment "in darkness on bread and water."[52] Thus did military authorities play a significant role in transforming a slave labor force into a semi-free labor force, as the rising tide of freedom swept away servitude owed to loyal as well as to disloyal masters. Louisiana and other states under Lincoln's plan of reconstruction soon formally abolished slavery.

In the meantime, N.P. Banks, Butler's successor in command of the Department of the Gulf, in campaigns against Port Hudson and up the Red River, swept the countryside of slaves, horses and mules, cattle, and other mainstays of the plantation. But in areas under his firm control he expected blacks to remain on their plantations, unless he directed otherwise.[53] His General Orders No. 12, January 29, 1863, noted that, although Lincoln's Proclamation designated areas of Louisiana not affected, the laws of the United States prohibited officers of the Army from returning runaway slaves, and conditions of war

inevitably deprived citizens of full control over their property. Public interest demanded that Negroes work, that those who left their plantations be compelled to support themselves by labor upon the public works. "Under no circumstances whatever can they be maintained in idleness, or allowed to wander through the parishes and cities of the State without employment." However, blacks deserved an equitable portion of crops they produced. A commission was directed to confer with planters and others to establish a yearly system of labor, which would provide for food, clothing, proper treatment, and just compensation for the blacks, at prescribed wages or portion of the crop. When accepted by the planter the "conditions of continuous and faithful service, respectful deportment, correct discipline, and perfect subordination shall be enforced on the part of the negroes by the officers of the Government." Wages would constitute a lien upon the crop. His plan might not be the best, Banks admitted, but it was the only practicable one, and "wise men will do what they can when they cannot do what they would."[54]

On February 16, 1863, General Banks issued a circular explaining his system of inducing blacks to return to their accustomed plantations. He believed thousands would die without regular work, and it was too expensive and impractical for the Army to support dependent and destitute persons. The cultivation of corn, sugar cane, cotton, and other crops was demanded by public interest and for this the labor of blacks was necessary. "On the plantations they will have secured to them by the officers of the Government sufficient and wholesome food, clothing, kind treatment and a share of the crop they produce." To pressure blacks to return to the plantations Banks reiterated his intention to employ those not on the plantations on public works or in the quartermaster department without pay except food and clothing, medical attention, and instruction and care as may be furnished to them and their women and children.[55] In orders issued two days later Banks forbade any officers without authority from headquarters to take any blacks from the plantations.[56]

Butler's and Banks's regulations provided the basis for the Secretary of War's regulations, Orders No. 9, Vicksburg, Mississippi, March 11, 1864, promulgated by General Lorenzo Thomas, who stated that the occupation of the plantations and employment of the freedmen had been directed by the president and was settled policy. The enlistment of soldiers from these plantations was suspended. Provost-marshals were to be placed at convenient points in the vicinity of leased plantations. It was their duty to see that justice and equity were observed in all relations between employers and freedmen. At least one school was to be established in each district for black children under 12.

Soldiers were not allowed to visit the plantations without written consent of their commanders, and never with arms, except when on duty accompanied by an officer. Plantation hands were not allowed to go from one plantation to another except as regulated by the provost-marshal of the district. Flogging and other cruel or unusual punishments were forbidden. Planters were to transmit a roll of their workers to the provost-marshal. In employment the family unit was to be respected. Questions between employers and workers were to be decided by provost-marshals, subject to appeal.

The sick and disabled were to be provided for on the plantations. Purchase of clothing or other property from the laborers was forbidden as was the sale of whiskey to them. Possession of arms or dangerous weapons, without authority, was prohibited. Laborers were to render, between daylight and dark, 10 hours in summer and nine hours in winter, respectful, honest, faithful labor, and receive healthful rations, comfortable clothing, quarters, fuel, medical attention, and instruction for children. The minimum wage, half of which was to be reserved

Provost Marshal's Headquarters at Corinth, Mississippi. During the transition from slavery to freedom provost-marshals supervised labor relations of freedmen and planters. Miller, ed., *The Photographic History of the Civil War* Vol, II, 157.

until the end of the year, was for males over 14 years of age $10 per month; for females over 14 $7; for children 12 to 14, and those unable to do a full day's work, half the above amounts. Foremen were to get additional wages. The schedule of wages could be commuted by agreement between the employer and the employee, subject to approval. Wages and rations could be deducted in case of frequent sickness. Indolence, insolence, disobedience of orders, and crime would be punished by forfeiture of pay to a fund for the support of the destitute, and such other punishment as provided for similar offenses by Army regulations.

Laborers would be held to their contract for one year. Those feigning sickness or refusing duty would be turned over to the provost-marshal for labor upon the public works without pay. Laborers would be permitted to cultivate land on private account, as agreed between them and their employer, subject to the approval of the provost-marshal of the district. That would "enable the laborer to take care of himself and prepare for the time when he can render so much labor for so much money, which is the great end to be attained." It was advised that employers provide extra pay for extra labor or provide for share cultivation. A bank would be established for the laborers' savings. The War Department's regulations contained a gratuitous pronouncement on the general necessity of labor aimed at the freedmen, who were being treated as semi-free, and the public:

> Freedmen are not relieved from the necessity of toil, which is the condition of existence with all the children of God. The revolution has altered its tenure, but not its law. This universal law of labor will be enforced upon just terms by the Government, under whose protection the laborer rests secure in his rights. Indolence, disorder, and crime will be suppressed. Having exercised the highest right in the choice and place of employment, he must be held to the fulfillment of his engagements until released therefrom by the Government. The several provost-marshals are hereby entrusted with plenary powers upon all matters connected with labor, subject to the approval of the commanding officer of the district.[57]

In response to the War Department's regulations concerning schools, on March 22, 1864, General Banks provided for a board of education in his command to establish "common schools" in districts defined by provost-marshals; acquire school sites to be transferred eventually to state authority; erect school houses; employ teachers; provide books and supplies, and libraries; regulate courses of study, discipline, hours (for children on weekdays and adults on Sundays), and records; exercise authority that school trustees in Northern states exercise, including levying school taxes that provost-marshals would collect. Freedmen who criticized Banks's labor policy as semi-slavery, approved his education program.[58]

Problems in dealing with freedmen in the Mississippi Valley and conflicts over jurisdiction plagued the Lincoln Administration. Treasury officials took charge of the abandoned plantations and, complained General Lorenzo Thomas, instead of improving on what the military had done, introduced a new and impractical system. In consequence many who had leased plantations became dissatisfied and left the country, returning the freedmen "upon our hands for support." Treasury officials claimed that they were in charge of the blacks, but Thomas countered that the Negroes were under his control, and argued, "the military authorities must have command of the Negroes or there will be endless confusion."[59]

General E.R.S. Canby, Banks's successor, warned district commanders to be watchful lest planters operating under Treasury Department regulations attempt to take blacks into the interior with the intention of returning them to slavery. If any planters defrauded workers of wages or their share of the crop, their property was to be seized. In a general order of February 1, 1865, Canby required that the leased plantations be limited to the Mississippi and its tributaries and interior localities within military control. Freedmen were not to be placed in areas where they might be carried off and enslaved. Troops were to be stationed not on plantations but in strong positions for protection of whole districts. If troops had to be withdrawn for offensive operations, freedmen were to be brought to safe places. Owners or lessees of plantations were to build defenses against small raiding parties. Freedmen were not to be taken except by military authorities for enlistment or draft or special labor. Draft animals and provisions were not to be seized from the protected plantations except in cases of military necessity. Freedmen except those in the military or hired by the military were to be turned over to agents of the Treasury Department.[60]

General Sherman, who had been concerned about attacks on leased plantations along the Mississippi by guerrillas, asserted to General Lorenzo Thomas, April 12, 1864: "All the people of the South, old and young, rich and poor, educated and ignorant, unite in this, that they will kill as vipers the whites who attempt to free their slaves, and also the 'ungrateful slaves' who attempt to change their character from slave to free." Thus federals had to combat not only the Confederate forces but the "entire people of the South." Sherman would have preferred to colonize the blacks on land forfeited by rebels. He saw the alluvial land between Memphis and Vicksburg as the very country in which "we might collect the Negroes," where they would find good land that would enable them "at once to be useful." But if the government preferred the "lessee system," he would use a black brigade to protect the leased plantations. However, the first object, Sherman insisted, must be to whip Lee and Johnston.[61]

In their campaigns Union generals were fortunate to find in otherwise enemy country many black friends. Major-General O.M. Mitchel, writing from Huntsville, Alabama, to Secretary of War E.M. Stanton, May 4, 1862, stated that the blacks were "our only friends," that he owed his life to them, and that he hoped to have informers among them on every plantation bordering the Tennessee River in Northern Alabama.[62] Although this help was not the full-fledged help the Union would ask of the blacks later, Stanton replied that Mitchel was fully justified in employing the assistance of slaves and not to use it would be a failure to employ means to suppress the rebellion. Protection of those who furnished information or other assistance was a high duty. When pursuing General Jubal Early down the Shenandoah Valley in March, 1864, General P.H. Sheridan would have abandoned his mired wagons but for two thousand blacks who had attached themselves to his column and who literally lifted the wagons out of the mud.[63]

Sherman gathered valuable information about the enemy from blacks who streamed into his lines at Memphis. They kept him posted on Confederate troop disposition, strength, and movements; and on the state of Southern society, its economic condition and its morale.[64] The inland Navy, too, relied on the blacks for intelligence. David Porter, commanding the Union's Mississippi Squadron, got information, as in January, 1863, from blacks on river plantations where the Confederate

Blue Wing had gone.[65] Informants some-times paid dearly for helping the Union invaders. Colonel S.W. Ferguson, C.S.A., reported, April 8, 1863, that he hanged a slave who, mistaking two of his men for the "Abolitionists, hailed them across the creek, and volunteered to conduct them to the rebel camp, so as to surprise it; informed them of my strength and posi-tion, asked for a gun to kill his master, and said that he would knock down and rape any white woman."[66] After Union forces seized the Mississippi to the Gulf, Confed-erate General Kirby Smith tried to break up plantations within 10 miles of the west bank of the River, and carry off the slaves and remove or destroy the cotton. One rea-son for his action was to prevent Union forces from getting information about his movements.[67] As in other places the Union Army on the Elk River in Tennessee regu-larly got reports from a slave informer at Winchester, Tennessee.[68]

Confederates counted on slaves to erect fortifications and to provide other auxiliary military services as well as labor on the plantations and wherever needed to sustain the Confederacy. As the Union gained increasing support from Southern blacks the Confederacy was that much weakened. Early in the war the Confeder-acy was able to marshal much of its slave manpower. In Virginia, especially, Con-federates hired and impressed large num-bers of slaves, many of them highly skilled, to labor in transportation, mining, rail-roading, and manufacturing, in saw-milling, hauling, erecting fortifications, and in a thousand other ways to sustain combat troops. Virginia slaves largely con-structed entrenchments General B. McClellan faced before Richmond. To check the Union advance down the Mis-sissippi Valley in the fall and winter of 1861–1862, Confederate engineers assem-bled slaves to fortify Nashville, Forts Henry and Donelson, and other strategic places.[69] Governor John Shorter of Alabama collected 500 slaves and sent them north to General A.S. Johnston in Bowling Green, Kentucky, for work on the fortifications.[70]

In February, 1862, an anxious band of legislators in the Confederate Congress urged President Jefferson Davis to make haste to fortify the Mississippi River cities Memphis, Helena, Vicksburg, Natchez, Baton Rouge, and New Orleans with slave labor to be made available by a cutback in cotton production. According to their plans slaves freed from cotton culture could also be put to work manufacturing armaments for the projected fortifications. The legisla-tors believed that "our slaves, which our enemies consider an element of weakness, can be converted into a powerful and reli-able means of defense," but if the enemy were to "penetrate down the Mississippi he would encounter large numbers of slaves on extensive plantations, with very grave consequences." Davis responded that the executive needed more than their zeal to achieve such an object.[71]

Confederate field officers were autho-rized to call upon the people along the Mississippi to contribute slaves as needed by the military. Some 400 slaves were used to lay down obstructions on the Tombig-bee River in December, 1862. After failing to check General Grant upriver, Confed-erates ordered slaves to Vicksburg to strengthen fortifications there. Slaves also strengthened barriers, constructed a boom, and created other obstacles to Union gunboats on the Yazoo River approaches to Vicksburg. In March, 1863, General Dabney Maury ordered the cav-alry to ride out and bring in slaves with tools to throw up fortifications along Deer Creek to frustrate General Sherman's moves against Vicksburg.[72]

The invasion of the Union Army pro-vided such a stimulus for slaves to escape that the Confederacy established depots as holding places for recaptured slaves, and put them to military labor pending their return to their masters.[73] Planters feared that slaves impressed for Confederate military labor might escape or be ill-treated, and compensation for their slaves' labor would be inadequate or left unpaid. Governor John Pettus of Mississippi relayed such fears to General J.C. Pemberton, who had authorized the impressment of slaves for the fortification of Vicksburg.[74]

Slaves could be used to release support personnel in the Confederate Army for service on the battlefield. Thus General Kirby Smith, in July, 1862, urged planters in his Trans-Mississippi Department to hire some of their slaves to the military as teamsters to release soldiers detailed for that duty for battle. Smith warned the planters that if they did not voluntarily hire the requisite number of their slaves to his army, he would take all he needed by impressment. By September, 1862, he noted that planters were worried about the loyalty of their slaves, and they wanted the able-bodied males securely held in the service of the Confederate Army.[75]

Some of Smith's sub-commanders wanted up to three-fourths of the able-bodied male slaves, but Smith limited the toll to one-in-four. However, in December, 1863, General J.B. Magruder called for Texas planters to send all their able-bodied male slaves, except one for each plantation, to Brazoria, Houston, Gonzales, Austin, and San Antonio, to work on the fortifications. Smith reduced Magruder's demand to conform to orders from Richmond that not more than one-fifth of male slaves, aged 17–50, be taken by the army. But in January, 1864, Magruder ordered the impressment of all slave men, women, and children of working age of one county to build and repair roads. By the end of 1864, with defeat imminent, Magruder was unable to get any men and supplies whatsoever.[76]

As the situation became increasingly desperate, Confederate generals demanded more labor, increasing their competition with planters for the diminishing supply of slave labor. T.H. Watts, governor of Alabama, April 9, 1864, felt obliged to ask General Leonidas Polk to spare as many slaves as possible for spring planting, especially where husbands and sons were away fighting. Slaveholders of Taladega County complained to the governor that they had been excessively burdened by the impressment of so many of their slaves.[77] On May 6, 1864, petitioners of Randolph County, also in Alabama, complained to Jefferson Davis that a higher proportion of their slaves were being impressed than in neighboring counties, causing distress to many women and children, and in turn leading some of the women to seize government wheat and corn to feed their starving families. Moreover, the petitioners argued, to take slaves from fields when crops needed cultivation would reduce necessary food production.[78] Faced with this shortage of labor the chief engineer at Mobile, searching for 3000 slaves to build fortifications, offered $360 a year for the lease of a slave and asked the Confederate Government to send him blacks captured from the Union Army. Others competed with him for captured blacks for work on the railroads.[79] General Joseph Johnston employed impressed slaves in his resourceful resistance to General Sherman's advance on Atlanta in 1864.[80] It was, of course, necessary to use military force both to impress slaves and keep them under guard, but in the last stages of the war the Confederacy had become too weak either to impress or to guard them.[81]

As the Union Army pushed down the Mississippi, planters vainly struggled to hold on to their slaves and keep them under discipline. In the spring of 1862 Governor John Pettus of Mississippi got the support of General P.G.T. Beauregard to form mounted companies to keep down disorders among slaves along the Mississippi and other rivers of the state open to Union gunboats.[82] But Union forces soon seized control of the land bordering the rivers and set the freedmen to cultivating plantations in the area. Confederate forces which not long before had defended the area and kept slaves in subjection now attacked Union controlled plantations cultivated by freedmen and made off with the former slaves.[83]

Slaveholders often took servants with them to the Confederate military to look after their personal needs and serve the army in various capacities. Slaves would serve their masters and perhaps a small group of men by cooking, washing, tending horses, and, rarely, by shouldering a rifle and joining in battle. William Byrd went to war with his master and remained with him until sent home after Lee's surrender. Sam Brooks marched off to the Confederate Army with his young master, as his older brother Jack had gone with "old master three years earlier, and as a heap of young slaves" did. Ike Pringle served his master through the Perryville, Chattanooga, and Atlanta campaigns. He "walked, walked, walked," and participated in campfires with thousands of men when it seemed that the "whole world was lighted up." When Ike heard of the surrender he "scattered" for home. Himself wounded while serving by his master's side, Henry Warfield was horrified by the carnage of war. Simon Durr accompanied his master until the war's end, and like other soldiers, was often footsore and hungry. With his master during the Siege of Vicksburg, Isaac Stier sought to allay his hunger with meat of cats and dogs and soup of sweat-soaked saddle blankets.[84]

Eloda Bradford cooked for his master and nine other soldiers until his master was taken prisoner at Atlanta; then he and other servants walked for weeks to their homes at Port Gibson, Mississippi. Peter Blewit served his master and also cared for horses during the Siege of Vicksburg. When his master was killed he returned to "Old Miss" in Newton County, Mississippi. As a wagoneer Dempsey Pitts hauled food for Confederate soldiers. Ransom Simmons was bodyguard to General Wade Hampton, for which service he later received a $25-a-year pension from South Carolina. Henry Turner served with General Patrick Cleburne during campaigns at Shiloh, Murfreesboro, Ringgold Gap, and Atlanta, and, like Cleburne, was killed at Franklin.[85]

Richard Mack served his master and, in battle, was stretcher bearer for the dead and wounded; Sam Kilgore built breastworks, hedges, and other Confederate military works in Alabama, Tennessee, and Kentucky; Nick Carter dug trenches for Southern soldiers. Tom Bones fished for shad in the James River with about 50 other slaves, and seined in the Chickahominy, to feed Confederate soldiers, and served the Confederacy through the Siege of Vicksburg. Fannie Mintner nursed Confederate soldiers for the duration of the war. Holt Collier was not a servant but a soldier, he said, with his master Colonel Howell Hinds.[86]

Some black soldiers served with both armies. George Rogers stayed with his master in the Confederate Army until his master died, then he went over to the Union Army. Jake Goodridge was captured with his master, who was imprisoned. Then Jake was made a "waitin' boy" by Union soldiers, who "cussed all the time." On the way to the Battle of Mansfield Katie Darling's father ran away and, complained his disappointed master, "jines up with them damn Yankees." Frank Childress was servant and dispatch carrier in the Confederare Army until captured at Helena, Arkansas, then soldiered for the next two and a half years with the Union Army.

William H. Harrison also began his military career as a servant, was captured, and transformed into a Union soldier. When mustered out at Chattanooga he had been given all the schooling he ever received by Yankee teachers in the Army. Cella Perkins's father went to war with his master, was captured, became a Union soldier, and never came home. Captured as a servant of a Confederate soldier at Vicksburg, Isaac Stier was held prisoner until, he said, he was willing to join the Union Army; in 1866 he was discharged.[87]

When it was clear that the war could have no quick end but would be decided by a desperate struggle of endurance, both sides became acutely aware of the critical importance of the slaves in determining the outcome. The North increased its efforts to magnify its strength with black fighters and workers and to weaken the South by encouraging massive black defection from the plantation economy. Steadily losing control of its slave labor, the South at last made a bid for the voluntary support of its blacks by offering them freedom if they would fight for Southern independence. By then the region's blacks had chosen the Union as guarantor of their freedom, and were contributing mightily to its imminent victory.

In the struggle over black manpower, Confederate raiding parties, such as one, May 2, 1863, near Ashton, Louisiana, seized and carried away 15 to 20 blacks who had gone over to the enemy.[88] Continued deterioration of Confederate strength in the area led General Kirby Smith to warn his subordinates Sterling Price and Richard Taylor, September 4, 1863, that the Northern government was pushing its policy of organizing black regiments and turning plantations into recruiting stations. Unless checked, a powerful force would be formed, expanded, and strengthened as Union armies advanced. When Confederate forces fell back, Smith recommended that able-bodied male Negroes be removed to safe localities, for "every sound male black left for the enemy becomes a soldier, whom we have afterward to fight."[89] After the loss of Vicksburg other Confederates, seeing the heightened danger of defeat, urged their government to employ slaves in a military capacity as wagoneers, pioneers, sappers and miners, in hospitals, and on railroads, to release whites to shore up depleted combat units.[90]

On January 2, 1864, General Patrick R. Cleburne, of the Army of Tennessee, supported by various brigade and regimental commanders, judged the war lost without large numbers of recruits and therefore recommended to his commanding general, Joseph Johnston, that the Confederacy enlist able-bodied male slaves and reward them with freedom. The army, Cleburne stated, weakened by long lists of dead and wounded, was hard pressed by superior forces on every front, and the soldiers were weary of costly effort that promised no beneficial results.

The North was winning because of superior numbers and material, and because slavery, from being a source of strength at the beginning of the war, "has now become, in a military point of view, one of our chief sources of weakness." The North was steadily increasing its preponderance by enlisting blacks. Every raid it made and every bit of territory it took added to the 100,000-man force of blacks already under arms. Moreover, antagonism to slavery encouraged European powers to oppose the Confederacy, even to permitting many of their citizens to join the Union Army. Also, at the approach of federal forces slaves became restless and the planters could "no longer with safety to their property openly sympathize with our cause. The fear of their slaves is continually haunting them;" many soon wished the "war stopped on any terms." The North could concentrate its forces but the South had to scatter its men, for it was vulnerable at every point there was a slave to be set free. All along the lines slavery made "an omnipresent spy system, pointing out our valuable men to the enemy, revealing our positions, purposes, and resources, and yet acting so safely and secretly that there is no means to guard against it."

What to do? President Davis wanted absent soldiers to return to duty, hiring of substitutes ended, exemption tightened, men serving in support services replaced by blacks and sent into combat. But these actions were not enough. Cleburne recommended "that we immediately commence training a large reserve of the most courageous of our slaves, and further, that we guarantee freedom within a reasonable time to every slave in the South who shall remain true to the Confederacy in this war. As between the loss of independence and the loss of slavery, we assume that every patriot will freely give up the latter." Cleburne thought that enlisting and freeing the slaves would also bring support from England and France and other countries that held back because of their opposition to slavery. The Northern people's crusade against slavery would be ended, leaving them only a war for ambition and power. Emancipation and enrollment of Negroes would, on the other hand, greatly strengthen the Southern Army and "instantly remove all the vulnerability, embarrassment, and inherent weakness which result from slavery. The approach of the enemy would no longer find every household surrounded by spies"; fear and avarice would no longer motivate masters. "There would be no recruits awaiting the enemy with open arms, no complete history of every neighborhood with ready guides, no fear of insurrection in the rear, or anxieties for the fate of loved ones when our armies move forward. The chronic irritation of hope deferred would be joy-

fully ended with the negro, and the sympathies of his whole race would be due to his native South." It would remove "all selfish taint from our cause and place independence above every question of property." This great sacrifice would "fill our hearts with a pride and singleness of purpose which would clothe us with a new strength in battle."... "The Negro has been dreaming of freedom."... "To attain it he will tempt dangers and difficulties not exceeded by the bravest soldier in the field." Cleburne advocated emancipating at once the hoped–for black soldiers and their families. He urged that slave marriages and parental rights be made sacred in the eyes of the law and that the slave trade be prohibited. He recommended "emancipating the whole race upon reasonable terms, and within such reasonable time as will prepare both races for the change."

The blacks would fight bravely, Cleburne reiterated, as they did in Santo Domingo and Jamaica, and as they were fighting, though half-trained, for the Yankees. After the war they would work hard, stimulated by wise legislation, in freedom. Prompt emancipation could give the South independence, but, Cleburne warned, "this concession to common sense may come too late." Cleburne's proposal, read in the presence of General Johnston and most of his corps commanders, received Johnston's tacit approval.[91]

As Cleburne feared, opposition within the Confederate Army and government delayed action. Major-General W.H.T. Walker wrote Jefferson Davis, January 2, 1864, that further agitation of Cleburne's proposal would "involve our cause in ruin and disgrace." Davis replied, January 13, 1864, that he had asked General Johnston that discussion of enlistment of blacks and emancipation be kept private.[92] Some months later, September 26, 1864, with the collapse of the Confederacy accelerating,

Henry W. Allen, Governor of Louisiana, wrote Secretary of War James W. Seddon that every able-bodied black man ought to be freed and put into the Confederate Army to fill its depleted ranks. "He caused the fight," Allen declared, "and he will have his portion of the burden to bear. We have learned from dear-bought experience that negroes can be taught to fight."[93] Union General E.R.S. Canby countered Allen by publicly proclaiming, October 11, 1864, that all slaves coming into his lines would be freed, that able-bodied males would be accepted as volunteers in his army or offered employment, and families would be provided for. Corporal James Henry Gooding of the 54th Massachusetts hoped the Confederacy would enlist black troops, for he was confident they would come over to the Union side at the first opportunity, trained and equipped at cost to the Confederacy. Lincoln did not believe slaves would fight for the Confederacy, but he was glad to hear of the project because it meant Confederates had reached the bottom of their resources.[94]

On January 11, 1865, General Robert E. Lee added his great influence to the movement to enlist blacks, urging that it be done without delay. On March 13, 1865, Jefferson Davis signed legislation authorizing enlistment of blacks, but with the restriction that they could be emancipated only with the consent of their masters and their states. When Confederate authorities finally decided to enlist blacks it was beyond their capacity to do so. Only days before surrender General Richard Taylor announced his readiness to enlist blacks as soldiers, in accordance with recent legislation of the Confederate Congress, if he could get the requisite arms.[95]

8

Black Fighting Men

Besides raising troops to win in battle, Union recruiters had other aims. General John Palmer wanted to continue recruiting blacks in Kentucky as "an argument forcible" to pressure the state legislature to pass the Thirteenth Amendment to end slavery in the state and in the nation.[1] R.D. Mussey, of the 100th U.S. Colored Infantry, looked on military service as citizenship training. He regarded the organization of black troops as an important social and humanitarian as well as military measure, and "as a providential means of fitting the race freed by the war for their liberty." Mussey endeavored to impress this view on his troops, that their recognition as men would follow their service as soldiers. After a year's experience with black troops he had "more hope and more faith than ever in the capability of the negro to make a good soldier and a good citizen."[2]

General Sherman conceded that in the Union slave states of Kentucky, Maryland, and Missouri military service for slaves might be "wisely used to secure their freedom with the consent of owners," and was worthy of a fair but not hurried trial in the rest of the South, but he was above all determined to protect his labor supply from being raided for soldiers. He believed that Southern blacks better served the army as teamsters and pioneers than as soldiers and preferred "300 negroes armed with spades and axes than 1,000 as soldiers." He employed large numbers of black workers along the Mississippi, on railroads, and as pioneer companies attached to his divisions. He thought that the first step in the liberation of blacks was to get them in a place of safety and provide them with the means to support their families, then to gradually increase their numbers as soldiers and sailors. In the meantime he threatened to arrest any officer who interferred with his "necessary gangs of hired negroes," by seeking to enlist them as soldiers.[3]

During the Vicksburg campaign General P.J. Osterhaus, like Sherman wanting laborers more than soldiers, requested that black men being organized in regiments be temporarily detached to help his working parties.[4] One way around assigning black combat troops to an inordinate amount of work duty was to organize two regiments of troops of "African descent," as General George Thomas did at Chattanooga, in March, 1864, one to consist of men who could pass the regular military exam, the other to be made up of all black men able to perform military fatigue duty.[5] Colonel John Eaton organized a special force in the Helena, Arkansas, area of troops who were,

These soldiers at Fort Lincoln in 1862 came from black communities in the Free States. Miller, ed., *Photographic History of the Civil War*, Vol IX, 177.

according to General N.B. Buford, good for nothing, "old, diseased, unfit for soldiers, and indifferently officered."[6]

When the federal government began to recruit freedmen to fight against their former masters it encountered opposition in the military as well as in civil society. When in March, 1863, General Halleck urged Grant to persuade his officers to accept freedmen as fellow soldiers, Grant replied that his corps commanders would carry out the government's policy even though they would not have initiated such a policy and that he himself would execute any policy ordered by proper authority. Charles A. Dana, visiting Grant's Army for the Administration, reported that by mid–April, 1863, officers who had earlier declared that they would never serve with black troops had come to accept them.[7]

Dana also reported in April, 1863, that General Hurlbut proposed to settle the "Negro question" in Memphis by enrolling as pioneers, teamsters, and general military workers all who were fit for service. Hurlbut also proposed to enlist a regiment of artillerymen out of this group to garrison Fort Pickering at Memphis. He expected to find excellent material and believed that the men would not be troubled by white soldiers.[8]

After Vicksburg fell, July 4, 1863, Lincoln asked Grant to support General Lorenzo Thomas's efforts to raise still more black troops in the Mississippi Valley, "a resource which, if vigorously applied now, will soon close this contest. It works doubly-weakening the enemy and strengthening us. We were not fully ripe for it, until the river was opened. Now I think at least

100,000 can and ought to be organized along its shores." Lincoln was glad that the Emancipation Proclamation had helped Grant's military operations.[9]

More black troops would have been put into the Army but for pressing demands for laborers by field commanders. The forts on the Mississippi River were mainly built by freedmen. When white and black troops were in the same command, blacks had to do more than their share of the work, because of the prejudice against them as fighting men. However, prejudice declined and things changed as black soldiers demonstrated their courage and fighting qualities, and as the lists of killed and wounded lengthened and made Northern whites ready to fill the depleted ranks with blacks.[10]

Recruiting of black troops in the Border states may be represented by events in Kentucky, which, along with Tennessee, Mississippi, and Louisiana raised the largest number of black troops. At first there was considerable opposition to enlisting blacks in the state. Provost-marshals were needed to quell dissent.[11] But when the loyal white people at last realized that blacks would be enrolled, peaceably or forcibly, and that black troops would reduce the demand for white troops, citizens of the state gave up much of their earlier resistance.[12] Lincoln himself required that blacks be enrolled properly in Kentucky. He wrote General Lorenzo Thomas, then in Louisville, June 13, 1864, that complaints were made to him that blacks were being forced into the military arbitrarily and violently. He ordered Thomas to see that making soldiers of Negroes be done according to the rules so that unnecessary provocation and irritation be avoided.[13]

In consequence on June 13, 1864, General Thomas issued General Orders, No. 20, providing that officers be placed in each county in Kentucky to receive able bodied blacks who presented themselves

or who were delivered by their owners. "The unconditional Union men will," Thomas believed, "cheerfully bring forward their slaves to assist in crushing the rebellion; and if others do not, it makes no difference, as all who present themselves for enlistment will be received and enlisted into the service of the United States." Camps were to be organized in each Congressional district where the blacks would be received, organized into companies and regiments, armed, equipped, and trained.[14] Thomas further ordered that black recruits were to be speedily trained, hence they were to perform only their fair share of fatigue duty with white troops, whereas they had been required by local commanders to perform most of the labor on fortifications and in camps.[15]

General Sherman thought that such dissidents as pestered Thomas ought to be dealt with severely. On June 21, 1864, from near Big Shanty, Georgia, he wrote Secretary of War Stanton that malcontents ought to be deported to Central America, the Caribbean, Lower California, Madagascar, or some such place. "One thing is certain," he stated, "there is a class of people men, women, and children, who must be killed or banished before you can hope for peace and order, even as far south as Tennessee."[16]

Such opposition as there was did not deter General Thomas from hurriedly organizing 3000 blacks in Lexington, Kentucky, and assembling white officers for them, since General J.M. Schofield had ordered several regiments of white troops from Kentucky to the front. The employment of black troops in Kentucky, Thomas wrote, "will thus become a necessity." He believed the loyal people realized that slavery had almost ceased to exist and that black men should be enlisted, while Southern sympathizers saw the same fact, and knowing they could not prevent enlistment of blacks, kept quiet. Thomas required the women and children to remain on the plantations, where they would be useful in securing the crops. In areas exempted by the Emancipation Proclamation, as in Kentucky, certificates of enlistment were furnished loyal owners of slaves who enlisted, in connection with claims by these owners.[17]

Thomas did have some trouble with slaves in Kentucky who left their owners without entering military service, and gathered in towns or roamed the countryside. He ordered these men forced into the ranks when their owners signified such a desire to the provost-marshals. By the end of 1864, with the end of the war in sight, enlistment of black troops was all but suspended in Kentucky as elsewhere. On December 27, 1864, black troops organized in and on duty in Kentucky included 9623 enlisted men stationed at Lexington, Columbus, Paducah, Munfordville, Smithland, Louisa, Covington, Henderson, Maysville, and Louisville.[18]

Agents for substitute brokers in Northern states enticed black men from Union-controlled areas in the South to take the places of draftees in their states. They offered bounties to blacks brought in by raiding troops intended for their own units, causing dissatisfaction among those already enlisted without benefit of bounties. Some agents encouraged black soldiers to desert their posts for promised bounties from Northern states. Other agents from bordering free states persuaded some Kentucky slaves to run away and enlist in their states for a small bounty, thus helping these states to fill their troop quotas.[19]

The Union Army conducted raids not only to disrupt the plantation economy but also to recruit laborers and soldiers. In July, 1862, before inaugurating its policy of enlisting slaves as soldiers, the Union Army was sweeping clean of blacks vicinities such as Oxford, Mississippi, and Helena, Arkansas. A year later a Union raiding party of black and white soldiers, with the black soldiers "fighting with hearty good will," defeated a Confederate force and secured, besides horses, mules, and food-stuff, 125 recruits from plantations bordering the Mississippi near Napoleon, Arkansas, for the Second Regiment Arkansas Volunteers, of African descent. The black population, here as elsewhere, hailed with joy the appearance of soldiers of their race.[20] In September, 1862, Governor John Gill Shorter of Alabama reported that Union raiding parties broke up coastal salt works and made off with the slave workers. A month later the governor wrote Jefferson Davis that if Union forces were to capture Mobile the 230,000 slaves in the river counties of the Alabama and the Tombigbee would be open to subversion; in consequence any amount of slave labor to strengthen Mobile could be had by the Confederacy. In June 1863, whites on the Combahee River fled in all directions from black raiders of the 54th Massachusetts while slaves ran to the boats of their liberators; over 400 of the 840 brought back to Beaufort enlisted in the 3rd South Carolina regiment. Physicians examining recruits secured in the raids were appalled by the scarred backs and cropped ears.[21] Union raiders in the Red River country of Louisiana led away innumerable black recruits, and raids by Union river boats on the Mississippi and tributaries became so effective that Confederates cast about for any means to check them, even entertaining a suggestion to organize draft-dodgers lurking in the swamps to prey on Federals along the rivers. Many citizens in the region carried on a cotton trade with the Federals. The side that controlled the rivers secured the trade along their banks, and, noted Captain John C. Kay of the Confederate River Rangers, nothing could be done to change the order of things but to "whip the

Federals away or whip the natives out of these counties."[22]

By mid-1863 vulnerable areas of the South were in great distress. Alabamian Thomas J. Foster reported to the Confederate Secretary of War that the area around Courtland was reduced to misery; slaves and stock abducted; factories burned; supplies destroyed. If a home guard were given weapons and ammunition by the War Department it could, he hoped, protect what was left. Local citizens had given their arms to volunteers at the beginning of the war, then "destroying angels" and "prowling brigades," as their federal officers designated them, had conducted wanton raids, forced women and children from their homes, which were often torched, destroyed provisions, and left the people homeless and destitute, reported Foster.[23] Jefferson Davis asked citizens of Mississippi during the Vicksburg Campaign, when their state was under siege, to organize in home guards those who could not take the field with regular military units but who could go out for hours or days in an emergency to repel plundering and devastating raiders in their localities.[24]

The Union Navy enlisted blacks as acclimated laborers, ranked as "boys" at $8, $9, or $10 per month with one ration, for service in boat crews on the Southern coast. Off Vicksburg in July, 1862, black "boys," escapees from Fort Pillow, where they had been used on Confederate fortifications, were employed as stokers at $10 a month on the gunboat Cincinnati, and six black firemen, captured from Confederate ships, served on the Mound City. The secretary of Navy permitted C.H. Davis, September 15, 1862, to employ "contrabands" as coal heavers, but not to allow them pay at that grade. Davis in turn informed his officers from his flagship Eastport, at Helena, Arkansas, September 23, 1862, that contrabands would in no case, whatever their employment, receive

a higher rating and pay than that of first-class boys.[25] General T. Williams employed contrabands on the canal cut-off in the Vicksburg Campaign, and when he abandoned that project he also abandoned workers on the Louisiana bank of the Mississippi. These men sought protection from Alfred Ellet, commanding U.S. Ram Switzerland, who employed many of them because of sickness in his crew.[26]

Admiral David Porter reduced expenses by substituting contrabands collected along the Mississippi in the fall of 1862 for firemen and coal heavers, and ordered all his commanders to use them in place of whites. He also employed contrabands in storing the Navy's coal at Memphis and Helena. Porter found, however, that with the men came their families. General Sherman, who had housed all the blacks, with their families, that he had employed, was reluctant to break up the families, but he would supply Porter's needs if necessary. He suggested Porter require that the workers' wages go to the maintenance of their families. Porter replied that, as his forces were liable to move anytime, he wanted single men, not families and requested that his own officers send single men to him at Cairo, Illinois.[27]

On November 27, 1862, Lieutenant James W. Shirk, U.S.S. Lexington, off Helena, informed Admiral Porter that slaves had heard of Lincoln's Preliminary Proclamation and had rushed to get to the river. He was surprised at the amount of information they possessed: "All of those who came on board the Lexington tell me that they are to be free on the 1st of January, but that their owners are getting ready to move them back from the river as soon as possible."[28] This flood of refugees provided a ready source of laborers and recruits for the Navy as well as the Army.

In December, 1862, Secretary of Navy Gideon Welles ordered that blacks not be enlisted with a higher rating than landsman. They could be advanced by the commanders of the ship in which they served to the rating of seaman, ordinary seaman, fireman, or coal heaver, but they could not be transferred from one vessel to another with a higher rating than landsman, though they could be discharged with the higher rating.[29] Like the generals he was unready for equality of opportunity in the armed forces.

Admiral Porter got plenty of help from blacks. He wrote from Yazoo City, Mississippi, to the chief of Equipment and Recruiting, Washington, D.C., January 3, 1863, "Don't be astonished at the lists of niggers I send you. I could get no men, so I work in the darkies. They do first-rate work and are far better behaved than their masters." To get the men, Porter now had to protect the women also. He reported, January 16, 1863, that contrabands were claiming his protection continually, among them many women. "I can not reject them under the law. They belong to persons in arms against the United States."[30]

The Navy, like the Army, liberated slaves in raids. The *Forrest Rose*, February 18, 1863, fired at from the Arkansas bank, near Buck Island, landed a party, destroyed a dwelling, storehouses, and "negro houses" nearby, and took away 21 blacks and carried them to Memphis. On February 1, 1863, the Gunboat *Juliet* left the mouth of the Yazoo for Cairo, with 211 contrabands. Sometimes Confederate military parties recaptured the runaways just before they got under cover of the Union guns. On other occasions Union naval forces liberated slaves being driven by Confederates across the Mississippi, as did the *U.S.S. General Sterling Price*, Selim E. Woodworth, commander, below Vicksburg, June 18, 1863. The *Sterling Price* brought to Grand Gulf 120 men, women, and children. There Lieutenant Commander E.K. Owen gave them small boats to

forage for themselves, to conserve his ship's supplies. Owen reported that blacks were coming in to Grand Gulf at the rate of about 500 per day. Up river, near Helena, Union forces broke up an attempt by two women to cross 200 of their slaves over the Mississippi to secure Confederate Territory in Arkansas.[31]

Influenced by prejudice of the day, yet expressing some appreciation of the military value of blacks, Lieutenant-Commander R.B. Lowry, *U.S. Supply Steamer Union*, wrote Secretary of the Navy Gideon Welles, May 19, 1863, that ex-slaves were fearful as infantrymen but were cool, quick, and apt in handling rammers, sponges, powder, shot, and shell of the great guns. "The sense of security behind the bulwarks of ships or the walls and casements of forts keeps them free from the apprehension of danger, either from shot or the wrath and vengeance of their former white owners. Their exhausting labor of loading and running in and out heavy guns, while their docility and aptness for military subordination would make them excellent garrison soldiers."[32]

By the summer of 1863 Admiral David Porter was using increasing numbers of "contrabands" because, he thought, the Southern climate made his white sailors sick; except when performing ordinary duty on their ships. Thus blacks were used as boat crews and for duty in the sun. They were to help defend the vessels where crews were unfilled, for in emergencies "blacks will make efficient men." Porter wanted to recruit none but the best of black men and then to open promotions of them to "second-class firemen, coal heavers, landsmen, ordinary seamen, but not to petty officers." They would be "kept distinct from the rest of the crew," be "stationed at guns when vacancies exist, to pass shot and powder, handle handspikes, at train-tackles and side-tackles, pumps, and fire buckets; and can be exercised

A great force of blacks who fled to the Union Army built and repaired railroads for offensive operations of generals U.S. Grant and W.T. Sherman. Miller, ed., *Photographic History of the Civil War*,
Vol II, 175.

separately at great guns and small arms."
Porter thought blacks were not naturally
clean, so special attention would, he supposed, have to be paid to their hygiene.[33]

Black construction units, enlisted and
hired, worked to repair and extend railroads used in great campaigns, such as the
Chattanooga and Atlanta Campaigns. Railroads were built and repaired as Sherman
advanced to Atlanta, and branch lines constructed or put in good condition.
Destroyed bridges were rebuilt; one over
the Chattahoochee was 780 feet long and
90 feet high. The roads were graded and
track laid and railroad yards built. White

and black construction units did the work,
including the Twelfth and Thirteenth Regiments United States Colored Infantry.
Much work was done on the roads, also in
machine shops, rolling mills for making
railroad iron, saw mills, and blacksmith
shops during the Nashville Campaign. In
some cases men carried cross-ties 300 to
400 yards for repairs and construction,
while waiting for work-oxen from the
Commissary Department. Construction
corps laid 170 miles of track on the Chattanooga and Knoxville Railroad, Chattanooga and Atlanta Railroad, Cleve-
land and Dalton Railroad, Nashville and

Northwestern Railroad, Nashville and Clarkville Railroad, and the Chattanooga Yard. The workers cut 500,000 cross-ties, 4 million board-feet of bridge timber, and about 2 million board-feet of other timber on the Chattanooga and Atlanta Railroad.[34]

In addition to performing much fatigue duty black troops were more likely to be assigned to dull garrison duty than white troops. As an example, when General S.G. Burbridge, commander of the District of Kentucky, wanted to use black troops as garrison troops, and white troops for more active duties, the great recruiter of black troops General Lorenzo Thomas objected; the Secretary of War sustained Burbridge, "on account of the peculiar condition of things in Kentucky."[35] After the Union seized the Mississippi in 1863, the main battles shifted eastward. Then recently enlisted black troops garrisoned the Mississippi from Columbus, Kentucky, to Forts Jackson and St. Philip below New Orleans, releasing veteran white troops for service farther east.[36]

By midsummer, 1864, six regiments of colored troops had been raised in Missouri and distributed down river, one at Memphis, two at Helena, two at Port Hudson, and one at Baton Rouge. In Middle and East Tennessee there were three regiments, one of which was made up of Kentucky recruits, and several companies, together with an artillery battery. On the line of the Nashville and Northwestern Railroad were the Twelfth and Thirteenth Regiments, doing guard duty. Three regiments and a part of another were on guard duty on the Nashville to Decatur line. At Chattanooga there were seven or eight companies, several of them labor companies, and two regiments on the fortifications. At Knoxville was the First Regiment of United States Colored Artillery.[37] Other forts and camps in Florida and South Carolina and other Southern states were held by black troops.

On an inspection trip down the Mississippi in September, 1864, General Lorenzo Thomas found the black troops garrisoning Forts Jackson and St. Philip in excellent condition, as were those at Morganza, Louisiana. More recruits were expected to come into Union lines then established on the Gulf Coast of Alabama, while expeditions into the interior would fill the regiments along the Mississippi. Eight companies were guarding a settlement of blacks cultivating on their own account a large "home farm" and doing well, at Vicksburg. Up the river at Goodrich's Island and Milliken's Bend there were several regiments of black troops. Two regiments of black infantry and a battery of black artillery were stationed at Helena. Expeditions into the interior kept these units at full strength. A colony of self-supporting blacks on Island No. 63, below Helena, was protected by black troops. At Memphis there was a "fine regiment" of artillery garrisoning Fort Pickering. Other black units were further up the Mississippi at Columbus, Kentucky, and Cairo, Illinois.[38]

On November 7, 1864, General Lorenzo Thomas reported black troops in: Iowa, near the Missouri line, one regiment of infantry; Arkansas, six regiments of infantry; Tennessee, two regiments of heavy artillery, one company of light artillery, and two regiments of infantry; Mississippi, one regiment of cavalry, two regiments of heavy artillery, and five regiments of infantry; Louisiana, one regiment of cavalry, three companies of light artillery, and six regiments of infantry; Alabama, three regiments of infantry; Florida, one regiment of infantry; Kentucky, two regiments of cavalry, two regiments of heavy artillery, and 11 regiments of infantry.

In all there were 4800 in four regiments of cavalry; 10,800 in six regiments of heavy artillery; 720 in four companies of light artillery; and 40,000 in four regiments of infantry. There were additional black troops in Tennessee and Louisiana. In January, 1865, General Thomas reported that there were 12 regiments of black troops in East and Middle Tennessee at Knoxville, Chattanooga, and other places.

Almost all the officers were white. There were a few black officers in New England units and in Louisiana's *Corps d'Afrique*, and some black physicians and chaplains. Lincoln conceded that officers should be white to reduce opposition in the military and society to enlisting blacks. Many of the non-commissioned officers were white, though an increasing proportion were black. Difficulty in getting medical officers was overcome by sending a medical officer through New England to recruit physicians for appointments in the black forces.[39]

Chaplains in the Union Army advocated education of ex-slaves among the soldiers to equip them for their new freedom; some organized their own programs of education. William K. Talbot, a hospital chaplain at Beaufort, South Carolina, taught convalescing black soldiers the elements of reading, writing, and figuring. He was heartened by the soldiers' eagerness to learn. Chaplain William Eaton organized regular instruction for the men of the 12th United States Colored Troops. Black chaplain Henry M. Turner energetically conducted his school for black soldiers. Others set up instructional programs for both black soldiers and refugees.[40]

Chaplain John Eaton of the 27th Ohio Infantry, in charge of refugees who fled to Union lines as Grant advanced to Vicksburg, organized a comprehensive program, including education, to aid the freedmen. Eaton believed that, although immediate attention to the refugees' necessities was important, their educational advancement should be the principal goal. Eaton solicited the aid of chaplains and other benevolent persons, and also the support of the American Missionary Association, the Western Freedmen's Aid Commission, and the Society of Friends for volunteer instructors and educational materials. General Grant supplied transportation, housing, rations, and

Black troops exhibit smartness and polish at Vicksburg in 1864. Miller, ed., *Photographic History of the Civil War*, Vol. IX, 173.

classrooms. In September, 1863, Secretary of War Stanton formally authorized such aid as Grant had been giving. At the same time Eaton, as Grant's Superintendent of Freedmen, coordinated from Memphis educational efforts in the Department of the Tennessee, which included Mississippi, Arkansas, Kentucky, Tennessee, and parts of Louisiana.[41]

Although the War Department supported education of black soldiers, for illiterate soldiers could not be the best soldiers, it did not develop a comprehensive policy. Education was pretty much left to the chaplains and field commanders. Some commanders took their responsibility seriously. General Godfrey Weitzel, commander of the black 25th Army Corps, required his officers to provide schools for their men. At the end of the war most black privates could not sign their names, but one-fourth of the men in Northern free black regiments could sign their names. Noncommissioned officers were mostly literate. The 62nd U.S. Colored Infantry boasted that of 431 men, 99 had learned to read and write by 1866, while others were at various stages on the road to that goal. About 250 men of the 59th U.S. Colored Infantry learned to read and write in a school in Memphis conducted by a chaplain and his wife. The Union Army was utilized to a degree as a training school for black soldiers and civilians.[42]

When a Union army marched through an area during the latter part of the war, the sight of black soldiers lifted the hearts of women, children, and old men being liberated with the help of their own fighting men.[43] It was no wonder that the advent of Yankee soldiers, black or white, in their blue jackets with buttons that looked like gold, so rich and grand on their beautiful horses, made young blacks want to join them, noted Mark Oliver. Such a band lured young Mose Rogers away with a promise of a "spotted horse and a pair of red boots," but Mose's mother followed the recruiters day and night until she got her son back.[44]

Doubtless most black men who ran away to join the Union Army were motivated, most of all, by desire to win freedom for themselves and their people. For this reason Southern black soldiers endured discrimination in pay and in other ways with less complaint than Northern free black soldiers. When the Union Army approached Baton Rouge, Louisiana, and entered Pike County, Mississippi, many young male slaves went off to join up, as they did elsewhere when news spread that the Yankees were fighting to free the slaves. Robert Wilson fought, he said, "to make things better." Similarly, John Ogee fled to Sherman's Army and served, probably as a laborer, at Vicksburg and on through Georgia and South Carolina. Mack Henderson served as a bugler. Alex Huggins became a cabin boy on the convoy ship *Nereus*. Vergil Jones's father fought in the field and, at war's end, brought home his musket as a trophy. George Washington Albright's father was killed in action at Vicksburg. Rose Russell served the Union medical corps in the Vicksburg Campaign as a volunteer nurse. A grazing bullet left a scar on her throat.[45]

Many blacks were drafted. Yankees took Landy Rucker's two brothers, saying they were "fightin' to free the niggers," and Lemuel Fox, whose sister Phyllis never saw him again. Though forced into the artillery, Tom Windham was treated so well that he was sorry when the war "broke up." Edmond Bradley, drafted into the 96th Louisiana Colored Regiment, became frightened and would have run from battle, he said, but for the knowledge that he would have been shot. Solomon Lambert believed that he and other black men were forced into the Union Army when the ranks became thin, and made to fight in a "white man's war."[46]

Union officers sometimes punished delinquents with time "Riding the Sawbuck." Miller, ed., *Photographic History of the Civil War*, Vol. VII, 191.

Black troops fought in about 450 engagements, some of them major engagements, from 1862 until the end of the war in 1865. Often employed as military laborers and garrison troops, they proved their mettle in combat on many occasions. Their courage and skill under fire earned them commendation, even from surprised commanders who held the notion that including blacks in the armed forces remained an experiment of uncertain outcome. Confounding sceptics, blacks fought hard in great campaigns of U.S. Grant and George Thomas, and gave a good account of themselves in many less famous military operations. Kansas, Louisiana, and

South Carolina regiments were the first to come under fire, in raids in 1862. The South Carolina Colored Volunteers, organized by General Rufus Saxton, raided rivers, bays, and islands along the coasts of South Carolina, Georgia, and Florida in late 1862 and early 1863 and gained recruits.[47]

In May 1863, blacks in Louisiana regiments joined in the assault on Port Hudson, Confederate stronghold on the Mississippi north of Baton Rouge. About a thousand black soldiers of the 1st and 3rd Louisiana Native Guards and a black engineer regiment, in cooperation with white units, bravely and repeatedly charged entrenched Confederates. Although the attacks were repulsed with heavy casualties, blacks won praise from fellow white soldiers and the commanding general N.P. Banks, and proved, as they would time and again, that the "experiment" of making soldiers of them was a decided success.[48]

At Milliken's Bend, Louisiana, June 7, 1863, during the Vicksburg Campaign, black troops joined white Union soldiers in repulsing a fierce Confederate attack. Because they were inexperienced, some of them having been drilled only a few days, and equipped with inferior guns, the attacking Confederates succeeded in breaking into their works before they could fire more than one or two volleys, according to General Elias S. Dennis. "Here ensued a most terrible hand-to-hand conflict of several minutes' duration, our men using the bayonet freely and clubbing their guns with fierce obstinacy, contesting every inch of ground, until the enemy succeeded in flanking them, and poured a murderous enfilading fire along our lines." Not until they were overpowered by superior numbers did they retreat behind the bank of the river, pouring volley after volley into the advancing Rebels. Gunboats got into position and fired a broadside into the Confederates who then retreated behind a levee, kept up their fire and tried to extend their lines. But they were held in check by two companies of the Eleventh Louisiana Infantry, of African descent, situated behind cotton bales and the old levee. The slugging fight continued until the worsted Confederates suddenly retreated. In his comments on Milliken's Bend Grant noted that, although most of the African troops had little experience with firearms, their conduct was reported to have been "most gallant, and I doubt not but with good officers they will make good troops."[49]

In July, 1863, Northern blacks of the 54th Massachusetts Volunteers bravely though unsuccessfully assaulted Fort Wagner, near Charleston. They met murderous fire from entrenched Confederates, and took heavy casualties. The soldiers and their fallen white commander, Colonel Robert G. Shaw, won a national reputation as heroes. Port Hudson, Milliken's Bend, and Fort Wagner demonstrated that black soldiers, ex-slave or free, could, because of their courage and skill and growing numbers, play an important part in winning the grinding and bloody war.[50]

With Union control of the Mississippi and environs after Vicksburg and Port Hudson, black troops in the West were employed mainly in garrisoning forts and camps along the Mississippi to protect Union-controlled plantations, contraband camps, transportation and communication lines, and occupied territory. Black engineers with Banks in the unsuccessful Red River Campaign constructed dams that enabled naval units stranded by low water to escape in the general retreat.[51]

On April 12, 1864, General Nathan B. Forrest's Confederate troops overran a garrison of African American troops at Fort Pillow, on the Mississippi in Tennessee. After resisting bravely, many of the blacks threw down their arms and, according to a report by Grant, were then mercilessly killed by Forrest's men. Confederates denied committing atrocities and claimed that they killed in battle those who refused to surrender or tried to escape.[52] Outraged, black troops in nearby Memphis took an oath to avenge their comrades at Fort Pillow. There were also reports of the shooting of wounded and captured black soldiers at Poison Spring and Marks Mill, Arkansas, a short time after Fort Pillow. In retaliation at Jenkins Ferry, on the Sabine River in Arkansas, the 2nd Kansas Colored Regiment overran a Confederate battery shouting, "Remember Poison Spring!"[53] and killed about 150 Confederates. Elsewhere when storming Confederate positions African Americans shouted, "Remember Fort Pillow!" "Remember Poison Spring!" Black cavalrymen captured and killed 17 Confederate soldiers in Louisiana in remembrance of Fort Pillow, and in an assault at Fort Blakely, Alabama, black troops killed surrendering Rebels. The reported atrocity at Fort Pillow increased the number of blacks desiring to join the armed forces and made it easier for Thomas Webster, for example, to recruit men for the Twenty-Fourth U.S. Colored Troops. To increase volunteers Webster recommended that blacks be placed on an equality with white soldiers.[54]

Black troops fought well with General George Thomas in his victorious Franklin-Nashville Campaign, December–January, 1864–1865. The Thirteenth U.S. Colored Infantry was, on December 16, 1864, for the first time under fire with veterans of Stone's River, Missionary Ridge, and Atlanta, and vied with the tested warriors in "bravery, tenacity, and deeds of noble daring." The loss of over 25 percent of those engaged, sustained in less than 30 minutes, included 80 killed, 388 wounded, and one missing.[55] The men of the Forty-Fourth U.S. Colored Infantry also fought with steadiness during an earlier clash of this campaign, as did the Fourteenth and Sixteenth U.S. Colored Infantry, and other units.[56]

Troops of the Twelfth Regiment U.S. Colored Infantry smartly attacked retreating Confederate forces of General John B. Hood in this same Nashville Campaign, crossing the Tennessee River into Alabama. The hardships of the winter campaign, including a shortage of tents and blankets, had a serious effect. Many of the men had to be left along the route because of sickness.[57] In operations against Hood's communications with Mobile, the Third U.S. Colored Cavalry, a part of a 2200-man cavalry unit commanded by Colonel E.D. Osband, destroyed cotton, corn, and wheat, and bridges and railways, brought back more recruits than men lost in the operation, and won high praise.[58] Farther east, Grant employed African American troops in his great Virginia Campaign that resulted in the capture of Richmond, the surrender of Lee, and the imminent fall of the Confederacy. Men of the Colored First, Fourth, Sixth, and Twenty-Second regiments convinced E.W. Hines, General Third Division, of the Eighteenth Army Corps, that blacks, when properly trained and led, made outstanding soldiers. But, Hines warned, "in our exuberance of satisfaction at their deportment, we should be cautious lest we imperil the success of the project of arming colored men, as well as the success of our armies by assuming that the negro is a soldier ready made, rather than that he will make a soldier by patient, persistent, and intelligent drill and instruction."[59]

Blacks did make fine soldiers. Besides fighting in great campaigns, they participated in raids to destroy supplies and disrupt transportation lines. In the Southeast region they fought bravely, though unsuccessfully, at Olustee, Florida, February, 1864, and Honey Hill, South Carolina, November, 1864. Although they were not included in Sherman's Army which captured Savannah at Christmastime, 1864, they did take and hold forts in areas around Savannah, and participated in expeditions against Fort Fisher, North Carolina in December, 1864, and January, 1865.[60]

Thousands of black soldiers held their positions in Grant's lines in the final assault on Lee's army. They attacked courageously while suffering heavy losses at the bloody Battle of the Crater in July, 1864. They constituted almost one-eighth of the troops besieging Petersburg, last major obstacle to Richmond. By the end of 1864 colored regiments in Grant's army had been consolidated into the black 25th Army Corps, commanded by General Godfrey Weitzel. Many black soldiers had the great satisfaction of marching into Richmond with the victorious Union Army in April, 1865.[61]

Slaves in insurrection were subject to execution, thus the first reaction of Confederates to slaves joining the enemy as soldiers was to judge them as deserving death, along with their officers who "incited" them to insurrection. In denouncing Benjamin Butler's military rule in New Orleans, Confederate President Jefferson Davis charged that African slaves had not only been incited to insurrection, "but numbers of them have

Black fighting men, such as these troops recovering from heavy losses at the Battle of the Crater in 1864, had a significant part in defeating the Confederacy. Miller, ed., *Photographic History of the Civil War*, Vol. III, 195.

actually been armed for a servile war -a war in its nature far exceeding in horrors the most merciless atrocities of the savages." Davis proclaimed that commissioned officers serving with armed slaves when captured were to be executed and that slaves captured in arms were to be turned over to the authorities of the states to be dealt with according to their laws.[62] Following Davis's lead, on November 30, 1862, the Confederate Secretary of War James Seddon wrote General P.G.T. Beauregard that slaves in rebellion were subject to death and "for example and to repress any spirit of insubordination it is deemed essential that slaves in armed insurrection should meet condign punishment. Summary executions must therefore be inflicted on those taken," the general commanding in the locality where they were captured deciding and ordering execution.[63]

Ex-slave soldiers when captured were not executed, as threatened. When black soldiers and their officers were captured in battle, as at Milliken's Bend in June, 1863, Confederate policy softened, partly because Union authorities threatened retaliation if their soldiers, black or white, were mistreated. But captured ex-slave soldiers were still thought of as slaves. In this vein H.L. Clay, assistant adjutant-general, Confederate States of America Army, wrote General E. Kirby Smith, "Considering the negroes as deluded victims, they should be received and treated with mercy and returned to their owners"; to refuse them quarter would only make them fight desperately.[64] General Smith wrote his subordinate generals that if captured black soldiers were executed by military authorities retaliation would certainly be provoked but, he thought, no exception could be taken to their being turned over to civil authorities of the states. This policy was embodied in a joint resolution of the Confederate Congress, in May, 1863,[65] which

provoked President Lincoln to condemn this policy "as a crime against the civilization of the age." He stated that the government would protect all its soldiers and ordered: "That for every soldier of the United States killed in violation of the laws of war a rebel soldier shall be executed, and for every one enslaved by the enemy or sold into slavery a rebel soldier shall be placed at hard labor on the public works and continued at such labor until the other shall be released and receive treatment due a prisoner of war."[66]

Some black soldiers captured at Jackson, Louisiana, in August, 1863, were killed when, it was alleged, they had attempted escape, and an investigation could not prove otherwise. In his report to General John Logan, Colonel John Powers declared: "Four of the negroes attempted to escape. I ordered the guard to shoot them down. In the confusion the other negroes attempted to escape likewise. I then ordered every one shot, and with my six shooter assisted in the execution of the order."[67] Later, on February 7, 1864, Union General George L. Andrews, commander of the post and *Corps d'Afrique*, Port Hudson, Louisiana, reported that he was "satisfied that rebel soldiers, with the connivance and assistance of their officers, have abused and shot some of our captured colored soldiers."[68]

The most notorious alleged abuse and killing of captured soldiers occurred April, 1864, at Fort Pillow, Tennessee, where, as we have seen, African American soldiers were, it was said, shot by General Nathan B. Forrest's men as they surrendered.[69] Black soldiers wanted the federal government to retaliate harshly for Confederate mistreatment of captured black soldiers. Secretary of War Stanton recommended that the Union retaliate by executing a like number of Confederate soldiers to those "massacred" at Fort Pillow, but his recommendation was not followed out of humanity and concern about endless retaliation.[70]

Some of the black soldiers captured at Fort Pillow, along with others captured by General Forrest at Athens, Alabama, September 24–25, 1864, were put to work by General D.H. Maury on the fortifications of Mobile. Confederates maintained that if the captured soldiers had been slaves they could be so employed legitimately. Grant forced abandonment of such practices on another occasion by putting an equal number of Confederate prisoners to work. In this connection, he wrote General Lee, October 20, 1864, "I shall always regret the necessity of retaliation for wrongs done our soldiers, but regard it my duty to protect all persons received into the Army of the United States, regardless of color or nationality."[71]

One of the soldiers worked at Mobile, Private Joseph Howard, Company F, One Hundred and Tenth Regiment United States Colored Infantry, escaped, and gave the following account:

> I was taken prisoner at the surrender of Athens, Alabama, September 24, 1864. We were marched to Mobile, Alabama, stopping at various places on the route. We were twelve days going to Mobile. After we were captured the rebels robbed us of everything we had that they could use. They searched our pockets, took our clothing, and even cut the buttons off of what little clothing they allowed us to retain. After arriving at Mobile, we were placed at work at the fortifications there, and impressed colored men who were at work when we arrived were released, we taking their places. We were kept at hard labor and inhumanly treated. If we lagged or faltered or misunderstood an order we were whipped and abused, some of our own men being detailed to whip the others. They gave as a reason for such harsh treatment that we knew very well what they wanted us to do, but that we feigned ignorance; that if we were with the Yankees we could do all they wanted, etc. For the slightest causes we were subjected to lash. We were very poorly provided for with food, our rations being corn meal and mule meat, and occasionally some poor beef.

On December 7, 1864, Howard stole a skiff and went down the river to the bay and was taken on board a Union gunboat.[72]

With Union victory, controversy over the treatment of black soldiers was supplanted by controversy over the status of African Americans as citizens.

On July 15, 1865, there were 123,156 black soldiers in the Union Army, about 12 percent of the total at the war's end. About 178,895 black troops served during the war, between 9 and 10 percent of the Union total. Losses were 68,178, over one-third of those enrolled. Of these, 2,751 were killed in action, the rest died of wounds or disease or were missing.[73]

In "The Colored Soldier," Paul Laurence Dunbar celebrated the achievements of the African American soldiers:

> Yes, the Blacks enjoy their freedom,
> And they won it dearly, too;
> For the life blood of their thousands
> Did the southern fields bedew.
> In the darkness of their bondage,
> In the depths of slavery's night,
> Their muskets flashed the dawning,
> And they fought their way to light.
>
> They were comrades then and brothers,
> Are they more or less to-day?
> They were good to stop a bullet
> And to front the fearful fray.
> They were citizens and soldiers,
> When rebellion raised its head;
> And the traits that made them worthy, —
> Ah ! those virtues are not dead.[74]

PART THREE

RECONSTRUCTION

9

First Freedom

Freedom for many blacks was formally announced: ex-masters, forced by agents of the victorious federal government, called their ex-slaves up with sound of bell, conch, or horn to the big house to inform them, often with a Union officer present, that they were henceforth and forever free. The ex-masters usually asked the freedmen to stay on, at least until the crop was made, in exchange for part of the crop. Henry Smith's old master called the people up one morning and, unfurling a long paper, told them that they were free to go or stay.[1] Another former master declared, "Liza, you don't belong to me any longer, you belong to yourself."[2] A Mississippian underlined his announcement of freedom by ceremoniously white-washing and putting away his bull whip.[3] An Arkansas planter "unrolled the Government paper," read it, and, said Ella Wilson, "just sot us free and turned us loose naked."[4] After he read the "freedom papers," a Texas planter added, "If you go, lots of white folks ain't gwine treat you like I does."[5] A Georgia planter visited the cabins one by one to inform each family of the new freedom. When Jerry Boykins's ex-master announced freedom he gave his former slaves a "big day," with barrels of whiskey rolled out and hogs barbecued.[6]

Some old masters could hardly admit that their former slaves were free. When one tried to announce freedom to the assembled blacks he burst into tears, and "never did tell it," said Emma Johnson.[7] Another said: "You are as free as I am now. The damn Yankees have come and set you free. I hope you are satisfied."[8] Still another, drunk, called his ex-slaves to the big house "and us not knowin' whether we's gwinter get whipped or what and he say, 'Niggers, I hates to tell you but you is as free as I is.'"[9] Cindy Anderson's master "come stompin' aroun' cussin' an' tol' us to git out. We didn't have nowheres to git to, but we had to go."[10] James Turner McLean's master, though he cried when he announced freedom, invited the people to a big dinner and asked them to stay and divide the crop. Some left but others stayed for 15 years, because he was a "feeling man."[11]

The old mistress might be the one who "blowed the conk" and announced freedom. When one old master read the freedom papers "he didn' seem to min', but Miss Em, she bawled and squalled" that her property was "taken 'way from her."[12] Miss Mary, however, simply called up the blacks, told them they were free, "gave them their age," and told them that they were free to go or stay.[13] Loss of slaves caused at least one mistress to go mad; and killed another.[14]

Often Union soldiers, not ex-masters, informed the blacks that they were free. Mollie Campbell recalled that Yankee

139

soldiers rode in and told them that they were free to leave whenever they wished. Big black men with uniforms "trimmed with eagle buttons" told Pinkey Howard's people that they did not have to wait on white folks anymore.[15] A Yankee soldier in Georgia said "you are free," and "if your mistress calls you 'John', call her 'Sally'."[16] Soldiers came to a Texas place, announced freedom, ransacked the big house, and left the old master in a "cussing spree what lasts as long as he lives."[17] In one area of Texas "Dey was gwine 'roun in dey blue uniform' and a big long sword hangin' at dey side" proclaiming freedom, said Fred Dibble.[18] Soldiers in Arkansas rode around telling blacks that "you didn't have no master, that you could go and come as you pleased."[19]

On a Mississippi plantation the old master continued to work the hands as if they remained slaves until Union cavalrymen rode up, assembled them, and proclaimed their freedom.[20] A Union officer in Arkansas said, "Aunt Dinah, you can do as you please. You're free." Afterwards he and his troops "carried on" all night, sent some confiscated food to the freed folks, and rode away next morning.[21] When one Yankee general announced freedom, his South Carolina audience burst into celebration and rejoicing. On some places soldiers required the old master to call up the blacks and announce freedom while they stood by in ostentatious command.[22]

Blacks sometimes heard about freedom not by special announcement but by word spread among the people. Prince Johnson saw wagon loads of freed people traveling through the country proclaiming freedom.[23] Others heard about freedom from messengers who slipped about from place to place, whispering the good news.[24] Dora Franklin's brother slipped into the big house to tell her that she was free and to urge her to leave. "Fore sundown dere woan one nigger left on de place," Dora said.[25] Blacks on a Texas place had to get their ex-master to acknowledge that, as they had heard from neighbors, slavery had been abolished.[26] When asked if they had been freed, a Mississippi planter responded, "No! Git to work or be tore up."[27] A "drove" of celebrating freedmen came by and urged one woman to go with them to Atlanta, but she refused, for she had small children to care for.[28] Sarah Poindexter recalled "de excitement in de neighborhood when roving crowds of niggers come 'long de big road, shoutin' and singin' dat all niggers am free."[29] Charlie Moses heard freedmen sing:

> Free at las'
> Free at las'
> Thank God Almighty
> I's free at las.'[30]

Blacks often greeted confirmation of their freedom with concern as well as joy. On one place freedmen carried on, shouting, "Free at Last!"[31] While on another place "all had different ways ob thinking 'bout hit, but most ob 'em wuz like me, dey didn't know what freedom meant," said James Lucas.[32] Another group welcomed freedom "so dey cud do like dey please wid no boss over dem, an' den dey wanted to go places an' dey wanted to make money like de white folks an' do deir own buyin'."[33]

Tom Robinson said that even the well-fed, well-cared for, rejoice when the cage door is thrown open. Accordingly, freedmen on an Arkansas place did not wait to see if they would get another meal, but took to the road rejoicing. On a North Carolina plantation ex-slaves greeted their freedom with whooping and laughing, and "acting like they were crazy" while their ex-master and mistress humbly observed the celebration. It was a heavenly day! said Tines Kendricks. It was a joyful time, declared Josephine Hamilton. All day long some Georgia blacks rallied around a liberty pole.[34] A Virginia group, rejoicing and shouting, sang:

> Mamy don't yo' cook no mo',
> Yo' ar' free, yo' ar' free.
> Rooster don't yo' crow no mo',
> Yo' ar' free, yo' ar' free.
> Ol' hen, don't yo' lay no mo' eggs,
> Yo' free, yo' free.[35]

Among an Alabama group some were happy while others were sad at their uncertain prospect. Georgians "Sarah Ann and Aunt Mary, dey throwed down deir hoes and jus' whooped and hollered 'cause dey was so glad," but Georgia Baker "wasn't even studyin' nothin' 'bout leavin'" her old master.[36] Mrs. John Barclay jumped up and down, clapped her hands and shouted "Glory to God!" and Victoria Perry's mother rejoiced that God had answered their prayers. James Boyd and friends threw their hats in the air. Another group jumped, hollered, danced, and stirred "'roun like bees workin' in and out a hive."[37] "Hallelujah" broke out among some blacks in East Texas who sang:

Abe Lincoln freed the nigger
with the gun and the trigger;
and I ain't goin' to get whipped any more.
I got my ticket
Leavin' the thicket,
and I'm a-headin' for the Golden Shore.[38]

Everyone was singing, feeling like heroes, "walkin' on golden clouds" out in the field. Lucindy Shaw "commenced dancin' an' shoutin' an' 'nockin' down de corn."[39]

Silas Smith said that on their South Carolina plantation the announcement of freedom was followed by confusion: "Didn't narry nigger on dat entire plantation know what to do widout his master. It was de awfulest feeling.... you felt jes' like you had done strayed off a-fishing and got

lost."[40] Others felt that they had been turned loose naked. Clara C. Young's people shouted and sang for a few days, then began to wonder what good freedom would bring.[41] Hamp Santee said that his people "jes rung bells, blowed horns, and shouted like deys crazy. Den dey all bought a brand new rope, and cut hit up into little pieces and dey gives every nigger a piece of hit to keep and say, dat when ever dey look at de rope dey remember dat dey is free from bondage."[42] Rachel Hankins, an Arkansas slave, like many Texas slaves, did not hear that she was free until June 19, 1865, thereafter she and her relatives and friends danced and feasted on that anniversary.[43]

Blacks suffered much during the transition from slavery to freedom, however limited their freedom might be. Disruption of the plantation economy, and their possession of next to nothing, made life difficult even when ex-masters tried to be fair. Planters were land poor. Fences were gone, buildings destroyed or in disrepair, stock down to one or two worn-out horses or mules, food stocks carried away or destroyed, finances wrecked. Planters were unable to pay wages except with a part of the crop. "Fer a time after de war everything wuz topsy turvey," Myra Jones said. Almost everything had to be rebuilt. "It was lak starting from the ground up."[44] Molly Horn said that her ex-masters did not give the freedmen anything, but "truth of it was they didn't have much to keep less givin' the niggers something. We all had little to eat and wear." There was no stock but a scrub or so. There was no garden seed except what could be borrowed 'round about.[45] At the end of the year Adam Singleton's old master had to pay off hands in cotton which was worth almost nothing "an' dar wus nuffin but starvation in de land fur bofe white and black." When his impoverished master took to drink and became cross Adam's family moved away.[46]

"After de war it took a mighty long time to get things goin' on smooth," John Cameron stated. "Mos' everything was tore up an' burned down to de groun'. It took a long time to build back wid-out no money an' den it warnt de grand old place it was de fus' time." Things were "ruint" for everybody.[47] Lewis Jefferson said, "All de white folks wus pore an' dey cud not pay de black folks fur wurk, an' de black folks had no credit an' some uf dem went to stealin' an' den de Bull Dozers wud git dem fur dat."[48] Hannah Hancock's ex-mistress let much of her land grow up in tree sprouts because she had no money to pay hands to work it.[49]

In trying to get started on their own freedmen found work scarce and wages low. John Moore's first weekly wages were 50 cents, a peck of cornmeal, three pounds of bacon, and a quart of syrup. Sarah Ashley worked as a cook for her food and clothes.[50] Henry Bobbitt, like many others, struggled to survive on whatever work he could get: "Well de first year I slept in folkses woodhouses an' barns an' in de woods or any whar else I could find. I wucked hyar an' dar, but de folkses jist give me sompin' ter eat an' my clothes wuz in strings 'fore de spring o' de year."[51] When indigent blacks resorted to the Freedmen's Bureau they experienced hardship too: crowding, unaccustomed food, unsettled conditions, and disease.[52]

When freedom was declared some former slaves knew just what to do: leave their place of bondage in haste. Many of these found the outside world inhospitable, and returned to work for "old master." Still others remained on the old place sometimes for years, before venturing abroad. Choices of what to do and where to go were severely limited by lack of resources: money, education, established friends and relations, and experience. Many had no alternative but to remain on the old place as hired hands or sharecroppers until time and experience of freedom brought opportunity to strike out on their own. Some stayed on until death of their white folks forced them to depart.

Ella Wilson noted the principal obstacle to getting a start was, "They just sot us free and turned us loose naked."[53] Silas Smith thought that not a single black on his place knew what to do at freedom. Smith himself stayed on but some left in the vain hope of getting a grant of land from carpetbaggers and scalawags, while others were forced out because "old mistress" herself had become too poor to keep them. James Bolton, who remained on the old place for 40 years after the war, said it took a long time for ex-slaves to learn how to buy and sell and take care of what they made. Dependency fostered by slavery was difficult for some to overcome.[54]

The aged could not risk striking out. One grandmother made and wore a new dress at the news of freedom but stayed with "her white folks" until her death. Few mothers of young children would chance accompanying a group heading somewhere, in search of uncertain opportunity. Ten year old Isaac Johnson stayed with his former master and mistress until they died, then went to their relatives. Diana Rankins's father kept his family on the old place, fearing that if they left they would freeze or starve. Peter Blewit's family stayed on because they "didn't have no udder place to go," and Andrew Boone's family also "had nothin' an' nowhere to go." W.L. Pollack's family could not accumulate enough money to buy food, if they left, and John Cole could find no means to go anywhere.[55] Minerva Bendy said that when turned loose, "Dey didn't even give us a hoecake or a slice of bacon."[56]

Some freedmen chose to stay on their old places because they judged their former masters as good people who needed their help. John Barker felt obliged to stay with his old master and mistress, even though the pay was not much, because "de war done took dere money and all." Georgia Baker stayed with her "two good masters" for several years.[57] So did Clara Young who loved her former master and mistress but had no use for "Old Mister Yankee, think he is so grand, wid his blue coat tail a draggin' on de ground!"[58] James Turner McLean served his former master, "a feeling man," until his master's death.[59]

Some freedmen who stayed received gifts out of their ex-masters' sense of obligation or as enticements to stay. All the hands stayed, most of them until death, on a Georgia plantation. One of them, Henry Bland, received when he became of age two mules and a wagon, a horse and buggy, and 10 pigs. Clara Walker's former mistress gave something to all. Clara's mother got a horse, a milk cow, eight hogs, and 50 bushels of corn. She moved to a little house on the place and made several crops on halves. Sylvia Watkins's ex-master gave her father, who stayed on, a hog, some chickens, and a milk cow. An Alabama planter gave families clothes, some money, a mule and wagon, a hog, and some corn. A Texas woman gave her ex-slaves $500 each in Confederate money — all the money she had.[60]

A small percentage of ex-slaves who remained with their former masters received gifts of land. Andrew Jackson Gill as late as the 1930s still owned and lived on land given him by his ex-master. Della Briscoe received, but later lost a three-acre plot and house. She had also been given a mule and buggy, a cow, hogs, and other property. Blacks created a community east of Fort Worth, Texas, as they did in scattered places throughout the South, on land donated by their ex-master. John Sneed's mother got two cows, a team of horses and a wagon, and 70 acres of land south of Austin.[61]

Young blacks without family or friends sometimes had to stay with old master and mistress after the rest of the ex-slaves had left to seek their fortune. Some were bound as apprentices. Fannie Tatum, for example, stated that her old master, who was also her father, had her bound to him until she was 21, during which time, she said, she was treated like a dog: "I wasn't allowed to eat at the table. I et on the edge of the porch with the dogs with my fingers. I worked around the house and washed until I was nine and then I started plowing. At ten I started splitting rails. My task was two hundred rails a day. If I didn't cut them I got a beating. I did not know what a coat was. I wore two pieces, a lowell undershirt and a lowell dress, bachelor brogans and sacks and rags wrapped around my legs for stockings. That was in winter. Summer I went barefooted and wore one piece. My sun hat was a rag tied on my head." She was, she said, never taken to church nor allowed to learn the ABCs from the white children of the family.[62] When the rest of the plantation's slaves were set free, the sheriff apprenticed Gabe Butler to his old mistress. Gabe, nominally an apprentice, was kept practically a slave for three more years, until a friendly neighbor at last got him released. Sam McCallum was bound out to gain some learning along with knowledge of farming. He worked hard on the farm, he said, but never saw a speller.[63]

A few young blacks became so closely identified with white folks in the big house that they did not want to leave. Jane Sutton ran away twice from her father, who had come with the sherrif to get her, to return to "Old Miss."[64] When Ida Rigby's mother returned after a long absence for her daughter, "It was," said Ida, "like taking me off from my own home."[65]

Some young blacks who remained on the plantation after the rest of the freedmen had left were held against their will, though not apprenticed, or remained because there was no one else to care for them. Harriet Miller stayed with her white folks until her grandfather finally came for her. Katie Darling was held for six years after the war by "Missy," who whipped her just the same as during slavery. At last she and her brother ran away.[66] Sarah Benjamin said that when the rest of the slaves scattered, her "mistress" said, "I wasn't no slave no more but I had to stay and he'p her for my board 'till I's grown." At 16 Sarah ran away and got married.[67] Viney Baker's ex-mistress let her go when her mother came for her only because, Viney said, she feared that she would be reported to the "Carpetbaggers." Squire Irvin's former master tried to keep him and other young blacks until they were 21, but the Yankees wouldn't hear of that. Some mothers came armed with an order from the provost-marshal to free their children. Emma Turner stayed, working for "victuals and clothes," until she was 20. Frank Bell's master kept him working for one dollar a month, threatening to kill him if he tried to leave. Frank gained freedom some years after the war when his ex-master himself was killed.[68]

At announcement of freedom some entire black communities left their places of bondage at once. Robert Falls, of Tennessee, remembered the roads being full of folks walking along in search of something better "somewhere else." Falls himself found an employer who offered him corn, molasses, pork, and clothes to make a crop. He was elated: "I knowed then I could make a living for my own self, and I never had to be a slave no more."[69] Roaming groups of blacks likely as not ended up in a camp established by the U.S. Army or Freedmen's Bureau, until individuals and families could be settled on old or new places as workers under contract.

Nathan Best saw droves of people making their way to an Army camp near New Bern, North Carolina where they lived in makeshift huts and drew from the provost-marshal hardtack, codfish, and "ole pink beefs dat was left from de army," until they were provided train tickets to a place of employment. At a camp in Atlanta the Freedmen's Bureau worked to get jobs for the people and "push 'em out," but it was nearly a year before some got work. Matilda Hatchett's family found a resting place in a church before getting settled. Tom Wylie Neal remembered everybody drifting around, drawing rations from the Yankees, wearing old uniforms, and sleeping anywhere until they could become self-supporting. These people likely would get work first as hirelings then as sharecroppers.[70]

Following the announcement of freedom, the plantation community usually split, with some of the people electing to remain on the old place as hired hands or sharecroppers while others went looking for a happier life elsewhere. One group that stayed made a bad bargain: they got no pay, because their ex-master claimed they "et it all up." Those who left took all their possessions (mostly clothes) tied in a bag. On an Arkansas place some of the hands laughed and danced and ran right off; others sharecropped a few years before departing. On a Mississippi plantation the freedmen threw down their tools and left, but came back by dark and stayed on some years more.[71] Many others went in search of a bright new life but soon returned to the security of the old place. Some North Carolina blacks went off to town, found hardtack and pickled meat doled out by Yankees, and returned to their old plantation, until in a few years they could leave in greater security.[72] Many who got help from the Freedmen's Bureau also had to return to their old places for a spell. Henrietta Murray went back to her white folks after two years away and stayed with them until they died. Solomon Lambert, who found little difference between slavery and freedom, returned to the old place and remained there many years. Others, after celebrating in town, came back to the old place, or some place "around."[73] Freedmen from a North Carolina plantation wandered from place to place for about a year until their former master and mistress hitched up their carriage and at length found them. "Some were so glad to get back they cried," Mary Anderson said, because their fare had been so poor while they rambled around — "they were hungry."[74]

Most of the freedmen unable to leave the old place in time got the experience and means to move on. At first many of them worked for little more than food, clothes, and shelter but after a while, as Peter Mitchell noted, they "larns to take care demselves." Robert Glenn made a contract with his ex-master, supervised by the Freedmen's Bureau, and took his freedom by degrees until he felt ready to leave. Others, like Charles Crawley and family, wanted to leave but, having no prospects, stayed until "we wuz able wid God's help to pull us selves together." Lucy Donald's family stayed on for a few years, then managed to homestead a place and get their own land. Jerry Eubanks worked for his ex-master until he made $183, then he went to Mobile and on to New Orleans, following jobs.[75]

Freedmen who remained on the old place to hold together their community would, in most cases, soon see their community begin to break up. One member would die, a second get married and leave, and a third start farming in the next county. Thus Minnie Davis's mother stayed a while, then left and rented a room, worked hard and saved, and bought a house. An employer enticed Jerry Boykins away to oversee his mule barn.[76]

Some people found mutual support and opportunity by migrating in groups. W.D. Miller joined a band of about 100 people from North Carolina on the way to Mississippi to pick cotton. Later he was drawn with others to Arkansas, where the fresh land was good but did not, as rumor had it, produce cotton so high it had to be picked from muleback. R.F. Parker also went with a group heading for the "promised land" of Arkansas. Josh Miles stayed with his former master until, one day, he migrated with a bunch of people to Texas where folks were going "all de time from de old states."[77] Sally Foltz and others went to Dyersburg, Tennessee, where laborers were in demand. There, she said, "they sorted us out like they was sorting hogs or corn-this man take this one to work and that man take that one."[78]

Many blacks encountered extreme hardship when released from bondage. When Yankee soldiers "give out news of freedom," Jake Goodridge waited to see what they would do next. The Yankees took their tents and departed, leaving Jake and his family and friends with "no place to stay and nuthin' to eat, naked and cold." Cindy Anderson's family found shelter in a chicken coop. Thomas Ruffin's family seasoned their greens with salt from the dirt floor of a smokehouse and marrow from thrown-away bones. Mothers who were sole support of children had a particularly hard time. Primus Magee's mother supported her five children "first one way den tuther for two or three years" before getting settled on a farm. Alex Montgomery's mother, abandoned by her husband, stayed on the old place and sharecropped, but, said Alex, "we kno'd nuffin but hard times."[79] Every one was "free ter 'tend ter his own bus'ness," said Simon Hare. "Trouble was, we didn't know *how ter*."[80] Yet, "Dere is sumpin' 'bout bein' free and dat makes up for all de hardships," said Thomas Jones.[81] Pauline Howell's people left the old place, returned, left again and returned once more, because, although their ex-master told them to "go on away," they had "no place to go and nothing to eat." Some of them sickened and died; the rest finally scattered.[82] Tina Johnson said that before things got settled around Raleigh, North Carolina, freedmen lived on "kush, co'n-bread, 'lasses an' what dey can beg an' steal frum de white folks. Dem days shore wuz bad."[83] The first winter, Willis Cozart was forced to go back to his former master to beg for bread. "Root hog or die!" seemed to be the only choice just after the war.[84] "Freedom meant we could leave whar we'd been bawn en bred, but hit also meant, we had to scratch fur ourselves," said Charlie Davenport.[85]

Surplus officers of the shrinking post-war army were a ready source of personnel for the semi-military Freedmen's Bureau, established to help the newly freed people. General O.O. Howard headed the bureau. Other generals, such as Clinton B. Fisk, who directed the bureau in Kentucky and Tennessee, had charge of districts, and officers of lesser rank like J.W. De Forrest, agent of the Bureau in South Carolina, served on the local level.

The Army provided the power, also, to protect the freedmen and enforce the policies of the Freedmen's Bureau and, before the Bureau got well underway, exercised federal authority over both ex-slaves and their ex-masters. The Department of the Gulf had, by June, 1865, established "contraband" hospitals and furnished large sums to the Freedmen's Bureau for various programs, including education. Generals provided employment to freedmen in their carrying out broad administration of affairs in the conquered South. General J.H. Wilson, for example, put 3000 blacks to work on the Chattanooga and Atlanta Railroad.[86]

As executors of federal authority in the interum between the collapse of the Confederacy and the full operation of the Freedmen's Bureau generals, afraid of chaos in the broken–down South, gave

advice and orders to freedmen concerning their conduct. On May 9, 1865, General C.C. Andrews, commanding the Second Division of the Thirteenth Army Corps at Selma, Alabama, advised the freedmen to contract with planters to work for wages or a share of the crop. He warned them to avoid leaving their homes to congregate in towns or Army posts, because, he said, they would suffer hardship on the road and in camps and at their journey's end have to work for a living still. He praised the freedmen for their peaceable behavior and urged them to be industrious, kind, and charitable in behavior.[87]

Planters urged the generals to check wandering and compel freedmen to perform steady agricultural labor. One such group in and around Columbus, Mississippi, requested, May 22, 1865, that General B.H. Grierson order blacks to stay on the plantations and work the crops rather than congregate in Columbus where they would, predicted the planters, become demoralized, impoverished, and disorderly. For his part, Grierson feared that freedmen would be mistreated if sent back to their ex-masters.[88]

He and other generals sought to balance liberty and order in their districts. General John Pope, commander of the Military Division of the Missouri, recommended, April 10, 1865, that, since white employers wished to exact as much labor from freedmen as possible, emancipated blacks be taken under the protection of the federal government, and state governments be required to protect the person and property of freedmen. The federal government could make such demands, Pope said, in connection with the readmission of the Southern states to the Union.[89] General J.H. Wilson, at headquarters in Macon, Georgia, also made recommendations for reorganizing the South, including using military and civil authority to transform the region's race relations. He wanted every vestige of slavery thoroughly destroyed, and the freedmen protected from injustice, before the "people of Georgia get the State government under their own control. If a single particle of life is left in the institution, or the original guardians of it are allowed any influence in the reorganization of the State, they will resuscitate and perpetuate its iniquities if possible." In the meantime Wilson urged planters to make fair contracts with freedmen for wages or a share of the crop until the Freedmen's Bureau could lay down proper regulations concerning the matter. He would not countenance idleness among the freedmen, who had, he said, generally behaved well. He would, in the interest of family life, force the dispersal of the black population to family leases on the plantation, to escape what he regarded as corrupting influences of common life in the quarters. He thought that every planter should be compelled to give every trustworthy freedman a life lease upon as much land as he and his family could cultivate, and require the lessee to live upon his own possessions and pay a fair rent in money or in kind. Having extended to all the protection of law and the privilege of free schools, with compulsory attendance of the children, this system would promote independence, respectability, and good morals. Wilson believed the Southern people must wait for the federal government's inspiration in all matters pertaining to the public welfare.[90]

General John E. Smith, commanding District of West Tennessee, at Memphis, recommended that since, as he believed, most freedmen, if not required to work, would take whatever they could, contracts for their labor be made under the supervision of the Superintendent of Freedmen, who would protect both worker and planter.[91] In the Selma, Alabama, district, General J. McArthur reported that freedmen generally remained on the plantations and worked well where planters acknowledged their freedom and agreed to compensate them with a share of the crop, all that most planters could offer.[92] In Northern Louisiana freedmen were told to stay on their plantations and were warned that they would not be permitted to be idle or to congregate at military posts. Post commanders and provost-marshals were to enforce these orders until the arrival of agents of the Freedmen's Bureau.[93]

In General Orders No. 24, the commander of the Northern Division of Louisiana stated that the transition from slavery to freedom was causing suffering and danger manifested by the blacks setting out for military posts "with no definite purpose except to leave the scene of their former bondage." The results could be the ruin of the agricultural interest and "suffering, starvation, and misery among the blacks." To prevent these disasters the commanding general therefore ordered: "That all persons heretofore held as slaves remain for the present with their former masters and by their labor secure the crops of the present season." If found wandering or gathering at military posts they would be arrested and punished. The planters were required to treat their laborers fairly, and to make definite contracts with them for the rest of the season. The chief thing, explained Captain William H. Clapp, was "To keep the negroes quiet and at work" until both employers and employed came to know what they must do.[94] General F.J. Herron, commanding Northern Division of Louisiana, went on to report that on the arrival of the agent of the Freedmen's Bureau contracts for wages could be fixed and other details settled. At the same time he promised to look after the interests of the blacks until the agent arrived and to see that they were not oppressed. Herron used the cavalry to "quiet the negroes."[95]

Other commanders warned freedmen that they would not be permitted to live in idleness or congregate at military posts but that their freedom would be protected and their employers required to deal with them justly.[96] An alarmed local commander at Okolona, Mississippi, Lieutenant Colonel H.C. Forbes, reported that the blacks were:

> ... becoming more and more de-moralized daily, notwithstanding the most constant and consistent efforts of the military to enjoin industry and quiet. A large portion of the able-bodied are al-ready vagrants and more are daily be-coming so. The slightest friction of the home harness is enough to drive them into vagabondism. As soon as they cease to work they subsist by stealing, and even the railroad, which has been rationing and paying them $25.00 per month, can-not retain them in its employ. They desert their agreements in whole gangs, always leaving in the night. The most trivial and childish reasons are sufficient to cause them to adopt courses which jeopardize not only their security and comfort, but also their lives.

The vagrancy of the able left the ineffective a dead weight on the planters' hands who forced these out to follow their providers. Forbes thought that the blacks of interior regions were unable to be free yet; for them to be free was for them "first to beg, then to steal, and then to starve." The nearest superintendent of the Freed-men's Bureau at Meridian "announces some very fine theories for the regulation of the labor question intended" to affect an area of 10,000 square miles. Few hear of him. So Forbes recommended that the Army compel the freedmen to labor. "Meanwhile, what am I to do, or to attempt toward restraining the vagrancy and violence of the negroes, and the cru-elty and heartlessness of the bad masters? Starving people are coming in from every direction, from five to sixty miles away, for relief. I am clean worn out with their wan and haggard beggary. I would rather face

an old-fashioned war-time skirmish line any time than the inevitable morning eruption of lean and hungry widows that besiege me at sun up and ply me until night with supplications that refuse to be silenced."[97] A similarly harassed comman-der of the Southern Division of Louisiana, at New Orleans, June 24, 1865, ordered that blacks remain on the plantations and that just compensation be paid them, and added, "Negroes must not be allowed to come to this city, where there are too many already, unless passed by their employers, approved by the military authorities."[98]

The commander of the District of Texas also acted to protect and coerce blacks until the arrival of the officers of the Freedmen's Bureau. "They cannot be forced to work," he wrote, "except in fulfillment of a proper contract, as vagrants from whom labor is demanded as compensation for subsistence, clothing, lodging, or as a duty to the public, shared in by others, or as an urgent necessity to the military service of the United States." Military necessity demanded that they not congregate at military posts. Persons mis-treating the blacks were to be tried before a provost-marshal.[99] Some blacks held back from agreeing to contracts for their labor in the hope of receiving land of their own. A naval officer on the Red River in Louisiana, Lieutenant-Commander James P. Foster, encountered wandering blacks who stated that they would not work "until the land is divided among them, as it belongs to them." He forced these blacks to work for half of what they produced as woodchoppers or as agricultural laborers, "with which arrangement they seemed well pleased."[100]

When the Confederacy was defeated, the Union Army exercised public author-ity until state governments satisfactory to the Union were established. Disruption and destruction of war reduced many Southern people, black and white, to near starvation. In these circumstances the Army became a relief agency for the destitute of both races. General Edward Hatch reported from Eastport, Mississippi, May 15, 1865, that there were many citizens in his area in a starving condition and in urgent need of rations.[101] Colonel B. Dornblaser, at Meridian, Mississippi, recommended, May 17, 1865, that since the war had stripped the country of supplies and means of production, the Army distribute subsistence rations to prevent suffering and starvation, and make mules and horses available for future production.[102] Captain O.S. Coffin also underlined the need of the people for draft animals, pointing out that many small farms in the vicinity of Meridian were owned by widows with children unable to cultivate their farms, having no horses, mules, or work oxen. Most of them had planted a few acres of corn, which required plowing, and it was time for planting sweet potatoes, which could not be done "without the assistance of the plow." Captain Coffin, therefore, urged that mules and horses seized from Confederates be made available to these small farmers, to help them escape destitution.[103] General P.J. Osterhaus furnished some Mississippi farmers with draft animals on loan, because Union cavalry units had carried away their stock. General J. McArthur, in May, 1865, sent corn on the Talladega Railroad to relieve 10,000 starving people in the mostly white mountain country of Alabama. In Louisiana local commanders concerned themselves with relief; and corn and "Confederate bacon" were distributed to blacks and whites in all parts of Alabama in early June, 1865.[104]

General George H. Thomas authorized General Hatch to distribute to destitute families of North Mississippi and Alabama Confederate corn of that country and to "Say to the holders that they disposed of it to their Government and have no right to it whatever, and should be thankful that the United States Government elects to distribute this corn rather than to require them to divide with the poor of their section what of subsistence they still have in their private possession."[105] Hatch seized the "Confederate corn" and gave it to the hungry, and assessed the well-off to supply the poor. General E.R.S. Canby sent 50,000 rations to General J.H. Wilson to feed the starving. In Arkansas military authorities relieved the utterly destitute in many parts of the state as far as they could.[106] General E.F. Winslow reported, July 3, 1865, that the condition of blacks regarding subsistence in counties in the vicinity of Atlanta was "generally provided for," "good," "good as the whites," "indifferent," and that "crops now growing will probably supply the population after harvest."[107]

Military men charged with maintaining order were concerned with displaced and disorderly whites, as with uprooted blacks. In May, 1865, General J.H. Wilson forced the Georgia Railroad, under threat of seizing it, to transport paroled Confederate prisoners on their way home, reducing destitution of the soldiers in that respect. General John B. Smith, at Memphis, in June, 1865, also found a large number of paroled officers and men in Memphis in need of transportation to their homes. While wandering about in Memphis they endangered the good order of the city and burdened the Army with their need of rations.[108]

The army of occupation had to break up guerrilla gangs, administer oaths of loyalty, feed the desperately hungry, supervise local government, and protect the freedmen. General George H. Thomas, for example, in exercising his extraordinary authority, on May 22, 1865, ordered General Hatch, at Eastport, Mississippi to "exercise command over as much territory surrounding your post as you can control, by threats to the bad, and encouragement to the good and law-abiding citizens."[109] Although the Union Army was a victorious army it could not control every area of the South. As General P. Joseph Osterhaus reported in early June about Mississippi: "There is a good deal of marauding going on in such sections of this state as are without the protection of our troops–that is to say, over by far the greater portion of the state." There were many reports of gangs amidst confusion and demoralization disturbing Alabama, Mississippi, and Tennessee.[110]

The extraordinary control of the collapsed Confederacy by the Union Army is illustrated in a dispatch of General Thomas, commanding in Nashville, to General H.M. Judah, in Chattanooga, May 22, 1865: "No civil officer of any of the counties in your district who is not undoubtedly loyal to the United States Government will be permitted to exercise the functions of his office. No one is eligible to office unless he has taken the oath of allegiance to the United States, and his neighbors can testify under oath that he is loyal to the Government of the United States. No one is entitled to vote until he has taken the oath of allegiance to the United States."[111] The use of the army in restoring loyal civil governments in the Southern states is revealed also in a dispatch of Andrew Johnson, later president of the United States, then military governor of Tennessee, to President Lincoln, January 13, 1865: "The convention composed of more than 500 delegates from all parts of the State have unanimously adopted an amendment to the constitution forever abolishing slavery in this state and denying the power of the Legislature passing any law creating property in man. Thank God that the tyrant's rod has been broken."[112]

Because of willfulness and ingrained habit planters were so reluctant to give up their former power as masters that Freedmen's Bureau agents backed by the military were needed in every locality, reported Colonel Horace N. Howland, June 27, 1865, on a tour through Southwestern Georgia. Away from army posts, he wrote, planters were abusing blacks as if they were still slaves, and endeavoring to keep them in practical slavery.[113] A few days later the acting assistant adjutant-general responded with orders governing relations between freedmen and planters until the Freedmen's Bureau could issue its own orders. The authority of parents would replace that of former masters, however, former masters would act as guardians of the aged and infirm in the absence of relatives who could support them, and were compelled to give them food and shelter. On the other hand, able-bodied freedmen were required to support their families, and unmarried youth under 20 were to help their parents and younger brothers and sisters. Planters were obliged to pay freedmen for work. Freedmen were advised to obey the law, but all brutal punishment was forbidden. Persons of age not bound to remain at home to support families could seek new homes and employment, but they would not be supported in idleness by the government or former masters. Freedmen and planters were to agree on wages and conditions, but "freedmen were advised that for the present they ought to expect only moderate wages, and when their employers cannot pay them money they ought to be contented with a fair share in the crops to be raised." Local commanders were to enforce these rules.[114]

In Alabama, Mississippi, and Louisiana, as elsewhere in the subjugated Confederacy, the military sought to promote the welfare of freedmen, to forestall idleness, and prevent maltreatment of blacks and was convinced that the only sure means to protect freedmen was the military power of the federal government.[115]

Black soldiers constituted a significant part of the army of occupation in the first years after the war. Some of their regiments were, however, employed principally in such labor as reconstructing torn-up railroads for the Army's use, laying track and building trestles. A few regiments of black troops were still being organized in the spring of 1865.[116] In June, 1865, black units in Mississippi were located at Vicksburg, Yazoo City, Davis's Bend, Natchez, Jackson, and other places. Two hundred and fifty of the Eighty-fourth United States Colored Infantry were stationed at Camden, Arkansas, in June, 1865, to maintain peace and order in that area. There were a number of black units in the occupying forces of southern Louisiana. In July, 1865, black outfits stationed at Memphis included: Third U. S. Colored Cavalry; Third U.S. Colored Heavy Artillery; Eleventh U.S. Colored Infantry; Eighty-eighth U.S. Colored Infantry; Fifty-ninth U.S. Colored Infantry; Company F, Second U.S. Colored Light Artillery; Company I, Second U.S. Colored Light Artillery. In August, 1865, General P.H. Sheridan had in Texas 24,000 white troops and 21,000 black troops.[117]

Black troops along with white troops were needed in the region because, as General John E. Smith noted, submission was that of a military necessity. Among all classes the majority was unwilling to cooperate in state restoration. People still retained the pride of caste. They were obliged to acknowledge publicly the abolition of African slavery, but "covertly they purpose, knowing not how and abiding a time they know not when, to again make color the badge of servitude and of oppression." It was Smith's opinion that "the safety of the Union requires that the armies of the United States should hold, occupy, and possess the territory lately in rebellion for a yet indefinite period."[118]

In a campaign to regain control of their region, begun at war's end in the spring of 1865, Southern whites agitated against federal troops, especially against black troops, occupying the defeated states. Complaints were sent up to Secretary of War Stanton in May, 1865, that black soldiers in West Tennessee were commiting outrages on persons and property and General R.A. Cameron in the La Fourche district of Louisiana was, he reported in June, 1865, pestered by prejudice against his black troops on the part of some educated and wealthy people who, he believed, hoped for the return of slavery.[119]

President Andrew Johnson joined the opposition. In September, 1865, he wrote General George Thomas that black troops in Greenville, Tennessee, were, he was informed, domineering over the people and had turned his home into a "negro brothel." He requested that Thomas remove the black troops from East Tennessee, or better, muster them out of service. Johnson wrote that "in the event of an insurrection it is feared that the Colored troops, so great in numbers, could not be controlled." Emissaries were, he was informed, "inciting the negro population to acts of violence, revenge, and insurrection." Johnson wanted an end to military occupation, a quick restoration of the Southern states and renewal of their former relations with the federal government, with little changed except the abolition of slavery. General Thomas responded to Johnson that he expected to dispense with 5000 colored troops in Tennessee but that the black troops there were under good discipline. In most collisions between white and black soldiers, he wrote, whites had provoked trouble by attempting to bully blacks, "for it is exceedingly repugnant to the Southerners to have negro soldiers in their midst." He had to employ black troops, he said, because white troops, themselves hostile to blacks, were clamoring to be discharged. He thought he could insure the supremacy of the federal government in his region by garrisoning 5000 or so well disciplined troops, white or black, in Atlanta or Chattanooga. Later, in 1867, Johnson removed General P.H. Sheridan from command of the Fifth Military District, comprising Louisiana and Texas, because Sheridan too vigorously exercised his authority in defense of blacks, Southern Unionists, and resident Northerners in support of the more thorough Congressional Reconstruction rather than lenient Presidential Reconstruction.[120]

U.S. Grant, commanding general of the U.S. Army, soon began to dispatch black troops out of sight of their former masters. On October 31, 1865, he informed General W.T. Sherman that he had sent to General John Pope four regiments of black troops "with the view of having them sent as far west as possible." He believed that these soldiers, later known as the Buffalo Soldiers, would do well on the plains, and after discharge provide labor for the railroads and mines.[121] Some African American troops remained for a time east of the Mississippi. Those stationed at Fort Pickering, in Memphis, provided an occasion for white supremacists to provoke a bloody riot in May, 1866. Later black militiamen were recruited by governors of some Southern states to support their administrations against white supremacists. When whites regained control of the Southern states they excluded African Americans from the state militias.

When Colonel L.L. Zulavsky called on his men in the First Division, U.S. Colored Troops, Mobile, Alabama, to contribute to a memorial to the martyred Lincoln, he might have acknowledged their partnership with the Great Emancipator in advancing freedom. Instead, he declared that they and all black people owed "freedom, justice, consideration, fame, and every other blessing" to Lincoln, "redeemer" of the colored race. Lincoln's name must forever, Zulavsky said, be held by them as a sacred name.[122]

Many blacks knew little of Lincoln until after the war, but quite a few of them believed that had slaveholders heeded his warning and freed their slaves, there would not have been a war.[123] Julius Jones thought Lincoln was a wonderful man who did what God put him here to do: set the slaves free. He did think, however, that the South was winning the war until Lincoln agreed to enlist black soldiers and promised that if they fought on his side he would set all the slaves free. "When them niggers heard that free part," Jones said, "They all joined the army."[124] To many freedmen Lincoln was a mythical figure, an instrument of God, a very great man. Stories circulated that he had visited various neighborhoods before the war, in disguise. Mary Wallace Bowe said he came to their plantation as a peddler, and later wrote her mistress thanking her for a drink of cool milk. Charlie Davenport said Lincoln "what called hisself a rail splitter came here to talk wid us. He went all through the country jest a rantin' and preachin' 'bout us being his black brudders." Adrianna Kerns believed Lincoln traveled through the South disguised as a beggar urging masters to free their slaves. Frank Patterson declared that Lincoln had breakfast with his master and denounced the buying and selling of people. William Edward Black thought that if slave owners had listened to the "Ox-driver" Lincoln, war would have been avoided.[125]

Generally, Lincoln was portrayed as an instrument of God to free the slaves. Frank Hughes thought that Lincoln's role was simply to carry out God's plan. Charles W. Dickens said that Lincoln was a mighty good man "but what he done was intended through de higher powers." Reuben Rosborough declared that "Mr. Lincoln was raised up by de Lord, just like

Moses, to free a 'culiar people." Sallie Paul said that God freed the slaves; Lincoln did what God gave him the power to do.[126]

When freedom's glow was dimmed by hardship Lincoln's greatness seemed limited. Disappointed blacks had thought, Gabe Butler said, that Lincoln would give them land, good things to eat, leisure, everything. Turner Jacobs said that at first his people thought Lincoln was a "young Christ come to save us," but when they did not get the expected "forty acres and a mule," they were disenchanted, but still "lakked him and thought he was a great man." Although William Kirk thought Lincoln was a seven-foot, four-inch war-captain who "believed in right," James Brittian saw him somewhat blemished because slaves got nothing when freed. Annie Stephenson believed that Lincoln would have done more for black people had he not been shot. Isaac Stier said that although Lincoln was a good man he was a poor white who never cut much of a figure in his clothes, and lacked "quality." John Bectom was, however, convinced that Lincoln was one of the greatest men who ever lived, who without a doubt "was the cause of us slaves being free."[127]

In an encomium at Lincoln's birthplace in February, 1909, ex-slave Isaiah Montgomery characterized Lincoln as "chosen of God the prophet of human liberty." In opposing slavery he was a true friend of the South and a "liberator of the minds and hearts of his countrymen." He was " a beacon light marking the pathway of truth and righteousness until the culminating act of his career: the promulgation of the immortal 'Emancipation Proclamation'." Montgomery said that the black people, still faced with "grave and unsolved difficulties," cherished the "life and example of this great man" and looked with hope and faith to the "Author of our national destiny."[128]

Beginning life as free men some blacks rejected sundry vestiges of slavery including names imposed on them in bondage, and chose new ones. Many kept their old names in solidarity with scattered family members or out of respect for family history. Sam McInnis, like those who rejected the name of a recent master, reverted to Sam Williams, his name under an earlier master, when he and Mandy dignified their jumping-the-broom under slavery with a regular "white folks" ceremony after freedom came. Most kept their given names, which their mothers most likely had given them anyhow. Their descendants more readily broke with the past and experimented with new names. Whether or not freedmen changed their names it was difficult to find lost relatives whose surnames had been changed by new masters. As Sylvia Floyd noted, "dey wouldn't know what name de 'ud be taken' as de colored folks had to go by de name of deir masters."[129]

Besides the problem of name changes most families were unable to find separated members because they had no idea where to look. Tines Kendricks noted that although a great many freed families searched for sold-away relatives, "De mostest of 'em never git togedder ag'in even after dey sot free 'cause dey don't know where one or de other is."[130] Mattie Curtis's parents did find three of their 14 children who had been taken away by slave traders. Most families had to get someone to write for them in their search for relatives. An occasional scamp would take money for letters he never mailed.[131]

Many couples who had married jumping-the-broom or who had merely taken up with one another regularized their marriages after freedom with religious or civil ceremonies. In some communities most of the freed couples were remarried on the same day. John Williams's parents formalized their marriage after all but one of their children had been born, and Eliza Hays's parents, who had lived together with permission of their master, when free married "accordin' to the law." Some couples went separate ways and took other spouses.[132]

Many freedmen greatly enjoyed exercising their right, denied or limited during slavery, to choose spouses and have their marriages blessed by the clergy. Emaline Neland was proud that a black clergyman conducted the ceremony at her marriage. Pauline Johnson and Felice Boudreaux were both married in a Catholic church in Opelousas, Louisiana, and Sarah Louise Augustus was married in a "white folks church." Franklin Binns rode 20 miles on horseback to court Arrie and, when he had won her hand, married her in the presence of a white minister.[133]

Unlike slave marriages freedom marriages could last. Sarah Wells was widowed but not until after 50 years of marriage. Allen and Clara Ward, married for more than half a century, brought 10 children into the world. Lawrence Evans made it fine with his wife and "stuck to her as long as she lived." Separation, divorce, and death, rather than the slave trader, broke up marriages and brought sorrow to families. Charlie Vaden divorced one wife, separated from another, and outlived two others. Sickness and death of a spouse impoverished and then broke apart the families of many freedmen, such as that of Anna Huggins, whose husband suffered a stroke and lingered for years. Unable to keep up mortgage payments on her income alone, Anna lost her home. When Edmond Smith's father died and left a house full of little children, the Smith family lived hand-to-mouth, just surviving on hard work and prayer. Lula Coleman outlived one husband and, abandoned by a second, kept going washing clothes for her "livin', right on." Neely Gray buried two of four husbands.[134]

Some women were glad to be rid of their husbands. Manda Boggan thought that she had the sorriest husband in the country until, after his death, she married a second one as good-for-nothing as the first. Ella Wilson's second husband married her on Thursday and, when she would not keep him in money, ran off on Monday.[135] Jane Sutton sang:

> Husban don't you 'buse me
> carry me back to Mama;
> Mama's chimney corner
> Is big enough fer me![136]

Rachel Bradley, in contrast, ran off her disloyal husband.[137] Instead of establishing families by formal marriage, some freedmen continued the slave practice of just living together. Toby and Govie Jones did not bother with any ceremony at all; they simply agreed to live together "as man and wife."[138]

Freedmen's unions bore fruit in many children who gave aid and comfort to their parents in old age, scattered to distant and unknown places, or died young. Poverty and scant means for communication and travel often separated parents from children who went off to new lives in cities, perhaps dropping altogether out of the lives of their parents. In the 1930s, ex-slave Lizzie Norfleet, mother of six children, with many grandchildren and great grandchildren, was still able to look after some of the young ones while their mothers worked in the fields. Celeste Avery was the mother of 14 children, but in her old age all but three were already dead. Emma Morris was sheltered in old age by her daughters, who supported her and kept her in a little money. Adeline Crump was the mother of 21 children, 10 of whom died young. Molly Ammond's 30 children died or wandered away, leaving their mother alone in old age. Lydia Stewart had, in 1935, 491 descendants: 11 children,

96 grandchildren, 248 great grandchildren, and 136 great, great grandchildren. Jennie Washington's children were unable to help her in her old age, because, she said, they did well just to help themselves.[139] Julia Frances Daniels's 17 children "done scatter to the four winds," as did Charles Bell's 14 children. Of Frank Larkin's 13 children seven were "living somewhere, but," he said, "they ain't no service to me."[140]

10

Politics and the Ku Klux Klan

During the first years of Reconstruction, Southern blacks anticipated rapid progress from slavery to freedom. Extension of the franchise, educational advancement, and economic development, they believed, would transform the South into a land of liberty and justice. Accordingly, at the end of the Civil War in 1865 blacks began a movement to win equal civil and political rights. They based their claims on the doctrine set out in the Declaration of Independence that all men are created equal and are endowed by their Creator with the inalienable rights of life, liberty, and the pursuit of happiness. All men, they added, also had a right to an existence worthy of human beings. The electoral franchise, they went on to say, was an indispensable means by which these rights were secured and maintained.

Black leaders argued their case in the year after Appomattox at public meetings all over the South. They declared that the former slaves were native-born Americans who had earned the suffrage by generations of toil and by fighting on the battlefields of the nation's wars, especially the recent War for the Union. And they asserted that if they were ignorant, they were yet wise enough to cast ballots for good men and good principles and to advance in knowledge of politics. Despite their optimism

they understood how great were the obstacles to be overcome. In September, 1865, in a petition to the South Carolina Constitutional Convention, African Americans of Charleston stated: "We fully understand what prejudices and preconceived opinions must be overcome before our prayers can be granted; but we try to believe that the people of South Carolina are capable of rising superior to the prejudices of habit and education, and buoyed up by this hope we respectfully ask that our prayer may be granted and we will ever pray."[1]

All of the ex–Confederate states, then being reorganized under the formula set out by President Andrew Johnson, rejected the blacks' petitions. Johnson himself told a delegation of blacks that extension of the suffrage to the freedmen would inaugurate a war of races. Northern states, also, rejected black men's petitions. At this juncture Southern whites precipitated a crisis. Their state legislatures enacted black codes that thrust freedmen into a lower caste, and their mobs unleashed general violence, especially intense in Memphis and New Orleans in 1866, against blacks.[2] According to the majority report of a congressional select committee that investigated the Memphis riot, "burglary, robbery, arson, mayhem, rape, assassination, and murder" were committed by the anti-Negro rioters. The North reacted swiftly. Congress, with Radical Republicans at the height of power, forced over Johnson's opposition the former Confederate States, except Tennessee, which alone among them had ratified the Fourteenth Amendment, to organize new governments which would guarantee black suffrage. Before this moral and political attack ebbed, the Fourteenth and Fifteenth Amendments were adopted, and black suffrage was imposed on a reluctant North, as well as on the South.

Political expediency, as well as moral fervor, prompted Congress in 1867-68 to hear the prayers of freedmen for equal civil and political rights. Without black political support Southern white Republicans faced certain defeat by Democratic ex-secessionists, and a reunited Democratic Party threatened national Republican supremacy as well. Supported by white equalitarians, African Americans gained the franchise in part because the Republican Party needed their votes.

When Congress extended them the suffrage in early 1867, freedmen held grand celebrations. They marched in torchlight parades and offered prayers of thanksgiving in public meetings. At last they felt really free. At mass meetings blacks and their white friends confidently anticipated a reign of impartial justice and equal rights.[3]

Having gained the suffrage blacks had next to organize. For this purpose they needed an effective press. In this, as in other respects, they were at a disadvantage. Newspapers published by Southern black men had small circulations among mostly illiterate freedmen. Except for a few, such as the New Orleans *Louisianian*, these journals survived for only a season. Radical Republican papers published by whites generally appealed to concentrations of Unionists, as in East Tennessee, and really were not very radical; or, like the Memphis *Post*, were supported by a small group of white radicals and a large mass of poor blacks. Most of these papers, too, were short-lived. Some of them began boldly, then moved to compromise, and finally, joined the white supremacists. Although such newspapers helped the blacks to organize, they were weakened by racism within their own ranks and by assaults from authoritarians of white supremacy.

The Memphis *Post*, for example, struggling against enemy newspapers in the Mid-South, continued publication only by begging and borrowing in the North. General John Eaton, the editor, explained that he had to have Northern support because of the mean opposition of intolerant rebels, who whipped his newsboys, boycotted his merchant patrons, excluded his paper from railroads and steamboats, and drove his black subscribers from the plantations. In Louisiana, Jasper Blackburn of the Homer *Iliad* was twice mobbed by his neighbors. By 1869 the *Post* had lost much of its militancy. Within a few years the radical press of Louisiana, founded "to correct the prejudices of society and reform the passions of the hour," was also in decline.[4]

Black Southerners meanwhile did not wait for white radicals to organize them but began their own organization, even as they petitioned for the suffrage. To cite an example, 2000 African Americans met in August, 1866, at Denison's Grove, Memphis, to select delegates for a Colored Convention to be held in Nashville, not, they said, to plan warfare against whites but to gain equal rights for all citizens.[5] Freedmen, here as elsewhere in the South, welcomed the aid of educated Northern blacks, who flocked South to help their brethren and to find a wider field for leadership than the North afforded, and also the assistance of white Republicans, who brought with them the strength of the party in control of the national government. Yet freedmen and

Political campaign in Baton Rouge. Black suffrage transformed Southern politics during a decade of Reconstruction. Miller, ed., *Photographic History of the Civil War*, IX, 305.

the ante-bellum free blacks provided much of the skill and energy for the organization of a network of local political groups within the Republican Party.

Semi-secret Union or Loyal Leagues spearheaded political organization. Local Abraham Lincoln and Frederick Douglass councils of the Leagues provided a focus of unity as well as means to formulate policies and direct campaigns. Members often came to meetings armed because there was hardly a square mile in the South where blacks and whites could hold a political

meeting without bitter opposition. In some areas blacks would not move unless led by disciplined Union Leaguers and encouraged by fife and drum. In chapel and grove, black and white leaders educated freedmen through political oratory and aroused in them emotional intensity to sustain fierce political struggle.[6]

On April 12, 1870, Memphis blacks celebrated the adoption of the Fifteenth Amendment which prohibited any state from depriving a citizen of his vote on account of race, color, or previous condition of servitude. Impressively organized, the blacks paraded down Main Street to Beale Street and on to James Park, in order: a brass band of the Sons of Ham, in a wagon; 24 marshals on horseback; two bearers of batter axes, with blue swallow-tail coats and striped pants; a band, dressed in Zouave, with red breeches; chaplain in black, bearing the Scriptures; Independent Order of Pole-Bearers, 250 strong, with banners; 36 girls in white, riding in a wagon drawn by four horses; United Sons of Ham, dressed in dark suits, with blue sashes and red, white, and blue rosettes; Young Men's Association, in dark suits and sashes; United Sons of Zion No.1, about 250, in dark clothes, with purple sashes; a band (fife, fiddle, and accordion); United Forever Society, 100 strong; Young Men's Association, No. 2, about 200; Laborers' Union; Daughters of Zion; St. John's Relief Society; Draymen's Association; women and children in carriages, omnibuses, wagons, and carts; and other citizens on foot. In James Park the crowd celebrated with food and drink. In the evening about 2000 blacks and a sprinkling of whites gathered at the Greenlaw Opera House for speeches by local political leaders Barbour Lewis and A. S. Mitchell and visiting dignitary John Lynch, black secretary of state of Mississippi.[7]

Blacks also had to develop group power within the Republican Party, for their goals were more radical than those of white Republicans. They wanted state and federal aid for education, troops to break the power of terrorist organizations, and a complex of legislation to rapidly improve the economic condition of the black people, all of which might have stimulated depressed classes in the Union to demand like benefits. Wedded to policies of social uplift, the Republican Party could not have developed a strong business orientation. Thus white Republicans stressed the need for unity, not only to win elections but also to muffle divisive radical demands.

Few among the most radical of whites stood for unqualified racial equality. Most liberals expected blacks to keep their place and vote for white Unionists in return for conservative gains and minor posts, such as justice of the peace. On every level of government, blacks held fewer offices than their numbers in the Republican Party warranted. Still their increasing demands for equal rights within the party as well as the general society forced whites to make concessions in the matter of officeholding if they wished to prevent internal dissension that would hand victory to united white supremacists. Splits occured everywhere, in fact, in part because blacks demanded racial equality within the party, even though they moderated their economic and social demands for the sake of unity. Threatening to turn against party bosses, the New Orleans *Louisianian* declared, May 30, 1874, that blacks would no longer pay a bonus in officeholding to white leadership "that has been too frequently their shame and injury." White supremacists, taking advantage of the dissension, made common cause with conservative Republicans and defeated white and black equalitarians. Within this coalition, usually called the Conservative Party, Democrats gained ascendancy, and, except in a few areas, white Republicans joined, during the 1870s, white supremacy Democrats to form the "Solid South."

Political developments in Tennessee illustrate the transformation of many white Republicans into white supremacy Democrats. As a consequence of military defeat of secessionists in the Civil War, Unionists gained precarious political control of the state. A minority forced to strengthen their position, they disfranchised many ex-Confederates and reluctantly extended the suffrage to blacks, whom they continued to bar from public office and service on juries. Dissatisfied with half-citizenship, blacks demanded and received civic equality. Ex-Confederates, on the other hand, loosed the Ku Klux Klan, a creature of Tennessee, against black and white Reconstructionists alike. In response to pressure from blacks for equal rights and from ex-Confederates for white supremacy, Republicans split into conservative and liberal factions. Removing political disabilities from ex-Confederates, conservatives gained support from Democrats and defeated their rivals. In turn the Democratic Party absorbed the conservative Republicans except in East Tennessee, where Unionists retained local influence by turning their remnant party into a "lily white" organization.[8]

When Radical Reconstruction began to fail Southern blacks faced a dilemma. If they remained in the Republican Party, they might be abandoned, as, in fact, they were in 1876; certainly they could expect few gains from the increasingly conservative Republican Party. If they turned to the Southern Democrats, they had to surrender to declared enemies. There was little hope in a third party, as the abortive Louisiana unification movement proved.

In Louisiana in 1873 black and white leaders formed a biracial Committee of One Hundred to promote political cooperation, known as unification, between blacks and native whites of the state. The committee adopted resolutions calling for racial integration in the schools, equal access to public facilities, and equality of economic opportunity. Resulting public clamor forced whites to withdraw from the coalition. Blacks, on the other hand, feared that whites intended to use the unification movement to gain control of the black electorate, which certainly was the intention of some white leaders, as General P. G. T. Beauregard later acknowledged. Yet many blacks continued to believe that political harmony between themselves and native whites was necessary to the solution of the problems of reconstruction. Thus in

October, 1874, blacks in convention in New Orleans, hoping to revive the unification movement, declared: "We are still the same quiet and well disposed people as ever, cherishing no animosities, animated by a desire of peace and good will towards all men, and exerting our efforts and influence to conduce to a union of the two races in which the interests of whites would be respected and the rights of the blacks preserved." Acknowledging serious defects in the Reconstruction regime in Louisiana, the convention offered to cooperate with Democrats to achieve reform.[9] But efforts to promote political unification came to nothing, and blacks continued to suffer neglect from white Republicans and opposition from Democrats.[10]

Editorials of the black New Orleans *Louisianian* record the frustration of blacks as they were abandoned by Republicans and attacked by Democrats. On October 24, 1874, the *Louisianian* complained that overtures of union based on ideas of justice and equal rights were not only spurned but "our people are offered the *absolute denial*, not only of their rights as men and citizens, but even the bare protection to life and security." On November 7, 1874, the *Louisianian* reported that a considerable number of blacks had voted Democratic in recent elections because they would no longer accept mistreatment from white Republican manipulators, but April 24, 1875, the journal expressed fear that recent compromises between Republicans and Democrats in Louisiana spelled doom for blacks of the state. On May 22, 1875, the *Louisianian* complained that blacks were being taunted as unfit for citizenship, when they asked "not for a division of the land, not to deprive white people of any of their advantages, but simply for a fair start and an equal chance in the race of life." As hope for unification with local whites or support from Northern Republicans faded, the *Louisianian* declared, March 30, 1878, that black people "will not follow in this campaign, or ever again, the men who wave the *bloody* shirt before the election and leave the consequences to be endured by the people whose only share in the victory or defeat is desertion by pretended friends and persecution by political foes."

Caught in this situation, blacks achieved what they could within the Republican Party. They continued to vote in a bloc, such that, as Ivory Osborne declared, "You never seed a colored person a Democrat."[11] Before white supremacists gained the power to disfranchise blacks by legal devices they were able to coerce a few blacks into voting their ticket. Blacks gained some legal rights, which were in part enforced during a brief period, won some educational assistance, and gained a few privileges and opportunities from Republican administrations in the states.

Meanwhile, blacks flocked to register as voters on the first days of registration. Unlettered freedmen began to ask questions and express opinions and bring freedom of discussion to every part of the South, where tyranny of thought had prevailed. Protected by federal troops and state militiamen, they went to polling places and elected black and white representatives to city councils, county courts, state legislatures, and to the United States Congress. White Republicans, as we have seen, partly because of their superior education and experience, partly because of their skill in political manipulation, received the lion's share of the major offices. In areas where to be Republican was tantamount to being black, black politicians rose highest. In South Carolina Jonathan Wright became a member of the State Supreme Court; in Louisiana P. B. S. Pinchback was chosen lieutenant-governor; in Mississippi Hiram Revels and Blanche Bruce were elected to the United States Senate.[12]

Local black officials, too, served their communities. William Finch, born a slave in 1832, came to Atlanta in 1868, a mecca for freedmen who hoped to acquire economic security, and opened a tailor's shop which prospered. In 1870, Finch was elected to the city council. As councilman, he was important in the creation of the Atlanta public school system, in which he secured the employment of black teachers. He also promoted the paving of streets and establishment of water works. He was defeated for reelection in December, 1871, after white supremacists organized against the "Africanization" of Atlanta.[13] Louis Joseph Piernas held several minor elective and appointive posts in Bay St. Louis, Mississippi, including auditor and postmaster. Blacks of Biscoe, Arkansas, elected John Clay constable, and Oscar Clark magistrate, and others of their race to the school board. In Texas, as in other Southern states, blacks, protected by Loyal Leaguers and federal troops, and in alliance with Carpetbaggers (Northern white men in the South who supported Reconstruction governments) and Scalawags (Southern white supporters of Reconstruction governments) elected a number of black men to state and local office.[14] Despite corruption and opportunism in the Reconstruction government, which white opponents exaggerated, blacks generally nourished a democratic spirit. The new state governments protected civil rights to the extent that they were able, made state prisons more humane, and secured the pardon of prisoners who had been sentenced to long terms for trifling offenses. They established a system of free education, administered the courts so as to defend the freedmen from the powerful, exempted homesteads from sale for debt, protected workmen's wages by laborers' liens, and established racially integrated militias.

The Northern public hoped that creation of popularly based governments in the South would end the need to protect black citizens by federal intervention.

H.R. Revels, U.S. Senator from Mississippi, 1870–1871; James T. Rapier, U.S. Congressman from Alabama, 1873–1875; B.K. Bruce, U.S. Senator from Mississippi, 1875–1881; J.H. Rainey, U.S. Congressman from South Carolina, 1869–1879; John R. Lynch, U.S. Congressman from Mississippi, 1873–1877, 1881–1885. James G. Blaine, *Twenty Years of Congress; From Lincoln to Garfield*, 2 vols. (Norwich, Conn., 1886), II, 304.

White supremacists, however, by means of economic coercion, fraud, and violence, seized control of one Southern government after another, and deprived blacks of much of their liberty. By 1877 all the Southern states had fallen into the grip of white supremacy, and Northern whites acquiesced in this triumph of Ku Kluxism. After white supremacists consolidated their power they began to enact segregationist laws known as Jim Crow legislation. When deprived of the vote William Lattimore protested that that was not right because all men were God's children;[15] Frank Green felt, "We ain't nothin' now, we can't vote."[16] Ivory Osborne also said that he could not vote, because "I ain't nobody;"[17] Dave Weathersby quit voting, he said, "as some folks didn't lak it;"[18] John Peterson stayed away because whites went to the polls with guns to "keep de colored folks from votin'."[19] Jerry Cook passed over practical disfranchisement when he said "dat any cullud man aroun' here, who knows de Constitution of de law, has paid his taxes, an' ain' no law violator" could vote in the general elections. (Selection of candidates in primary elections was reserved for white voters-the white primary).[20]

As Reconstruction came to an end in Louisiana, blacks of that state, according to the editor of the New Orleans *Louisianian*, November 17, 1877, were forced into accepting racial separation while maintaining hope for a good life in a future South: "We have our churches and schools, benevolent and co-operative societies, ministers, teachers, doctors, lawyers, planters, merchants and newspapers."... "The establishment of our full equality is sure to come." Some disenchanted blacks departed from white society to form their own towns, such as Mound Bayou, Mississippi. Others gave up on the South and began an exodus to the North and West that continued for a hundred years. The "Exodus" of many thousands to Kansas, led by Benjamin Singleton, Columbus Johnson, and others, and greatly stimulated by Henry Adams, was a remarkable effort to escape political, economic, and social tyranny.[21]

In an "Address of the Colored People of Alabama in Convention Assembled, to the People of the United States," in 1874, blacks stated that to prevent their being reduced to practical slavery the nation had given them the suffrage which they had used to place in office men "friendly to the elevation of our race." But white supremacists had employed all the political and economic power they possessed, and violence against the colored people to make the clauses of the Constitution of Alabama that guarantee equal rights for all citizens "mere words set upon paper, to be scoffed at." The convention, therefore, announced the formation of an "Emigration Association" to promote the emigration of Alabama blacks to the West where they could "have an equal chance in the struggle for life and fortune."[22]

White supremacists founded the Ku Klux Klan and related Knights of the White Camilia, Red Shirts, and assorted "Councils" to subordinate freedmen. Although the federal government in 1871 jailed some Klansmen under the Ku Klux Klan Acts, the spirit of the Klan triumphed with the victory of white men's governments during the 1870s.

The Klan and the slave patrol were essentially the same, "old Pharoah [sic] exactly," believed James Reeves.[23] Isaac Stier said that the Klan would not bother those who "behaved" but "sho' disastered dem what meddled wid de white folks."[24] The Klan was formed, said Robert Weathersby, "to make de colored folks do what dey wanted 'em to do."[25] Like the slave patrol, the Klan would drive blacks in if they were out after a certain time and whip those who "done anything dey didn't lak."[26] The Klan's purpose, whether masquerading as ghosts or whipping a freedman, "was getting submission over the country," declared Happy Day Green.[27] John Crawford said the Ku Klux around Manor, Texas, was "always chasing some wild nigger and beatin' him up," but left Crawford's people alone "'cause we stays on de farm and works and don't have no truck with dem wild niggers."[28] Eli Davison, also a Texan, said he "never done no votin', 'cause them Klu Kluxers was allus at the votin' places."[29] After the Klan as an organization had all but vanished, many officers of the law carried on their work in their day-to-day enforcement of white supremacy. Richard Jackson heard a white man making a speech on the square in Marshall, Texas, declare that "he was gwine tell us darkies why they didn't low us to vote," but the "law come out and made him git out the wagon and leave."[30] In South Carolina Ku Kluxers whipped black and white political activists; and before long, Lucy Withers said, had "run the Yankees plumb out of the country."[31] Cal Woods remembered that after the war in South Carolina some folks came and said that blacks were free and equal but then the Ku Klux came whipping, shooting, and hanging, declaring that "they was not goiner have equalization if they have to kill all the Yankees and niggers in the country."[32] In neighboring North Carolina the Ku Kluxers similarly terrorized the freedmen in order to establish a new tyranny to replace the fallen tyranny of slavery.[33]

Ku Kluxers usually operated in their own neighborhoods where they were known by local blacks. A Ku Kluxer who came dressed in his robes to warn Anderson Furr's family to act right if they wished to do well was, Furr's family well knew, the old master under his robes putting on a strange voice.[34] Others knew the "ghosts" as white men "wid dem garments on 'em" hunting blacks who had "deserted" them

and taken up with the Yankees.[35] Talitha Lewis who worked for a Ku Kluxer found "them rubber pants what they filled with water" when pretending to drink enormous quantities of water to quench a thirst unslaked since their death at the Battle of Shiloh.[36] Dora Franks overheard a gathering of white neighbors planning a raid as Ku Kluxers.[37] Blacks recognized well-disguised Klansmen by their mounts. Lorenza Ezell knew all the Ku Klux in the neighborhood: "Spite dey sheets and things, I knowed dey voices and dey saddle hosses."[38] James Lucas knew the local Ku Kluxers but dared not tell; they were known to take their enemies right out of the fields and kill them.[39]

A few ex-slaves betrayed their people to the Klan. Fount Howard, according to Wesley Graves, helped the Ku Klux catch people he disliked. Prince Johnson rode with the Ku Klux, and prospered. Ned Chaney knew black men who snooped around for Klansmen who cut his uncle's throat.[40] Will Adams defended the Klan because, he said, "Carpetbaggers come round larnin' niggers to sass the white folks what done fed them."[41]

To coerce whites to join the white supremacists or leave the country and to drive freedmen into a lower cast, Ku Kluxers resorted to all manner of intimidation, violence, and terror. Charlie Moses saw Klansmen parading down the streets of Brookhaven, Mississippi, on their way to tar and feather a black man.[42] "Cat" Ross witnessed Ku Kluxers demonstrate their power in Arkansas by parading two abreast in a column a quarter of a mile long. A smaller gang ran down Ross's uncle, a great dancer, and lorded it over him by making him dance the pigeon wing.[43] Ku Kluxers near Village Creek, Texas, came to a dance and picked out a black man and whipped him, "jus' to keep de niggers scart," remembered William Hamilton.[44] If an ex-slave got a farm and prospered, Pierce

Harper said, the Ku Klux would get after him, and if freedmen got a school house, they were liable to burn it down.[45] In January, 1870, a band of about 30 disguised men took two blacks accused of stealing horses from a jail in Lebanon, Tennessee, and hanged them.[46] In February, 1870, a gang of hooded men fired into a black man's cabin when he refused to come out, wounding him and killing his wife. Then they burned down his cabin. Children forced to stay in the burning cabin were rescued when the Klansmen rode away.[47]

Ku Kluxers did not stop with intimidation, or even beatings, but sometimes resorted to murder. They killed her father, said Sarah Whitmore.[48] They killed Agatha Babino's uncle near Carencro, Louisiana, because he opposed the Democrats. "Dey tie him by de feet. Dey drag him through de bresh."[49] They hung a Yankee near Livingston, Alabama, for telling freedmen they ought to get 40 acres and a mule.[50] In North Carolina Klansmen, said Ben Johnson, hung a black man for insulting a white woman and threatened to hang anyone who took the body down. The sheriff, after four days, took it down.[51] Ku Kluxers dragged two blacks from a jail in Manchester, Tennessee, and hung them on a chestnut tree.[52] Ida Blackshear Hutchison said the Klan ran her brother out of Alabama over politics, and in 1874 killed Tom Ivory, a leader of Republicans, and cut out his tongue, as an example to the rest of the blacks.[53] Earlier, but not for long, the federal government put a stop to the Klan's violence in Alabama, and elsewhere.[54]

If a few blacks spied for the Klan, others actively resisted the Klan. Freedmen tied grapevines across country roads to unhorse Klansmen as they had unhorsed the patrol in former times.[55] When ordered out of his North Carolina neighborhood, Sam Allen killed two of the Klansmen with his knife, it was said, before leaving.[56] The Klan did not dare to whip certain strong

and courageous men, unless they had swept the black communities clear of weapons.[57] Polly Turner Cancer said that after the Civil War blacks bought guns with their wages "to hunt rabbits and sich but de Ku Klux didn't want dem to have guns," and seized their guns.[58]

Near Enfield, North Carolina, a group of blacks laid plans to ambush Ku Kluxers who had whipped some of them. The Ku Kluxers learned of their plan and stayed away.[59] At Jefferson, Texas, according to report, Dick Walker organized a black militia to keep the Klan off the blacks. One night after Union soldiers had departed Klansmen attacked the militiamen, who were meeting at a church, and killed several and wounded others.[60] Near Meridian, Mississippi, Ku Kluxers took black political leader Miles Hampton from a party and murdered him. The next day black men went in a drove to Meridian to buy guns and ammunition and to ask whites for help. The Ku Klux waited a while, then struck again, killing and dispersing the blacks and their white allies. Black Charles Caldwell, Mississippi state senator and commander of black militiaman, was assassinated in Clinton, in December, 1875.[61]

Where the Klan became intolerable many blacks departed in search of greater freedom and security. Casper Rumple left South Carolina with a group to escape the Klan, which had killed several blacks and "scared them all up." Klansmen became so bold after federal troops were withdrawn that they sometimes struck in broad daylight, undisguised.[62] Following a bloody riot in Barnwell County, South Carolina, Louise Pettis's family emigrated with a trainload of refugees to Biscoe, Arkansas. Dr. D. B. Gaines's people also joined an exodus from South Carolina to Arkansas, because of a reign of terror by the Ku Klux and Red Shirts.[63] In the late 1870s large numbers of blacks migrated to Kansas, as we have seen, to escape the Klan spirit of the South. Individuals and families often went away without waiting for a general exodus. John Beckwith ran off to Raleigh when the Klan got after him for fighting with a white boy.[64] When the Klan got bad around Morgan City, Louisiana, John Ogee headed for Texas. When the Klan made life miserable in a rural area in North Texas, Scott Hooper's family moved to Fort Worth.[65] The Ku Klux spirit of violence cost Texan Rufus Jackson his life because he accidentally stepped on a white man's foot.[66] But when Benjamin Kennedy, an engineer on the *Mary Alice*, below Memphis, cursed Alexander Henderson, a black fireman, Henderson threw Kennedy overboard, and Kennedy drowned.[67]

11

Education and Religion

As freedmen needed political power to protect their interests in government, they needed public assistance to break out of the ignorance of slavery. As a matter of policy, slaves had been denied educational opportunity, but advancing armies of the North gave what the South withheld. Some runaway slaves joined these armies and learned to read and write as they fought the men who had kept them in darkness. Black troops paid tuition for instruction from missionary tutors or attended schools of various sorts staffed by benevolent white soldiers, usually chaplains. Although Charles Francis Adams, Jr., of the Fifth Massachusetts Cavalry, organized an excellent educational program, the schooling furnished black troops as a whole was haphazard. The armies did, however, aid and protect civilian teachers who opened schools for black children along the tracks of invasion.[1]

After the war the Freedmen's Bureau built on the educational foundations laid by the Treasury Department and the War Department in the Sea Islands of South Carolina, and on the work of the military in the Lower Mississippi Valley, such as that of Grant and Eaton and that of General N. P. Banks in Louisiana, who created a board of education, levied taxes for educational purposes, and, by 1865, had brought into existence many schools for freedmen.[2]

Despite demonstrations of benefits that might be expected from a thorough program for the social and economic uplift of the freedmen, the federal government decided to open the gates of opportunity to freedmen principally through education. Thus the Freedmen's Bureau devoted a substantial part of its energy and resources to the establishment of an educational system for its charges. Unfortunately, if the bureau had concentrated its whole effort in one state its educational program would have been inadequate to meet the needs of the black children in that state alone. Officials of the bureau, therefore, chose to initiate educational systems, which they would leave to the Southern states to perfect.[3]

The Freedmen's Bureau received cooperation from numerous religious and philanthropic groups in the North, among which the American Missionary Association, the Home Mission Society, and the Freedmen's Aid Society were especially active. These associations sent food and clothing, seeds and tools, to black refugees, but, like the bureau itself, channeled their energy above all into schools. They supplied teachers; the Freedmen's Bureau protected these teachers, provided them with transportation, and erected many of the buildings in which they kept school. In towns and cities the bureau and the missionaries opened a fair number of schools;

in many rural counties they were unable to organize any schools at all. Yet compared with what had gone before, their work was admirable.[4] The Yankee teachers were mainly young women "of intelligence, of education, and of the most unblemished character," according to a congressional committee on the Memphis riot of 1866, who answered the call of duty to help elevate an oppressed people "in the face of scorn and obloquy," and at the peril of their lives.[5]

Mary Anngady's school in Chapel Hill, North Carolina, and Mandy Tucker's in Pine Bluff, Arkansas, like most Freedmen's Bureau schools, were staffed by the Yankee volunteers, and a sprinkling of blacks, such as Mary Lathrop, of Philadelphia, who taught in a school in the Second Baptist Church, Chapel Hill, North Carolina. Elias Hill was the only black teacher in his part of South Carolina of whom Erwin Smith knew.[6]

Elijah Hopkins, Charlie Mitchell, and Hannah Austin all began their education after the war under white teachers from the North, most of whom were women. Joseph Leonidas Star attended a Yankee-run school in the First Presbyterian Church in Knoxville, Tennessee, that dispensed clothing as well as learning, and Charlie Hunter sat at the feet of Northern teachers at the African Methodist Episcopal Church in Raleigh, North Carolina. Betty Cofer learned her lessons in a log school in North Carolina, from Moravians, and Quakers taught Charlotte Stephens in Little Rock, Arkansas. Jasper Battle's white teacher in a church in Georgia, strict and good, did not allow "fussin' and fightin' and foolin' 'round," in school or coming and going, a rule he enforced with a hickory switch. Jesuits and Religious of the Sacred Heart in their schools around Grand Coteau, Louisiana, besides imparting secular knowledge made their charges models to their black and white

neighbors in religious knowledge and fidelity. Blacks and whites of the area worshipped in the same church until 1932, when the black parish, St. Peter Claver, was established. Colored Sisters of the Holy Family conducted a school for blacks at Bellevue, Louisiana.[7]

Virginia Varris's first teachers were white, because, she said, "the colored didn't know nothing to teach." But Elisha Doc Garey's teacher on a Georgia plantation was an "Injun" who carried his flute everywhere. Ella Johnson experienced black teachers succeeding white teachers in her Little Rock, Arkansas, school, and J. M. Parker observed similar evolution in his South Carolina school when his white teacher was followed by a black clergyman, then by a black woman.[8] Northern white teachers returned home when their task of initiating education of ex-slaves was completed, or when driven away by Ku Kluxers.

In these early days when education promised to open all avenues to advancement, many blacks had a hunger for knowledge and a dedication to study. Wherever schools were opened the old and young flocked to them. When Celia Winchester, a black graduate of Oberlin College, arrived in the St. Francis River bottoms of Arkansas, the freedmen of the vicinity welcomed her with enthusiasm. Children attended her school in the daytime; the old gathered at night after the field work was done. Here and there people huddled in groups around the flickering light of pine-knot torches and little lamps to study their lessons. In warm weather groups came together outdoors to sing the A B Cs. The older folks practiced their lessons in the kitchens and the fields. In many places men and women joined the children in school after the crops were laid by. In some areas children attended school only after their day's work in the fields was done.[9]

Although enlightened whites favored the education of freedmen, many white people of the South were, during the early days of Reconstruction, unrelenting in their opposition to education for former slaves, especially education dominated by Northerners. Out of this group sprang mobs which stoned and whipped teachers and burned down "Nigger schools." Even churches which sheltered small bands of pupils were sometimes destroyed. In some rural communities black men quietly resolved to replace, after the expected Ku Klux attack, the school houses they were then raising. In other communities they banded together to defend their schools, as in Shelbyville, Tennessee, where, in January, 1869, they killed four of the Ku Kluxers who raided their school. Afterwards, these blacks posted warnings that if the school were burned or the teacher killed prominent whites would pay a fearful penalty.[10]

Southern whites harrassed Yankee teachers in varying degrees, from ostracising them to "busting up" their schools. The Ku Klux drove Yankee teachers from a school near Mexia, Texas, and shut down their school, and a gang of men drove a teacher from his school on Williamson Creek, south of Austin.[11] Betty Krump's Northern teachers left Helena, Arkansas, because "folks didn't do 'em right. They set 'em off to theirselves. Wouldn't keep 'em, wouldn't walk 'bout wid 'em. They wouldn't talk to 'em. The Yankees sont 'em down here to egercate us up wid ... white folks."[12]

In numerous ways black people promoted their own education. As early as 1867 about one-half of the teachers in Freedmen's Bureau schools were black. Parents paid tuition of .50 cents to $1.25 per month for their children; those who had no cash furnished chickens, eggs, and vegetables. Through their religious organizations freedmen encouraged education.

In 1867 the Centenary Methodist Church in Memphis, for example, conducted school for about 120 pupils. The Lincoln Chapel, also in Memphis, offered instruction on Sunday afternoons to 301 pupils, including a group of illiterate adults. Both of these churches conducted weekday schools.[13]

Black people in rural districts, where most blacks lived, faced more severe handicaps than did their brethren in the cities. In some areas planters forced 12-year-olds to drop out of school to work in the fields, and parents often could not support their families without their children's labor. Schools usually were distant. Then missionary teachers often departed before black replacements could be trained. Inevitably there was the lack of funds. Still, rural blacks established schools, even though sessions would last only a few months.

Charlie Hinton, Bill Crump, A. C. Pruitt, and Ike Worthy, like thousands of school-age freedmen, went to school for a few days to a few weeks. Louis Davis's mother bought him a school book but was unable to send him to school. Similarly, Annie Hill's parents could not afford tuition. Alice Wise was "apt about washin' and ironin' and sewin'," and her family needed her income. Scott Martin had to leave school after two sessions to go to work, and Cresa Mack dropped out after one month to help support his widowed mother. Enterprising Viney Foster learned to read from a boy who did go to school, became an omnivorous reader of literary, historical, and religious works, and sent his children to Fisk and Howard.[14] Some children were able to stay in school long enough to get at least a start in knowledge. Ben Hite learned to read a little but not write much. Willie Wallace and Hardy Miller learned the rudiments of reading, writing, and figuring. Jeptha Choice got "through fractions," and Ivory Osborne completed the eighth grade. Charley Hayes was home-schooled by his grandmother who had been taught by her mistress. John Jones got a start in his seven days at school, so that by "ketch as ketch can" he went on to read and write.[15] Charlie Barbour regretted his scant education and wished that he had learned at least to write a letter. Ike Worthy consoled himself that, unlike some others he knew, he had, though remaining illiterate, kept out of the penitentiary. Emma Grisham got little schooling because, she said, her daddy "thought ef 'n you knowed yo a,b,c's en could read a line, dat wuz 'nuff."[16]

A goodly number of local blacks with little or no college experience became teachers in the postwar South. One of them, Belle Carruthers, taught in the Holly Springs, Mississippi, schools. She also taught Sunday school in a local Methodist church and contributed to the Negro section of the county newspaper, *The South-Reporter*. James Turner McLean went to a plantation school under black Isaac Brantley, whose method, complained McLean, was to read aloud while the children repeated after him. Harre Quarls, who said that he was the only black adult who could read at the end of the war in two settlements in Madison and Leon Counties, Texas, was taught by his mistress and passed on his skills to black children in the local school. Zek Brown's mother, also taught by her mistress, began her teaching career when freedom came. Peter Robinson conducted school, served as a school trustee, and helped organize the Colored Cumberland Presbyterian Church in Meridian, Texas. Esther King Casey paid fees of .50 cents a month for school, and, at 18, herself became a teacher. Nettie Van Buren, sent by her father to a boarding school in Cotton Plant, Arkansas, then to Jacksonville, Illinois, returned to teach in Clarendon, Arkansas.[17] Teachers during First Freedom often came cheap, as John

Peterson remembered: "Dere was a colored fellow had a little learnin' and we hired him two nights a week for three dollars a month."[18]

Many of the teachers during the early years were remarkable people. Taylor Z. Thistle, for example, found dense ignorance and poverty all around Cedar Hill, Tennessee, in 1872–73. His 19 pupils each paid tuition of a dollar per month, which brought him, after room and board, $9 in monthly salary. Yet Thistle struggled to educate both himself and his pupils and to enrich the life of the community.[19] Later, W. E. B. Du Bois, like other Fisk University students, offered instruction to rural black children during summer vacation. Frequently, able men taught school to finance their own training for the professions, and subsequently provided indispensable support for the education of blacks, especially for their higher education. As the collapse of Reconstruction blocked opportunity in other directions, schools attracted a high proportion of the most intelligent blacks. For black women, teaching was practically the only avenue of advancement.[20]

Black teachers hoped to initiate the elevation of the black community by enlightening the young. The subsequent growing virtue of the black community, would, their leaders believed, command the respect of the whites and bring an end to oppression. To prepare teachers, and to provide a comprehensive system of education, black leaders joined with their white friends to establish colleges in every one of the Southern states. Fisk University, to cite an example, was founded in 1866 by the American Missionary Association in cooperation with the Western Freedmen's Aid Commission, with the assistance of General Clinton B. Fisk of the Freedmen's Bureau and the black people of Nashville. The Peabody Fund supported selected students in the teacher training department.

A small percentage of students found opportunity at institutions of higher education for blacks founded during Reconstruction by religious and legislative bodies. *Harper's*, Vol. XLIX, No. CCXCII (September 1874), 460.

During Reconstruction and for long afterwards, a high percent of the graduates of Fisk and other black colleges and universities became teachers or clergymen.[21]

Thomas Rutling, Benjamin Holmes, and Emma Grisham were among a regiment of teachers trained at Fisk University. Wiley and Bishop Colleges prepared A. M. Moore for teaching in Louisiana and preaching in East Texas. Henry Butler, a veteran of the Union Army, attended grade school in Pine Bluff, Arkansas, studied at Washburn College, Topeka, Kansas, and taught school in Fort Worth, Texas. After graduating from Hampton University in 1874, Mary Jane Wilson established her own school. James C. James graduated from Howard in 1873 and began a teaching career in Virginia, North Carolina, and Maryland; and J. B. Combs studied at Straight University and Holly Springs Normal School and taught in Tennessee and Mississippi and served as principal at St. John's School, Tippah County, Mississippi.[22]

Black colleges also focused on service to their communities. They encouraged clergymen to continue their studies and found Sunday schools. Their students preached in the streets and provided social services for the destitute. Students themselves, like the Jubilee Singers of Fisk, actively sustained their institutions. At opening ceremonies in 1866 a black barber pronounced the foundation of Fisk to be part of a movement that was destined to sweep over the South and bring enlightenment to a people kept under a cloud of ignorance for 200 years. But at this ceremony Governor W. G. Brownlow advised the teachers to be prudent, lest they offend the dominant party which, he said, would close the school within a week of the withdrawal of federal troops.[23] Existing in this hostile environment, black colleges abandoned hope for immediate improvement in race relations in favor of long range programs of uplift, the sort of idea Booker T. Washington later made famous. The ardor of these colleges and that of the teachers they sent among the black people was somewhat dampened by omnipresent discrimination, and so the results they obtained fell short of their aspirations.

Before the sanguine expectations of rapid progress through education had weakened, schools became exciting social as well as academic centers for blacks. Their public exercises attracted crowds who responded to the recitations of the youth as demonstrations of the capacity of the black race. At closing ceremonies, adults joined in the parades and picnics. In some cities black children from all the schools, accompanied by parents, supported by a galaxy of benevolent societies, and led by a brass band, would parade down the principal streets. The throng would perhaps gather at the railroad station for an excursion to the picnic grounds.[24] At a public examination of students in Aberdeen, Mississippi, the black community swelled with pride at the progress of children who worked two days a week to earn tuition for the other three days, and who, despite this handicap, proved false their former masters, who had told them a thousand times that they could not benefit from education.[25]

The spirit which stirred these people was expressed by Frederick Douglass at the opening exercises of the Douglass Institute in Baltimore on October 1, 1865. Douglass declared that a people who had been pronounced fit only for the coarse labor of society dared to establish institutions devoted to the higher aspirations of the human soul. Because of the contempt of a portion of the people for the black race and because of their determination to hold black people in a degraded position, it was unfortunately necessary, Douglass said, for blacks to join together, for the present, to develop themselves in separate institutions.

Their achievement, he believed, would in time bring the public consideration they deserved.[26]

Immediately after the Civil War, blacks all over the South launched a movement to secure free schools. At first they petitioned for, then, after obtaining the suffrage, demanded, the creation of public schools. As a consequence, the Radical Constitutional Conventions, in which black delegates sat, provided for the education of children at the expense of the states. Black delegates successfully opposed motions for segregation of the races in schools, but state legislatures inevitably provided, under loosely drawn constitutional prohibitions against discrimination, separate schools. Louisiana alone prohibited, for a time and with some success, racial segregation in public schools.[27]

Segregation made possible discrimination in the allocation of funds which later became a general policy of white-dominated governments. But the immediate consequence of the school laws was a rapid increase in both black and white schools. As the Radical governments collapsed, white students gained at the expense of blacks, although both suffered from the niggardly policy of white supremacists. In portions of Tennessee in 1867–68 the black scholastic population could not be counted for purposes of state aid, because of threats against the lives of those who dared to take a census of black children. In a number of counties superintendents were selected because it was understood by their advocates that they would unfairly execute the law. In other counties superintendents were deprived of funds necessary to organize schools for blacks. Added to these difficulties was the diversion of school funds to pay interest on railroad bonds. In consequence, during the 1867–68 year, school districts received from the state of Tennessee only 48 cents for each enumerated child of

school age. During this year eight counties did not establish any schools, despite constant prodding from the distinguished State Superintendent of Instruction, General John Eaton. In 1869 only 300 of 27,000 black youth of several counties of West Tennessee were in school. In North Carolina thousands of black children gained admission to public schools, while other thousands never had a chance to go to school a single day. Conditions were approximately the same in each of the ex-Confederate states. Despite difficulties in translating the idealism of the Radical constitutions into practice, the black people of the South played a significant role in the establishment and extension of the public schools.[28]

At the end of Reconstruction the potentialities of black schools were not fully realized. Stagnation alternated with progress; growth in one place contrasted with inertia in another. Too much depended on the impoverished black masses. White administrators often manipulated resources to give educational advantages to white over black children. The triumph of white supremacy in education, as in every area of life, retarded the advance of blacks from slavery to freedom. Nevertheless, white supremacists were unwilling to discriminate against black school children to the same degree that they discriminated against their parents. Thus public schools, however inadequate, continued to elevate the mind of the black South and thereby helped prepare for a later, more powerful assault on caste than Reconstruction itself had been.

After emancipation blacks withdrew from interracial but internally segregated churches to form Baptist, Methodist, Pentecostal, and other Protestant denominations under their own governance. Separate black parishes often were organized in the Catholic Church, often under the direction of the Josephites. Jesuits had strong centers of mission among blacks at Grand Coteau, Louisiana, and Mobile, Alabama.[29]

Some blacks preferred integrated churches with equal rights, but the whites did not accept them as equal. For this and other reasons the trend toward separation was strong, and these blacks were eventually pulled into racially separated churches. For example, in 1863 Quakers established a relief, educational, and religious program near Helena, Arkansas. After the war a regiment of black soldiers bought land, erected a building on it, and gave the whole to the Quakers, which became in 1872 Southland College. Meanwhile, in 1866 a Quaker meeting was organized, with most of its members black. By 1879 all but four of 142 members were black. However, most of those classified as Quakers were students in the college who, when they moved away, joined black churches, especially black Baptist or Methodist churches.[30]

Most churches under control of whites encouraged blacks to secede and go into black churches by continuing the segregation of slave times. Although the Mississippi Mission Conference of the Methodist Episcopal Church resolved, December 19, 1867, that "we are, and will remain, unalterably opposed to all distinctions made in the House of God on account of race or color," in March, 1874, the Ames Church of this conference denied blacks admission to the main floor and sent them to the gallery, as did other congregations around the South.[31] Blacks would not freely accept segregation by whites; it had to be imposed upon them by later Jim Crow legislation. Before Jim Crow they did choose self-segregation in their churches rather than accept badges of inferiority.

Black churches and parishes became centers of solidarity, education, and social service as well as focuses of spiritual life. They promoted clubs and associations; provided a forum for lectures, debates, and political activity; and held festivals. They gave people experience in managing organizations and sustaining cooperative effort. They marshaled resources for costly programs including helping the sick and indigent.[32]

In their haste to form their own churches and congregations blacks often organized brush-arbor churches or met in members' homes until they could obtain the means to erect more substantial structures. Anderson Furr, among others, helped replace a brush-arbor meeting-place with a "sho' 'nough church house." Jane Hunter baked the first sacrament bread for the Colored Methodist Episcopal Church, organized in Little Rock in 1870. Cora Horton served as president of the Women's Missionary Society of several Arkansas conferences of the Colored Methodist Episcopal Church. Hannah Plummer's Colored Methodist Church had a white pastor for some years after freedom. After withdrawing from white controlled churches some blacks never joined another church. Among them Joe Rollins ruefully admitted, "I ought I knows."[33]

Black clergymen were intellectual and social leaders. Some were men of force and originality, self-made, imaginative, eloquent. Most elevated their communities. The Reverend L. Hawkins of the Centenary Methodist Episcopal Colored Church of Memphis, for example, designed and built his church (performing much of the labor himself), directed religious life, and superintended the church's free school.[34]

Inheritors of the disabilities of slavery, many of the black clergy had little or no formal training. They depended on native wit and eloquence, industrious reading of the Bible, and presentation of the Gospel to the hearts of their unlearned congregations. Thus did Bell Williams's father, who, it was claimed, had read the Scriptures 77 times by his death at that age, preach in Methodist churches in and around Murfreesboro, Tennessee. William Weatherall was taught to read by his wife before he could achieve much as a preacher. His son William Carrol combined preaching and manual labor. Carey Davenport, a Methodist clergyman, got most of his education from a German college "principal."[35] One of this band of unlearned but hard working and conscientious clergy, Robert Laird, stated, "I'se jes' gone 'round whar de folks need to hear de Gospel an' preached it to 'em de bes' I could."[36]

Many clergymen combined preaching with other occupations. William H. McCarthy served both as teacher and preacher in and around New Orleans; Robert Wilson earned his living as a cook, in order to practice his profession as

The clergy provided spiritual, educational, and social leaership for their people. *Harper's*, Vol. XLIX, No. CCXCII (September 1874), 463).

clergyman; Moses Mitchell laid down asphalt, repaired shoes, carpentered, farmed, and served as a Methodist clergyman; Dempsey Pitts supported himself by farming, and preached at the first Colored Methodist Church, Coffeyville, Mississippi; Manus Robinson blazed trees for turpentine, and preached on the side; Needham Love cut wood and hauled it to market with his own team of mules, and served as clergyman also. Frank Childress, on the other hand, was able to pursue formal studies for the Methodist ministry and preach in Tennessee, Mississippi, and Arkansas.[37]

Powerful preaching and a responsive congregation had a potent effect on July Ann Halfen, who had never been a church member until she was moved to join Shiloh Baptist Church. "I don't kno' why I jined," July said. "De man wus preachin' an' some uf de folks wus clappin' deir hands an' some uf dem wus pattin deir feet an' some uf dem wus shoutin' an' all to once I felt de spirit move an' den I went to shoutin' like de rest uf de folks, an' I went down in front an' got down on my knees an' I prayed hard an' de spirit seem to say to me dat I wus a chile uf God." The next Sunday July was baptized at Osyka, Mississippi, in the Tangipaho River.[38] Malinda Edwards, however, unnerved by signs and portents, hastened to join the church and became a "great shouter."[39] Not everyone was admitted into the fold. If the congregation did not judge a person "ready to be tuk in de church," according to Benny Dillard, "dey was told to wait and pray 'til dey had done seed de light."[40]

Baptisms, especially in Baptist churches, sometimes brought out large assemblies, churchgoers and spectators. In the years after the war black Baptist churches of Nashville coordinated their baptizing in the Cumberland River on the first Sunday in May. Thousands of people, black and white, would line the banks of the river to witness the joyful administration and reception of the Sacrament. Congregations would process from their churches "singin' en shoutin' en keep dat up 'til dey got ter de river." Some of the worshippers and newly baptized would fall to the ground in ecstacy.[41]

Being a member of a church was expected to have a marked effect on behavior. Talitha Island thought that church goers should stay away from parties, which she supposed were always wild.[42] Gabe Emanuel declared "De Lord God Almighty takes good care o' his children, if dey be's good an' holy."[43] Lucindy Shaw was, she said, a devil until she got religion, then she "wuz tellin' a different tale."[44] Smith Simmons allowed that people outside the church were apt to be no 'count while church people were mostly good people.[45] Mary Weldon Jones, of St. Michael's Church, Ridge, Maryland, said that dancing and Holy Communion kept her bright and cheerful. Her guiding principle was "the darker the night, the brighter you'se got to shine."[46]

Many of the ex-slaves expressed a humble relationship with Jesus Christ. Old, blind, impoverished Clara Jones said, "De Lord helps me, I am depending on him."[47] Many another ex-slave lived out his life confident of the friendship of "sweet Jesus." Adeline Marshall declared, "Jes' look at me! I's old with mis'ry and 'lone in de world. My husband and chillen done die long ago and leave me here, and I jes' go from house to house, tryin' to find a place to stay. Dat why I prays Gawd to take me to his bosom, cause He de onlies' one I got to call on."[48]

"I got a religion that will do to die with," said Caroline Watson, "I done give up everything."[49]

Robert Falls said that the Lord never failed him; when in need he stood, raised his arms, and prayed, "Lord, help me!"[50] Peace did not come without a struggle to

Charlie Moses who declared, "I knows it ain't right to hev' hate in de heart, but God Almighty, it's hard to be forgivin'."[51]

Poor, sick, aged, isolated ex-slaves sometimes looked back on better days, even as slaves. Dilcie Raborn said, "Seed more hardness since I got old than ever I did in mah life."[52] Elodga Bradford declared, "Us old uns knows dat slavery times wa'nt so bad."[53] Clara Davis, old and poor, her children scattered and giving her no help, saw her youth as a better time, but, she said, "Dey tuk me away f'om dat a long time ago."[54]

Rather than looking back to a happier youth, many of the aged ex-slaves looked forward to a day of glory. Fanny Hodges, who could hardly get about, sustained herself with a pension of four dollars a month, wages from doing a little washing, and by begging. She did not know whether her children were alive, or whether she had any grandchildren. Despite bad times she carried on as a member of Flowery Mount Baptist Church, McComb, Mississippi, while waiting for Jesus to come for her.[55] Sonia Rassberry, who had cooked, washed, and ironed for a living, and had been blind for years, thanked the Lord for life and sang out, "Glory to Jesus."[56] Laura Montgomery, who was blind and unable to work, and who lived with a daughter, said, "I sho wants to go to Heaven when I die. I is tryin' to make my las' days my bes' days. I can't stay here much longer. I is seen some good days an' some bad ones. Praise de Lord, I is one of his chilluns."[57] Manda Edmondson, getting "powerful ole," was still able to "sing and shout" praise to God.[58] Phyllis Fox, dependent on her children, said, "Been here 'bout long 'nuff an' when my Jesus do say *Come!* I's ready."[59]

12

Sharecroppers, Laborers,
and Businessmen

Of great immediate importance was the freedmen's need for economic opportunities in place of the forced labor of slavery. As slaves, they had been paid with little more than coarse clothing, corn meal, bacon, molasses, and crude shelter. As freedmen, they expected a fair return for their labor. Most of all, they wanted the economic independence of 40 acres and a mule. Then they could escape the vestiges of slavery and enjoy the fruits of their labors. Some few white Radicals advocated confiscation of the slaveowners' lands for distribution among former slaves, and, for a moment, the federal government toyed with the idea, and, here and there, located freedmen on abandoned lands in an abortive attempt to provide them with an economic foundation for citizenship. But the idea of confiscation was dropped, so the federal government ejected most freedmen from lands it had settled them on, employing military force where necessary, and returned to pardoned Confederates plantations they had abandoned to invading Union armies. Farms might also have been provided as homesteads from federal land in the South and West, except that millions of impoverished freedmen would have needed a substantial subsidy to get established on their own lands, while the economy of the South would have been dislocated by the withdrawal of black laborers from the plantations. For these reasons, except for some few blacks settled on homesteads in such states as Mississippi and Arkansas, the federal government adopted the policy of requiring blacks to make contracts as hired hands or sharecroppers, and to wait for evolutionary integration into Southern society. If the federal government had guaranteed sustained protection for freedmen, this policy might have worked reasonably well.

The Freedmen's Bureau helped, and in some instances forced, blacks to contract their labor to white landowners, and required both parties to keep their contracts. Bureau officers, from General O. O. Howard down, also exhorted freedmen to labor faithfully, form stable families, educate their children, and accumulate savings with which to buy farms. Howard saw that freedmen were looking for economic opportunity, while planters were looking for labor. His solution was to advocate equality before the law, urge blacks to work for white landowners, and trust to time and education to overcome prejudice and ignorance.[1]

By autumn of 1865, after the first season of labor after Appomattox, freedmen were desperate. They had worked from the war's end through spring and summer for wages or a share of the crop that could not support them. Venus, for example, worked on a plantation in South Carolina for one-tenth of the crop she made, and, when it was brought in, had, after rations and housing, one quart of molasses and a bushel of corn. Freedmen on the Williamson plantation in Fayette County, Tennessee, received one-sixth of the crop. Even the one-half share, which later became standard, was little compensation for farm families, especially when they purchased supplies on credit, at high interest, and at marked-up prices, in the plantation store.[2]

More than ten thousand freedmen in one month went out to the plantations in the vicinity of Memphis. They rebuilt fences, erected houses in the places of those destroyed by war, and cultivated the fields until they blossomed white with cotton.[3] In other places freedmen at first worked hard, and then came drought, followed by hard rains and rapid growth of weeds. Faced with low yields, many freedmen lost heart and worked listlessly. Planters, also in hard straits, were tempted to cheat freedmen out of what little share was theirs. A great cause of discontent was the employers promising to pay wages at the end of each month, or at the end of three months, only to put off payday until the end of the year.[4]

Crops grown on shares turned out better than on farms where wage work prevailed, because "croppers" enjoyed more liberty in their work and were spurred by the incentive to increase earnings by increasing yields. Planters too preferred a stable work force during the crop year. Besides, they had little cash to pay wages before the crop was made and were themselves dependent on Northern economic institutions. As a consequence, sharecropping generally replaced wage work. But blacks, and poor whites too, who advanced from sharecropping to farm ownership

were rare. Most of them were barely able to square accounts in December before going into debt again at the plantation store in February. An exception, Scott Bond, of St. Francis County, Arkansas, because of his unflagging energy and sleepless calculation, became a rich planter and businessman, the "Black Rockefeller of the South."[5]

When the crop was sold the "cropper" would pay for the food and clothing advanced while the crop was making, from his share of the proceeds. If he worked hard, the weather cooperated, and the price of cotton stayed high, he could pay off his debt and accumulate savings to rent or buy a farm of his own. Unfortunately, most sharecroppers were stuck in debt year after year, condemned to cultivate someone else's land.

The sharecropper's part of the crop varied. If he could furnish a team of mules and a few farm implements, which he rarely could, he received a larger portion than if he furnished labor only. A renter could pay in cash or a smaller part of his crop than the sharecropper paid, one-third, perhaps, rather than one-half. Jake Dawkins sharecropped with his family a year after freedom for one-third of the corn and one-fourth of the cotton and cleared about a bale of cotton and two wagonloads of corn, before moving on to another place, hoping to do better. Columbus Williams and his family received one-half of the cotton when the landowner furnished the mules, but kept two-thirds of the corn and three-fourths of the cotton when they finally got their own team.[6]

Ebenezer Brown started working for wages due at the end of the year, but there was next to nothing left after rations advanced by the planter had been paid for. If he left for another place he would, he said, have nothing to take with him, not even "lasses or taters." Later he managed to borrow money to buy a horse and wagon

"Croppers" picked cotton by hand until replaced by mechanical pickers in the 20th century. Julian A.C. Chandler and others, editors, *The History of the Southern States: The South in the Building of a Nation*, 12 vols. (Richmond, VA, 1909), Vol. III, 429.

and a season's supply of food and clothing, then had a good year sharecropping. He made 12 bales of cotton and 400 barrels of corn.[7] Ann Drake, of Pike County, Mississippi, described her people's experience sharecropping: "Money wuz mighty scarce in de country, an' black people could not git credit, an' dey hed nuffin to make er crop wid, an' so dey hed to hire out on shares, an' dey made nuffin, an' whut lil'l dey did make, de white man got it" so they were "kep' movin' frum place to place."[8]

Like Ann Drake's people, Edmond Jones never had any luck sharecropping. On top of everything else the river overflowed and his crop failed. He gave up farming to become a janitor. Tom Robinson, on the other hand, a farmer until old age, started as a sharecropper with nothing but his labor, rose to supplying his food and clothing, then his team and farm implements, and at last became a cash renter entitled to the whole of his crop. As renter he raised corn, potatoes, and truck to feed his family and animals, and cotton for cash.[9]

Henrietta Evelina Smith was convinced that sharecroppers never prospered. If a man made a good crop, she said, the landowner would run him off and take everything.[10] Gabe Butler was equally pessimistic: "Dey wus so deep in debt de white folks tuk all dey made."[11] Jane Lassiter discribed sharecropping as "like dis, a crowd of tenants would get dissatisfied on a certain plantation, dey would move, an' another gang of niggers move in. Dat wus all any of us could do."[12] Jane Arrington's parents moved from place to place all their lives in the vain hope of getting ahead.[13] Willis Cofer's family was more fortunate: "Us started out widout nothin' and had to go in debt to de white folkses at fust but dat wuz soon paid off."[14]

Not all landlords cheated their tenants, said Addy Gill. But Columbus Williams believed he was furnished supplies at exorbitant prices. Food provided on credit was little more than pickled pork, molasses, cornmeal, and flour. When Sarah Williams Wells's family "settled up" they had $12 in cash. Richard McDaniel thought that sharecroppers worked as hard as during slavery and received slaves' compensation, and their right to move about and visit did not "lighten the work none but it lightened the rations right smart."[15]

A small percentage of sharecroppers became farm owners. Gus Bradshaw, formerly a cropper, was able to buy a 50 acre farm in Texas in 1877. More than half a century later he was still on his farm. Mary Ann Patterson owned a farm near Roger's Hill in Travis County, Texas, that her husband had bought.[16] Betty Powers's family advanced in four years from sharecropping to farm ownership when they purchased a wooded place near Marshall, Texas, and improved it. "We uns all pitches in and clears it and builds de cabin," she said. "Was we'uns proud? There twas, our place to do as we pleases, after bein' slaves. Dat sho' am de good feelin'. We works like beavers puttin' de crop in, and my folks stays dere till dey dies." Betty herself left home at age 13 to marry, and slipped back into sharecropping.[17]

Alex Woodward of South Carolina managed to buy a house and some land but still found it hard to make ends meet some years. Bunk Ratliff became a successful farm owner, given a boost by his Union veteran's pension. A few landowners got a start homesteading and then "lived like the white folks." Others, like Louis Johnson, of Pine Bluff, Arkansas, bought on credit, but, unable to survive crop failures, fell back into croppers' ranks.[18]

Day laborers found it hard to get by on their wages, let alone save for a better future. Parker Pool thought of himself as a wage-slave responsible for his own keep. Sam Jones, near Wharton, Texas, was paid $15 a month by his ex-master for three

years, until he found work in a Fort Worth packing plant. Similarly, Annie Young earned 50 cents a day clearing new ground. James Henry Nelson, of Pine Bluff, worked for anyone who would hire him. "Some paid me and some didn't," he said.[19] George Greene made a dollar and a half a day, then a dollar, sometimes 75 cents a day. Juda Dantzler earned from a doctor at Goose Pond, Mississippi $4 a month. Workers such as Dantzler usually received food and shelter in addition to their wages. James Cornelius hauled cotton to New Orleans for four years after the war for 50 cents a day, and dinner. Frank Patterson stayed on with his ex-master for $2 a month, plus food, clothes, and housing, with a raise to $5 a month.[20]

After the war many freedmen in search of better pay migrated to the Southwestern states. There the land was still being settled, and the demand for labor was greater, and wages higher. Labor contractors came to the Southeast promising a bright future with good wages. Such a recruiter roamed through Georgia after the war looking for laborers for new cotton country in Arkansas. Ishe Webb's father was the sort the labor agents were looking for. He took his family to Arkansas to earn higher wages picking cotton and bigger crop shares than they could get in their part of Georgia. The first year the family cleared five bales of cotton as their share, raised corn, and bought a horse and a cow. Mary Jane Mooreman's family was lured from Bowling Green, Kentucky, to Woodruff County, Arkansas, also by a labor contractor promising high wages, and Ambers Gray met a man "huntin' hands" in Georgia and went with him to Sardis, Mississippi, and then on to help develop Biscoe, Arkansas, from swamp and woods. A planter went to Chattanooga, found hands, and paid their way by rail to Memphis, and by boat to Linden, Arkansas, on the St. Francis River. Bill

Simms walked from Osceola, Missouri, to Lawrence, Kansas, where he found higher wages and better opportunity. In time, he was able to send his daughters to college, and see them become teachers in Oklahoma.[21]

Freedmen were skilled in all sorts of labor connected with rural life. In consequence, many of them combined farming and working in timber: felling trees, hewing railroad crossties, making pine pitch and tar, and sawmilling. They labored as woodsmen, sharecroppers, or day laborers depending on the availability of employment. Larkin Payne farmed in season and cut and hauled wood in winter, then tried railroading, returned to farming, and ended doing "all I can git to do." Pink Holly lost his job when the timber of his locality was exhausted, then he went to carpentering and farming. Henry Nelson cleared new ground, hauled logs, worked on steamboats plying between Memphis and Helena, and wielded a pick and shovel on the railroad. Robert Solomon labored in sawmills in Arkansas and Louisiana, laid crossties and rails, worked in an oil mill, and farmed.[22]

"Gwine to Georgy": Some blacks sold to the Southwest or later lured there by higher wages returned home to family and friends. Harper's, Vol. LIX, No. CCCLIII (October 1879), 717.

Many blacks held jobs with steamboat lines, railroads, and freight companies, generally performing hard labor. Harrison Boyd worked on the Texas and Pacific Railroad, from Marshall to Longview, he said, for $1.50 and three drinks of whiskey a day. Augustus Robinson had his jaw broken

Worker collecting turpentine sap by cup in Pine Country. Chandler and others, eds., *History of the Southern States*, Vol. VI, 257.

and four front teeth knocked out by a piece of flying steel; lost his right eye to a hot cinder from a furnace; and suffered a hernia from carrying heavy pieces of iron. He was saved from further harm, though impoverished, when forced to retire because of old age. Tony Piggy served as roustabout on steamboats between Cairo, Illinois, and New Orleans, and Memphis and Newport, Arkansas, and at other times laid railroad track and farmed; Wash Anderson worked on steamboats and railroads and at sawmills in Arkansas, Oklahoma, Louisiana, and Texas; William Hunter was a section hand on the railroad, a logger, and a cotton mill hand; Frank Wise farmed until 1879, then went to steamboating and railroading; and Berry Smith spiked crossties on the railroad, steamboated between New Orleans and St. Louis, and farmed. Austin Grant hauled cotton, flour, and whiskey in Texas.[23]

Some freedmen continued to practice arts learned in slave days. Others mastered new skills under freedom. Cicero Finch had run a mill and threshed wheat, pressed cider, and ginned cotton, and made wagons and carriages, as a slave; in freedom he started with a pick and shovel and then became a painter and plasterer in Atlanta. Henry Probasco's father, a blacksmith, carpenter, and shoemaker during slavery, after emancipation operated his own shoeshop in Waco, Texas. George W. Harris became a brick moulder, and Jake Walker a building contractor in Pine Bluff, Arkansas. Sylvester Sostan Wickliffe operated blacksmith shops in Lafayette, Louisiana, and Liberty, Texas.[24]

Blacks also made a living as ranch hands in the Southwest. Jack Bess, for example, "punched cows" from ranch to ranch around San Angelo, Texas, and Henry Lewis rode the Texas prairie until he was 94. Hiram Mayes also herded cattle until old age, and John Price broke many a wild horse. John Sneed drove cattle up the Chisholm Trail, and hauled supplies in a six-wheeled wagon in the Austin area. After serving in the Ninth United States Cavalry, James Martin drove cattle, even to faraway Dakota, and Tom Mills, also a former soldier in the West, rode the Hill Country of Texas. Ben Kinchlow built fences, broke horses to the saddle, and minded cattle in Texas for $7 to $8 a month and keep, but he feasted on javelinas and deer. Walter Rimm cooked for the hands on the King Ranch and other Texas ranches.[25]

Some freedmen joined or stayed in the Army after the war and served in the Great Plains as "Buffalo Soldiers," as the Indians called them. William Branch fought Comanches and Apaches in Texas and Oklahoma. Madison Bruin skirmished with Indians on Devils River, in Brazos Canyon, and in the Rattlesnake and Guadalupe Mountains, with the Eighth and Tenth Cavalry. William Davis was sent to Fort Stockton, Texas, from Nashville, Tennessee, with the Twenty Fourth Infantry, but like many other soldiers when mustered out, set to work in the West, in his case as deckhand on the *Dinah* and the *Lizzie* hauling freight between Galveston and Houston, and then "jobbed" from place to place.[26]

Skills supplementing agricultural labor gave slaves work other than following the plow or swinging the hoe, while special talents led to unusual jobs. Sam Scott ran a minstrel company of eight to 10 performers, and served as property manager at the Old Opera House, Russelville, Arkansas. He took shows around about, once making $47 "clear money" at Clarksville, Arkansas. He remembered other minstrel groups that provided opportunity for black performing artists: "Richard's and Pringle's Georgia Minstrels, de Nashville Students, Lyman Twins, Barlow Brothers' Minstrels, Daisy, de Missouri Girl, with Fred Raymond, and Billy

Kersands, with his mouf a mile wide." Scott's group sang and danced in shows at the Old Opera House, and on circuit to Holla Bend, Dover, Danville, Ola, Charleston, Nigger Ridge and other rural communities in the area. At performances, blacks sat on one side and whites on the other. In his old age Scott occasionally took out shows to Pope, Yell, and Johnson County towns.[27] Black musicians also played at big "to do's" of white people, and black dancers taught whites the latest steps, said Warren Taylor.[28]

Blacks often led hunting and fishing parties. Holt Collier, famous as a hunter of big game, especially bear, and a champion in shooting contests, accompanied Theodore Roosevelt on a bear hunt in Mississippi, and was rewarded with a dupli-cate of Roosevelt's own rifle. Joe Golden, with his dog "Abraham Lincoln," hunted all sorts of wild animals, and sold quail at 25 cents each to a local doctor. Golden also had a bootblack stand, then a butcher shop, and raised garden vegetables for sale.[29] Texas hunter Edgar Bendy boasted: "I used to be plumb give up to be de best hunter in Tyler and in de whole country. I kilt more deer dan any other man in de country and I been guide for all de big men what come here to hunt."[30]

Pensions for military service helped some workers who found the job market uncertain and unprofitable. James Spikes, who served in the Union Army in Mississippi said his pension "comes in right nice — it does that."[31] Many other black laborers went from job to job, patiently

Atlanta was a mecca for these musicians. *Harper's,* Vol LX, No. CCCLV (December 1879), 42.

struggling to make a living. John Love worked in a sorghum mill, laid cross ties on the Houston and Central Texas Railroad, broke wild horses for 25 cents a day and keep, and carried mail for eight years through the Brazos River bottoms from Marlin to Eddy. Jenny Proctor's children held jobs in hotels, cafes, and filling stations, and in homes. Ellis Ken Kannon toiled at one odd job after another until he finally got steady work at St. Mary's Church, Nashville, where the priests did not treat him "lak a nigger." After freedom Andy Odell plowed, hoed, cut wood, "en wuk'd in quarries pecking rock." Lewis Jones worked at a cotton gin in LaGrange, Texas, then at a meat packing plant, and, when laid off, at anything he could get.[32] "Since freedom I done most everything anybody could do," James Jackson said. "I been porter and waiter in hotels and rest'rants. I been factory hand, and worked for carpenters and in de roun' houses. I picked cotton and worked on de farm."[33] Barney Alford turned from saw-milling at a dollar a day to preaching, which he quit when the congregation stopped paying him. Henry Murray farmed, made baskets and chair bottoms, and built dirt chimneys. John Logan farmed, operated a lathe in a cabinet maker's shop in Little Rock, worked in the water works of Hot Springs, fired a furnace in a bath house, gardened for a hotel, hauled freight, and built rock walls.[34]

Had they found any chance of prosperity on the farm many blacks never would have exchanged the countryside where they were born and raised for squalid sections of towns and cities. As it was, rural freedmen came to join old residents and war refugees in the spectacular life of the city, where social institutions abounded, and where a variety of work was to be done. Most city blacks were, of course, unskilled and took such odd jobs as came along. They loaded and unloaded

trains, steamboats, and ships, carried messages, swept floors, laid down street pavement, hauled goods in wagons, and toiled at hundreds of jobs which required little or no skill and paid wages inadequate to sustain a family.

To supplement income of their husbands, wives often worked as domestic servants, washers, and ironers. As a consequence, many women were unable to give adequate attention to their own children. The mother of Scott Bond, successful Arkansas planter and businessman, was so burdened as a servant that her son grew up almost a stranger to her.[35] Where the problem of eking out an existence was solved, there was a house to buy and children to educate. Often women provided the sole means of support for their families, and savings which sustained freedmen's banks and insurance companies came in part from their earnings.

Women toiled in the fields, cooked, washed, ironed, cleaned house, and cared for children. Mary Harris, for example, washed, ironed, and sewed to make a living.[36] And Rosa Simmons washed and cooked and "done 'bout everything." In her old age, she said, "Sometimes I have something to eat and sometimes I don't."[37] Susan Castle, of Athens, Georgia, like many domestics, worked years for one family until disabled and "misery tuk up wid" her. Sarah Poindexter held a job in a North Carolina tobacco factory. After years of farming and taking in washing and ironing, Emma Johnson saved enough to buy a house. Not so fortunate, Nora Goodwin cooked for a judge for many years, until her eyes went bad. Mary Gaines ran a cafe with her husband until widowed, then washed, ironed and cooked–when she could find work. Tilday Collins made a living, such as it was, as a midwife and "doctor" for minor ailments. Maggie Wesmoland cooked, plowed, and washed and ironed mountains of clothing. Accomplished Mand Morrow cooked for Governor

Stephen Hogg, of Texas, for many years. Becky Hawkins, of Pine Bluff, Arkansas, nursed white folks' babies, and, she said, "washed and ironed and ironed and washed and ironed." Gracie Mitchell, also of Pine Bluff, cooked, took care of others' children, farmed, and sewed. She made and sold quilts of 22 designs, from "Railroad Crossing" to "Lily in the Valley." After freedom Rosina Hoard, of Garfield, Texas, "had to do de man's work, chop down trees and plow de fields and pick cotton."[38]

Although black workers made up the bulk of the unskilled labor force, in every Southern city there were black carpenters, machinists, shoemakers, blacksmiths, stonecutters, and wagonmakers whose wages were double or triple those of the unskilled. In 1865 100,000 of the artisans of the South were black. By the end of Reconstruction many of these skilled blacks had been squeezed out of their trades by white workers, who received apparent economic benefits in exchange for allegiance to the doctrines of white supremacy. These displaced artisans, together with the unskilled, supplied recruits for strike-breaking agents in the North and South. The mere rumor that blacks would be brought in often was enough to end a strike or set off a riot.

To prevent ruinous competition black workmen tried to persuade white workers to make common cause with them. In New Orleans in 1866, black bricklayers sought admission, on terms of equality, to a labor union of white bricklayers, which needed their aid during a strike. In 1869 Isaac Myers, of the Colored Caulkers Trade Union Society of Baltimore, and Chairman of the National Labor Union's Committee on Cooperation, declared that black workers would gladly cooperate with white workers, if the latter would end the need of blacks to cut the price of labor to obtain employment. White locals rejected Myers's plea.[39]

Faced with exclusion and discrimination, African Americans formed separate

Cutting sugar cane in Louisiana. Many women in freedom as in slavery toiled in the fields. Chandler and others, eds., *History of the Southern States*, Vol. V, 191.

unions, but made frequent declarations of their desire to disband these unions in favor of unions of blacks and whites. In 1869 they organized the Colored National Labor Union, with Myers as president. The union's leaders denounced the exclusion of blacks from white trade unions as an insult to God and a disgrace to humanity. Their central purpose, they said, was to organize all black laborers until the necessity for separate organization ceased to exist. In 1871 the C.N.L.U. elected Frederick Douglass president and turned to politics in the vain hope of changing conditions it alone was powerless to alter.[40]

Opportunities for African American businessmen were, like job opportunities for black tradesmen, very limited during Reconstruction. And the chance to go into business did not mean that they would avail themselves of it, for the majority of them could not think of themselves as having possibilities in business. The number of black businessmen during Reconstruction, therefore, did not greatly exceed the number of free black businessmen before the Civil War. The lack of capital was a basic problem. Privileged whites experienced difficulty in obtaining capital; untried African Americans found it nearly impossible to raise money. Wages of the mass of freedmen were, of course, too low to generate much capital through savings.[41]

Black businessmen were likely to be barbers or caterers or grocers. Some enjoyed considerable success. James Tait opened a grocery in Atlanta in 1866 that became the nucleus of a sizeable estate; Samuel Harris of Williamsburg, Virginia, kept a store through Reconstruction, doing a thriving business; in North Carolina, Warren Coleman began dealing in rags, bones, and old iron in 1876, and in a few years had an establishment worth $100,000; William Sumner, starting as a drayman in Nashville, accumulated considerable property by 1868; in Memphis,

R. R. Church began building a large fortune in real estate; in Texas, veteran of the Civil War and Indian Wars Sam Kilgore gained the experience and savings in military and civilian construction that enabled him to establish a cement company.[42] Other black businessmen were hotel keepers, florists, poultry dealers, ice cream makers, contractors, merchants, tailors, undertakers, realtors, hackmen and teamsters, hucksters and peddlers, livery stable keepers, packers and shippers, and, in some cities, jewelers and goldsmiths. A few blacks organized ambitious enterprises, such as textile factories and sassafras oil mills, most of which failed.[43]

Black business ventures in truth were more often failures than successes. The trouble was, African American businessmen were inexperienced and had to depend on the patronage of an impoverished black community and operate within a nexus of political, social, and economic relationships of white supremacy. The most spectacular failure was that of the Freedmen's Bank. The existence of military savings banks for black soldiers led to the chartering of the Freedmen's Savings Bank and Trust Company, organized with government aid, with 36 branches, most of them in the old slave territory. From 1865 to 1879 the bank prospered. Freedmen greeted it with enthusiasm and entrusted their savings to its care. But troubles set in. White and black officials looted the bank and called in black leaders to save it. Frederick Douglass, misled into accepting the presidency, soon reported the true state of affairs to the Senate Committee on Finance. Nearly $3 million in deposits were involved in the bankruptcy, of which 62 percent was at length returned to depositors. This colossal failure dampened the desire of black people to invest their savings in any bank, and their confidence in black and white leaders, and also in the federal government, waned.[44]

Vendors hawked their wares on city streets. *Harper's*, Vol. LX, No. CCCLV (December 1879) 32.

Insurance companies were more successful than other large enterprises. Through their churches blacks looked out for the sick, fed the hungry, and buried the dead. Church insurance societies broadened into fraternal organizations, which became, in turn, large insurance associations. Another factor which contributed to the development of insurance enterprises was the organization of excursions for the celebration of holidays. As part of these celebrations freedmen held parades, in which members of the insurance societies were decked out in colorful regalia. Excursions, arranged at half-fare on steamboat or railroad, brought thousands of freedmen to the celebrations, where they developed a longing to join the insurance societies. The old and young, men and women, participated.[45] At a celebration in Memphis, in April, 1870, of the adoption of the Fifteenth Amendment, as we have seen, hundreds of representatives of the United Sons and Daughters of Ham, United Sons of Zion, United Forever Society, and the St. John's Relief Society, handsomely dressed, and accompanied by brass bands, led a procession of several thousand strong to James Park for speeches, feasting, and dancing.

In working out insurance plans the societies at first made the mistake of taking in indiscriminately poor risks, and in setting the monthly premium too low to pay the amount promised. Societies which adopted up-to-date business practices weathered the early experimental period and prospered. The necessity for efficient management was emphasized as the societies changed from mystic orders into business organizations. Out of the experiences of associations such as the True Reformers came the Southern Aid Society, the National Benefit Life Insurance Company, and other insurance groups. These in turn promoted the establishment, late in the 19th century, of African American banks.[46]

African Americans celebrated every step toward their freedom, the Emancipation Proclamation, ratification of the Fourteenth and Fifteenth Amendments, passage of the Reconstruction and Civil Rights Act, and the great national and religious holidays. On these and other occasions they welcomed association with whites on terms of equality, but formed their own institutions rather than accept treatment as inferiors. Separated, they were slowed, not halted, in their movement to achieve the promise of American life, because, as the New Orleans *Louisianian*, June 6, 1874, declared:

> Of one flesh God made us all; the national bill of rights, the immortal Declaration, affirms that we are all free and equal in our inalienable rights; the Constitution in organic form expresses the truths, inspired and traditional, that underlie our civilization, and the statutes render the speculative, organic right, operative and practical, therefore we dare come before the American people — reinforced with the unexampled growth in all the qualities and virtues of citizens, that have been made by us since our emancipation and enfranchisement ... [and] say boldly, with the full appreciation of the dignity and value of American citizenship, that [our] rights must and will find their protection in the Great Republic so long as the national integrity and honor survive.

Notes

Chapter 1

1. Liza Strickland, in *Mississippi Narratives*, Supplement, Series 1, Vol 10, Part 5, 2064, of *The American Slave: A Composite Autobiography*, ed. by George P. Rawick, 19 vols. (Westport, Connecticut: Greenwood, 1972–1979); hereafter cited with names of states abbreviated, and Sup for Supplement, Ser for Series, and P for Part. Martha Wheeler, *MS*, Sup, Ser 1, Vol 10, P 5, 2263–2264; Rina Brown, *MS*, Sup, Ser 1, Vol 6, P 1, 275; Mandy Jones, *MS*, Sup, Ser 1, Vol 8, P 3, 1228; Mose King, *AR*, Ser 1, Vol 9, P 4, 207.

2. Bill Homer, *TX*, Ser 1, Vol 4, P 2, 153.

3. Foster Weatherby, *MS*, Sup, Ser 1, Vol 10, P 5, 2228; Harriet Payne, *AR*, Ser 2, Vol 10, P 5, 301.

4. Amos Clark, *TX*, Ser 1, Vol 4, P 1, 221.

5. Jasper Battle, *GA*, Ser 2, Vol 12, P 1, 63; Vinnie Busby, *MS*, Sup, Ser 1, Vol 6, P 1, 308–309.

6. Mary Moriah Susanna James, *MD*, Ser 2, Vol 16, 37; Gabriel Gilbert, *TX*, Ser 1, Vol 4, P 2, 68; Benjamin Whitley Smith, *MS*, Sup, Ser 1, Vol 10, P 5, 1997; James Henry Stith, *AR*, Ser 2, Vol 10, P 6, 239; Virginia Harris, *MS* , Sup, Ser 1, Vol 8, P 3, 937; Mose Davis, *GA*, Ser 2, Vol 12, P 1, 268; M. S. Fayman, *MD*, Ser 2, Vol 16, 13.

7. Mand Morrow, *TX*, Ser 1, Vol 5, P 3, 140; Rev. Squire Dowd, *NC*, Ser 2, Vol 14, P 1, 265; Evie Herrin, *MS*, Sup, Ser 1, Vol 8, P 3, 989.

8. Marion Johnson, *AR*, Ser 2, Vol 9, P 4, 117; Henry Daniels, *MS*, Sup, Ser 1, Vol 7, P 2, 549; Frederick Law Olmsted, *Cotton Kingdom*, ed. by A.M. Schlesinger, Sr. (1861; New York: Knopf, 1953), 346.

9. Dave Walker, *MS*, Sup, Ser 1, Vol 10, P 5, 2148; John Spencer Bassett, ed., *The Southern Plantation Overseer as Revealed in His Letters* (reprint; 1925, Westport, Connecticut: Negro Universities Press, 1972), 262; George Patterson, *SC*, Ser 2, Vol 3, P 3, 227; Wash Anderson, *TX*, Ser 1, Vol 4, P 1, 18; Solomon Northup, *Twelve Years A Slave*, ed. by Sue Eakin and Joseph Logsdon (1853; reprint, Baton Rouge: Louisiana State University Press, 1968), 80.

10. Caroline Holland, *AL*, Ser 1, Vol 6, 185; Georgia Baker, *GA*, Ser 1, Vol 12, P 1, 39; Hannah Plummer, *NC*, Ser 2, Vol 15, P 2, 179; James Tubbs, *AR*, Ser 2, Vol 10, P 6, 355; James V. Deane, *MD*, Ser 2, Vol 16, 6; Olmsted, *Cotton Kingdom*, 447.

11. Richard Wade, *Slavery in the Cities: The South 1820–1860*, (New York: Oxford University Press, 1964), 56–75.

12. Josephine Cox, *MS*, Sup, Ser 1, Vol 7, P 2, 526; Louis Davis, *MS*, Sup, Ser. 1, Vol 7, P 2, 526; Mary Island, *AR*, Ser 2, Vol 9, P 3, 390; Malindy Maxwell, *AR*, Ser 1, Vol 10, P 5, 59; Jasper Battle, *GA*, Ser 2, Vol 12, P 1, 63; Jeff Chandler, *TX*, Ser 1, Vol 4, P 1, 188; Lizzie Williams, *MS*, Ser 1, Vol 10, P 5, 2335; Lucy Donald, *MS*, Sup, Ser 1, Vol 7, P 2, 637; Sylvia Floyd, *MS*, Sup, Ser 1, Vol 7, P 2, 743; Charlie Meadow, *SC*, Ser 1, Vol 3, P 3, 180; Harriet Barrett, *TX*, Ser 1, Vol 4, P 1, 49; Sena Moore, *SC*, Ser 1, Vol 3, P 3, 210; Georgia Baker, *GA*, Ser 2, Vol 12, P 1, 39.

13. Molly Ammonds, *Al*, Ser 1, Vol 6, 9; Nap McQueen, *TX*, Ser 1, Vol 5, P 3, 36; Frank Patterson, *AR*, Ser 2, Vol 10, P 5, 277; George Green, *AR*, Ser 2, Vol 9, P 3, 106; Richard Carruthers, *TX*, Ser 1, Vol 4, P 1, 197.

14. George Green, *AR*, Ser 2, Vol 9, P 3, 107; John Hunter, *AR*, Ser 2, Vol 9, P 3, 360; Laura Montgomery, *MS*, Sup, Ser 1, Vol 9, P 4, 1553; Rev. James Washington, *MS*, Sup, Ser 1, Vol 10, P 5, 2200; Augustus Robinson, *AR*, Ser 2, Vol 10, P 6, 56; Lillie Williams, *AR*, Ser 2, Vol 11, P 7, 177.

15. Laura Ford, *MS*, Sup, Ser 1, Vol 7, P 2, 756; Glascow Norwood, *MS*, Sup, Ser 1, Vol 9, P 4, 1655; Maria Robinson, *TX*, Ser 1, Vol 5, P 3, 255.

16. Vinnie Busby, *MS*, Sup, Ser 1, Vol 6, P 1, 308–309; Nathan Best, *MS*, Sup, Ser 1, Vol 6, P 1, 129; James Reeves, *AR*, Ser 1, Vol 10, P 6, 28; Tom Holland, *TX*, Ser 1, Vol 4, P 2, 145; Calley Rolley, *MS*, Sup, Ser 1, Vol 9, P 4, 1885; Joe Rollins, *MS*, Sup, Ser 1, Vol 9, P 4, 1896; Wash Anderson, *TX*, Ser 1, Vol 4, P 1, 18; Amos Clark, *TX*, Ser 1, Vol 4, P 1, 220.

17. Olmsted, *Cotton Kingdom*, 447–448.

18. Rev. Silas Jackson, *MD*, Ser 2, Vol 16, 30; Ebenezer Brown, *MS*, Sup, Ser 1, Vol 6, P 1, 245–246; Frank Patterson, *AR*, Ser 2, Vol 10, P 5, 277; Dicey Thomas, *AR* , Ser 2, Vol 10, P 6, 290; Della Briscoe, *GA*, Ser 2, Vol 12, P 1, 128; Celeste Avery, *GA*, Ser 2, Vol 12, P 1, 23–24.

19. George Taylor, *AL*, Ser 1, Vol 6, 371; Prince Smith, *SC*, Ser 1, Vol 3, P 4, 116–117; Henry Walker, *AR*, Ser 2, Vol 11, P 7, 30.

20. Vinnie Busby, *MS* , Sup, Ser 1, Vol 6, P 1, 308–309.

21. Thomas Cole, *TX*, Ser 1, Vol 4, P 1, 226; William Dosite Postell, *The Health of Slaves on Southern Plantations* (1951; reprint, Gloucester, Mass.: Peter Smith, 1970), 35.

22. Tom McAlpine, *AL*, Ser 1, Vol 6, 270; Harper Lewis, *TX*, Ser 1, Vol 5, P 3, 5.

23. Mattie Gilmore, *TX*, Ser 1, Vol 4, P 2, 72.

24. Tines Kendricks, *AR*, Ser 2, Vol 9, P 4, 178; Sarah Gudger, *NC*, Ser 2, Vol 14, P 1, 354; Hagar Lewis, *TX*, Ser 1, Vol 5, P 3, 4–7; Cato Carter, *TX*, Ser 1, Vol 4, P 1, 22.

25. Charlie Crump, *NC*, Ser 2, Vol 14, P 1, 214.

26. Annie Row, *TX*, Ser 1, Vol 4, P 1, 35; Lula Jackson, *AR*, Ser 2, Vol 9, P 4, 9, 12; Julius Jones, *MS*, Sup, Ser 1, Vol 8, P 3, 12, 6; "One of Dr. Gale's 'Free Niggers'," *Unwritten History of Slavery*, in *The American Slave*, Ser 2, Vol 18, 1–16; Beth Powers, *TX*, Ser 1, Vol 4, P 1, 35; Wes Brady, *TX*, Ser 1, Vol 4, P 1, 133; Mary Raines, *SC*, Ser 1, Vol 3, P 4, 2.

27. Happy Day Green, *AR*, Ser 2, Vol 9, P 3, 88; Henry Barnes, *AL*, Ser 1, Vol 6, 22; Sam Mitchell, *SC*, Ser 1, Vol 3, P 3, 200; Barnes Alford, *MS*, Sup, Ser 1, Vol 6, P 1, 24.

28. Henry Lee, *AR*, Ser 2, Vol 9, P 4, 248; Clara Young, *MS*, Ser 1, Vol 7, 171; Henry Pettus, *AR*, Ser 2, Vol 10, P 5, 340.

29. Rachel Adams, *GA*, Ser 2, Vol 12, P 1, 4; Pinkie Howard, *AR*, Ser 2, Vol 9, P 3, 337; Callie Gray, *MS*, Sup, Ser 1, Vol 8, P 3, 863; Alek Woodward, *SC*, Ser 1, Vol 3, P 4, 254.

30. Charity Jones, *MS*, Sup, Ser 1, Vol 8, P 3, 1193–1194; Anthony Taylor, *AR*, Ser 2, Vol 10, P 6, 262.

31. Isaac Stier, *MS*, Ser 1, Vol 7, 147; Arrie Burns, *GA*, Ser 2, Vol 12, P 1, 76; Allen Johnson, *AR*, Ser 2, Vol 9, P 4, 65; Sally Nealy, *AR*, Ser 2, Vol 10, P 5, 185; Rachel Harris, *AR*, Ser 2, Vol 9, P 3, 181; Olmsted, *Cotton Kingdom*, 433–434.

32. Georgia Baker, *GA*, Ser 2, Vol 12, P 1, 41.

33. Betty Powers, *TX*, Ser 1, Vol 5, P 3, 190.

34. Nancy Washington, *SC*, Ser 1, Vol 3, P 4, 185–186; William Williams, *OH*, Ser 2, Vol 16, 116.

35. Callie Gray, *MS*, Sup, Ser 2, Vol 8, P 3, 864.

36. Minnie Davis, *GA*, Ser 2, Vol 12, P 1, 255.

37. Austin Pen Parnell, *AR*, Ser 2, Vol 10, P 5, 264–265; Tilda Johnson, *MS*, Sup, Ser 1, Vol 10, P 5, 1961–1963.

38. Tilda Johnson, Mary Joiner, Millie Young, *MS*, Sup, Ser 1, Vol 10, P 5, 1961–1963.

39. Ellen Gooden, *MS*, Sup, Ser 1, Vol 10, P 5, 1965–1966.

40. Della Buckley, *MS*, Sup, Ser 1, Vol 6, P 1, 302; William Wheeler, *MS*, Sup, Ser 1, Vol 10, P 5, 2273–2274.

41. Millie Boyd, *MS*, Sup, Ser 1, Vol 10, P 5, 1964–1965.

42. Harriet Jones, *TX*, Ser 1, Vol 4, P 2, 233.

43. Isom Weathersby, *MS*, Sup, Ser 1, Vol 10, P 5, 2237.

44. Callie Washington, *MS*, Sup, Ser 1, Vol 10, P 5, 2185–2186; Reuben Fox, *MS*, Sup, Ser 1, Vol 7, P 2, 770; Thomas Ruffin, *AR*, Ser 2, Vol 10, P 6, 99–100; Charlie Moses, *MS*, Ser 1, Vol 7, 115; Ben Moon, *AR*, Ser 2, Vol 10, P 5, 119–120; Victoria Randle, *MS*, Sup, Ser 1, Vol 8, P 3, 1305; Mom Genia Woodberry, *SC*, Ser 1, Vol 3, 222; Liza Strickland, *MS*, Sup, Ser 1, Vol 10, P 5, 2064–2067; Wade, *Slavery in the Cities*, 132–142.

45. Polly Turner Cancer, *MS*, Sup, Ser 1, Vol 7, P 2, 341.

46. Dicey Thomas, *AR*, Ser 2, Vol 10, P 6, 291; Ank Bishop, *AL*, Ser 1, Vol 6, P 360; Joe Barnes, *TX*, Ser 1, Vol 4, P 1, 46; Ebenezer Brown, *MS*, Sup, Ser 1, Vol 6, P 1, 248.

47. Squire Irvin, *MS*, Sup, Ser 1, Vol 8, P 3, 1080; Mary Jane Mooreman, *AR*, Ser 2, Vol 10, P 5, 131; Israel Jackson, *AR*, Ser 2, Vol 9, P 4, 5; Benny Dillard, *GA*, Ser 2, Vol 12, P 1, 291; Harriet Miller, *MS*, Sup, Ser 1, Vol 9, P 4, 1499; John Belcher, *MS*, Sup, Ser 1, Vol 6, P 1, 107;

Ned Chaney, *MS*, Sup, Ser 1, Vol 7, P 2, 375; Alex Montgomery, *MS*, Sup, Ser 1, Vol 9, P 4, 1523–1524; Lewis Jefferson, *MS*, Sup, Ser 1, Vol 8, P 3, 1138; Joe Barnes, *TX*, Ser 1, Vol 4, P 1, 46.

48. Henry Murray, *MS*, Sup, Ser 1, Vol 9, P 4, 1614; Adam Singleton, *MS*, Sup, Ser 1, Vol 10, P 5, 1949; Lizzie Williams, *MS*, Sup, Ser 1, Vol 10, P 5, 2335.

49. Mahalia Shores, *AR*, Ser 2, Vol 10, P 6, 155. Many plantations had dairies: see Postell, *Health of Slaves*, 35.

50. Mary Anderson, *NC*, Ser 2, Vol 14, P 1, 22.

51. "Owns the House he Lived in as a Slave," *Unwritten History of Slavery*, in *American Slave*, Vol 18, 130; Emma Tidwell, *AR*, Ser 2, Vol 10, P 6, 330; Henry Green, *AR*, Ser 2, Vol 9, P 3, 99; Dempsy Pitts, *MS*, Sup, Ser 1, Vol 9, P 4, 1711.

52. Tom Huntley, *MS*, Sup, Ser 1, Vol 8, P 2, 1069; Charlie Davenport, *MS*, Sup, Ser 1, Vol 7, P 2, 561; Frances Willis, *MS*, Sup, Ser 1, Vol 10, P 5, 2358.

53. Larnce Holt, *TX*, Ser 1, Vol 4, P 2, 151; Adaline Hodges, *AL*, Ser 1, Vol 6, 183–184; Henry Kirk Miller, *AR*, Ser 2, Vol 10, P 5, 78; Ella Gillespie, *AR*, Ser 2, Vol 9, P 3, 44; Sally Dixon, *MS*, Sup, Ser 1, Vol 7, P 2, 627; Postell, *Health of Slaves*, 41.

54. Lizzie Williams, *MS*, Sup, Ser 1, Vol 10, P 5, 2336.

55. Monroe Brackens, *TX*, Ser 1, Vol 4, P 1, 124.

56. Tempie Herndon Durham, *NC*, Ser 2, Vol 14, P 1, 285–286; Olmsted, *Cotton Kingdom*, 346–347, 451; Betty Coffer, *NC*, Ser 2, Vol 14, P 1, 168–170.

57. Rachel Bradley, *AR*, Ser 1, Vol 2, 11; Georgia Baker, *GA*, Ser 2, Vol 12, P 1, 4; Sarah Gudger, *NC*, Ser 2, Vol 14, P 1, 341; Lucindy Shaw, *MS*, Sup, Ser 1, Vol 10, P 5, 1926.

58. Tempie Herndon Durham, *NC*, Ser 2, Vol 14, P 1, 285-286; Ellen Polk, *TX*, Ser 1, Vol 5, P 3, 188.

59. Celeste Avery, *GA*, Ser 2, Vol 12, P 1, 24; Georgia Baker, *GA*, Ser 2, Vol 12, P 1, 48; C.W. Hawkins, *AR*, Ser 2, Vol 9, P 3, 215; Squire King, *AR*, Ser 2, Vol 9, P 4, 214; Callie Elder, *GA*, Ser 2, Vol 12, P 1, 312.

60. Hannah Austin, *GA*, Ser 2, Vol 12, P 1, 20; Mollie Williams, *MS*, Ser 1, Vol 7, 1581; Hannah Hancock, *AR*, Ser 2, Vol 9, P 3, 142.

61. Minnie Davis, *GA*, Ser 2, Vol 12, P 1, 256; Jane Morgan, *MS*, Sup, Ser 1, Vol 9, P 1, 1576; Calline Brown, *MS*, Sup, Ser 1, Vol 6, 236; Henrietta Isom, *AR*, Ser 2, Vol 9, P 3, 392; James Lucas, *MS*, Sup, Ser 1, Vol 8, P 3, 1345.

62. Delia Garlic, *AL*, Ser 1, Vol 6, 132.

63. Adeline Marshall, *TX*, Ser 1, Vol 4, P 1, 277.

64. Callie Washington, *MS*, Sup, Ser 1, Vol 10, P 5, 2186; Lizzie Norfleet, *MS*, Sup, Ser 1, Vol 9, P 4, 1639–1651; Ellen Betts, *TX*, Ser 1, Vol 4, P 1, 75; Callie Elder, *GA*, Ser 2, Vol 12, P 1, 312.

65. John Barclay, *TX*, Ser 1, Vol 4, P 1, 40; Henry Lewis, *TX*, Ser 1, Vol 5, P 3, 10.

66. Sarah Anne Green, *NC*, Ser 2, Vol 14, P 1, 34; Martha Bradley, *AL*, Ser 1, Vol 6, 47; Annie Cole, *MS*, Sup, Ser 1, Vol 7, P 2, 440.

67. Jasper Battle, *GA*, Ser 2, Vol 12, P 1, 65.

68. Jane Morgan, *MS*, Sup, Ser 1, Vol 9, P 1, 1576.

69. Rev. Silas Jackson, *MD*, Ser 2, Vol 16, 30; Gabe Emmanuel, *MS*, Sup, Ser 1, Vol 8, P 3, 1060; Frank Hughes, *MS*, Sup, Ser 1, Vol 7, P 2, 682; Henry Bland, *GA*, Ser 2, Vol 12, P 1, 82; Alice Houston, *TX*, Ser 1, Vol 4, P 2, 160–161; Postell, *Health of Slaves*, 41.

70. Memphis *Daily Appeal*, 1847–1852.

71. Mattie Curtis, *NC*, Ser 2, Vol 14, P 1, 218; Jasper Battle, *GA*, Ser 2, Vol 12, P 1, 65; James Burton, *MS*, Sup,

Ser 1, Vol 6, P 1, 305; Robert Weathersby, *MS*, Sup, Ser 1, Vol 10, P 5, 2241; Albert Cox, *MS*, Sup, Ser 1, Vol 7, P 2, 513; Charlie Rigges, *AR*, Ser 2, Vol 10, P 6, 39; Virginia Harris, *MS*, Sup, Ser 1, Vol 8, P 3, 938.

Chapter 2

1. Mom Genia Woodberry, *SC*, Ser 1, Vol 3, P 4, 224; Rose Brown, *MS*, Sup, Ser 1, Vol 6, P 1, 285.

2. Jane Sutton, *MS*, Ser 1, Vol 7, 152; Lawrence Hampton, *AR*, Ser 2, Vol 9, P 3, 139; Andrew Jackson Gill, *MS*, Sup, Ser 1, Vol 8, P 3, 845; Randall M. Miller, "Slaves and Southern Catholicism," in John A. Boles, ed., *Masters and Slaves in the House of the Lord: Race and Religion in the American South, 1740–1870*, (Lexington, KY: University Press of Kentucky, 1988), 127–152, 135; Robert Weathersby, *MS*, Sup, Ser 1, Vol 10, P 5, 2241.

3. Ned Chaney, *MS*, Sup, Ser 1, Vol 7, P 2, 372; Squire Irvin, *MS*, Sup, Ser 1, Vol 8, P 3, 1083; Sidney Bonner, *AL*, Ser 1, Vol 6, 39–40; Louis Fowler, *TX*, Ser 1, Vol 4, P 2, 51; Andrew Goodman, *TX*, Ser 1, Vol 4, P 2, 76.

4. Malindy Maxwell, *AR*, Ser 2, Vol 10, P 5, 58; Gus Clark, *MS*, Sup, Ser 1, Vol 7, P 2, 405; Charlie Moses, *MS*, Ser 1, Vol 7, 115; Frances Willis, *MS*, Sup, Ser 1, Vol 10, P 5, 2358; Essex Henry, *NC*, Ser 2, Vol 14, P 1, 396.

5. Miller, "Slaves and Southern Catholicism," in Boles, ed., *Masters and Slaves in the House of the Lord*, (Lexington, KY., 1988), 127–152.

6. Prince Johnson, *MS*, Sup, Ser 1, Vol 8, P 3, 1171–1172; Willis Cofer, *GA*, Ser 2, Vol 12, P 1, 208; James V. Deane, *MD*, Ser 2, Vol 16, 7; Louis Davis, *MS*, Sup, Ser 1, Vol 7, P 2, 580.

7. Lizzie Norfleet, *MS*, Sup, Ser 1, Vol 9, P 4, 1644.

8. Tines Kendricks, *AR*, Ser 2, Vol 9, P 4, 179.

9. Bill Crump, *NC*, Ser 2, Vol 14, P 1, 210.

10. Andrew Moody, *TX*, Ser 1, Vol 5, P 3, 117; Hamp Kennedy, *MS*, Ser 1, Vol 7, 86; Jasper Battle, *GA*, Ser 2, Vol 12, P 1, 66–67; Richard Macks, *MD*, Ser 2, Vol 16, 54.

11. Catherine Beale, in John W. Blassingame, ed., *Slave Testimony: Two Centuries of Letters, Speeches, Interviews and Autobiographies* (Baton Rouge: Louisiana State University, 1977), 579–580.

12. Alec Bostwick, *GA*, Ser 2, Vol 12, P 1, 110.

13. Hannah Austin, *GA*, Ser 2, Vol 12, P 1, 20.

14. Lizzie Williams, *MS*, Sup, Ser 1, Vol 10, P 5, 2334–2338.

15. Crozier Moore, *MS*, Sup, Ser 1, Vol 9, P 4, 1571.

16. Dempsey Pitts, *MS*, Sup, Ser 1, Vol 9, P 4, 1715; Liza Jones, *AR*, Ser 2, Vol 9, P 4, 156; Olivier Blanchard, *TX*, Ser 1, Vol 4, P 1, 91; Mary Smith, *SC*, Ser 1, Vol 3, P 4, 114; Lindsey Faucette, *NC*, Ser 2, Vol 14, P 1, 303; Gabe Emanuel, *MS*, Sup, Ser 1, Vol 7, P 2, 682; Rachel Hawkins, *AR*, Ser 2, Vol 9, P 3, 155; Manda Boggan, *MS*, Sup, Ser 1, Vol 6, P 1, 157; Pauline Johnson and Felice Boudreaux, *TX*, Ser 1, Vol 4, P 2, 226.

17. Lucy to Rev. C.C. Jones, December 30, 1850, Blassingame, *Slave Testimony*, 90.

18. Olmsted, *Cotton Kingdom*, 228.

19. Louis Joseph Piernas, *MS*, Sup, Ser 1, Vol 9, P 4, 1702.

20. Charles Coles, *MD*, Ser 2, Vol 16, 4–5; Victor Duhon, *TX*, Ser 1, Vol 4, P 1, 308; Edward D. Reynolds, S.J., *Jesuits for the Negro*, (New York: The America Press, 1949), 162–164; Donaville Broussard, *TX*, Ser 1, Vol 4, P 1, 152.

21. Susan Boggs, in Blassingame, *Slave Testimony*, 418; Isaac Throgmorton, in Blassingame, *Slave Testimony*, 435.

22. Benny Dillard, *GA*, Ser 2, Vol 12, P 1, 290–291.

23. Annie Coley, *MS*, Sup, Ser 1, Vol 7, P 2, 439; Randall M. Miller, ed., *"Dear Master": Letters of a Slave Family* (Ithaca: Cornell University Press, 1978), 197.

24. Bill Williams, *SC*, Ser 1, Vol 3, P 4, 200; Isiah Jefferies, *SC*, Ser 1, Vol 3, P 3, 19.

25. Simon Hare, *MS*, Sup, Ser 1, Vol 8, P 3, 914.

26. Robert Weathersby, *MS*, Sup, Ser 1, Vol 10, P 5, 2239–2244.

27. Jeptha Choice, *TX*, Ser 1, Vol 4, P 1, 218.

28. Harrison Beckett, *TX*, Ser 1, Vol 4, P 1, 54–55.

29. Will Adams, *TX*, Ser 1, Vol 4, P 1, 2.

30. James Bolton, *GA*, Ser 2, Vol 12, P 1, 97.

31. "All My Bosses Were Nigger Traders," *Unwritten History of Slavery*, in *American Slave*, Vol 18, 261.

32. Robert Lofton, *AR*, Ser 2, Vol 9, P 4, 371; Charlotte Beverly, *TX*, Ser 1, Vol 4, P 1, 85; James Smith, in Blassingame, *Slave Testimony*, 276–277; Sarah Ford, *TX*, Ser 1, Vol 4, P 2, 44; John Bates, *TX*, Ser 1, Vol 2, P 1, 51.

33. Washington Allen, *GA*, Ser 2, Vol 12, P 1, 11; Mark Oliver, *MS*, Sup, Ser 1, Vol 9, P 4, 1664; Richard Parker, in Blassingame, *Slave Testimony*, 465–466.

34. Mary Watson, *AR*, Ser 1, Vol 7, P 7, 67.

35. Clara Young, *MS*, Sup, Ser 1, Vol 10, P 5, 2403.

36. Rev. Silas Jackson, *MD*, Ser 2, Vol 16, 32.

37. Ellen Claiborne, *GA*, Ser 2, Vol 12, P 1, 187; Richard Mack, *MD*, Ser 2, Vol 16, 54; Olmsted, *Cotton Kingdom*, 375; Charlie Meadow, *SC*, Ser 1, Vol 3, P 3, 181; Gabe Butler, *MS*, Sup, Ser 1, Vol 6, P 1, 315.

38. Wade, *Slavery in the Cities*, 83–84, 175–177.

39. Olmsted, *Cotton Kingdom*, 241–244.

40. Randy Sparks, "Religion in Amite County Mississippi, 1800–1861," in Boles, ed., *Masters and Slaves in the House of the Lord*, 69–79; Laura Ford, *MS*, Sup, Ser 1, Vol 7, P 2, 757.

41. George Owens, *TX*, Ser 1, Vol 5, P 3, 168; Ellen Butler, *TX*, Ser 1, Vol 4, P 1, 177; Lizzie Hughes, *TX*, Ser 1, Vol 4, P 2, 167.

42. Molly Campbell, *MS*, Sup, Ser 1, Vol 7, P 2, 664; Lizzie Johnson, *AR*, Ser 2, Vol 9, P 4, 103; Nancy Robinson, *MS*, Sup, Ser 1, Vol 9, P 4, 1864; Cora Horton, *AR*, Ser 2, Vol 9, P 3, 322.

43. W.L. Bost, *NC*, Ser 2, Vol 14, P 1, 143.

44. Simon Hare, *MS*, Sup, Ser 1, Vol 8, P 3, 914; Maggie Woods, *AR*, Ser 2, Vol 11, P 1, 232; Lucy Donald, *MS*, Sup, Ser 1, Vol 7, P 2, 639.

45. Stearlin Arnwine, *TX*, Scr 1, Vol 4, P 1, 33.

46. Silvia King, *TX*, Ser 1, Vol 4, P 2, 294.

47. John Macy, *TX*, Ser 1, Vol 5, P 3, 33.

48. Sylvia Floyd, *MS*, Sup, Ser 1, Vol 7, P 2, 747.

49. Steve Weathersby, *MS*, Sup, Ser 1, Vol 10, P 5, 2247. See also Lawrence W. Levine, *Black Culture and Black Consciousness: Afro-American Folk Thought From Slavery to Freedom* (New York: Oxford University Press, 1977), 28–30.

50. Carey Davenport, *TX*, Ser 1, Vol 4, P 1, 282.

51. Jacob Branch, *TX*, Ser 1, Vol 4, P 1, 139–140.

52. Anderson and Minerva Edwards, *TX*, Ser 1, Vol 4, P 2, 6–7.

53. James Green, *TX*, Ser 1, Vol 4, P 2, 89.

54. Walter Calloway, *AL*, Ser 1, Vol 6, 52.

55. Lina Anne Pendergrass, *SC*, Ser 1, Vol 3, P 3, 248–249.

56. Arrie Binns, *GA*, Ser 2, Vol 12, P 1, 77; Clara Young, *MS*, Sup, Ser 1, Vol 10, P 5, 2403; Blount Baker, *NC*, Ser 2, Vol 14, P 1, 64.

57. "Slaves Have No Soul," *Unwritten History of Slavery* in *American Slave*, Vol 18, 47–49.

58. Alec Bostwick, *GA*, Ser 2, Vol 12, P 1, 109.

59. Pet Franks, *MS*, Ser 1, Vol 7, 58.

60. Easter Lockhart, *SC*, Ser 1, Vol 3, P 3, 109–110.

61. Dora Jackson, *MS*, Ser 2, Vol 8, P 3, 1111.

62. Sarah Thomas, *MS*, Sup, Ser 1, Vol 10, P 5, 2107.

63. Rachel Santee Reed, *MS*, Sup, Ser 1, Vol 9, P 4, 1815.

64. Tom Robinson, *AR*, Ser 2, Vol 10, P 6, 64.

65. Mary Colbert, *GA*, Ser 2, Vol 12, P 1, 224.

66. Harriet Tubman, in Blassingame, *Slave Testimony*, 463.

67. Fannie Moore, *NC*, Ser 2, Vol 15, P 2, 130.

68. Andrew Moss, *TN*, Ser 2, Vol 16, 49; Annie Row, *TX*, Ser 1, Vol 5, P 3, 259; W.L. Bost, *NC*, Ser 2, Vol 14, P 1, 143.

69. "*Granny*," in Blasingame, *Slave Testimony*, 539–541.

70. Delia Garlic, *AL*, Ser 1, Vol 6, 131.

71. George Gurtner, "*Color Blind in New Orleans*," *Our Sunday Visitor* (January 7, 1996), Vol 84, No. 36, 12; Cyprian Davis, O.S.B., *The History of Black Catholics in the United States* (New York: Crossroad, 1990) 105–108.

72. Davis, *Black Catholics*, 99–101.

73. Isaac Wilson, *MS*, Sup, Ser 1, Vol 10, P 5, 2361.

74. Dora Jackson, *MS*, Sup, Ser 1, Vol 8, P 3, 1111.

75. Malinda Edwards, *MS*, Sup, Ser 1, Vol 7, P 2, 680.

76. Mary Williams, *AR*, Ser 2, Vol 11, P 7, 182; "White Folks' Pet," *Unwritten History of Slavery*, in *American Slave*, 27; Ann Palmer, *SC*, Ser 1, Vol 3, P 3, 223–225.

77. Mary Jane Hardridge, *AR*, Ser 2, Vol 9, P 3, 160.

78. Clara Walker, *AR*, Ser 2, Vol 11, P 7, 19–20; Elax Bonner, *MS*, Sup, Ser 1, Vol 6, P 1, 175–176; Mary Williams, *AR*, Ser 2, Vol 11, P 7, 181–182.

79. Hamp Kennedy, *MS*, Ser 1, Vol 7, 86; Minnie Ross, *GA*, Ser 1, Vol 12, P 1, 29; William Adams, *TX*, Ser 1, Vol 4, P 1, 4–8; Clara Walker, *AR*, Ser 2, Vol 11, P 7, 20–21; Rosanna Frazier, *TX*, Ser 1, Vol 4, P 2, 64.

80. Hamp Santee, *MS*, Sup, Ser 1, Vol 10, P 5, 1917; Manus Brown, *MS*, Sup, Ser 1, Vol 6, P 1, 271.

81. Martha Colquitt, *GA*, Ser 2, Vol 12, P 1, 245.

82. J.M. Keating, *History of Memphis and Shelby County, Tennessee*, 2 vols. (Syracuse, New York: D. Mason, 1888), Vol 1, 124–128. See also Frances Wright, *Views of Society and Manners in America*, edited by Paul R. Baker (1821; reprint, Cambridge, MA: Belknap Press of Harvard University Press, 1963), xv–xviii.

83. Memphis *Daily Appeal*, August 17, 1847; March 29, May 22, July 10, December 13, 1851; March 25, 1852.

84. Memphis *Daily Appeal*, June 16, August 15, 1851; Willie Lee Rose, *Slavery and Freedom*, edited by William W. Freehling (New York, Oxford University Press, 1982) 25.

85. Laura Ford, *MS*, Sup, Ser 1, Vol 7, P 2, 756–757.

86. Cecelia Chappel, *TN*, Ser 2, Vol 16, 6.

87. Milton Marshall, *SC*, Ser 1, Vol 3, P 3, 173; Sam McCallum, *MS*, Sup, Ser 1, Vol 9, P 4, 1351.

88. Frances Willis, *MS*, Sup, Ser 1, Vol 10, P 5, 2358.

89. Minnie Davis, *GA*, Ser 2, Vol 12, P 1, 257; W.L. Bost, *NC*, Ser 2, Vol 14, P 1, 141; Anderson Williams, *MS*, Sup, Ser 1, Vol 10, P 5, 2298; C.H. Hall, in Blassingame, *Slave Testimony*, 417; Frederick Douglass, *Life and Times of Frederick Douglass Written by Himself* (1882; reprint, New York: Collier Books, 1962), 79.

90. Tom McAlpine, *AL*, Ser 1, Vol 6, 269.

91. James Singleton, *MS*, Sup, Ser 1, Vol 10, P 5, 1960; Cora Gillam, *AR*, Ser 2, Vol 9, P 3, 28; Jimmie Johnson, *SC*, Ser 1, Vol 3, P 3, 53; Miller, ed., "*Dear Master*": *Letters of a Slave Family*, 197–208.

92. Hagar Lewis, *TX*, Ser 1, Vol 5, P 3, 4; Jerry Moore, *TX*, Ser 1, Vol 5, P 3, 121; Olmsted, *Cotton Kingdom*, 348–349; Harre Quarles, *TX*, Ser 1, Vol 5, P 3, 223; Rev. Lafayette Price, *TX*, Ser 1, Vol 5, P 3, 204.

93. Adora Rienshaw, *NC*, Ser 2, Vol 15, P 2, 214; James C. James, *MD*, Ser 2, Vol 16, 35; W. Solomon Debham, *NC*, Ser 2, Vol 14, P 1, 244; Robert Glenn, *NC*, Ser 2, Vol 14, P 1, 333.

94. "Noted Personalities in Warren County," *MS*, Sup, Ser 1, Vol 9, P 4, 1532–1533.

95. Louis Davis, *MS*, Sup, Ser 1, Vol 7, P 2, 580.

96. Susan Castle, *GA*, Ser 2, Vol 12, P 1, 182.

97. Memphis *Daily Appeal*, May 26, June 21, 1852.

98. *Ibid.*, March 4, 1853.

99. *Ibid.*, August 18, 1853; Postell, *Health of Slaves*, 68.

100. Olmsted, *Cotton Kingdom*, 449; Postell, *Health of Slaves*, 54–55.

101. James Bunton, *MS*, Sup, Ser 1, Vol 6, P 1, 306; Mom Agnes James, *SC*, Ser 1, Vol 3, P 3, 9; Lindsey Faucette, *NC*, Ser 2, Vol 14, P 1, 303; Sylvia King, *TX*, Vol 4, P 2, 294.

102. Clara Walker, *AR*, Ser 2, Vol 11, P 7, 21–22; Postell, *Health of Slaves*, 113–115.

103. Minerva Wells, *MS*, Sup, Ser 1, Vol 10, P 5, 2257.

104. Porter Bond, *MS*, Sup, Ser 1, Vol 6, P 1, 168; Fred James *SC*, Ser 1, Vol 3, P 3, 15; Benjamin Russell, *SC*, Ser 1, Vol 3, P 4, 54.

105. Georgia Baker, *GA*, Ser 2, Vol 12, P 1, 49.

106. Arrie Binns, *GA*, Ser 2, Vol 12, P 1, 76; James Bolton, *GA*, Ser 2, Vol 12, P 1, 94; Sherry Barnes, *AL*, Ser 1, Vol 6, 21; Harriet Barrett, *TX*, Ser 1, Vol 4, P 1, 50; Scott Hooper, *TX*, Ser 1, Vol 4, P 2, 158.

107. Rena Clark, *MS*, Sup, Ser 1, Vol 7, P 2, 409–410; Harriet Collins, *TX*, Ser 1, Vol 4, P 1, 244–245; Mary Kincheon, *TX*, Ser 1, Vol 4, P2, 16; Jacqueline Jones, *Labor of Love, Labor of Sorrow: Black Women, Work and the Family from Slavery to the Present* (New York: Vintage Books, 1985), 40.

108. Josephine Cox, *TX*, Sup, Ser 1, Vol 7, P 2, 526; Jake McLeod, *SC*, Ser 1, Vol 3, P 3, 160; Postell, *Health of Slaves*, 130.

109. Clara Davis, *AL*, Ser 1, Vol 6, 109–110.

110. Isaac Stier, *MS*, Ser 1, Vol 7, 2048–2051; Susan Castle, *GA*, Ser 2, Vol 12, P 1, 182; Smith Simmons, *MS*, Sup, Ser 1, Vol 10, P 5, 140; Rev. James W. Washington, *MS*, Sup, Ser 1, Vol 10, P 5, 2200; Ben Moon, *AR*, Ser 2, Vol 10, P 5, 119; Henry Bland, *GA*, Ser 2, Vol 12, P 1, 85; Tom Wilson, *MS*, Sup, Ser 1, Vol 10, P5, 2378; Leta Gray, *KS*, Ser 1, Vol 16, 3–4.

111. Harriet Jones, *TX*, Ser 1, Vol 4, P 2, 234; Northup, *Twelve Years A Slave*, 113–116.

112. Annie Stanton, *AL*, Ser 1, Vol 6, 354; John Smith, *NC*, Ser 2, Vol 15, P 2, 275; Molly Ammond, *AL*, Ser 1, Vol 6, 11; Pauline Grice, *TX*, Sup, Ser 1, Vol 4, P 2, 99–100; Andrew Goodman, *TX*, Ser 1, Vol 4, P 2, 76; Tilday Collins, *AL*, Ser 1, Vol 6, 85; Sarah Ann Green, *NC*, Ser 2, Vol 14, P 1, 342; Cinte Lewis, *TX*, Ser 1, Vol 5, P 3, 2.

113. Ann Drake, *MS*, Sup, Ser 1, Vol 7, P 2, 643–644.

114. Needham Love, *AR*, Ser 2, Vol 9, P 4, 295; Harriet Walker, *MS*, Sup, Ser 1, Vol 10, P 5, 2159.

115. James Boyd, *TX*, Ser 1, Vol 4, P 1, 117–120; Henry Bland, *GA*, Sup 2, Vol 12, P 1, 81; Midge Burnett, *NC*, Ser 2, Vol 14, P 1, 157; Dock Wilborn, *AR*, Ser 2, Vol

11, P 7, 145; George Fisher, *MS*, Sup, Ser 1, Vol 7, P 2, 731; Leta Gray, *KS*, Ser 2, Vol 16, 3–4.

116. Sarah Fitzpatrick, in Blassingame, *Slave Testimony*, 644.

117. Simon Durr, *MS*, Sup, Ser 1, Vol 7, P 2, 656; Bill Crump, *NC*, Ser 2, Vol 14, P 1, 209; Preston Kyles, *AR*, Ser 2, P 4, 220–222.

118. Hannah Crasson, *NC*, Ser 2, Vol 14, P 1, 191; Lucy Lewis, *TX*, Ser 1, Vol 5, P 3, 15; Ellen Betts, *TX*, Ser 1, Vol 4, P 1, 79; Northup, *Twelve Years A Slave*, 167.

119. Anda Woods, *MS*, Sup, Ser 1, Vol 10, P 5, 2390.

120. Lizzie Hughes, *TX*, Ser 1, Vol 4, P 2, 167.

121. Harriet Jones, *TX*, Ser 1, Vol 4, P 2, 234–235.

122. Bill Homer, *TX*, Ser 1, Vol 4, P 2, 155; A.C. Pruitt, *TX*, Ser 1, Vol 5, P 3, 219; Fred Brown, *TX*, Ser 1, Vol 4, P 1, 158; William Adams, *TX*, Ser 1, Vol 4, P 1, 10; Anderson and Minerva Brown, *TX*, Ser 1, Vol 4, P 3, 7; Marshal Butler, *GA*, Ser 2, Vol 12, P 1, 167; Reuben Laird, *MS*, Sup, Ser 1, Vol 8, P 3, 1299; Harriet Miller, *MS*, Sup, Ser 1, Vol 9, P 4, 1502; Diccy Windfield, *MS*, Sup, Ser 1, Vol 10, P 5, 2385.

123. "Owns The House He Lived In as a Slave," *Unwritten History of Slavery*, in *American Slave*, Vol 18, Ser 2, 131; Richard Mack, *SC*, Ser 1, Vol 3, P 3, 151; Ephriam Lawrence, *SC*, Ser 1, Vol 3, P 3, 97–99; Louis Fowler, *TX*, Ser 1, Vol 4, P 2, 51; Bill Crump, *NC*, Ser 2, Vol 14, P 1, 209; Andrew Goodman, *TX*, Ser 1, Vol 4, P 2, 76.

124. Henry Lewis, *TX*, Ser 1, Vol 5, P 3, 11; Aaron Russell, *TX*, Ser 1, Vol 5, P 3, 271.

125. Tinie Force and Elvira Lewis, *KY*, Ser 2, Vol 16, 114–116.

126. Ben Leitner, *SC*, Ser 1, Vol 3, P 3, 100.

127. Charlie Davenport, *MS*, Sup, Ser 1, Vol 7, 558.

128. Salem Powell, *MS*, Sup, Ser 1, Vol 9, P 4, 1748; Ann Drake, *MS*, Sup, Ser 1, Vol 7, P 2, 646.

129. Charity More, *SC*, Ser 1, Vol 3, P 3, 205–206.

130. Henry Warfield, *MS*, Sup, Ser 1, Vol 10, P 5, 2183.

131. James Bolton, *GA*, Ser 2, Vol 12, P 1, 93; Gus Clark, *MS*, Sup, Ser 1, Vol 7, P 2, 404.

132. Virginia Newman, *TX*, Ser 1, Vol 5, P 3, 149.

133. Emma Blalock, *NC*, Ser 2, Vol 14, P 1, 105–106; Zeb Crowder, *NC*, Ser 2, Vol 14, P 1, 22; Sam Polite, *SC*, Ser 1, Vol 3, P 3, 272; Amos Clark, *TX*, Ser 1, Vol 4, P 1, 221.

134. Olmsted, *Cotton Kingdom*, 448; Lucy Lewis, *TX*, Ser 1, Vol 5, P 3, 18; Carter J. Jackson, *TX*, Ser 1, Vol 4, P 3, 180; Henry Ryan, *SC*, Ser 1, Vol 3, P 4, 71; W. Solomon Debham, *NC*, Ser 2, Vol 14, P 1, 243.

135. Daphney Wright, *SC*, Ser 1, Vol 3, P 4, 269; Valmar Cormier, *TX*, Ser 1, Vol 4, P 1, 253.

136. Susan Kelly, *VA*, Ser 2, Vol 16, 45.

137. Marion Johnson, *AR*, Ser 2, Vol 9, P 4, 112.

138. Israel Jackson, *AR*, Ser 2, Vol 9, P 4, 6.

139. Harriet Jones, *TX*, Ser 1, Vol 4, P 2, 234.

140. Lizzie Hughes, *TX*, Ser 1, Vol 4, P 2, 167.

141. Isaac Wilson, *MS*, Sup, Ser 1, Vol 10, P 5, 2360–2361.

142. Pauline Grice, *TX*, Ser 1, Vol 4, P 2, 99.

143. Lizzie Hughes, *TX*, Ser 1, Vol 4, P 2, 167.

144. John Goodson, *AR*, Ser 2, Vol 9, P 3, 57.

145. Ebenezer Brown, *MS*, Sup, Ser 1, Vol 6, P 1, 243.

146. Ambus Gray, *AR*, Ser 2, Vol 9, P 3, 78; Minerva Grubbs, *MS*, Sup, Ser 1, Vol 8, P 3, 892; George Weathersby, *MS*, Sup, Ser 1, Vol 10, P 5, 2234; Allen Ward, *MS*, Sup, Ser 1, Vol 10, P 5, 2171.

147. Philip Johnson, *MD*, Ser 2, Vol 16, 41–43.

148. Susan Kelly, *VA*, Ser 2, Vol 16, 45.

149. Edwin Walker, *MS*, Sup, Ser 1, Vol 10, P 5, 2154.

150. Ebenezer Brown, *MS*, Sup, Ser 1, Vol 6, P 1, 2441.

151. Rachel Adams, *GA*, Ser 2, Vol 12, P 1, 294; Eliza Washington, *AR*, Ser 1, Vol 11, P 7, 51–52; Martha Colquitt, *GA*, Ser 2, Vol 12, P 1, 244; Claiborne Moss, *AR*, Ser 2, Vol 10, P 5, 161; Charlie Graham, *AR*, Ser 2, Vol 9, P 3, 68; Sara Colquitt, *AL*, Ser 1, Vol 6, 88–89; Chaney Hews, *NC*, Ser 2, Vol 14, P 1, 407; James V. Deane, *MD*, Ser 2, Vol 16, 8–9; James Boyd, *TX*, Ser 1, Vol 4, P 1, 118; Green Cumby, *TX*, Ser 1, Vol 4, 261.

152. George Woods, *SC*, Ser 1, Vol 3, P 4, 249; Junius Quattlebaum, *SC*, Ser 1, Vol 3, P 3, 283–284; Prince Johnson, *MS*, Sup, Ser 1, Vol 8, P 3, 1173.

153. Manus Robinson, *MS*, Sup, Ser 1, Vol 9, P 4, 1858–1859.

154. Fred Brown, *TX*, Ser 1, Vol 4, P 1, 158; Jim and Sally Nickerson, *MS*, Sup, Ser 1, Vol 9, P 3, 1638; William Grant, *AR*, Ser 2, Vol 9, P 3, 12; Frank Hughes, *MS*, Sup, Ser 1, Vol 8, P 3, 1060.

155. Henry Cheatam, *AL*, Ser 1, Vol 6, 68; Valmar Cormier, *TX*, Ser 1, Vol 4, P 1, 253.

156. Charlie Davenport, *MS*, Ser 1, Vol 7, 36; Adam Singleton, *MS*, Sup, Ser 1, Vol 10, P 5, 1947; Mary Anderson, *NC*, Ser 2, Vol 14, P 1, 23; John Price, *TX*, Ser 1, Vol 5, P 3, 198; Jennie Webb, *MS*, Sup, Ser 1, Vol 10, P 5, 2250; Minerva Grubbs, *MS*, Sup, Ser 1, Vol 8, P 3, 892; Ann Drake, *MS*, Sup, Ser 1, Vol 7, P 2, 645.

157. Isaac Johnson, *NC*, Ser 2, Vol 15, P 2, 17; Charlie Barbour, *NC*, Ser 2, Vol 14, P 1, 75; Jane Arrington, *NC*, Ser 2, Vol 14, P 1, 48.

158. Tony Cox, *MS*, Sup, Ser 1, Vol 7, P 2, 533.

159. Emily Dixon, *MS*, Sup, Ser 1, Vol 7, P 2, 622.

160. Olmsted, *Cotton Kingdom*, 234–235.

161. Keating, *Memphis*, 154.

Chapter 3

1. Virginia Sims, *AR*, Ser 2, Vol 10, P 6, 163.

2. Olmsted, *Cotton Kingdom*, 357.

3. Ephom Banks, *MS*, Sup, Ser 1, Vol 6, P 1, 103; John Cole, *GA*, Ser 2, Vol 12, P 1, 228.

4. "Autobiography of Ebenezer Brown," *MS*, Sup, Ser 1, Vol 6, P 1, 243.

5. Andy Marion, *SC*, Ser 1, Vol 3, P 3, 167.

6. William Hunter, *AR*, Ser 2, Vol 9, P 3, 317; Moses Jeffries, *AR*, Ser 2, Vol 9, P 4, 39; John Matthews, *MS*, Sup, Ser 1, Vol 9, P 4, 1454; Nelson Dickerson, *MS*, Sup, Ser 1, Vol 7, P 2, 601.

7. Nelson Dickerson, *MS*, Sup, Ser 1, Vol 7, P 2, 601; Betty Powers, *TX*, Ser 1, Vol 5, P 1, 191.

8. Temple Wilson, *MS*, Sup, Ser 1, Vol 10, P 5, 2370; James V. Deane, *MD*, Ser 2, Vol 16, 7; Jake Dawkins, *MS*, Sup, Ser 1, Vol 7, P 2, 595.

9. Lizzie Brown, *MS*, Sup, Ser 1, Vol 6, P 1, 263.

10. Willis Easter, *TX*, Ser 1, Vol 4, P 1, 2; Richard Moring, *NC*, Ser 2, Vol 15, P 2, 139–140; Mom Agnes James, *SC*, Ser 1, Vol 3, P 3, 11.

11. Charlie Robinson, *SC*, Ser 1, Vol 3, P 4, 36.

12. Tempie Herndon Durham, *NC*, Ser 2, Vol 14, P 1, 288; Susan Snow, *MS*, Ser 1, Vol 7, 137; Virginia Jackson, *AR*, Ser 2, Vol 9, P 4, 26.

13. Parke Johnston, in Blassingame, *Slave Testimony*, 490–491.

14. Vinnie Busby, *MS*, Sup, Ser 1, Vol 6, P 1, 310.
15. Manda Walker, *SC*, Ser 1, Vol 3, P 4, 170–171.
16. Warren Taylor, *AR*, Ser 2, Vol 10, P 6, 273; Sena Moore, *SC*, Ser 1, Vol 3, P 3, 24.
17. Julia Bunch, *GA*, Ser 2, Vol 12, P 1, 159.
18. Lydia Stewart, *MS*, Sup , Ser 1, Vol 10, P 5, 2047; Adeline Crump, *NC*, Ser 2, Vol 14, P 1, 205.
19. Jim Allen, *MS*, Sup, Ser 1, Vol 6, P 1, 57; Casper Rumple, *AR*, Ser 2, Vol 10, P 6, 103; Viney Foster, *MS*, Sup, Ser 1, Vol 7, P 2, 760–762.
20. Mary Estes Peters, *AR*, Ser 2, Vol 10, P 5, 328–329; Lizzie Hawkens, *AR*, Ser 2, Vol 9, P 3, 205; Martha Johnson, *AR*, Ser 2, Vol 9, P 4, 122; Nanny Madden, *AR*, Ser 2, Vol 10, P 5, 39; Dora Franks, *MS*, Sup, Ser 1, Vol 7, P 2, 782; Betty Powers, *TX*, Ser 1, Vol 5, P 3, 191–192; Sella Martin, in Blassingame, *Slave Testimony*, 703–704.
21. Mary Reynolds, *TX*, Ser 1, Vol 5, P 3, 243; Hattie Rogers, *NC*, Ser 2, Vol 15, P 2, 230; Donaville Broussard, *TX*, Ser 1, Vol 4, P 1, 151; Elvira Boles, *TX*, Ser 1, Vol 4, P 1, 107; Gabriel Gilbert, *TX*, Ser 1, Vol 4, P 2, 69; Olmsted, *Cotton Kingdom*, 239–240.
22. Fanny Berry, *VA*, Ser 2, Vol 16, 2.
23. W.L. Bost, *NC*, Ser 2, Vol 14, P 1, 142.
24. Martha Bradley, *AL*, Ser 1, Vol 6, 46.
25. Mattie Curtis, *NC*, Ser 2, Vol 14, P 1, 220.
26. James Brittian, *MS*, Sup, Ser 1, Vol 6, P 1, 217–218; "All My Bosses Were Nigger Traders," *Unwritten History of Slavery*, in *American Slave*, Vol 18, 261; "My Old Master was a Methodist Preacher," *Unwritten History of Slavery,* in *American Slave,*Vol 18, 298; Augustus Robinson, *AR*, Ser 2, Vol 10, P 6, 55–56; Chaney Spell, *NC*, Ser 2, Vol 15, 308; Eakin and Logsdon, eds., *Twelve Years a Slave*, 142–143.
27. Mary Gaines, *AR*, Ser 2, Vol 9, P 3, 7; Tom Stanhouse, *AR*, Ser 2, Vol 10, P 6, 216; Robert Solomon, *AR*, Ser 2, Vol 10, P 6, 208; Eugenia Weatherall, *MS*, Sup, Ser 1, Vol 10, 2214–2215; J.N. Gillespie, *AR*, Ser 2, Vol 9, P 3, 34; Becky Hawkins, *AR*, Ser 2, Vol 9, P 3, 209; Elizabeth Hines, *AR*, Ser 2, Vol 9, P 3, 273.
28. Wade, *Slavery in the Cities*, 124; Olmsted, *Cotton Kingdom*, 228–240; Lyle Saxon, Edward Dreyer, and Robert Tallant, *Gumbo Ya Ya: A Collection of Louisiana Folk Tales* (New York: Bonanza Books, 1945) 159–160.
29. Adora Rienshaw, *NC*, Ser 2, Vol 15, P 2, 213–214; Millie Markham, *NC*, Ser 2, Vol 15, P 2, 102–107; George Patterson, *SC*, Ser 1, Vol 3, P 3, 226–227.
30. Ervin Smith, *AR*, Ser 2, Vol 10, P 6, 187–188; Adaline Johnson, *AR*, Ser 2, Vol 9, P 4, 53; Andrew Moss, *TN*, Ser 2, Vol 16, 50; Dora Franks, *MS*, Sup, Ser 1, Vol 7, P 2, 782.
31. Alexander Robertson, *SC*, Ser 1, Vol 3, P 4, 34.
32. Jack Johnson, *SC*, Ser 1, Vol 3, P 3, 41.
33. Cato Carter, *TX*, Ser 1, Vol 4, P 1, 205.
34. *"Massa's Slave Son," Unwritten History of Slavery,* in *American Slave,* Vol 18, 84.
35. Davis, *Black Catholics in the United States* (New York: Crossroad, 1990), 146–152.
36. See Michael Tadman, *Speculators and Slaves: Masters, Traders, and Slaves in The Old South* (Madison, WI: University of Wisconsin Press, 1980), 170–219.
37. Foster Weathersby, *MS*, Sup, Ser 1, Vol 10, P 5, 2229.
38. Sarah Wells, *AR*, Ser 2, Vol 11, P 7, 90; Julia Brown, *GA*, Ser 2, Vol 12, P 1, 144.
39. Clay Bobbit, *NC*, Ser 2, Vol 14, P 1, 118.
40. Virginia Bell, *TX*, Ser 1, Vol 4, P 1, 62; Tom Morris, *MS*, Sup, Ser 1, Vol 9, P 4, 1579–1580.
41. Harriet Hill, *AR*, Ser 2, Vol 9, P 3, 258; Rose

Holman, *MS*, Sup, Ser 1, Vol 8, P 3, 1037; James Singleton, *MS*, Sup, Ser 1, Vol 10, P 5, 1960; Carolyn Stout, *AR*, Ser 2, Vol 10, P 6, 245; Robert Glenn, *NC*, Ser 2, Vol 14, P 1, 329–331; Laura Clark, *AL*, Ser 1, Vol 6, 72–73.
42. George Washington Miller, *MS*, Sup, Ser 1, Vol 9, P 4, 1487.
43. Aunt Mary Ferguson, *GA*, Ser 2, Vol 12, P 1, 326–328.
44. Jane Williams, *MS*, Sup, Ser 1, Vol 10, P 5, 2223.
45. Elmira Hill, *AR*, Ser 2, Vol 9, P 3, 254; Martha Johnson, *AR*, Ser 2, Vol 9, P 4, 122.
46. Anna King, *AR*, Ser 2, Vol 9, P 4, 202; George Williamson, *MS*, Sup, Ser 1, Vol 10, P 5, 2352; Mattie McLain, *MS*, Sup, Ser 1, Vol 7, P 2, 614; Martha Wheeler, *MS*, Sup, Ser 1, Vol 10, P 5, 2262.
47. Julia Casey, *TN*, Ser 2, Vol 16, 3; Bill Homer, *TX*, Ser 1, Vol 4, P 2, 154; Adeline Jackson, *SC*, Ser 1, Vol 3, P 3, 2; Jane Harrington, *NC*, Ser 2, Vol 14, P 1, 47; Jonathan Thomas, in Blassingame, *Slave Testimony*, 251–252; J.W.C. Pennington, "The Fugitive Blacksmith," in Arna Bontemps, ed., *Great Slave Narratives* (Boston: Beacon Press Boston, 1969), 258.
48. Abram Harris, *AR*, Ser 2, Vol 9, P 3, 171.
49. Mamie Thompson, *AR*, Ser 2, Vol 10, P 6, 318; Dave Lawson, *NC*, Ser 2, Vol 15, P 2, 44–50; Mary Moriah Anne Susanna Jones, *MD*, Ser 2, Vol 16, 39.
50. Tom Holland, *TX*, Ser 2, Vol 4, P 2, 146.
51. Clara Jones, *NC*, Ser 2, Vol 15, P 2, 31–32; Andy J. Anderson, *TX*, Ser 1, Vol 4, P 1, 5.
52. Mary Anderson, *NC*, Ser 2, Vol 14, P 1, 33; Millie Simpkins, *TN*, Ser 2, Vol 16, 66; James V. Deane, *MD*, Ser 2, Vol 16, 7; Lula Nichols, *NC*, Ser 2, Vol 15, 148–149.
53. Tadman, *Speculators and Slaves*, 127–129.
54. Maggie Stanhouse, *AR*, Ser 2, Vol 10, P 6, 223; Ida Blackshear Hutchinson, *AR*, Ser 2, Vol 9, P 3, 370; Viney Baker, *NC*, Ser 2, Vol 14, P 1, 71; Lewis Jones, *TX*, Ser 1, Vol 4, P 2, 237; Millie Williams, *MS*, Vol 7, Ser 1, 157–158.
55. Rose Williams, *TX*, Ser 1, Vol 5, P 3, 177–178.
56. Mary Jane Jones, *MS*, Sup, Ser 1, Vol 8, P 3, 1243; Annie Coley, *MS*, Sup, Ser 1, Vol 7, P 2, 440–441; Mary Barbour, *NC*, Ser 2, Vol 14, P 1, 79; Martha Jackson, *AL*, Ser 1, Vol 6, 222.
57. Eustace Hodges, *NC*, Ser 2, Vol 14, P 1, 447; Betty Simmons, *TX*, Ser 1, Vol 5, P 3, 23; J. Harry Bennett, *Bondsmen and Bishops: Slavery and Apprenticeship on the Codrington Plantations of Barbados, 1710–1838.* (Berkeley, CA: University of California Press, 1958).
58. Mandy McCullough Cosby, *AL*, Ser 1, Vol 6, 90.
59. David Blount, *NC*, Ser 2, Vol 14, P 1, 113.
60. Taylor Jackson, *AR*, Ser 2, Vol 9, P 4, 22–23; Willie Lee Rose, ed., *A Documentary History of Slavery in North America* (New York: Oxford University Press, 1976), 169.
61. Tadman, *Speculators and Slaves*, 98–100.
62. Olmsted, *Cotton Kingdom*, 229–230.
63. Keating, *Memphis*, 328.
64. Memphis *Daily Appeal*, January 25, 1853.
65. Betty Simmons, *TX*, Ser 1, Vol 5, P 3, 20–21.
66. Charlotte Willis, *AR*, Ser 2, Vol 11, P 7, 193.
67. Minerva Wells, *MS*, Sup, Ser 1, Vol 10, P 5, 2257.
68. Richard Macks, *MD*, Ser 2, Vol 16, 51.
69. John Smith, *NC*, Ser 2, Vol 15, P 2, 282–283.
70. W.L. Bost, *NC*, Ser 2, Vol 14, P 1, 140.
71. Sella Martin, in Blassingame, ed., *Slave Testimony*, 704–705.
72. James Brown, *TX*, Ser 1, Vol 4, P 1, 161.
73. Green Cumby, *TX*, Ser 1, Vol 4, P 1, 260.
74. Cato Carter, *TX*, Ser 1, Vol 4, P 1, 207.

75. Henry Warfield, *MS*, Sup, Ser 1, Vol 10, P 5, 2180.

76. Frederick Bancroft, *Slave Trading in the Old South*, (New York: Ungar Publishing Co., 1959), 250–265.

77. Memphis *Daily Appeal*, February 27, 1852; May 27, 1853. For typical advertisements see the *Daily Appeal*, September 4, 1847; November 1, 1848; May 28, 1851; July 19, October 12, 1853.

78. *Ibid.*, June 15, 1852; September 1, 1853.

79. *Ibid.*, January 8, 1851.

80. *Ibid.*, January 29, 1853.

81. *Ibid.*, September 11, December 5, 1847; January 6, January 21, 1851; March 30, April 7, April 20, December 7, 1852; March 22, December 5, 1853.

82. *Ibid.*, January 3, January 10, May 24, 1851; December 1, December 29, 1852; December 2, 1853.

83. *Ibid.*, January 26, February 9, July 14, July 16, 1852.

84. Northup, *Twelve Years a Slave*.

Chapter 4

1. Mark Oliver, *MS*, Sup, Ser 1, Vol 9, P 4, 1661; Isom Blackshear, *AR*, Ser 2, Vol 9, P 3, 372; Frank Freeman, *NC*, Ser 2, Vol 14, P 1, 321; John Hunter, *AR*, Ser 2, Vol 9, P 3, 362; Hannah Plummer, *NC*, Ser 2, Vol 15, P 2, 180–181; Anna Baker, *MS*, Ser 1, Vol 7, 13.

2. Ellis Jefson, *AR*, Ser 2, Vol 9, P 4, 44; Frances Patterson, *MS*, Sup, Ser 1, Vol 9, P 4, 1679; Lula Coleman, *MS*, Sup, Ser 1, Vol 7, P 2, 427–430.

3. Lizzie, McCloud, *AR*, Ser 2, Vol 10, P5, 4.

4. Cinte Lewis, *TX*, Ser 1, Vol 5, P 3, 2.

5. Abram Harris, *AR*, Ser 2, Vol 9, P 3, 172; William Ball Williams, *AR*, Ser 2, P 7, 191.

6. Tom Randall, *MD*, Ser 2, Vol 16, 58; Blassingame, *Slave Testimony*, 268–274.

7. Felix Haywood, *TX*, Ser 1, Vol 4, P 2, 132; Walter Rimm, *TX*, Ser 1, Vol 5, P 3, 249.

8. Blassingame, *Slave Testimony*, 457–465.

9. Mac Johnson, *AR*, Ser 2, Vol 9, P 4, 108–109; Louis Johnson, *AR*, Ser 2, Vol 9, P 4, 104; Julia Brown, *GA*, Ser 2, Vol 12, P 1, 147; Hannah Chapman, *MS*, Sup, Ser 1, Vol 7, P 2, 381; Joe Rollins, *MS*, Sup, Ser 1, Vol 9, P 4, 1897; Abe Kelley, *MS*, Sup, Ser 1, Vol 8, P 3, 1270; Charlotte Moore, *MS*, Sup, Ser 1, Vol 9, P 4, 1566; Amanda Ross, *AR*, Ser 2, Vol 10, P 6, 82; Leah Garret, *GA*, Ser 2, Vol 12, P 2, 14–15; Edinbur Randall, in Blassingame, *Slave Testimony*, 321–325.

10. Gill Ruffin, *TX*, Ser 1, Vol 5, P 3, 263.

11. Louis Johnson, *AR*, Ser 2, Vol 9, P 4, 104; Laura Thornton, *AR*, Ser 2, Vol 10, P 6, 326; Happy Day Green, *AR*, Ser 2, Vol 9, P 3, 87; George Ward, *MS*, Sup, Ser 1, Vol 10, P 5, 2176; Olmsted, *Cotton Kingdom*, 388; Memphis *Daily Appeal*, August 13, 1851.

12. Evie Herrin, *MS*, Sup, Ser 1, Vol 8, P 3, 988–989.

13. Tom Wilson, in Blassingame, *Slave Testimony*, 338–340.

14. Fanny Cannady, *NC*, Ser 2, Vol 14, P 1, 163–164; Aunt Jane Morgan, *MS*, Sup, Ser 1, Vol 9, P 4, 1574; Page Harris, *MD*, Ser 2, Vol 16, 24; Essex Henry, *NC*, Ser 2, Vol 14, P 1, 397; Northup, *Twelve Years a Slave*, 101–107.

15. Moses Jeffries, *AR*, Ser 2, Vol 9, P 4, 39; Fanny Cannady, *NC*, Ser 2, Vol 14, P 1, 163–164; Eugenia Weatherall, *MS*, Sup, Ser 1, Vol 10, P 5, 2219–2220; Tom Wilson, *MS*, Sup, Ser 1, Vol 10, P 5, 2379; Anna Woods, *AR*, Ser 2, Vol 11, P 7, 226; George Washington Miller, *MS*, Sup, Ser 1, Vol 9, P 4, 1488; Will Glass, *AR*, Ser 2, Vol 9, P 3, 38.

16. Jack Frowers, in Blassingame, *Slave Testimony*, 451; Lavima Bell, in Blassingame, *Slave Testimony*, 341–345; Louis Cain, *TX*, Ser 1, Vol 4, P 1, 186; Memphis *Daily Appeal*, August 30, 1852.

17. Charles McClendon, *AR*, Ser 2, Vol 10, P 5, 2; John Williams, *AR*, Ser 2, Vol 11, P 7, 175; William Jackson, *AR*, Ser 2, Vol 9, P 4, 29; Bassett, *The Southern Plantation Overseer*, 78–81; Gabe Emanuel, *MS*, Sup, Ser 1, Vol 7, P 2, 683; Pennington, "The Fugitive Blacksmith," 216.

18. Wade, *Slavery in the Cities*, 214–222.

19. Memphis *Daily Appeal*, May 3, 1851; September 1, 1853.

20. Memphis *Daily Appeal*, September 14, 1848; March 11, 1845; October 30, November 24, December 6, 1851; June 15, 1852; April 12, 1853.

21. *Ibid*, December 15, 1847; August 23, August 26, 1848; March 3, June 18, July 14, 1851; July 15, 1852; June 11, 1853.

22. James McPherson, *Battle Cry of Freedom: The Civil War Era*, (New York: Oxford University Press, 1988), 119–120.

23. Polly Turner Cancer, *MS*, Sup, Ser 1, Vol 7, P 2, 342.

24. Isiah Jefferies, *SC*, Ser 1, Vol 3, P 3, 19.

25. Manda Walker, *SC*, Ser 1, Vol 3, P 4, 171.

26. Lewis Clark, in Blassingame, *Slave Testimony*, 157; Harriet Barrett, *TX*, Ser 1, Vol 4, P 1, 49; Ervin Smith, *AR*, Ser 2, Vol 10, P 6, 188–189; Arrie Binns, *GA*, Ser 2, Vol 12, P 1, 75.

27. Jane Sutton, *MS*, Sup, Ser 1, Vol 7, 153–154; Allen Ward, *MS*, Sup, Ser 1, Vol 10, P 5, 2172–2173.

28. Tom Holland, *TX*, Ser 1, Vol 4, P 2, 146; Henry Green, *AR*, Ser 2, Vol 9, P 3, 95.

29. See, for example, Perry Lewis, *MD*, Ser 2, Vol 16, 49–50; Preston Kyles, *AR*, Ser 2, Vol 9, P 4, 220–221; Ada Woods, *MS*, Sup, Ser 1, Vol 10, P 5, 2390; Walter Rimm, *TX*, Ser 1, Vol 5, P 3, 249.

30. Austin Pen Parnell, *AR*, Ser 2, Vol 10, P 5, 268.

31. Sam Broach, *MS*, Sup, Ser 1, Vol 6, P 1, 224; Hattie Suggs, *MS*, Sup, Ser 1, Vol 10, P 5, 2077; Adrianna Kerns, *AR*, Ser 2, Vol 9, P 4, 192.

32. Sally Dixon, *MS*, Sup, Ser 1, Vol 7, P 2, 628; Rose, ed., *A Documentary History of Slavery*, 337–344; Bassett, *The Southern Plantation Overseer*, 263.

33. Olmsted, *Cotton Kingdom*, 373.

34. W.B. Allen, *GA*, Ser 2, Vol 12, P 1, 14–15; Gabe Butler, *MS*, Sup, Ser 1, Vol 6, P 1, 317.

35. Mose Davis, *GA*, Ser 2, Vol 12, P 1, 270; Sally Dixon, *MS*, Sup, Ser 1, Vol 7, P 2, 627; Henry Ryan, *SC*, Ser 1, Vol 3, P 3, 71; James C. James, *MD*, Ser 2, Vol 16, 35; Marshall Butler, *GA*, Ser 2, Vol 12, P 1, 167; Emily Dixon, *MS*, Sup, Ser 1, Vol 7, P 2, 621; Harrison Beckett, *TX*, Ser 1, Vol 4, 55; Willis Cozart, *NC*, Ser 2, Vol 14, P 1, 184–185.

36. William Byrd, *TX*, Ser 1, Vol 4, P 1, 184; Andrew Boone, *NC*, Ser 2, Vol 14, P 1, 133–134; Martha Jackson, *AL*, Ser 1, Vol 6, 222; Lizzie Williams, *MS*, Sup, Ser 1, Vol 10, P 5, 2336–2337.

37. Green Cumby, *TX*, Ser 1, Vol 4, P 1, 2600; C.B. McCray, *TX*, Ser 1, Vol 5, P 3, 42; Richard Carruthers, *TX*, Ser 1, Vol 4, P 1, 198; Pauline Grice, *TX*, Ser 1, Vol 4, P 2, 98; James C. James, *MD*, Ser 2, Vol 16, 35; Harry McMillan, in Blassingame, *Slave Testimony*, 381.

38. Lettie Nelson, *AR*, Ser 2, Vol 10, P 5, 209; James Morgan, *AR*, Ser 2, Vol 10, P 5, 143.

39. Sarah Wells, *AR*, Ser 2, Vol 11, P 7, 90; Tom Morrison, *AR*, Ser 2, Vol 10, P 5, 148; Prince Smith, *SC*, Ser 1, Vol 3, P 4, 117–118; Ebenezer Brown, *MS*, Sup, Ser 1, Vol 6, P 1, 243–244; Susan Snow, *MS*, Ser 1, Vol 7, 137; Anthony Taylor, *AR*, Ser 2, Vol 10, P 6, 261.

40. Mary Tabon, *AR*, Ser 2, Vol 10, P 6, 253.

41. Alec Bostwick, *GA*, Ser 2, Vol 12, P 1, 107.

42. Solomon Bradley, in Blassingame, *Slave Testimony*, 371–373; Annie Row, *TX*, Ser 1, Vol 5, P 3, 259; Elizabeth Finley, *MS*, Sup, Ser 1, Vol 7, P 2, 728.

43. William Gant, *AR*, Ser 2, Vol 9, P 3, 12; Reuben Fox, *MS*, Sup, Ser 1, Vol 7, P 2, 772; Ella Booth, *MS*, Sup, Ser 1, Vol 6, P 1, 179; Gabe Butler, *MS*, Sup, Ser 1, Vol 6, P 1, 317; Henrietta Evelina Smith, *AR*, Ser 2, Vol 10, P 6, 194.

44. Jack Greene, *AL*, Ser 1, Vol 6, 168–169; Martha Jackson, *AL*, Ser 1, Vol 6, 222.

45. Mary Reynolds, *TX*, Ser 1, Vol 5, P 3, 241.

46. Katie Darling, *TX*, Ser 1, Vol 4, P 1, 279.

47. Austin Pen Parnell, *AR*, Ser 2, Vol 10, P 5, 270; Rachel Harris, *AR*, Ser 2, Vol 9, P 3, 179.

48. Maggie Westmoland, *AR*, Ser 2, Vol 11, 100; Leah Garrett, *GA*, Ser 2, Vol 12, P 2, 13; Charlie Moses, *MS*, Sup, Ser 1, Vol 9, P 4, 1597–1599; Charlie Hunter, *NC*, Ser 2, Vol 14, P 1, 454.

49. Charley Crawley, *VA*, Ser 2, Vol 16, 7–10.

50. Delia Garlic, *AL*, Ser 1, Vol 6, 129.

51. Prince Smith, *SC*, Ser 1, Vol 3, P 4, 117–118; Victoria Perry, *SC*, Ser 1, Vol 3, P 3, 260; Hector Smith, *SC*, Ser 1, Vol 3, P 4, 101.

52. "Blacks Have No More Chance Than Slaves Had," *Unwritten History of Slavery,* in *American Slave,* Ser 2, Vol 18, 197.

53. W.L. Bost, *NC*, Ser 2, Vol 14, P 1, 142; Frank Menefee, *AL*, Ser 1, Vol 6, 279; Pasa Barnwell, in Blassingame, *Slave Testimony*, 698; Mary Armstrong, *TX*, Ser 1, Vol 4, P 1, 25; Henry Walton, *MS*, Sup, Ser 1, Vol 10, P 5, 2168; Leah Garret, *GA*, Ser 2, Vol 12, P 2, 13; Vinnie Busby, *MS*, Sup, Ser 1, Vol 6, P 1, 310; Thomas Jones, *TX*, Ser 1, Vol 4, P 2, 202–203.

54. Hilliard Johnson, *AL*, Ser 1, Vol 6, 229.

55. Tory Jones, *TX*, Ser 1, Vol 4, P 2, 250; Mahalia Shores, *AR*, Ser 2, Vol 10, P 6, 155–156.

56. Celeste Avery, *GA*, Ser 1, Vol 12, P 1, 24–25; Douglass, *Life and Times*, 115–126, 139–143; Warren McKinney, *AR*, Ser 2, Vol 10, P 5, 27; Mother Anne Clark, *TX*, Ser 1, Vol 4, P 1, 224; Isom Hutchinson, *AR*, Ser 2, Vol 9, P 3, 372–374; J.L. Smith, *AR*, Ser 2, Vol 10, P 6, 198; Will Glass, *AR*, Ser 1, Vol 9, P 3, 38–39; Eugenia Weatherall, *MS*, Sup, Ser 1, Vol 10, P 5, 2215; Ervin Smith, *AR*, Ser 2, Vol 10, P 6, 189.

57. Anna Huggins, *AR*, Ser 2, Vol 9, P 3, 354; Annie Coley, *MS*, Sup, Ser 1, Vol 7, P 2, 441–442; Dianah Watson, *TX*, Ser 1, Vol 5, P 3, 145.

58. Wade, *Slavery in the Cities*, 97–106; 183–194; 226–260.

59. *Ibid.*, 183–191.

60. Keating, *Memphis*, 381.

61. Memphis *Daily Appeal*, September 9, October 6, 1852; July 25, 1853.

62. *Ibid.*, June 18, December 9, 1851; March 23, April 13, May 4, May 11, June 15, and October 9, 1852; July 1, July 12, 1853.

63. *Ibid.*, January 14, April 16, April 28, June 1, 1852; April 28, May 24, November 1, November 21, December 5, 1853.

64. *Ibid.*, June 1, 1851; February 24, April 14, May 4, May 10, May 20, June 15, June 19, 1852; May 24, July 25, October 22, October 25, November 1, November 22, 1853.

65. *Ibid.*, January 22, March 5, March 12, March 13, July 24, 1852.

66. *Ibid.*, September 6, 1852; July 25, July 26, July 29, 1853.

67. *Ibid.*, March 2, 1851; January 14, January 27, March 15, March 26, April 10, April 12, May 29, June 15, July 9, July 20, 1852; July 20, July 21, October 12, December 2, 1853.

Chapter 5

1. Charlotte Stephens, *AR*, Ser 2, Vol 10, P 6, 230; James Stith, *AR*, Ser 2, Vol 10, P 6, 238–243; John Jackson, *NC*, Ser 2, Vol 15, P 2, 2–3; Hannah Plummer, *NC*, Ser 2, Vol 15, P 2, 178–179; Keating, *Memphis*, 328.

2. Richard Starobin, *Industrial Slavery in the Old South,* (New York: Oxford University Press, 1970), 290–297; Wade, *Slavery in the Cities*, 38–51.

3. Memphis *Daily Appeal*, September 17, 1847; February 16, 1848; May 2, August 13, 1851; February 27, March 18, 1852.

4. J.W. Fairley, *MS*, Sup, Ser 1, Vol 7, P 2, 710; Prince Johnson, *MS*, Ser 1, Vol 7, 77; Parke Johnston, in Blassingame, ed., *Slave Testimony*, 386–395, 440, 490; Ellen Vaden, *AR*, Ser 2, Vol 11, P 7, 4; Ira Berlin, *Many Thousands Gone: The First Two Centuries of Slavery in North America* (Cambridge, MA: The Belknap Press of Harvard University Press, 1998), 274–275.

5. Olmsted, *Cotton Kingdom*, 231–233; Memphis *Daily Appeal*, February 14, 1851; April 27, April 28, 1852.

6. Ben Moon, *AR*, Ser 2, Vol 10, P 5, 119; Julie Bunch, *GA*, Ser 2, Vol 12, P 1, 157; Liza Strickland, *MS*, Sup, Ser 1, Vol 10, P 5, 2065; George Rogers, *NC*, Ser 2, Vol 15, P 2, 22; C.W. Hawkins, *AR*, Ser 2, Vol 9, P 3, 212.

7. James Gill, *AR*, Ser 2, Vol 9, P 3, 19–20; Henry Turner, *AR*, Ser 2, Vol 10, P 6, 364–366; Mark Oliver, *MS*, Sup, Ser 1, Vol 9, P 4, 1665; James Brown, *MS*, Sup, Ser 1, Vol 6, P 1, 231–232; Alex Huggins, *NC*, Ser 2, Vol 14, P 1, 450; Esther King, *AL*, Ser 1, Vol 6, 55; Amos Clark, *TX*, Ser 1, Vol 4, P 1, 220–221; Andrew Jackson Jarnagin, *MS*, Sup, Ser 1, Vol 8, P 3, 1128; Felix Street, *AR*, Ser 2, Vol 10, P 6, 246; Jeff Johnson, *MS*, Sup, Ser 1, Vol 8, P 3, 1163; Henry Walker, *AR*, Ser 2, Vol 11, P 7, 35.

8. Memphis *Daily Appeal*, August 13, October 23, 1851; March 18, 1852; July 1, 1853; Manus Robinson, *MS*, Sup, Ser 1, Vol 9, P 4, 1858.

9. Sneed Teague, *AR*, Ser 2, Vol 10, P 6, 281; Mom Genia Woodberry, *SC*, Ser 1, Vol 3, P 4, 223; Annie Coley, *MS*, Sup, Ser 1, Vol 7, P 2, 442–443.

10. Willis Cofer, *GA*, Ser 2, Vol 12, 205; Charles Bell, *MS*, Sup, Ser 1, Vol 6, P 1, 123; Charles Hayes, *AL*, Ser 1, Vol 6, 174; Doc Edwards, *NC*, Ser 2, Vol 14, P 1, 296; Henry Gibbs, *MS*, Sup, Ser 1, Vol 8, P 3, 826.

11. Abner Jordan, *NC*, Ser 2, Vol 15, P 2, 55; Esther King Casey, *AL*, Ser 1, Vol 6, 55; Ida Blackshear Hutchinson, *AR*, Ser 2, Vol 9, P 3, 370; "My Mother was the Smartest Black Woman in Eden," *Unwritten History of Slavery,* in *American Slave,* Ser 2, Vol 18, 285; Henry Probasco, *TX*, Ser 1, Vol 5, P 3, 205.

12. Joseph Leonidas Star, *TN*, Ser 2, Vol 16, 71; James Holmes, *MS*, Sup, Ser 1, Vol 8, P 3, 1044; Rube Jemison, *MS*, Sup, Ser 1, Vol 8, P 3, 1148; Melinda Maxwell, *AR*, Ser 2, Vol 8, P 5, 62; Andy Gill, *NC*, Ser 2, Vol 14, P 1, 325.

13. Jerry Eubanks, *MS*, Sup, Ser 1, Vol 7, P 2, 689;

Elisha Doc Garey, *GA*, Ser 2, Vol 12, P 2, 4; Josh Miles, *TX*, Ser 1, Vol 5, P 3, 80.

14. Andy Marion, *SC*, Ser 1, Vol 3, P 3, 168.

15. Henrietta E. Smith, *AR*, Ser 2, Vol 10, P 6, 194; Berry Clay, *GA*, Ser 2, Vol 12, P 1, 191.

16. Barney Alford, *MS*, Sup, Ser 1, Vol 6, P 1, 261; Memphis *Daily Appeal*, January 15, 1851; October 8, 11, 12, 19, 20, 21, 1853; Alexander Scaife, *SC.*, Ser 1, Vol 3, P 4, 77.

17. Happy Day Green, *AR*, Ser 2, Vol 9, P 3, 87; "Noted Personalities in Warren County," *MS*, Sup, Ser 1, Vol 9, P 4, 1538–1540; Daniel Phillips, *TX*, Ser 1, Vol 5, P 3, 183–184.

18. Ebenezer Brown, *MS*, Sup, Ser 1, Vol 6, P 1, 239; Lizzie Williams, *MS*, Sup, Ser 1, Vol 10, P 5, 2334; Betty Cofer, *NC*, Ser 2, Vol 14, P 1, 168.

19. Rosa Starke, *SC*, Ser 1, Vol 3, P 4, 148; John W. Blassingame, "Status and Social Structure in the Slave Community: Evidence From New Sources," in Harry P. Owens, ed., *Perspectives and Irony in American Slavery* (Jackson, MS: Ballantine Press, 1976), 137–149.

20. Andy J. Anderson, *TX*, Ser 1, Vol 4, P 1, 14; Olmsted, *Cotton Kingdom*, 431–433.

21. Robert Weathersby, *MS*, Sup, Ser 1, Vol 10, P 5, 2242–2243.

22. Lizzie Norfleet, *MS*, Sup, Ser 1, Vol 9, P 4, 1642; Jennie Webb, *MS*, Sup, Ser 1, Vol 10, P 5, 2250.

23. Henrietta Evelina Smith, *AR*, Ser 2, Vol 10, P 5, 194.

24. Marriah Hines, *VA*, Ser 2, Vol 16, 28; David Blount, *NC*, Ser 2, Vol 14, P 1, 111; Charles Coles, *MD*, Ser 2, Vol 16, 4; Wes Brady, *TX*, Ser 1, Vol 4, P 1, 134.

25. Reuben Fox, *MS*, Sup, Ser 1, Vol 7, P 2, 771; Jamar Lawson, *AR*, Ser 2, Vol 9, P 4, 30.

26. Prince Smith, *SC*, Ser 1, Vol 3, P 4, 116–118; Harry McMillan, in Blassingame, ed., *Slave Testimony*, 380.

27. Frank Menefee, *AL*, Ser 1, Vol 6, 279; Cecelia Chappel, *TN*, Ser 2, Vol 16, 6.

28. Olmsted, *Cotton Kingdom*, 249–250; 254–257.

29. Laura Hart, *AR*, Ser 2, Vol 9, P 3, 191; Henry Bland, *GA*, Ser 2, Vol 12, P 1, 81; Ambus Gray, *AR*, Ser 2, Vol 9, P 3, 77–78.

30. Abbie Lindsay, *AR*, Ser 2, Vol 9, P 4, 257; Henry Bland, *GA*, Ser 2, Vol 12, P 1, 81; James Morgan, *AR*, Ser 2, Vol 10, P 5, 143; William Wheeler, *MS*, Sup, Ser 1, Vol 10, P 5, 2272; Crozier Moore, *MS*, Sup, Ser 1, Vol 9, P 4, 1570; Allen Ward, *MS*, Sup, Ser 1, Vol 10, P 5, 2171; Mary Kincheon, *TX*, Ser 1, Vol 4, P 2, 16.

31. Susan Kelly, *VA*, Ser 2, Vol 16, 45.

32. Nathan Best, *MS*, Sup, Ser 1, Vol 6, P 1, 130; Lindley Hadley, *AR*, Ser 2, Vol 9, P 3, 127; Tom Wilson, *MS*, Ser 1, Vol 7, 165; Mollie Williams, *MS*, Ser 1, Vol 7, 158; Northup, *Twelve Years A Slave*, 116; Henrietta Williams, *AR*, Ser 2, Vol 11, P 7, 164; Adrianna Kerns, *AR*, Ser 2, Vol 9, P 4, 192; Henrietta McCullers, *NC*, Ser 2, Vol 15, P 2, 74; Clara Jones, *NC*, Ser 2, Vol 15, P 2, 131; Henry Essex, *NC*, Ser 2, Vol 14, P 1, 394; Lizzie Williams, *MS*, Sup, Ser 1, Vol 10, P 5, 2337.

33. Adam Singleton, *MS*, Sup, Ser 1, Vol 10, P 5, 1948; Georgianna Foster, *NC*, Ser 2, Vol 14, P 1, 315; Sarah Gudger, *NC*, Ser 2, Vol 14, P 1, 353; Ellen Payne, *TX*, Ser 1, Vol 5, P 3, 177.

34. Liza Strickland, *MS*, Sup, Ser 1, Vol 10, P 5, 2065.

35. Ebenezer Brown, *MS*, Sup, Ser 1, Vol 6, P 1, 244–249.

36. Olivier Blanchard, *TX*, Ser 1, Vol 4, P 1, 90–92; Rias Body, *GA*, Ser 2, Vol 12, P 1, 87; Julia Stubbs, *MS*,

Sup, Ser 1, Vol 6, P 1, 275; Rina Brown, *MS*, Sup, Ser 1, Vol 6, P 1, 275; Mary Island, *AR*, Ser 2, Vol 9, P 3, 389; Georgina Giwbs, *VA*, Ser 2, Vol 16, 15.

37. Jasper Battle, *GA*, Ser 2, Vol 12, P 1, 71.

38. Lillie Williams, *AR*, Ser 2, Vol 11, P 7, 177; Bell Wilkes, *AR*, Ser 2, Vol 11, P 7, 147; Julia E. Haney, *AR*, Ser 2, Vol 9, P 3, 149–151; Willis Easter, *TX*, Ser 1, Vol 4, P 2, 1; Rias Body, *GA*, Ser 2, Vol 12, P 1, 87; Fannie Moore, *NC*, Ser 2, Vol 15, P 2, 134.

39. Luvenia Coleman, *MS*, Sup, Ser 1, Vol 7, P 2, 435–437; Mahalia Shores, *AR*, Ser 2, Vol 10, P 6, 154, 156; Mom Genia Woodberry, *SC*, Ser 1, Vol 3, P 4, 219–223; "Autobiography of Rev. James W. Washington," *MS*, Sup, Ser 1, P 5, 2199; Agatha Babino, *TX*, Ser 1, Vol 4, P 1, 137; Sara Colquitt, *AL*, Ser 1, Vol 6, 88.

40. Ella Wilson, *AR*, Ser 2, Vol 11, P 7, 202; Laura Montgomery, *MS*, Sup, Ser 1, Vol 9, P 4, 1553; Mattie Jones, *MS*, Sup, Ser 1, Vol 7, P 2, 613; Alex Montgomery, *MS*, Sup, Ser 1, Vol 9, P 4, 1527; Manus Brown, *MS*, Sup, Ser 1, Vol 6, P 1, 269; Rias Body, *GA*, Ser 2, Vol 12, P 1, 87; Fannie Moore, *NC*, Ser 2, Vol 15, P 2, 134; Mom Genia Woodberry, *NC*, Ser 1, Vol 3, P 4, 220.

41. Emma Oats, *AR*, Ser 2, Vol 10, P 5, 221–222.

42. Dinah Hayes, *MS*, Sup, Ser 1, Vol 8, P 3, 962.

43. Ellen Claibourn, *GA*, Ser 2, Vol 12, P 1, 187; Rebecca Phillips, *MS*, Sup, Ser 1, Vol 9, P 4, 1694.

44. Betty Cofer, *NC*, Ser 2, Vol 14, P 1, 168.

45. Henry Daniels, *MS*, Sup, Ser 1, Vol 7, P 2, 549–550; Harriet McFarlin Payne, *AR*, Ser 2, Vol 10, P 5, 301; Mose Davis, *GA*, Ser 2, Vol 12, P 1, 269.

46. Hattie Jefferson, *MS*, Sup, Ser 1, Vol 8, P 3, 1131–1132; Rina Brown, *MS*, Sup, Ser 1, Vol 6, P 1, 275; Mandy McCullough Cosby, *AL*, Ser 1, Vol 6, 90.

47. Clark Hill, *AR*, Ser 2, Vol 9, P 3, 247; Rube Brown, *MS*, Sup, Ser 1, Vol 6, P 1, 289; Georgina Gwibs, *VA*, Ser 2, Vol 16, 15.

48. Jenny Proctor, *TX*, Ser 1, Vol 5, P 3, 209.

49. Mary Island, *AR*, Ser 2, Vol 9, P 3, 389; Henry Waldon, *AR*, Ser 2, Vol 11, P 7, 17; John Gregory, *MS*, Sup, Ser 1, Vol 8, P 3, 890; Adrianna Kerns, *AR*, Ser 2, Vol 9, P 4, 191; Eliza Scantling, *SC*, Ser 1, Vol 3, P 4, 78–79.

50. "Noted Personalities in Warren County," *MS*, Sup, Ser 1, Vol 9, P 4, 1532–1540.

51. John Williams, *MS*, Sup, Ser 1, Vol 10, P 5, 2327.

52. Georgia Baker, *GA*, Ser 2, Vol 12, P 1, 44; Henry Green, *AR*, Ser 2, Vol 9, P 3, 90; Charlie Davenport, *MS*, Sup, Ser 1, Vol 7, P 2, 559.

53. Walter Long, *SC*, Ser 1, Vol 3, P 3, 119.

54. John Sneed, *TX*, Ser 1, Vol 5, P 3, 49; Laura Cornish, *TX*, Ser 2, Vol 4, P 1, 254–255; Hagar Lewis, *TX*, Ser 1, Vol 5, P 3, 5–6.

55. Lewis Wallace, *MS*, Sup, Ser 1, Vol 10, P 5, 1265–1266; Emma Johnson, *MS*, Sup, Ser 1, Vol 8, P 3, 1153.

56. Harre Quarls, *TX*, Ser 2, Vol 5, P 3, 223; Northup, *Twelve Years a Slave*, 136–138.

57. Hattie Jefferson, *MS*, Sup, Ser 1, Vol 8, P 3, 1131; J.W. Terrill, *TX*, Ser 1, Vol 5, P 3, 81; Ben Simpson, *TX*, Ser 1, Vol 5, P 3, 28–29; Annie Griegg, *AR*, Ser 2, Vol 9, P 3, 114; Josephine Howell, *AR*, Ser 2, Vol 9, P 3, 339–340; Charlie Moses, *MS*, Ser 1, Vol 7, 113–115.

58. Tines Kendricks, *AR*, Ser 1, Vol 9, P 4, 178.

59. Barbara Haywood, *NC*, Ser 2, Vol 14, P 1, 387.

60. Thomas Hall, *NC*, Ser 2, Vol 14, P 1, 360–362.

61. Dora Brewer, *MS*, Sup, Ser 1, Vol 6, P 1, 201; Rosa Lindsey, *AR*, Ser 2, Vol 9, P 4, 260; Henrietta Williams, *AR*, Ser 2, Vol 11, P 7, 164; Charlie Rigger, *AR*, Ser 2, Vol 10, P 6, 39; Hattie Hill, *AR*, Ser 2, Vol 9, P 3, 262; Maria White, *MS*, Sup, Ser 1, Vol 10, P 5, 2276–2280.

62. Robert Weathersby, *MS*, Sup, Ser 1, Vol 10, P 5, 2242–2243; Lizzie Williams, *MS*, Sup, Ser 1, Vol 10, P 5, 2335; Northup, *Twelve Years A Slave*, 170.

63. Isaac Stier, *MS*, Ser 1, Vol 7, 144; Lee Guidon, *AR*, Ser 2, Vol 9, P 3, 120; Martha Colquitt, *GA*, Ser 2, Vol 12, P 1, 241; James Bolton, *GA*, Ser 2, Vol 12, P 1, 95; Annie Coley, *MS*, Sup, Ser 1, Vol 7, P 2, 441; Henry Gibbs, *MS*, Sup, Ser 1, Vol 8, P 3, 821; Bassett, *The Southern Plantation Overseer*, 6.

64. Virginia Harris, *MS*, Sup, Ser 1, Vol 8, P 3, 939; Abe McLennan, *MS*, Sup, Ser 1, Vol 9, P 4, 1409.

65. Maggie Perkins, *AR*, Ser 2, Vol 10, P 5, 312–313.

66. Dempsey Pitts, *MS*, Sup, Ser 1, Vol 9, P 4, 1712; James Lucas, *MS*, Sup, Ser 1, Vol 8, P 3, 1332; Miller "*Dear Master*": *Letters of a Slave Family*, 184–188.

67. Amy Chapman, *AL*, Ser 1, Vol 6, 60.

68. David Blount, *NC*, Ser 2, Vol 14, P 1, 111–113.

69. Olmsted, *Cotton Kingdom*, 437–443.

70. John Gilstrap, *MS*, Sup, Ser 1, Vol 8, P 3, 850; Sarah Taylor, *AR*, Ser 2, Vol 10, P 6, 271.

71. Rita Sorrell, *NC*, Ser 2, Vol 15, P 2, 301; Fannie Dunn, *NC*, Ser 2, Vol 14, P 1, 272–273; Richard Macks, *MD*, Ser 2, Vol 16, 52; Annie Young Henson, *MD*, Ser 2, Vol 16, 27; Georgia Baker, *GA*, Ser 2, Vol 12, P 1, 37–57; George Skipwith to John Cocke, June 17, 1847, in Blassingame, *Slave Testimony*, 66–68; Miller "*Dear Master*": *Letters of a Slave Family*, 147–148; 151–152.

72. Ellen Claibourn, *GA*, Ser 2, Vol 12, P 1, 185–187; Jane Johnson, *SC*, Ser 1, Vol 3, P 3, 49; Anna Baker, *MS*, Ser 1, Vol 7, 13.

73. See William Van DeBurg, *The Slave Driver; Black Agricultural Labor Supervisors in the Antebellum South* (New York: Oxford University Press, 1988), 3–43.

74. *Ibid.*, 50–59; 103–112; Rufus Dirt, *AL*, Ser 1, Vol 6, 117.

75. Squire Irvin, *MS*, Sup, Ser 1, Vol 8, P 3, 1082; Callie Washington, *MS*, Sup, Ser 1, Vol 10, P 5, 2187; Rina Brown, *MS*, Sup, Ser 1, Vol 6, P 1, 275; Sarah Fitzpatrick, in Blassingame, *Slave Testimony*, 640.

76. Robert Young, *MS*, Sup, Ser 1, Vol 10, P 5, 2409; James Holmes, *MS*, Sup, Ser 1, Vol 8, P 3, 1045; Isiah Green, *GA*, Ser 2, Vol 12, P 3, 51; Henry Williams, *AR*, Ser 2, Vol 11, P 7, 167; Charlie Aarons, *AL*, Ser 1, Vol 6, 2–3; Jane Johnson, *SC*, Ser 1, Vol 3, P 3, 49.

77. Prince Smith, *SC*, Vol 3, P 4, 117–118.

78. Josephine Howard, *TX*, Ser 1, Vol 4, P 2, 164.

79. Van DeBurg, *The Slave Drivers*, 115–116.

Chapter 6

1. *War of the Rebellion: A Compilation of the Official Records of the Union and Confederate Armies*, 128 vols. (Washington: GPO. 1880–1901), Series 2, Vol 5, 671–682. (Hereafter cited as *O.R., Armies*, Ser).

2. *Ibid.*, Ser 1, Vol 24, Part 2, (Hereafter cited as P), 435–436.

3. *Ibid.*, Ser 1, Vol 24, P 1, 502.

4. *Ibid.*, Ser 1, Vol 24, P 1, 504–505.

5. *War of the Rebellion: Official Records of the Union and Confederate Navies*, 30 vols. (Washington: GPO. 1894–1922), Ser 1, Vol 23, 431–432. (Hereafter cited as *O.R., Navies*).

6. *Ibid.*, Ser 1, Vol 45, P 1, 844–847.

7. Jane Sutton, *MS*, Ser 1, Vol 7, 155; Jane McLeod Wilborn, *MS*, Sup, Ser 1, Vol 10, P 5, 2287; Matilda Hatchett, *AR*, Ser 2, Vol 9, P 3, 198; Wadley Clemons, *AL*, Ser 1, Vol 6, 79; Mary Jane Mooreman, *AR*, Ser 2, Vol 10, P 5, 131; Felix Street, *AR*, Ser 2, Vol 10, P 6, 248; Ida Atkins, *NC*, Ser 2, Vol 14, P 1, 11; Joanna Thompson, *MS*, Sup, Ser 1, Vol 8, P 3, 1096; Mary Ella Grandberry, *AL*, Ser 1, Vol 6, 163; Calley Halsen Williamson, *AR*, Ser 2, P 7, 196–197; Ike McCoy, *AR*, Ser 2, Vol 10, P 5, 13; Willis Cozart, *NC*, Ser 2, Vol 14, P 1, 185; Ishe Webb, *AR*, Ser 2, Vol 11, P 7, 77; Jake Dawkins, *MS*, Sup, Ser 1, Vol 7, P 2, 597; Mattie Curtis, *NC*, Ser 2, Vol 14, P 1, 218; Allen Ward, *MS*, Sup, Ser 1, Vol 10, P 5, 2173; Aunt Jane Morgan, *MS*, Sup, Ser 1, Vol 9, P 4, 1574; K. Jack Bauer, ed., *Soldiering: The Civil War Diary of Rice C. Bull, 123rd New York Volunteer Infantry* (San Rafael, CA: Presidio Press, 1977), 185–186.

8. Louisa Adams, *NC*, Ser 2, Vol 14, P 1, 6; July Ann Halfen, *MS*, Ser 1, Vol 8, P 3, 902; Mollie Williams, *MS*, Ser 1, Vol 7, 162; Smith Simmons, *MS*, Ser 1, Vol 10, P 5, 1940; Florida Hewitt and Miles Stone, *MS*, Sup, Ser 1, Vol 8, P 3, 1004; Ebenezer Brown, *MS*, Sup, Ser 1, Vol 6, P 1, 250–251; Bauer, ed., *Soldiering*, 214.

9. Charlie Barbour, *NC*, Ser 2, Vol 14, P 1, 76.

10. John Bectom, *NC*, Ser 2, Vol 14, P 1, 96.

11. Talitha Lewis, *AR*, Ser 2, Vol 9, P 4, 252.

12. Louis Lucas, *AR*, Ser 2, Vol 9, P 4, 300.

13. Oliver Jones, *MS*, Sup, Ser 1, Vol 8, P 3, 1254; Bauer, ed., *Soldiering*, 188.

14. Sarah Jane Patterson, *AR*, Ser 2, Vol 10, P 5, 287; Henry Pristell, *SC*, Ser 1, Vol 3, P 3, 280–281; Jerry Hinton, *NC*, Ser 2, Vol 14, P 1, 430; Donald Yacovone, ed., *A Voice of Thunder: The Civil War Letters of George E. Stephens* (Urbana, IL: University of Illinois Press, 1997), 180; Frank Green, *AR*, Ser 2, Vol 9, P 3, 102.

15. Fannie Dunn, *NC*, Ser 2, Vol 14, P 1, 271; Charles W. Dickens, *NC*, Ser 2, Vol 14, P 1, 256–257; Lila Nichols, *NC*, Ser 2, Vol 15, P 2, 150; Josie Martin, *AR*, Ser 2, Vol 12, P 5, 51–52; Mandy Coverson, *NC*, Ser 2, Vol 14, 181; Elvira Collins, *MS*, Sup, Ser 1, Vol 7, P 2, 479; Adeline Jackson, *SC*, Ser 1, Vol 3, P 3, 3; Lindsey Faucett, *NC*, Ser 2, Vol 14, P 1, 305.

16. *O.R. Armies*, Ser 1, Vol 8, 642; Ser 1, Vol 49, P 2, 940, 1199; John W. DeForest, *A Volunteer's Adventures: A Union Captains Record of the Civil War*, ed., by James H. Croushore (New Haven: Yale University Press, 1946), 73–74; Ellen Briggs Thompson, *AR*, Ser 2, Vol 10, P 6, 311; Jane Lee, *NC*, Ser 2, Vol 15, P 2, 52.

17. Nelson Dickerson, *MS*, Sup, Ser 1, Vol 7, P 2, 604; Mandy Johnson, *AR*, Ser 2, Vol 9, P 4, 111.

18. Cornelia Ishmon, *AR*, Ser 2, Vol 9, P 3, 379; R.F. Parker, *AR*, Ser 2, Vol 10, P 5, 255; Frances Cobb, *MS*, Sup, Ser 1, Vol 7, P 2, 420.

19. Lizzie McCloud, *AR*, Ser 2, Vol 10, P 5, 5.

20. *O.R. Armies*, Ser 1, Vol 15, 706–707.

21. *Ibid*, Ser 1, Vol 24, P 1, 352.

22. Celeste Avery,*GA*, Ser 2, Vol 12, P 2, 26; Anna Baker, *MS*, Sup, Ser 1, Vol 6, P 1, 93; Willie Wallace, *AR*, Ser 2, Vol 12, P 7, 43; Bauer, *Soldiering*, 181.

23. Elizabeth Finley, *MS*, Sup, Ser 1, Vol 7, P 2, 729; Andrew Jackson Gill, *MS*, Sup, Ser 1, Vol 8, P 3, 843.

24. Henry Jenkins, *SC*, Ser 1, Vol 3, P 3, 26.

25. Mary Angady, *NC*, Ser 2, Vol 14, P 1, 35.

26. Martha Colquitt, *GA*, Ser 2, Vol 12, P 1, 218.

27. Cyntha Jones, *AR*, Ser 2, Vol 9, P 4, 138.

28. Melissa Munson, *MS*, Sup, Ser 1, Vol 9, P 4, 1607.

29. Rosa Thomas, *MS*, Sup, Ser 1, Vol 10, P 5, 2100–2101; Hector Hamilton, *NC*, Ser 2, Vol 14, P 1, 367; Rev. Jesse Washington, *MS*, Sup, Ser 1, Vol 10, P 5, 2201; "Cat" Ross, *AR*, Ser 2, Vol 10, P 6, 86; Ed Crum, *MS*, Sup, Ser 1, Vol 7, P 2, 537; Reuben Jones, *AR*, Ser 2, Vol 9,

P 4, 166; Lizzie Lucado, *AR*, Vol 9, P 4, 305; Frances Patterson, *MS*, Sup, Ser 1, Vol 9, P 4, 1680; Sam Crawford, *MS*, Sup, Ser 1, Vol 6, P 1, 188.

30. Martha Richardson, *SC*, Ser 1, Vol 3, P 4, 20–22; Alfred Peters, *AR*, Ser 2, Vol 10, P 5, 322.

31. Minerva Wells, *MS*, Sup, Ser 1, Vol 10, P 5, 2261.

32. Laura Ford, *MS*, Sup, Ser 1, Vol 7, P 2, 757–758.

33. Tony Cox, *MS*, Sup, Ser 1, Vol 7, P 2, 523.

34. Tom Morris, *MS*, Sup, Ser 1, Vol 9, P 4, 1583.

35. Jessie Rice, *SC*, Ser 1, Vol 3, P 4, 13.

36. Andrew Peale, *MS*, Sup, Ser 1, P 4, 188; Clara Cotton McCoy, *NC*, Ser 2, Vol 15, 66–70.

37. Mose King, *AR*, Ser 2, Vol 9, P 4, 208.

38. Netty Henry, *MS*, Ser 1, Vol 7, 64; DeForest, *A Volunteer's Adventures*, 197.

39. Henry Walker, *AR*, Ser 2, Vol 11, P 7, 281.

40. Tom Wilson, *MS*, Sup, Ser 1, Vol 10, P 5, 2379.

41. Maria Parham, *MS*, Sup, Ser 1, Vol 9, P 4, 1674.

42. Jane McLeod Wilburn, *MS*, Sup, Ser 1, Vol 10, P 5, 2287.

43. Julia Stubbs, *MS*, Sup, Ser 1, Vol 10, P 5, 2070; Emma Oats, *AR*, Ser 2, Vol 10, P 5, 223; Andrew Moss, *TN*, Ser 2, Vol 16, 51; Jake McLeod, *SC*, Vol 3, P 3, 162; George Coleman, *MS*, Sup, Ser 1, Vol 7, P 2, 425; Harry Bridge, *MS*, Sup, Ser 1, Vol 6, P 1, 209–210.

44. Dave Walker, *MS*, Sup, Ser 1, Vol 10, P 5, 2151.

45. Mary Kindred, *TX*, Ser 1, Vol 4, P 2, 286; Jane McCleod, *SC*, Ser 1, Vol 3, P 3, 162.

46. Wylie Nealy, *AR*, Ser 2, Vol 10, P 5, 188.

47. Annie Coley, *MS*, Sup, Ser 1, Vol 7, P 2, 440.

48. Frank Williams, *AR*, Sup, Ser 1, Vol 10, P 5, 150; Betty Cofer, *NC*, Ser 2, Vol 14, P 1, 171; Richard Slaughter, *VA*, Ser 2, Vol 16, 46–48; Elizabeth Sparks, *VA*, Ser 2, Vol 16, 52–53.

49. Gabe Butler, *MS*, Sup, Ser 1, Vol 6, P 1, 317.

50 Matilda Miller, *AR*, Ser 2, Vol 10, P 5, 91.

51. Kittie Stanford, *AR*, Ser 2, Vol 10, P 6, 214; Mary Reynolds, *TX*, Ser 1, Vol 5, P 3, 246; Molly Horn, *AR*, Ser 2, Vol 9, P 3, 320.

52. Pate Newton, *AR*, Ser 2, Vol 9, P 5, 216–217; Jane Oliver, *AR*, Ser 2, Vol 10, P 5, 229; Mary Myhand, *AR*, Ser 2, Vol 10, P 5, 177; Dinah Perry, *AR*, Ser 2, Vol 10, P 5, 318; John Wells, *AR*, Ser 2, Vol 11, P 7, 85; John Wesley, *AR*, Ser 2, Vol 11, P 7, 96.

53. Adeline Hodges, *AL*, Ser 1, Vol 6, 182.

54. Seabe Tuttle, *AR*, Ser 2, Vol 10, P 6, 370; Parrish Washington, *AR*, Ser 2, Vol 11, 60.

55. Clarice Jackson, *AR*, Ser 2, Vol 9, P 4, 3.

56. Minerva Lofton, *AR*, Vol 9, P 4, 264; Joe Golden, *AR*, Ser 2, Vol 9, P 3, 49; Susie King, *AR*, Ser 2, Vol 9, P 4, 210–213.

57. Hattie Sugg, *MS*, Sup, Ser 1, Vol 10, P 5, 2077; Ernest Branon, *MS*, Sup, Ser 1, Vol 6, P 1, 198; Rebecca Brown Hill, *AR*, Ser 2, Vol 9, P 3, 267; Myra Jones, *MS*, Sup, Ser 1, Vol 8, P 3, 1249.

58. Molly Horn, *AR*, Ser 2, Vol 9, P 3, 319.

59. Julia Bunch, *GA*, Ser 2, Vol 12, P 1, 159.

60. Sally Dixon, *MS*, Sup, Ser 1, Vol 7, P 2, 629.

61. Betty Krump, *AR*, Ser 2, Vol 9, P 4, 216–217; Richard Slaughter, *VA*, Ser 2, Vol 16, 47–48.

62. Rosa Lindsey, *AR*, Ser 2, Vol 9, P 4, 260; Rose, *Slavery and Freedom*, 49–70.

63. Lorenzo Ezell, *TX*, Ser 1, Vol 4, P 2, 29–30.

64. Ann Drake, *MS*, Sup, Ser 1, Vol 7, P 2, 647–648; Rosa Simmons, *AR*, Ser 2, Vol 10, P 6, 158.

65. David Blount, *NC*, Ser 2, Vol 14, P 1, 113–115; Mary Jane Moorman, *AR*, Ser 2, Vol 10, P 5, 131–132; James L. Roark, *Masters Without Slaves: Southern Planters in the Civil War and Reconstruction* (New York: Norton, 1977), 77–79.

66. Adaline Johnson, *AR*, Ser 2, Vol 9, P 4, 53; J.M. Parker, *AR*, Ser 2, Vol 10, P 5, 243; Lula Coleman, *MS*, Sup, Ser 1, Vol 7, P 2, 432.

67. Frank Patterson, *AR*, Ser 2, Vol 10, P 5, 279–280.

68. Tines Kendricks, *AR*, Ser 2, Vol 9, P 4, 180–181.

69. Chana Littlejohn, *NC*, Ser 2, Vol 15, P 2, 56; Dora Franks, *MS*, Ser 1, Vol 7, 54; Annie Young, *AR*, Ser 2, Vol 11, P 7, 253; William Adams, *TX*, Ser 1, Vol 4, P 1, 11; Elvie Lomack, *AR*, Ser 2, Vol 9, P 4, 283; Mary Jones, *AR*, Ser 2, Vol 9, P 4, 163.

70. John Cameron, *MS*, Sup, Ser 1, Vol 7, P 2, 333.

71. Victoria Sims, *AR*, Ser 2, Vol 10, P 6, 162.

72. Frank Patterson, *AR*, Ser 2, Vol 10, P 5, 278.

73. Temple Wilson, *MS*, Sup, Ser 1, Vol 10, P 5, 2372–2373.

74. Manda Boggan, *MS*, Sup, Ser 1, Vol 6, P 1, 158.

75. Talitha Island, *AR*, Ser 2, Vol 9, P 3, 385; Mandy Tucker, *AR*, Ser 2, Vol 10, P 6, 358; Turner Jacobs, *MS*, Sup, Ser 1, Vol 8, P 3, 1118–1119; John Jones, *AR*, Ser 2, Vol 9, P 4, 150.

76. Anna Williamson, *AR*, Ser 2, Vol 11, P 7, 194.

77. William Rose, *SC*, Ser 1, Vol 3, P 4, 49.

78. Elijah Hopkins, *AR*, Ser 2, Vol 9, P 3, 312; William Porter, *AR*, Ser 2, Vol 10, P 5, 362.

79. George Ward, *MS*, Sup, Ser 1, Vol 10, P 5, 2177; Jane Osbrook, *AR*, Ser 2, Vol 10, P 5, 232.

80. Edwin Walker, *MS*, Sup, Ser 1, Vol 10, P 5, 2155.

81. Hanna Chapman, *MS*, Sup, Ser 1, Vol 7, P 1, 382; Rina Brown, *MS*, Sup, Ser 1, Vol 6, P 1, 277; Glascow Norwood, *MS*, Sup, Ser 1, Vol 9, P 4, 1657–1658; William Gant, *AR*, Ser 2, Vol 9, P 3, 13; Tom Robinson, *AR*, Ser 1, Vol 10, P 6, 65; Elmira Hill, *AR*, Ser 2, Vol 9, P 3, 25–40; Tom Wylie Neal, *AR*, Ser 2, Vol 10, P 5, 182.

82. Julia Cox, *MS*, Sup, Ser 1, Vol 7, P 2, 521.

83. Sarah Anne Green, *NC*, Ser 2, Vol 14, P 1, 344–345; James Gill, *AR*, Ser 2, Vol 9, P 3, 22–24.

84. James Brittian, *MS*, Sup, Ser 1, Vol 6, P 1, 220.

85. Minnie Davis, *GA*, Ser 2, Vol 12, P 1, 257; Mary Anderson, *NC*, Ser 2, Vol 14, P 1, 24.

Chapter 7

1. *O.R. Armies*, Ser 1, Vol 3, 372–373.

2. *Ibid.*, Ser 1, Vol 3, 467.

3. *Ibid.*, Ser 1, Vol 4, 288.

4. *Ibid.*, Ser 1, Vol 4, 307.

5. *Ibid.*, Ser 1, Vol 4, 481–482.

6. *Ibid.*, Ser 1, Vol 4, 337–347.

7. *Ibid.*, Ser 1, Vol 7, 787.

8. *Ibid.*, Ser 1, Vol 7, 801–802.

9. *Ibid.*, Ser 1, Vol 8, 370, 444–445.

10. *Ibid.*, Ser 1, Vol 8, 693.

11. *O.R. Navies*, Ser 1, Vol 23, 149.

12. *O.R. Armies*, Ser 1, Vol 13, 525.

13. *Ibid.*, Ser 1, Vol 7, 668.

14. William T. Sherman, *The Sherman Letters: Correspondence between General and Senator Sherman from 1837 to 1891*, ed. by Rachel Sherman Thorndike (New York: C. Scribner's Sons, 1894), 160–161.

15. Roy P. Basler, ed., *The Collected Works of Abraham Lincoln*, 8 vols. Plus index vol. (New Brunswick, NJ: Rutgers University Press, 1953–1955), 420.

16. For the Butler — Phelps Controversy, see *O.R.*

Armies, Ser 1, Vol 15, 439–445, 486–491, 516, 526, 534–537, 542–543, 549–550.

17. Basler, ed., *Works of Lincoln*, V, 144–146, 152–153, 169, 223, 317–319, 327.

18. *Ibid.*, V, 433–436; VI, 28–30.

19. *Ibid.*, VII, 281–282.

20. *Ibid.*, VII, 507.

21. *Ibid.*, VII, 332–333.

22. *O.R. Armies.*, Ser 2, Vol 5, 807–808.

23. *Ibid.*, Ser 2, Vol 5, 940.

24. *Ibid.*, Ser 1, Vol 32, P 2, 39.

25. *Ibid.*, Ser 1, Vol 32, P 2, 89, 147.

26. Yacovone, *A Voice of Thunder*, 323–324; James M. McPherson, *The Negro's Civil War: How American Negroes Felt and Acted During the War for the Union* (New York: Macmillan Pub. Co., 1965), 65.

27. *O.R. Armies*, Ser 1, Vol 24, P 3, 701.

28. *Ibid.*, Ser 1, Vol 24, P 3, 588. See also C.A. Dana to Secretary of War E.M. Stanton, June 26, 1863, *Ibid.*, Ser 1, Vol 24, P 1, 110.

29. *Ibid.*, Ser 1, Vol 32, P 2, 408.

30. *Ibid.*, Ser 1, Vol 24, P 3, 156–157.

31. *Ibid.*, Ser 1, Vol 24, P 3, 186–187.

32. *Ibid.*, Ser 1, Vol 20, P 1, 15.

33. *Ibid.*, Ser 1, Vol 24, P 3, 46–47.

34. *Ibid.*, Ser 1, Vol 24, P 1, 18.

35. *Ibid.*, Ser 1, Vol 24, P 3, 65.

36. *Ibid.*, Ser 1, Vol 24, P 3, 105.

37. *Ibid.*, Ser 1, Vol 25, P 1, 71–72; Ser 1, Vol 15, 27–28.

38. *Ibid.*, Ser 1, Vol 24, P 2, 177; Ser 1, Vol 24, P 3, 479; Ser 1, Vol 24, P 3, 481–483.

39. *O.R. Navies*, Ser 1, Vol 23, 619; Ser 1, Vol 23, 639.

40. *O.R. Armies*, Ser 1, Vol 15, 491; DeForest, *A Union Captain's Record of the Civil War*, Yale University Press, 10, 22, 31–32, 40.

41. *O.R. Navies*, Ser 1, Vol 23, 473–475.

42. *O.R. Armies*, Ser 1, Vol 34, P 4, 93.

43. *Ibid.*, Ser 1, Vol 52, P 1, 302.

44. *Personal Memoirs of U.S. Grant*, 2 vols. (New York: The Century Co., 1885–1886), Vol 1, 424–426; See also Willie Lee Rose, *Rehearsal for Reconstruction* (New York: Vintage Books, 1967), 14–168.

45. *O.R. Armies*, Ser 1, Vol 24, P 3, 67–68.

46. *Ibid.*, Ser 1, Vol 24, P 3, 149–150.

47. *Ibid.*, Ser 3, Vol 4, 893–894.

48. Mary Barbour, *NC*, Ser 2, Vol 14, P 1, 81; George W. Harris, *NC*, Ser 2, Vol 14, P 1, 373; McPherson, *The Negro's Civil War*, 114.

49. Nathan Best, *MS*, Sup, Ser 1, Vol 6, P 1, 132–133.

50. *O.R. Armies*, Ser 3, Vol 4, 770–773.

51. Edwin S. Redkey, *A Grand Army of Black Men: Letters from African-American Soldiers in the Union Army, 1861–1865* (New York: Cambridge University Press, 1992), 56–59.

52. *O.R. Armies*, Ser 1, Vol 15, 592–595.

53. *Ibid.*, Ser 1, Vol 15, 709, 727–728; *O.R. Navies*, Ser 1, Vol 26, 236–237.

54. *O.R. Armies*, Ser 1, Vol 15, 666–667.

55. *Ibid.*, Ser 2, Vol 5, 279.

56. *Ibid.*, Ser 1, Vol 15, 678.

57. *Ibid.*, Ser 3, Vol 4, 166–170.

58. *Ibid.*, Ser 3, Vol 4, 193–194; McPherson, *The Negro's Civil War*, 129–131.

59. *O.R. Armies*, Ser 3, Vol 4, 124; Ser 2, Vol 4, 235–236. See also Lincoln to General Thomas, Ser 2, Vol 4, 143.

60. *Ibid.*, Ser 1, Vol 41, P 4, 828; Ser 1, Vol 27, 37–38.

See also *Ibid.*, Ser 1, Vol 49, P 2, 579.

61. *Ibid.*, Ser 3, Vol 4, 225–226.

62. *Ibid.*, Ser 1, Vol 10, P 2, 162–163.

63. *Ibid.*, 165; P.H. Sheridan, *Personal Memoirs*, 2 vols. (New York: C.L. Webster, 1888), II, 121.

64. *O.R. Armies*, Ser 1, Vol 52, P 2, 370–372.

65. *O.R. Navies*, Ser 1, Vol 24, 155.

66. *O.R. Armies*, Ser 1, Vol 24, P 1, 509.

67. *Ibid.*, Ser 1, Vol 32, P 2, 578.

68. *Ibid.*, Ser 1, Vol 39, P 1, 15.

69. *Ibid.*, Ser 1, Vol 4, 507; James H. Brewer, *The Confederate Negro: Virginia's Craftsmen and Military Laborers, 1861–1865* (Durham, NC: Duke University Press, 1969), *passim*; Bell Irvin Wiley, *The Life of Johnny Reb: The Common Soldier of the Confederacy* (reprint; 1943, Baton Rouge: Louisiana State University Press, 1978), 329.

70. *O.R. Armies*, Ser 1, Vol 52, P 2, 240.

71. *Ibid.*, Ser 1, Vol 52, P 2, 278–280.

72. *Ibid.*, Ser 1, Vol 52, P 2, 400; Ser 1, Vol 15, 809–810; Ser 1, Vol 52, P 2, 408; Ser 1, Vol 52, P 2, 441.

73. *Ibid.*, Ser 2, Vol 5, 844–845.

74. *Ibid.*, Ser 1, Vol 52, P 2, 449–450; Ser 1, Vol 24, P 3, 595.

75. *Ibid.*, Ser 1, Vol 32, P 2, 907, 994.

76. *Ibid.*, Ser 1, Vol 34, P 2, 927; Ser 1, Vol 41, P 4, 1107–1108.

77. *Ibid.*, Ser 1, Vol 32, P 3, 652–653, 763–765.

78. *Ibid.*, Ser 1, Vol 52, P 2, 667–668.

79. *Ibid.*, Ser 1, Vol 32, P 3, 797.

80. *Ibid.*, 753.

81. *Ibid.*, Ser 1, Vol 52, P 2, 653–654.

82. *Ibid.*, 309.

83. *O.R. Navies*, Ser 1, Vol 32, P 2, 856–857; Ser 1, Vol 26, 466.

84. Wiley, *The Life of Johnny Reb*, 328; William Byrd, *TX*, Ser 1, Vol 4, P 1, 184; Sam Brooks, *MS*, Sup, Ser 1, Vol 6, P 1, 225; "Uncle Ike Pringle," *MS*, Sup, Ser 1, Vol 9, P 4, 1762; Henry Warfield, *MS*, Sup, Ser 1, Vol 10, P 5, 2180; Simon Durr, *MS*, Sup, Ser 1, Vol 7, P 2, 657; Isaac Stier, *MS*, Sup, Ser 1, Vol 10, P 5, 2050.

85. Elodga Bradford, *MS*, Sup, Ser 1, Vol 6, P 1, 186; Peter Blewit, *MS*, Sup, Ser 1, Vol 6, P 1, 153; Dempsy Pitts, *MS*, Sup, Ser 1, Vol 9, P 4, 1721; Ransom Simmons, *SC*, Sup, Ser 1, Vol 3, P 4, 91; Henry Turner, *AR*, Ser 2, Vol 10, P 6, 368.

86. Sam Kilgore, *TX*, Ser 1, Vol 4, P 2, 259; Nick Carter, *MS*, Sup, Ser 1, Vol 7, P 2, 363; Tom Bones, *MS*, Sup, Ser 1, Vol 6, P 1, 171; Fannie Mintner, *MS*, Sup, Ser 1, Vol 9, P 4, 1510; Holt Collier, *MS*, Sup, Ser 1, Vol 7, P 2, 451.

87. George Rogers, *NC*, Ser 2, Vol 15, P 2, 223–224; Jake Goodridge, *AR*, Ser 2, Vol 9, P 3, 53; Katie Darling, *TX*, Ser 1, Vol 4, P 1, 278; Frank Childress, *MS*, Sup, Ser 1, Vol 7, P 2, 387; William H. Harrison, *AR*, Ser 2, Vol 9, P 3, 185; Cella Perkins, *AR*, Ser 2, Vol 10, P 5, 309; Isaac Stier, *MS*, Ser 1, Vol 7, 147–148, also in *MS*, Sup, Ser 1, Vol 10, P 5, 2053.

88. *O.R. Armies*, Ser 1, Vol 24, P 1, 694.

89. *Ibid.*, Ser 1, Vol 32, P 2, 990.

90. *Ibid.*, Ser 1, Vol 24, P 3, 7043–7044.

91. *Ibid.*, Ser 1, Vol 52, P 2, 586–592, 595–596, 598–599, 606–609.

92. *Ibid.*, 595–596.

93. *Ibid.*, Ser 1, Vol 41, P 3, 774.

94. *Ibid.*, 774; Corporal James Henry Gooding, *On the Altar of Freedom: A Black Soldier's Civil War Letters From The Front*, edited by Virginia Matzke Adams

(Amherst: University of Massachusetts Press, 1991), 54; Basler, ed., *Works of Lincoln*, VIII, 360–361.

95. McPherson, *The Negro's Civil War*, 243–244; *O.R. Armies*, Ser.1, Vol 49, P2, 1199.

Chapter 8

1. *O.R. Armies*, Ser 3, Vol 4, 1271.
2. *Ibid.*, 774.
3. *Ibid.*, Ser 1, Vol 39, P 2, 132; Ser 3, Vol 4, 434, 454, 455.
4. *Ibid.*, Ser 1, Vol 24, 222.
5. *Ibid.*, Ser 3, Vol 2, 149.
6. *Ibid.*, Ser 1, Vol 41, P 3, 750.
7. *Ibid.*, Ser 1, Vol 24, P 3, 156–157; Ser 1, Vol 24, P 1, 31.
8. *Ibid.*, Ser 1, Vol 24, P 1, 70.
9. *Ibid.*, Ser 1, Vol 24, P 3, 584.
10. *Ibid.*, Ser 3, Vol 4, 921–922.
11. *Ibid.*, 174–176; 177–179.
12. *Ibid.*, 201–202.
13. *Ibid.*, 429.
14. *Ibid.*, 429–430.
15. *Ibid.*, 431.
16. *Ibid.*, Ser 1, Vol 39, P 2, 131–133.
17. *Ibid.*, Ser 3, Vol 4, 248–249; 467–468.
18. *Ibid.*, 543; 995; 1017–1018.
19. *Ibid.*, 543; 559–560; 694–695.
20. *Ibid.*, Ser 1, Vol 52, P 2, 332; Ser 1, Vol 24, P 2, 430; Leon F. Litwack, *Been in the Storm So Long: The Aftermath of Slavery* (New York: Vintage Books, 1980), 93–94.
21. *Ibid.*, 354; 379–381; Gooding, *Altar of Freedom*, 27–29; Joseph T. Glatthaar, *Forged in Battle: The Civil War Alliance of Black Soldiers and White Officers* (New York: Free Press, 1990), 77–78.
22. *O.R. Navies*, Ser 1, Vol 26, 181–182; *O.R. Armies*, Ser 1, Vol 52, P 2, 599–601.
23. *O.R. Armies*, Ser 1, Vol 52, P 2, 486; 488–489.
24. *Ibid.*, 469–470.
25. *O.R. Navies*, Ser 1, Vol 23, 80–81; 253–254; 356–375.
26. *Ibid.*, Ser 1, Vol 15, 530.
27. *Ibid.*, Ser 1, Vol 23, 449–450.
28. *Ibid.*, 479, 508–510.
29. *Ibid.*, 638.
30. *Ibid.*, 603; Ser 1, Vol 24, 179, 196, 213.
31. *Ibid.*, 256–257, 428; Ser 1, Vol 25, 72–73, 74–76, 93, 322–323.
32. *Ibid.*, Ser 1, Vol 27, 499–500.
33. *Ibid.*, Ser 1, Vol 25, 327–328.
34. *O.R. Armies*, Ser 3, Vol 4, 957–960.
35. *Ibid.*, 468–469; 474.
36. Dudley T. Cornish, *The Sable Arm: Negro Troops in the Union Army, 1861–1865*, (New York: W.W. Norton, 1956), 265.
37. *O.R. Armies*, Ser 3, Vol 4, 433–434.
38. *Ibid.*, 708–709.
39. *Ibid.*, 921–922, 1058; Glatthaar, *Forged in Battle*, 182–185, 279–280.
40. Ira Berlin and others, eds., in *The Black Military Experience, Freedom: A Documentary History of Emancipation, 1861–1867*, Ser 2, (Cambridge: Cambridge University Press, 1982), 612–613.
41. Warren B. Armstrong, "Union Chaplains and the Education of Freedmen," *Journal of Negro History*, 52 (April, 1967), 104–115.

42. *Ibid.*, 104–115; Berlin and others, eds., *Black Military Experience*, 611–613; McPherson, *The Negro's Civil War*, 211–212.
43. Roger Hinton, *NC*, Ser 2, Vol 14, P 1, 439; Isaac Johnson, *NC*, Ser 2, Vol 15, P 2, 18.
44. Mark Oliver, *MS*, Sup, Ser 1, Vol 9, P 4, 1607; Will Ann Rogers, *AR*, Ser 2, Vol 10, P 6, 73–74.
45. Litwack, *Been in the Storm So Long*, 83–85. Fillmore Ramsey, *MS*, Sup, Ser 1, Vol 9, P 4, 1794; Julius Jones, *MS*, Sup, Ser 1, Vol 8, P 3, 1222; Ann May, *MS*, Sup, Ser 1, Vol 9, P 4, 1463; James Spikes, *AR*, Vol 10, P 6, 212; Ambus Gray, *AR*, Vol 9, P 3, 78; John Ogee, *TX*, Ser 1, Vol 5, P 3, 154–155; Mack Henderson, *MS*, Sup, Ser 1, Vol 8, P 3, 972; Alex Huggins, *NC*, Ser 2, Vol 14, P 1, 451; Vergil Jones, *AR*, Ser 2, Vol 9, P 4, 169; George Washington Albright, *MS*, Sup, Ser 1, Vol 6, P 1, 11; Rose Russell, *MS*, Sup, Ser 1, Vol 9, P 4, 1903–1904.
46. Landy Rucker, *AR*, Ser 2, Vol 10, P 6, 93; Phyllis Fox, *MS*, Sup, Ser 1, Vol 7, P 2, 767; Tom Windham, *AR*, Ser 2, Vol 11, P 7, 211; Edmond Bradley, *MS*, Sup, Ser 1, Vol 6, P 1, 194; William Ball Williams, *AR*, Ser 2, Vol 11, P 7, 192; Solomon Lambert, *AR*, Vol 9, P 4, 231.
47. Berlin and others, *Black Military Experience*, 517.
48. *Ibid.*, 518; Glatthaar, *Forged in Battle*, 123–129.
49. *O.R. Armies*, Ser 1, Vol 24, P 2, 446–448. See Also, Glatthaar, *Forged in Battle*, 130–135.
50. Berlin and others, *Black Military Experience*, 519.
51. *Ibid.*, 520.
52. U.S. Grant, *Report of Lieutinant General U.S. Grant of the Armies of the United States—1864–1865*. Adjutant General's Office, November 18, 1865 (Washington, 1865), 21; Glatthaar, *Forged in Battle*, 156–157.
53. Cornish, *Sable Arm*, 173–231.
54. *O.R. Armies*, Ser 3, Vol 4, 247–248. See also *Ibid.*, 920; Glatthaar, *Forged in Battle*, 157–158.
55. *O.R. Armies*, Ser 1, Vol 45, P 1, 543–544.
56. *Ibid.*, 534–541.
57. *Ibid.*, 546–548.
58. *Ibid.*, 777–779.
59. *Ibid.*, Ser 1, Vol 39, P 2, 490–491.
60. Berlin and others, *Black Military Experience*, 520–521; Redkey, *Grand Army of Black Men*, 31–32.
61. Berlin and others, *Black Military Experience*, 521–522; Glatthaar, *Forged in Battle*, 167.
62. *O.R. Armies*, Ser 1, Vol 15, 906–908.
63. *Ibid.*, Ser 2, Vol 4, 954.
64. *Ibid.*, Ser 2, Vol 6, 115. See also *Ibid.*, Ser 1, Vol 24, P 2, 457–459, 466; Ser 2, Vol 6, 73.
65. *Ibid.*, Ser 2, Vol 6, 139.
66. *Ibid.*, 163.
67. *Ibid.*, 259. See also *Ibid.*, 244, 258–259, 288–289.
68. *Ibid.*, 924–926.
69. *Ibid.*, Ser 3, Vol 4, 247–248, 920; Berlin and others, *Black Military Experience*, 570.
70. *O.R. Armies*, Ser 2, Vol 7, 113–114; Redkey, *Grand Army of Black Men*, 46–50; Berlin and others, *Black Military Experience*, 570.
71. *O.R. Armies*, Ser 2, Vol 7, 1018–1019. See also *Ibid.*, 156, 222–223, 990–993, 1117; *Ibid*, Ser 2, Vol 8, 109.
72. *Ibid.*, Ser 2, Vol 3, 153. For further discussion of the black soldiers who were prisoners of Confederates see, *Ibid.*, Ser 2, Vol 8, 175–176, 354–355, 396.
73. Cornish, *Sable Arm*, 288.
74. Lida K. Wiggins, *The Life and Works of Paul Laurence Dunbar*, (Naperville, IL: J.L. Nichols & Company, 1907), 50–52.

Chapter 9

1. Henry Smith, *AR*, Ser 2, Vol 10, P 6, 196.
2. Hannah Austin, *GA*, Ser 2, Vol 12, P 1, 20.
3. Hester Norton, *MS*, Sup, Ser 1, Vol 9, P 4, 1653–1654.
4. Ella Wilson, *AR*, Ser 2, Vol 11, P 7, 205.
5. Laura Cornish, *TX*, Ser 1, Vol 4, P 1, 255.
6. Celeste Avery, *GA*, Ser 2, Vol 12, P 2, 27; Jerry Boykins, *TX*, Ser 1, Vol 4, P 1, 122.
7. Emma Johnson, *MS*, Sup, Ser 1, Vol 8, P 3, 1155.
8. Henretta Gooch, *MS*, Sup, Ser 1, Vol 8, P 3, 859.
9. Jake Dawkins, *MS*, Sup, Ser 1, Vol 7, P 2, 597.
10. Cindy Anderson, *MS*, Sup, Ser 1, Vol 6, P 1, 67.
11. Turner McLean, *NC*, Ser 2, Vol 15, P 2, 86.
12. Ivory Osborne, *AR*, Ser 2, Vol 10, P 5, 230; Stearlin Arnwine, *TX*, Ser 1, Vol 4, P 1, 33.
13. Charlie Hinton, *AR*, Ser 2, Vol 9, P 3, 280.
14. Katie Rye, *AR*, Ser 2, Vol 10, P 6, 111; James Reeves, *AR*, Ser 2, Vol 10, P 6, 28.
15. Mollie Campbell, *MS*, Sup, Ser 1, Vol 7, 2, 664; Aunt Pinkey Howard, *AR*, Ser 2, Vol 9, P 3, 327.
16. Isiah Green, *GA*, Ser 2, Vol 12, P 2, 55.
17. Anderson and Minerva Edwards, *TX*, Ser 1, Vol 4, P 2, 8.
18. Fred Dibble, *TX*, Ser 1, Vol 5, P 3, 53.
19. Thomas Ruffin, *AR*, Ser 2, Vol 10, P 6, 99.
20. Harry Bridges, *MS*, Sup, Ser 1, Vol 6, P 1, 211.
21. Matilda Hatchett, *AR*, Ser 2, Vol 9, P 3, 198.
22. Victoria Perry, *SC*, Vol 3, P 3, 261; Mahalia Shores, *AR*, Ser 2, Vol 10, P 6, 154; Webster Thomas, *AR*, Vol 10, P 6, 306.
23. Prince Johnson, *MS*, Sup, Ser 1, Vol 7, 81.
24. Lillie Williams, *AR*, Ser 2, Vol 11, P 7, 178; Virginia Jackson, *AR*, Ser 2, Vol 9, P 4, 26.
25. Dora Franklin, *MS*, Sup, Ser 1, Vol 7, P 2, 786.
26. John Bates, *TX*, Ser 1, Vol 4, P 1, 52.
27. George Coleman, *MS*, Sup, Ser 1, Vol 7, P 2, 426.
28. Bessie Lawson, *AR*, Ser 2, Vol 9, P 4, 245.
29. Sarah Poindexter, *SC*, Ser 1, Vol 3, P 3, 268.
30. Charlie Moses, *MS*, Ser 1, Vol 7, 116.
31. Mark Oliver, *MS*, Sup, Ser 1, Vol 9, P 4, 1638–1689.
32. James Lucas, *MS*, Sup, Ser 1, Vol 8, P 3, 1344.
33. Rina Brown, *MS*, Sup, Ser 1, Vol 6, P 1, 277–278.
34. Tom Robinson, *AR*, Ser 2, Vol 10, P 6, 66; Casper Rumple, *AR*, Ser 2, Vol 10, P 6, 106; Mary Anderson, *NC*, Ser 2, Vol 14, P 1, 25; Tines Kendrick, *AR*, Ser 2, Vol 9, P 4, 183; Josephine Hamilton, *AR*, Ser 2, Vol 9, P 3, 135; Minnie Davis, *GA*, Ser 2, Vol 12, P 1, 262.
35. Fanny Berry, *VA*, Ser 2, Vol 16, 6.
36. Tildy Collins, *AL*, Ser 1, Vol 6, 85; Georgia Baker, *GA*, Ser 2, Vol 12, P 1, 50.
37. James Boyd, *TX*, Ser 1, Vol 4, P 1, 118; J.W. Terrill, *TX*, Ser 1, Vol 5, P 3, 82.
38. Felix Haywood, *TX*, Ser 1, Vol 4, P 2, 133.
39. Lucindy Shaw, *MS*, Sup, Ser 1, Vol 10, P 5, 1928.
40. Silas Smith, *SC*, Ser 1, Vol 3, P 4, 119; Ella Wilson, *AR*, Ser 2, Vol 11, P 7, 205.
41. Clara C. Young, *MS*, Ser 1, Vol 7, 173.
42. Hamp Santee, *MS*, Sup, Ser 1, Vol 10, P 5, 1919.
43. Rachel Hankins, *AR*, Vol 9, P 3, 156.
44. Myra Jones, *MS*, Sup, Ser 1, Vol 8, P 3, 1250.
45. Molly Horn, *AR*, Ser 2, Vol 9, P 3, 320.
46. Adam Singleton, *MS*, Sup, Ser 1, Vol 10, P 5, 1952.

47. John Cameron, *MS*, Sup, Ser 1, Vol 7, P 2, 334; Temple Wilson, *MS*, Sup, Ser 1, Vol 10, P 5, 2374.
48. Lewis Jefferson, *MS*, Sup, Ser 1, Vol 8, P 3, 1143.
49. Hannah Hancock, *AR*, Ser 2, Vol 9, P 3, 144.
50. Rev. John Moore, *TN*, Ser 2, Vol 16, 48; Sarah Ashley, *TX*, Ser 1, Vol 4, P 1, 36.
51. Victoria Perry, *SC*, Ser 1, Vol 3, P 3, 361. Fred James, *SC*, Vol 3, P 3, 16.
52. Warren McKinney, *AR*, Ser 2, Vol 10, P 5, 27–28.
53. Ella Wilson, *AR*, Ser 2, Vol 11, P 7, 205.
54. Silas Smith, *SC*, Ser 1, Vol 3, P 4, 119–120; James Bolton, *GA*, Ser 2, Vol 12, P 1, 103; Rose, *Slavery and Freedom*, Oxford University Press, 70.
55. Avalena McConico, *AR*, Ser 2, Vol 10, P 5, 11; Bessie Lawson, *AR*, Ser 2, Vol 9, P 4, 245; Diana Rankins, *AR*, Ser 2, Vol 10, P 6, 13; Peter Blewit, *MS*, Sup, Ser 1, Vol 6, P 1, 153; Andrew Boone, *NC*, Ser 2, Vol 14, P 1, 136–137; W.L. Pollacks, *AR*, Ser 2, Vol 10, P 5, 358.
56. Minerva Bendy, *TX*, Ser 1, Vol 4, P 1, 69.
57. John Barker, *TX*, Ser 1, Vol 4, P 1, 43; Georgia Baker, *GA*, Ser 2, Vol 12, P 1, 50.
58. Clara Young, *MS*, Ser 1, Vol 7, 173.
59. James Turner McLean, *NC*, Ser 2, Vol 15, P 2, 87.
60. Henry Bland, *GA*, Ser 2, Vol 12, P 1, 85; Clara Walker, *AR*, Ser 2, Vol 11, P 7, 26; Sylvia Watkins, *TN*, Ser 2, Vol 16, 77; Frank Menefee, *AL*, Ser 1, Vol 6, 281; Gus Johnson, *TX*, Ser 1, Vol 4, P 2, 210–211.
61. Andrew Jackson Gill, *MS*, Sup, Ser 1, Vol 8, P 3, 847; Della Briscoe, *GA*, Ser 2, Vol 12, P 1, 132; Andy Nelson, *TX*, Ser 1, Vol 5, P 3, 145–147; John Sneed, *TX*, Ser 1, Vol 5, P 3, 50.
62. Fannie Tatum, *AR*, Ser 2, Vol 10, P 6, 257–258.
63. Gabe Butler, *MS*, Sup, Ser 1, Vol 6, P 1, 318; Sam McCallum, *MS*, Ser 1, Vol 7, 103.
64. Jane Sutton, *MS*, Ser 1, Vol 7, 155.
65. Ida Berry, *AR*, Ser 2, Vol 10, P 6, 46; See also Molly Williams, *MS*, Ser 1, Vol 7, 164.
66. Harriet Miller, *MS*, Sup, Ser 1, Vol 9, P 4, 1505; Katie Darling, *TX*, Ser 1, Vol 4, P 1, 280.
67. Sarah Benjamin, *TX*, Ser 1, Vol 4, P 1, 71.
68. Viney Baker, *NC*, Ser 2, Vol 14, P 1, 72; Squire Irvin, *MS*, Sup, Ser 1, Vol 8, P 3, 1087; Anna Baker, *MS*, Ser 1, Vol 7, 15; Emma Turner, *AR*, Ser 2, Vol 10, P 6, 360; Frank Bell, *TX*, Ser 1, Vol 4, P 1, 60.
69. Robert Falls, *TN*, Ser 2, Vol 16, 16.
70. Nathan Best, *MS*, Sup, Ser 1, Vol 6, P 1, 132–133; Milton Richie, *AR*, Ser 2, Vol 10, P 6, 49; Matilda Hatchett, *AR*, Ser 2, Vol 9, P 3, 199; Tom Wylie Neal, *AR*, Ser 2, Vol 10, P 5, 185; George Hinton, *NC*, Ser 2, Vol 14, P 1, 445.
71. Hattie Jefferson, *MS*, Sup, Ser 1, Vol 8, P 3, 1135; Henry Daniels, *MS*, Sup, Ser 1, Vol 7, P 2, 551.
72. Chaney Hews, *NC*, Ser 1, Vol 14, P 1, 407.
73. Rev. Squire Dowd, *NC*, Ser 2, Vol 14, P 1, 266; Henrietta Murray, *MS*, Sup, Ser 1, Vol 9, P 4, 1611; Solomon Lambert, *AR*, Ser 2, Vol 9, P 4, 231; Mahalia Shores, *AR*, Ser 2, Vol 10, P 6, 155.
74. Mary Anderson, *NC*, Ser 2, Vol 14, P 1, 26.
75. Peter Mitchell, *TX*, Ser 1, Vol 5, P 3, 115; Robert Glenn, *NC*, Ser 2, Vol 14, P 1, 336–338; Charles Crawley, *VA*, Ser 2, Vol 16, 13; Jerry Eubanks, *MS*, Sup, Ser 1, Vol 7, P 2, 699.
76. Sam Broach, *MS*, Sup, Ser 1, Vol 6, P 1, 227; Jerry Boykins, *TX*, Ser 1, Vol 4, P 1, 123.
77. W.D. Miller, *AR*, Ser 2, Vol 10, P 5, 97; R.F. Parker, *AR*, Ser 2, Vol 10, P 5, 255; Josh Miles, *TX*, Ser 1, Vol 5, P 3, 81.

78. Sally Foltz, *MS*, Sup, Ser 1, Vol 7, P 2, 753.

79. Jake Goodridge, *AR*, Ser 2, Vol 9, P 3, 54; Thomas Ruffin, *AR*, Ser 2, Vol 10, P 6, 99; Primus Magee, *MS*, Sup, Ser 1, Vol 9, P 4, 1432; Alex Montgomery, *MS*, Sup, Ser 1, Vol 9, P 4, 1530.

80. Simon Hare, *MS*, Sup, Ser 1, Vol 8, P 3, 920. See also Vinnie Busby, *MS*, Sup, Ser 1, Vol 6, P 1, 311.

81. Thomas Jones, *TX*, Ser 1, Vol 4, P 2, 204. See also Elizabeth Finley, *MS*, Sup, Ser 1, Vol 7, P 2, 730.

82. Pauline Howell, *AR*, Ser 2, Vol 9, P 3, 43.

83. Tina Johnson, *NC*, Ser 2, Vol 15, P 2, 22.

84. Willis Cozart, *NC*, Ser 2, Vol 14, P 1, 185–186.

85. Charles Davenport, *MS*, Sup, Ser 1, Vol 7, P 2, 565.

86. *O.R. Armies*, Ser 1, Vol 48, P 2, 744; *Ibid.*, Ser 1, Vol 49, P 2, 828–829.

87. *Ibid.*, Ser 1, Vol 49, P 2, 728–729.

88. *Ibid.*, Ser 1, Vol 49, P 2, 878; 856–857.

89. *Ibid.*, Ser 1, Vol 48, P 2, 128–129.

90. *Ibid.*, Ser 1, Vol 49, P 2, 783–787.

91. *Ibid.*, Ser 2, Vol 8, 651.

92. *Ibid.*, Ser 1, Vol 49, P 2, 975–976.

93. *Ibid.*, Ser 1, Vol 48, P 2, 749.

94. *Ibid.*, 854–855, 867–868.

95. *Ibid.*, 903–918.

96. *Ibid.*, 970–971.

97. *Ibid.*, Ser 1, Vol 49, P 2, 1024–1025.

98. *Ibid.*, Ser 1, Vol 48, P 2, 986; 980–981, 1017–1018.

99. *Ibid.*, 1017–1018.

100. *O.R. Navies*, Ser 1, Vol 27, 294–295.

101. *O.R. Armies*, Ser 1, Vol 49, P 2, 791.

102. *Ibid.*, 826.

103. *Ibid.*, 835.

104. *Ibid.*, Ser 1, Vol 48, P 2, 957–958; *Ibid.*, Ser 1, Vol 49, P 2, 887, 890; 963–964.

105. *Ibid.*, 851.

106. *Ibid.*, 1015, 1020; *Ibid.*, Ser 1, Vol 48, P 2, 905.

107. *Ibid.*, Ser 1, Vol 49, P 2, 1061–1062.

108. *Ibid.*, 861, 969.

109. *Ibid.*, 859, 874.

110. *Ibid.*, Ser 1, Vol 48, P 2, 832, 1310; *Ibid.*, Ser 1, Vol 49, P 2, 812, 831, 911.

111. *Ibid.*, Ser 1, Vol 49, P 2, 874.

112. *Ibid.*, Ser 3, Vol 4, 1050.

113. *Ibid.*, Ser 1, Vol 49, P 2, 1041–1042.

114. *Ibid.*, 1068.

115. *Ibid.*, 954.

116. *Ibid.*, Ser 1, Vol 49, P 2, 790, 803; *Ibid.*, Ser 1, Vol 49, P 2, 828.

117. *Ibid.*, Ser 1, Vol 48, P 2, 720, 820, 829–830; *Ibid.*, Vol 49, P 2, 1079–1080; *Ibid.*, Ser 1, Vol 48, P 2, 1171.

118. *Ibid.*, Ser 1, Vol 49, P 2, 1101–1104.

119. *Ibid.*, 905–906; Ibid., Ser 1, Vol 48, P 2, 901.

120. *Ibid.*, Ser 1, Vol 49, P 2, 1112; Sheridan, *Personal Memoirs*, 256–280.

121. *O.R. Armies*, Ser 1, Vol 48, P 2, 1250.

122. *Ibid.*, Ser 1, Vol 49, P 2, 833–834.

123. Bell Carruthers, *MS*, Sup, Ser 1, Vol 7, P 2, 368.

124. Julius Jones, *MS*, Sup, Ser 1, Vol 8, P 3, 1223.

125. Mary Wallace Bowe, *NC*, Ser 2, Vol 14, P 1, 150–151; Charlie Davenport, *MS*, Sup, Ser 1, Vol 7, P 2, 562; Adriana Kerns, *AR*, Ser 1, Vol 9, P 4, 193; Frank Patterson, *AR*, Ser 2, Vol 10, P 5, 278; William Edward Black, *MS*, Sup, Ser 1, Vol 6, P 1, 144.

126. Frank Hughes, *MS*, Sup, Ser 1, Vol 8, P 3, 1065; Charles W. Dikens, *NC*, Sup, Ser 1, Vol 14, P 1, 257; Reuben Rosborough, *SC*, Ser 1, Vol 3, P 4, 47; Sallie Paul, *SC*, Ser 1, Vol 3, P 3, 247.

127. Gabe Butler, *MS*, Sup, Ser 1, Vol 6, P 1, 326; Turner Jacobs, *MS*, Sup, Ser 1, Vol 8, P 3, 1119; William Kirk, *AR*, Ser 2, Vol 9, P 4, 215; James Brittian, *MS*, Sup, Ser 1, Vol 6, P 1, 220; Annie Stephenson, *NC*, Ser 2, Vol 15, P 2, 323; Isaac Stier, *MS*, Sup, Ser 1, Vol 10, P 5, 2055; John Bectom, *NC*, Ser 2, Vol 14, P 1, 98.

128. "Noted Personalities During Period of Development, Warren County. Will Strong." *MS*, Sup, Ser 1, Vol 9, P 4, 1533–1535.

129. John Williams, *MS*, Sup, Ser 1, Vol 10, P 5, 2326–2332; Sylvia Floyd, *MS*, Sup, Ser 1, Vol 7, P 2, 742; Litwack, *Been in the Storm So Long*, 247–251.

130. Tines Kendricks, *AR*, Ser 2, Vol 9, P 4, 184.

131. Mattie Curtis, *NC*, Ser 2, Vol 14, P 1, 221; Molly Hudgens, *AR*, Ser 2, Vol 9, P 3, 345.

132. Waters McIntosh, *AR*, Ser 2, Vol 10, P 5, 21; John Williams, *MS*, Sup, Ser 1, Vol 10, P 5, 2331–2332; Eliza Hayes, *AR*, Ser 2, Vol 9, P 3, 222; William J. Stevens, *AR*, Ser 2, Vol 10, P 6, 234.

133. Emaline Neland, *AR*, Ser 2, Vol 10, P 5, 195; Pauline Johnson and Felice Boudreaux, *TX*, Ser 2, Vol 4, P 2, 228; Sarah Louise Augustus, *NC*, Ser 2, Vol 14, P 1, 57; Arrie Binns, *GA*, Ser 2, Vol 12, P 1, 78–79.

134. Sarah Wells, *AR*, Ser 2, Vol 11, P 7, 93; Allen Ward, *MS*, Sup, Ser 1, Vol 10, P 5, 2173–2174; Lawrence Evans, *MS*, Sup, Ser 1, Vol 7, P 2, 706; Charles Vaden, *AR*, Ser 2, Vol 11, P 7, 1; Anna Huggins, *AR*, Ser 2, Vol 9, P 3, 354; Lula Coleman, *MS*, Sup, Ser 1, Vol 7, P 2, 434; Neely Gray, *AR*, Ser 2, Vol 9, P 3, 83.

135. Manda Boggan, *MS*, Sup, Ser 1, Vol 6, P 1, 158; Ella Wilson, *AR*, Ser 2, Vol 11, P 7, 206.

136. Jane Sutton, *MS*, Sup, Ser 1, Vol 10, P 5, 2092.

137. Rachel Bradley, *AR*, Ser 1, Vol 2, 1–3.

138. Toby Jones, *TX*, Ser 1, Vol 4, P 2, 252.

139. Lizzie Norfleet, *MS*, Sup, Ser 1, Vol 9, P 4, 649; Celeste Avery, *GA*, Ser 2, Vol 12, P 2, 27; Emma Morris, *AR*, Ser 2, Vol 10, P 5, 154; Adeline Crump, *NC*, Ser 2, Vol 14, P 1, 205; Lydia Stewart, *MS*, Sup, Ser 1, Vol 10, P 5, 2047; Jennie Washington, *AR*, Ser 2, Vol 11, P 7, 59.

140. Julia Frances Daniels, *TX*, Ser 1, Vol 4, P 1, 277; Charles Bell, *MS*, Ser 1, Vol 6, P 1, 127; Frank Larkin, *AR*, Ser 2, Vol 9, P 4, 238.

Chapter 10

1. Quoted by Herbert Aptheker, "South Carolina Negro Conventions, 1865," *Journal of Negro History*, XXXI, No. 1 (January, 1946), 91–97, 95.

2. House of Representatives, 39th Congress, 1st Session, Report No. 101, *Memphis Riots and Massacres*, Washington, 1866, (Arno Press, Washington, 1969), 22.

3. Memphis *Post*, March-July, 1867.

4. *Ibid.*, 1866–1869.

5. *Ibid.*, August 2, 1866.

6. *Ibid.*, March-July, 1867.

7. Memphis *Daily Appeal*, April 13, 1870.

8. Memphis *Daily Appeal* and Memphis *Post*, 1867–1870. See also Richard O. Curry, "The Abolitionists and Reconstruction: A Critical Appraisal," *Journal of Southern History*, XXXIV (November, 1968), 527–545.

9. New Orleans *Louisianian*, October 10, 1874.

10. T. Harry Williams, "The Louisiana Unification

Movement of 1873," *Journal of Southern History*, XI, No. 3 (August, 1945), 349–369.

11. Ivory Osborne, *AR*, Ser 2, Vol 10, P 5, 231.

12. Otis A. Singletary, *Negro Militia and Reconstruction* (Austin: University of Texas Press, 1957), 10–36; R.H. Woody, "Jonathan Jasper Wright, Associate Justice of the Supreme Court of South Carolina, 1870–1877," *Journal of Negro History*, XVIII, No. 2 (April, 1933), 114–131; Edward F. Sweat, "Francis Cardoza — Profile of Integrity in Reconstruction Politics," *Journal of Negro History*, XLVI, No. 4 (October, 1961), 217–232.

13. Clarence Bacote, "William Finch, Negro Councilman and Political Activist in Atlanta During Early Reconstruction," *Journal of Negro History*, XL, No. 4 (October, 1955), 341–364.

14. Louis Joseph Piernas, *MS*, Sup, Ser 1, Vol 9, P 4, 1706–1708; Green Gray, *AR*, Ser 2, Vol 9, P 3, 81; Ella Gillespie, *AR*, Ser 2, Vol 9, P 3, 44; Parrish Washington, *AR*, Ser 2, Vol 11, P 7, 61; Clarice Jackson, *AR*, Ser 2, Vol 9, P 4, 4; Spart Quinn, *MS*, Sup, Ser 1, Vol 8, P 3, 1225; James Marten, *Texas Divided: Loyalty and Dissent in the Lone Star State, 1856–1874* (Lexington, KY:University Press of Kentucky, 1990) 161–173.

15. William Lattimore, *AR*, Ser 2, Vol 10, P 4, 243.

16. Frank Green, *AR*, Ser 2, Vol 9, P 3, 103.

17. Ivory Osborne, *AR*, Ser 2, Vol 10, P 5, 23.

18. Dave Weatherby, *MS*, Ser 1, Vol 10, P 5, 2226.

19. John Peterson, *AR*, Ser 2, Vol 10, P 5, 333.

20. Jerry Cook, *MS*, Sup, Ser 1, Vol 7, P 2, 499.

21. John G. Van Deusen, "The Exodus of 1879," *Journal of Negro History*, XXI, No. 2 (April, 1936), 111–129; Roy Garvin, "Benjamin, or 'Pap' Singleton and his Followers," *Journal of Negro History*, XXXIII, No. 1 (January, 1948), 1–23.

22. New Orleans *Louisianian*, December 26, 1874.

23. James Reeves, *AR*, Ser 2, Vol 10, P 6, 28.

24. Isaac Stier, *MS*, Sup, Ser 1, Vol 10, P 5, 2054.

25. Robert Weathersby, *MS*, Sup, Ser 1, Vol 10, P 5, 2243.

26. Wright Stapleton, *MS*, Sup, Ser 1, Vol 10, P 5, 2033.

27. Happy Day Green, *AR*, Ser 2, Vol 9, P 3, 89.

28. John Crawford, *TX*, Ser 1, Vol 4, P 1, 258.

29. Eli Davison, *TX*, Ser 1, Vol 4, P 1, 297.

30. Richard Jackson, *TX*, Ser 2, Vol 4, P 2, 197.

31. Lucy Withers, *AR*, Ser 2, Vol 11, P 7, 223.

32. Cal Woods, *AR*, Ser 2, Vol 11, P 7, 230.

33. W.L. Bost, *NC*, Ser 2, Vol 14, P 1, 146; Mandy Coverson, *NC*, Ser 2, Vol 14, P 1, 181.

34. Anderson Furr, *GA*, Ser 2, Vol 12, P 1, 351.

35. Abram Harris, *AR*, Ser 2, Vol 9, P 3, 173.

36. Talitha Lewis, *AR*, Ser 2, Vol 9, P 4, 254.

37. Dora Franks, *MS*, Ser 1, Vol 7, 54.

38. Rebecca Hill, *AR*, Ser 2, Vol 9, P 3, 271; Lorenza Ezell, *TX*, Ser 1, Vol 4, P 2, 31.

39. James Lucas, *MS*, Ser 1, Vol 8, P 3, 1343–1344.

40. Wesley Graves, *AR*, Ser 2, Vol 9, P 3, 74–75; Prince Johnson, *MS*, Sup, Ser 1, Vol 8, P 3, 1175–1177; Ned Chaney, *MS*, Sup, Ser 1, Vol 7, P 2, 377.

41. Will Adams, *TX*, Ser 1, Vol 4, P 1, 3.

42. Charlie Moses, *MS*, Ser 1, Vol 7, 116.

43. "Cat" Ross, *AR*, Ser 2, Vol 10, P 6, 86.

44. William Hamilton, *TX*, Ser 1, Vol 4, P 2, 107.

45. Pierce Harper, *TX*, Ser 1, Vol 4, P 2, 112.

46. Memphis *Daily Appeal*, February 1, 1870.

47. *Ibid.*, February 18, 1870.

48. Sarah Whitmore, *AR*, Ser 2, Vol 11, P 7, 140.

49. Agatha Babino, *TX*, Ser 1, Vol 4, P 1, 37–38.

50. Renfro Hangs, *AL*, Ser 1, Vol 6, 140–141.

51. Ben Johnson, *NC*, Ser 1, Vol 15, P 2, 10.

52. Ann Matthews, *TN*, Ser 2, Vol 16, 44.

53. Ida Blackshear Hutchison, *AR*, Ser 2, Vol 9, P 3, 376–377.

54. Mary Ella Grandberry, *AL*, Ser 1, Vol 6, 163.

55. Nancy King, *TX*, Ser 1, Vol 4, P 2, 289.

56. Ben Johnson, *NC*, Ser 2, Vol 15, P 2, 11.

57. Sarah Jane Patterson, *AR*, Ser 2, Vol 10, P 5, 288; William Henry Rooks, *AR*, Ser 2, Vol 10, P 6, 77.

58. Polly Turner Cancer, *MS*, Sup, Ser 1, Vol 7, P 2, 347.

59. John Hunter, *AR*, Ser 2, Vol 9, P 3, 363.

60. Lee Pierce, *TX*, Ser 1, Vol 5, P 3, 186–187; Marten, *Texas Divided*, 159.

61. Sam McCallum, *MS*, Sup, Ser 1, Vol 9, P 4, 1356–1357; Singletary, *Negro Militia*, 125–126.

62. Casper Rumple, *AR*, Ser 2, Vol 10, P 6, 106–107.

63. Dr. D.B Gaines, *AR*, Ser 2, Vol 9, P 3, 4.

64. John Beckwith, *NC*, Ser 2, Vol 14, P 1, 90.

65. John Ogee, *TX*, Ser 1, Vol 5, P 3, 155; Scott Hooper, *TX*, Ser 1, Vol 4, P 2, 158.

66. Annie Row, *TX*, Ser 1, Vol 5, P 3, 261.

67. Memphis *Daily Appeal*, April 26, 1870.

Chapter 11

1. Dudley T. Cornish, "The Union Army as a Training School for Negroes," *Journal of Negro History*, XXXVII, No. 4 (October, 1952), 368–382.

2. Edwin D. Hoffman, "From Slavery to Self Reliance: The Record of Achievement of the Freedmen of the Sea Island Region," *Journal of Negro History*, XLI, No. 1 (January, 1956), 8–42. *O.R. Armies*, Ser 3, Vol 4, 193–194.

3. See Report of the Commissioner of the Freedmen's Bureau, General O.O. Howard, in Memphis *Daily Appeal*, December 28, 1865; Report of the Assistant Commissioner of the Freedmen's Bureau for Tennessee, Memphis *Daily Appeal*, November 14, 1868; Martin Abbott, *The Freedmen's Bureau in South Carolina, 1865–1872*, (Chapel Hill: University of North Carolina Press, 1967), 130–135.

4. G.K. Eggleston, "The Work of the Relief Societies During the Civil War," *Journal of Negro History*, XIV, No. 3 (July, 1929), 272–299; Loretta Funke, "The Negro in Education," *Journal of Negro History*, V, No. 1 (January, 1920), 1–21.

5. Report of the Majority, *Memphis Riots and Massacres*, 20.

6. Mary Anngady, *NC*, Ser 2, Vol 14, P 1, 36; Mandy Tucker, *AR*, Ser 2, Vol 10, P 6, 358; Ervin Smith, *AR*, Ser 2, Vol 10, P 6, 191.

7. Joseph Leonidas Star, *TN*, Ser 2, Vol 16, 72; Charlie Hunter, *NC*, Ser 2, Vol 14, P 1, 454; Betty Cofer, *NC*, Ser 2, Vol 14, P 1, 170; Charlotte Stephens, *AR*, Ser 2, Vol 10, P 6, 227–228; Jasper Battle, *GA*, Ser 2, Vol 12, P 1, 69; Reynolds, *Jesuits for the Negro*, 166, 173.

8. Virginia Varris, *MS*, Sup, Ser 1, Vol 8, P 3, 946; Ella Johnson, *AR*, Ser 2, Vol 9, P 4, 180; J.M. Parker, *SC*, Ser 1, Vol 10, P 5, 246.

9. Dan A. Rudd and Theo. Bond, *From Slavery to Wealth: The Life of Scott Bond. The Rewards of Honesty, Industry, Economy and Perseverance* (Madison, AR: Journal Print Co., 1917), 25–26; Martha Patterson, *TX*, Ser 1, Vol 5, P 3, 176; "A Union Soldier," *Unwritten History of Slavery*, in *American Slave*, Vol 18, 124.

10. Memphis *Post*, January 11, 1869.

11. James Johnson, *TX*, Ser 1, Vol 4, P 2, 217; William Moore, *TX*, Ser 1, Vol 5, P 3, 137; Clarissa Scales, *TX*, Ser 1, Vol 5, P 3, 43.

12. Betty Krump, *AR*, Ser 2, Vol 9, P 4, 217.

13. Memphis *Post*, February 18, 1867.

14. Charlie Hinton, *AR*, Ser 2, Vol 9, P 3, 280; Bill Crump, *NC*, Ser 2, Vol 14, P 1, 210–211; A.C. Pruitt, *TX*, Ser 1, Vol 5, P 3, 221; Ike Worthy, *AR*, Ser 2, Vol 11, P 7, 242–243; Louis Davis, *MS*, Sup, Ser 1, Vol 7, P 2, 586; Annie Hill, *AR*, Ser 2, Vol 9, P 3, 245; Alice Wise, *AR*, Ser 2, Vol 11, P 7, 216; Scott Martin, *TN*, Ser 2, Vol 16, 40.

15. Ben Hite, *AR*, Ser 2, Vol 9, P 3, 281; Willie Wallace, *AR*, Ser 2, Vol 11, P 7, 42; Hardy Miller, *AR*, Ser 2, Vol 10, P 5, 75; Jeptha Choice, *TX*, Ser 1, Vol 4, P 1, 218; Ivory Osborne, *AR*, Ser 2, Vol 10, P 5, 230; Charles Hayes, *AL*, Ser 1, Vol 6, 175; John Jones, *AR*, Ser 2, Vol 9, P 4, 1507.

16. Charlie Barbour, *NC*, Ser 2, Vol 14, P 1, 77; Ike Worthy, *AR*, Ser 2, Vol 11, P 7, 242–243; Emma Grisham, *TN*, Ser 2, Vol 16, 29.

17. Belle Caruthers, *MS*, Sup, Ser 1, Vol 7, P 2, 368; James Turner McLean, *NC*, Ser 2, Vol 15, P 2, 87; Harre Quarls, *TX*, Ser 1, Vol 5, P 3, 223; Zek Brown, *TX*, Ser 1, Vol 4, P 1, 167; Mariah Robinson, *TX*, Ser 1, Vol 5, P 3, 255; Leta Gray, *KS*, Ser 2, Vol 16, 4; Esther King Casey, *AL*, Ser 1, Vol 6, 56–57; Nettie Van Buren, *AR*, Ser 2, Vol 11, P 7, 5–6.

18. John Peterson, *AR*, Ser 2, Vol 10, P 5, 333.

19. James H. O'Donnell III, ed., "A Freedman Thanks His Patrons: Letters of Taylor Thistle, 1872–1873," *Journal of Southern History*, XXXIII, No. 1 (February, 1967), 68–84.

20. Alrutheus A. Taylor, "Fisk University and the Nashville Community, 1866–1900," *Journal of Negro History*, XXXIX, No 2, (April, 1954), 111–126.

21. *Ibid.*, 111–126; L.P. Jackson, "The Origin of Hampton Institute," *Journal of Negro History*, X, No 2 (April, 1925), 131–149.

22. Thomas Rutling and Benjamin Holmes, in Blassingame, *Slave Testimony*, 615–620; Emma Grisham, *TN*, Ser 2, Vol 16, 29; A.M. Moore, *TX*, Ser 1, Vol 5, P 3, 119–120; Henry Butler, *TX*, Ser 1, Vol 4, P 1, 181; Mary Jane Wilson, *VA*, Ser 2, Vol 16, 55–56; James C. James, *MD*, Ser 2, Vol 16, 35; J.E. Combs, *MS*, Sup, Ser 1, Vol 7, P 2, 484–485.

23. Memphis *Post*, January 14, 1866.

24. *Ibid.*, May 29, 1869.

25. *Ibid.*, July 14, 1866.

26. Philip S. Foner, "Address of Frederick Douglass at the Inauguration of Douglass Institute, Baltimore, October 1, 1865," *Journal of Negro History*, LIV, No. 2 (April, 1969), 175–177.

27. Edgar W. Knight, *Public Education in the South* (New York, 1922), 324; Frederick Eby, *The Development of Education in Texas* (New York: The Macmillan Co., 1925), 266; F.B. Simkins and R.H. Woody, *South Carolina During Reconstruction* (Chapel Hill: The University of North Carolina Press, 1932), 439–440; Louis R. Harlan, "Desegregation in New Orleans Public Schools During Reconstruction," *American Historical Review*, LXVII, No. 3 (April, 1962), 663–675. See also Henry Allen Bullock, *A History of Negro Education in the South From 1619 to the Present* (Cambridge, Mass.: Harvard University Press, 1967), 46–52.

28. Memphis *Post*, February 9, 1869. See also *Ibid.*, February 12, 1867, and 1867–1869, *passim*.

29. Reynolds, *Jesuits for the Negro*, 165–180.

30. Henry J. Cadbury, "Negro Membership in the Society of Friends," *Journal of Southern History* XXI (April, 1936), 151–213.

31. New Orleans *Louisianian*, May 30, 1874.

32. R.A. Carter, "What The Negro Had Done," *Journal of Negro History*, XI (January, 1926), 1–7.

33. Anderson Furr, *GA*, Ser 2, Vol 12, P 1, 352; Cora L. Horton, *AR*, Ser 2, Vol 9, P 3, 322–324; Hannah Plummer, *NC*, Ser 2, Vol 15, P 2, 182; Santee Reed, *MS*, Sup, Ser 1, Vol 9, P 4, 1819; Joe Rollins, *MS*, Sup, Ser 1, Vol 9, P 4, 1898.

34. Memphis *Post*, January 4, 1866.

35. Bell Williams, *AR*, Ser 2, Vol 11, P 7, 149; Philip Johnson, *MD*, Ser 2, Vol 16, 43; Eugenia Weatherall, *MS*, Sup, Ser 1, Vol 10, P 5, 2216–2217; Carey Davenport, *TX*, Ser 1, Vol 4, P 1, 284.

36. Robert Laird, *MS*, Sup, Ser 1, Vol 8, P 3.

37. William H. McCarthy, *MS*, Sup, Ser 1, Vol 9, P 4, 1377–1379; Robert Wilson, *AR*, Ser 2, Vol 11, P 7, 209; Moses Mitchell, *AR*, Ser 2, Vol 10, P 6, 114–115; Dempsy Pitts, *MS*, Sup, Ser 1, Vol 9, P 4, 172; Manus Robinson, *MD*, Sup, Ser 1, Vol 9, P 4, 1859–1860; Needham Love, *AR*, Ser 2, Vol 9, P 4, 293–294; Frank Childress, *MS*, Sup, Ser 1, Vol 7, P 2, 390.

38. July Ann Halfen, *MS*, Sup, Ser 1, Vol 8, P 3, 903–904.

39. Malinda Edwards, *MS*, Sup, Ser 1, Vol 7, P 2, 680.

40. Benny Dillard, *GA*, Ser 2, Vol 12, P 1, 295.

41. Patsy Hyde, *TN*, Ser 2, Vol 16, 35; Frankie Goole, *TN*, Ser 2, Vol 16, 23.

42. Talitha Island, *AR*, Ser 2, Vol 9, P 3, 385.

43. Gabe Emanuel, *MS*, Sup, Ser 1, Vol 7, P 2, 686.

44. Lucindy Shaw, *MS*, Sup, Ser 1, Vol 10, P 5, 1930.

45. Smith Simmons, *MS*, Sup, Ser 1, Vol 10, P 5, 1942.

46. Reynolds, *Jesuits for the Negro*, 66.

47. Clara Jones, *NC*, Ser 1, Vol 15, P 2, 28.

48. Adeline Marshall, *TX*, Ser 1, Vol 5, P 3, 47.

49. Caroline Watson, *AR*, Ser 2, Vol 11, P 7, 63.

50. Robert Falls, *TN*, Ser 2, Vol 16, 16.

51. Charlie Moses, *MS*, Sup, Ser 1, Vol 9, P 4, 1603.

52. Aunt Dilcie Raborn, *AR*, Ser 2, Vol 9, P 3, 333.

53. Elodga Bradford, *MS*, Sup, Ser 1, Vol 6, P 1, 186.

54. Clara Davis, *AL*, Ser 1, Vol 6, 110. See also Aaron Carter, *MS*, Sup, Ser 1, Vol 7, P 2, 360.

55. Fanny Hodges, *MS*, Ser 1, Vol 7, 71.

56. Sonia Rassbury, *AR*, Ser 2, Vol 10, P 6, 16.

57. Laura Montgomery, *MS*, Sup, Ser 1, Vol 9, P 4, 1558–1559.

58. Manda Edmondson, *MS*, Sup, Ser 1, Vol 7, P 2, 678.

59. Phyllis Fox, *MS*, Sup, Ser 1, Vol 7, P 2, 768.

Chapter 12

1. Report of General O.O. Howard, commissioner of the Freedmen's Bureau, 1865, in Memphis *Daily Appeal*, December 28, 1865; Address of General Clinton B. Fisk at Collins Church, Memphis, December 4, 1865, in Memphis *Daily Appeal*, December 5, 1865.

2. Report of John A. Staley, captain and inspector of the Freedmen's Bureau, November 16, 1865, in Memphis *Daily Appeal*, November 18, 1865; Roger L. Ransom and Richard Sutch, *One Kind of Freedom: The Economic Consequences of Emancipation* (Cambridge: Cambridge University Press, 1977), 160–163.

3. Speech of General Clinton B. Fisk to Freedmen, of Tennessee, at Nashville, September 1, 1866, in Memphis *Daily Appeal*, September 7, 1866.

4. Report of Major H. Sweeny of the Freedmen's Bureau from Helena, Arkansas, in Memphis *Post*, January 16, 1867.

5. Rudd and Bond, *From Slavery to Wealth*; Roark, *Masters Without Slaves*, 147–165.

6. Jake Dawkins, *MS*, Sup, Ser 1, Vol 7, P 2, 597–598; Columbus Williams, *AR*, Ser 2, Vol 11, P 7, 157. See also Forrest McDonald and Grady McWhiney "The South From Self-Sufficency To Peonage: An Interpretation," *American Historical Review*, Vol 85, No. 5 (December, 1980), 1095–1118.

7. Ebenezer Brown, *MS*, Sup, Ser 1, Vol 6, P 1, 251–252.

8. Ann Drake, *MS*, Sup, Ser 1, Vol 7, P 2, 648–649.

9. Edmond Jones, *AR*, Ser 2, Vol 9, P 4, 142; Tom Robinson, *AR*, Ser 2, Vol 10, P 6, 67–68.

10. Henrietta Evelina Smith, *AR*, Ser 2, Vol 10, P 6, 195.

11. Gabe Butler, *MS*, Sup, Ser 1, Vol 6, P 1, 326.

12. Jane Lassiter, *NC*, Ser 2, Vol 15, P 2, 41. See also Mingo White, *AL*, Ser 1, Vol 6, 421.

13. Jane Arrington, *NC*, Ser 2, Vol 14, P 1, 49.

14. Willis Cofer, *GA*, Ser 2, Vol 12, P 1, 210.

15. Addy Gill, *NC*, Ser 2, Vol 14, P 1, 326–327; Columbus Williams, *AR*, Ser 2, Vol 11, P 7, 157; Moses Jefferies, *AR*, Ser 2, Vol 9, P 4, 40; Sarah Williams Wells, *AR*, Ser 2, Vol 11, P 7, 95; Richard McDaniel, *AR*, Ser 2, Vol 10, P 5, 15.

16. Gus Bradshaw, *TX*, Ser 1, Vol 4, P 1, 132; Mary Ann Patterson, *TX*, Ser 1, Vol 5, P 3, 172.

17. Betty Powers, *TX*, Ser 1, Vol 5, P 3, 192.

18. Alec Woodward, *SC*, Ser 1, Vol 3, P 4, 256; Bunk Ratliff, *MS*, Sup, Ser 1, Vol 9, P 4, 1798–1799; Ann May, *AR*, Ser 2, Vol 10, P 5, 67; Steve Weathersby, *MS*, Sup, Ser 1, Vol 10, P 5, 2248; Louis Johnson, *AR*, Ser 2, Vol 9, P 4, 106.

19. Parker Pool, *NC*, Ser 2, Vol 15, P 2, 190–191; Sam Jones, *TX*, Ser 1, Vol 5, P 3, 140; Annie Young, *AR*, Ser 2, Vol 11, P 7, 254; James Henry Nelson, *AR*, Ser 2, Vol 10, P 5, 206.

20. George Greene, *AR*, Ser 2, Vol 9, P 3, 110; Juda Dantzler, *MS*, Sup, Ser 1, Vol 7, P 2, 557; James Cornelius, *MS*, Sup, Ser 1, Vol 7, P 2, 505; Frank Patterson, *AR*, Ser 2, Vol 10, P 5, 281; Armstead Barrett, *TX*, Ser 1, Vol 4, P 1, 48.

21. Henry C. Pettus, *AR*, Ser 2, Vol 10, P 5, 341; Ishe Web, *AR*, Ser 2, Vol 11, P 7, 79; Mary Jane Mooreman, *AR*, Ser 2, Vol 10, P 5, 132; Ambus Gray, *AR*, Ser 2, Vol 9, P 3, 78; Tom Wylie Neal, *AR*, Ser 2, Vol 10, P 5, 183; Andrew Gregory, *AR*, Ser 2, Vol 9, P 3, 112; Bill Simms, *KS*, Ser 2, Vol 16, 10–12.

22. Larkin Payne, *AR*, Ser 2, Vol 10, P 5, 307; Larnce Holt, *TX*, Ser 1, Vol 4, P 2, 152; Pink Holly, *AR*, Ser 2, Vol 9, P 3, 306; Henry Nelson, *AR*, Ser 2, Vol 10, P 5, 201 Robert Solomon, *AR*, Ser 2, Vol 10, P 6, 209.

23. Harrison Boyd, *TX*, Ser 1, Vol 4, P 1, 113; Augustus Robinson, *AR*, Ser 2, Vol 10, P 6, 59; Tony Piggy, *AR*, Ser 2, Vol 10, P 5, 346; Wash Anderson, *TX*, Ser 1, Vol 4, P 1, 19–20; William Hunter, *AR*, Ser 2, Vol 9, P 3, 368; Louis Cain, *TX*, Ser 1, Vol 4, P 1, 187; Frank Wise, *AR*, Ser 2, Vol 11, P 7, 219; Berry Smith, *MS*, Sup,

Ser 1, Vol 10, P 5, 1981–1983; Austin Grant, *TX*, Ser 2, Vol 4, P 2, 86; Lindsey Faucette, *NC*, Ser 2, Vol 14, P 1, 305.

24. Cicero Frank, in Blassingame, *Slave Testimony*, 584; Seabe Tuttle, *AR*, Ser 2, Vol 10, P 6, 370; Henry Probasco, *TX*, Ser 1, Vol 5, P 3, 206; Lizzie Baker, *NC*, Ser 2, Vol 14, P 1, 68–69; George W. Harris, *NC*, Ser 2, Vol 14, P 1, 373; Jake Walker, *AR*, Ser 2, Vol 11, P 7, 37; Sylvester Sostan Wickliffe, *TX*, Ser 1, Vol 5, P 4, 159.

25. Jack Bess, *TX*, Ser 1, Vol 4, P 1, 74; Henry Lewis, *TX*, Ser 1, Vol 5, P 3, 13; John Price, *TX*, Ser 1, Vol 5, P 3, 199; John Sneed, *TX*, Ser 1, Vol 5, P 3, 50–51; James Martin, *TX*, Ser 1, Vol 5, P 3, 64; Tom Mills, *TX*, Ser 1, Vol 5, P 3, 98–100; Ben Kinchlow, *TX*, Ser 1, Vol 4, P 3, 263–277; Walter Rimm, *TX*, Ser 1, Vol 5, P 3, 250–251.

26. Madison Bruin, *TX*, Ser 1, Vol 4, P 1, 172–173; William Davis, *TX*, Ser 1, Vol 4, P 1, 293. See also Tom Mills, *TX*, Ser 1, Vol 5, P 3, 99; James Martin, *TX*, Ser 1, Vol 5, P 3, 64.

27. Sam Scott, *AR*, Ser 2, Vol 10, P 6, 131–133.

28. Warren Taylor, *AR*, Ser 2, Vol 10, P 6, 278.

29. Holt Collier, *MS*, Sup, Ser 1, Vol 7, P 2, 447; Joe Golden, *AR*, Ser 2, Vol 9, P 3, 49–52.

30. Edgar Bendy, *TX*, Ser 1, Vol 4, P 1, 67.

31. James Spikes, *AR*, Ser 1, Vol 10, P 6, 213. See also Ransom Simmons, *SC*, Ser 1, Vol 3, P 4, 91.

32. John Love, *TX*, Ser 1, Vol 5, P 3, 27; Jenny Proctor, *TX*, Ser 1, Vol 5, P 3, 217; Ellis Ken Kannon, *TN*, Ser 2, Vol 16, 39; Andy Odell, *TN*, Ser 2, Vol 16, 61; Lewis Jones, *TX*, Ser 1, Vol 4, P 2, 239.

33. James Jackson, *TX*, Ser 1, Vol 4, P 2, 184.

34. Barney Alford, *MS*, Sup, Ser 1, Vol 6, P 1, 30–33; Henry Murray, *MS*, Sup, Ser 1, Vol 9, P 4, 1617; John Logan, *AR*, Ser 2, Vol 9, P 4, 279.

35. Rudd and Bond, *From Slavery to Wealth*, 200.

36. Mary Harris, *AR*, Ser 2, Vol 9, P 3, 177.

37. Rosa Simmons, *AR*, Ser 2, Vol 10, P 6, 158.

38. Susan Castle, *GA*, Ser 2, Vol 12, P 1, 182–183; Sarah Poindexter, *SC*, Ser 1, Vol 3, P 3, 270; Emma Johnson, *MS*, Sup, Ser 1, Vol 8, P 3, 1156; Mary Gaines, *AR*, Ser 2, Vol 9, P 3, 9; Tilday Collins, *AL*, Ser 1, Vol 6, 85–86; Maggie Wesmoland, *AR*, Ser 2, Vol 11, P 7, 103; Mandy Morrow, *TX*, Ser 1, Vol 5, P 3, 140; Becky Hawkins, *AR*, Ser 2, Vol 9, P 3, 210; Gracie Mitchell, *AR*, Ser 2, Vol 10, P 5, 108–109; Rosina Hoard, *TX*, Ser 1, Vol 4, P 2, 143. See Also Jones, *Labor of Love, Labor of Sorrow*, 52–56.

39. Sumner Eliot Matison, "The Labor Movement and the Negro During Reconstruction," *Journal of Negro History*, XXXIII, No. 4, (October, 1948) 426–468, 440.

40. *Ibid.*,460–465.

41. J.H. Harmon, "The Negro as a Local Business Man," *Journal of Negro History*, XIV, No. 2, (April, 1929), 116–155; 122–123.

42. *Ibid.*, 126–128; for R.R. Church see *Planter's Journal*, Memphis, Tennessee, September 15, 1906.

43. Harmon, "The Negro as a Local Business Man," 126–128.

44. Arnett G. Lindsay, "The Negro in Banking," *Journal of Negro History*, XIV, No. 2, (April, 1929), 156–201.

45. C.G. Woodson, "Insurance Business Among Negroes," *Journal of Negro History*, XIV, No. 2, (April, 1929), 200–226; 204–205.

46. *Ibid.*, 208–209.

Bibliographical Essay

The books and articles mentioned below are principal sources used by the author in writing this book. Of special value is *The American Slave: A Composite Autobiography*, edited by George P. Rawick (19 vols., Greenwood Press, Westport, Conn., 1972–1979). *The American Slave* reprints, with an introductory volume by the editor, 2000 interviews with ex-slaves by Fisk University and the Federal Writers Project of the Works Progress Administration in the 1920s and 1930s. The greater portion of the interviews were made by the Federal Writers Project in the 1930s. These interviews express every aspect of the slaves' lives and their later experiences as a freed people. John W. Blassingame, ed., *Slave Testimony: Two Centuries of Letters, Speeches, Interviews, and Autobiographies* (Louisiana State University Press, Baton Rouge, 1977), like *The American Slave*, portrays the nature of slavery through the experiences of many who endured it.

Willie Lee Rose, ed., *A Documentary History of Slavery in North America* (Oxford University Press, New York, 1976), presents a representative collection of documents. Rose's *Slavery and Freedom*, edited by William W. Freehling (Oxford University Press, New York, 1982), is a work of perceptive interpretation.

A contemporary observer of great acuteness recorded his observations in Frederick Law Olmsted, *Cotton Kingdom*, edited by A.M. Schlesinger, Sr. (Knopf, New York, 1953).

Ira Berlin's *Many Thousands Gone: The First Two Centuries of North America* (The Belknap Press of Harvard University Press, Cambridge, Mass., 1988), is a recent comprehensive history of major changes in American slavery from its earliest days to its demise. Harry P. Owens, ed., *Perspectives and Irony in American Slavery* (Ballantine Press, Jackson, Miss., 1976), offers valuable interpretations. Richard Wade, *Slavery in the Cities: The South 1820–1860* (Oxford University Press, New York, 1964), depicts the conditions of urban slaves.

A valuable history of the life of a kidnapped slave in the Lower South is Solomon Northup, *Twelve Years a Slave*, edited by Sue Eakin and Joseph Logsdon (Louisiana State University Press, Baton Rouge, 1968).

J. Harry Bennett, *Bondsmen and Bishops: Slavery and Apprenticeship on the Codrington Plantations of Barbados 1710–1838* (University of California Press, Berkeley, Calif., 1958), shows how plantation managers reduced their dependence on the slave trade by increasing the plantation slave birth rate and decreasing childhood mortality through ameliorating conditions of the slaves' lives. William Dosite Postell, *The Health of Slaves on Southern Plantations* (Peter Smith, Gloucester, Mass., 1970), discusses the health of slaves. Richard Starobin,

Industrial Slavery in the Old South (Oxford University Press, New York, 1970), is a useful study of slaves in Southern industrial pursuits. Lyle Saxon, Edward Dreyer, and Robert Tallant, *Gumbo YaYa: A Collection of Louisiana Folk Tales* (Bonanza Books, New York, 1945), concentrates on Louisiana blacks.

John W. Blassingame, "Status and Social Structure in the Slave Community: Evidence from New Sources," in Harry P. Owens, ed., *Perspectives and Irony in American Slavery* (Ballantine Press, Jackson, Miss., 1976), appraises the hierarchy of the plantation slave community on the basis of the slaves' service to one another. Jacqueline Jones studies the role of women in *Labor of Love, Labor of Sorrow: Black Women, Work and the Family from Slavery to the Present* (Vintage Books, New York, 1985). In *Views of Society and Manners in America*, edited by Paul R. Baker (The Belknap Press of Harvard University Press, Cambridge, Mass., 1963), the nineteenth century feminist Frances Wright describes her education of slaves for colonization abroad. J.M. Keating in the *History of Memphis, Shelby County, Tennessee* (2 vols., D. Mason, Syracuse, New York, 1888), reveals a hostile attitude toward the education of slaves and free blacks.

Cyprian Davis, O.S.B., *The History of Black Catholics in the United States* (Crossroad, New York, 1990); Randall M. Miller, "Slaves and Southern Catholicism," in John A. Boles, ed., *Masters and Slaves in the House of the Lord* (University Press of Kentucky, Lexington, 1988, 127–152); Randy Sparks, "Religion in Amite County, Mississippi, 1800–1861," also in Boles, ed., *Masters and Slaves in the House of the Lord* (69–79); and Edward D. Reynolds, S.J., *Jesuits for the Negro* (The America Press, New York, 1949), all have interesting discussions of the religion of blacks. In *Black Culture and Black Consciousness: Afro-American Folk Thought from Slavery to Freedom* (Oxford University Press, New York, 1979), Lawrence W. Levine stresses the relationship of religion and culture.

Frederick Bancroft, *Slave Trading in the Old South* (Ungar Publishing Company, New York, 1931), and Michael Tadman, *Speculators and Slaves: Masters, Traders, and Slaves in the Old South* (University of Wisconsin Press, Madison, 1980), are instructive on the internal slave trade.

J.W.C. Pennington, "The Fugitive Blacksmith," in Arna Bontemps, ed., *Great Slave Narratives*, (Boston, 1969, 193–267), and Frederick Douglass, *Life and Times of Frederick Douglass Written by Himself* (Collier Books, New York, 1962), tell the story of two great runaway slaves. The Memphis *Daily Appeal* carried frequent advertisements for the discovery and the return of runaway slaves and published a great deal of additional material about all aspects of slavery.

John Spencer Bassett, ed., *The Southern Plantation Overseer as Revealed in His Letters* (Negro Universities Press, Westport, Conn., 1972), is an interesting and informative commentary on the overseer's role in plantation management. Randall M. Miller, *"Dear Master": Letters of a Slave Family* (Cornell University Press, Ithaca, 1978), reveals the considerable influence of an important house servant in the operation of a large Alabama plantation. William Van De Burg, *The Slave Driver: Black Agricultural Labor Supervisors in the Antebellum South* (Oxford University Press, New York, 1988), sympathetically portrays the black slave driver as an important figure in plantation management and an honorable character in the black community.

War of the Rebellion: A Compilation of the Official Records of the Union and Confederate Armies (128 vols., Government Printing Office, Washington, 1880–1901), and *War of the Rebellion: Official Records of the Union and Confederate Navies* (30 vols., Government Printing Office, Washington,

1894–1922), are massive collections of civilian and military documents that are of inestimable importance for the study of the Civil War. These documents contain much material on slaves, freedmen, and black soldiers as well as an abundance of material on every phase of the Civil War. Numerous individuals recount their experiences in the war in *The American Slave: A Composite Autobiography*, mentioned above.

Roy P. Basler, ed., *The Collected Works of Abraham Lincoln* (8 vols., Rutgers University Press, New Brunswick, N.J., 1953), includes letters and documents of Lincoln's dealings with the great question of slavery and freedom as well as innumerable other documents revealing his intense involvement in every aspect of the Civil War. Papers and writings of some of Lincoln's men that record the ending of slavery are: U.S. Grant, *Personal Memoirs* (2 vols., Century, New York, 1885–1886), and *Report of Lieutenant General Grant of the Armies of the United States 1864–1865* (Adjutant General's Office, November 18, 1865, Washington, 1865); William T. Sherman, *The Sherman Letters: Correspondence Between General and Senator from 1837–1891* (C. Scribner's Sons, New York, 1894); P.H. Sheridan, *Personal Memoirs* (2 vols., C.L. Webster, New York, 1888); John W. DeForest, *A Volunteer's Adventures: A Union Captain's Record of the Civil War* (edited by James H. Croushore, Yale University Press, New Haven, 1946); and Jack Bauer, ed., *Soldiering: The Civil War Diary of Rice C. Bull, 123rd New York Volunteer Infantry* (Presidio Press, San Raphael, Calif., 1977).

James L. Roark, *Masters Without Slaves: Southern Planters in the Civil War and Reconstruction* (W.W. Norton, New York, 1977), describes the slaveholders' reaction to the loss of their slaves.

For a one volume history of the Civil War see James McPherson, *Battle Cry of Freedom: The Civil War Era* (Oxford University Press, New York, 1988).

Contributions of black troops are treated in Dudley T. Cornish, *The Sable Arm: Negro Troops in the Union Army, 1861–1865* (W.W. Norton, New York, 1956); James M. McPherson, *The Negro's Civil War: How American Negroes Felt and Acted During the War for the Union* (Macmillan, New York, 1965); Ira Berlin and others, eds., *The Black Military Experience*, in *Freedom: A Documentary History of Emancipation, 1861–1867* (Ser. 2, Cambridge University Press, Cambridge, 1982); Joseph T. Glatthaar, *Forged in Battle: The Civil War Alliance of Black Soldiers and White Officers* (Free Press, New York, 1990).

Edwin S. Redkey, *A Grand Army of Black Men: Letters from African American Soldiers in the Union Army 1861–1865* (Cambridge University Press, New York, 1992); Donald Yacovone, ed., *A Voice of Thunder: The Civil War Letters of George E. Stephens* (University of Illinois Press, Urbana, 1997); and Corporal James Henry Gooding, *On the Altar of Freedom: A Black Soldier's Civil War Letters From the Front* (edited by Virginia Matzke Adams, University of Massachusetts Press, Amherst, 1991), honor the participation of some of the free black troops of the North.

Paul Laurence Dunbar celebrates the achievements of black troops in "The Colored Soldier," in Lida K. Wiggins, *The Life and Works of Paul Laurence Dunbar* (J.L. Nichols, Naperville, Ill., n.d., 50–52).

James H. Brewer writes of the extraordinary labor performed by slaves for the Confederate armies and governments in *The Confederate Negro: Virginia's Craftsmen and Military Laborers, 1861–1865* (Duke University Press, Durham, N.C., 1969), and Bell Irvin Wiley, *The Life of Johnny Reb: The Common Soldier of the Confederacy* (Louisiana State University Press, Baton Rouge, 1978), includes material on slaves in the Confederate army.

Educational and other services offered to black troops are found in Dudley T.

Cornish, "The Union Army as a Training School for Negroes," *Journal of Negro History*, XXXVII, No. 4 (October 1952, 368–382); Warren B. Armstrong, "Union Chaplains and the Education of Freedmen," *Journal of Negro History*, LII (April 1967), 104–115; and G.K. Eggleston, "The Work of the Relief Societies During the Civil War," *Journal of Negro History*, XIV, No. 3 (July 1929), 272–299.

Important issues in Reconstruction are dealt with in Willie Lee Rose, *Rehearsal for Reconstruction* (Vintage Books, New York, 1967); F.B. Simkins and R.H. Woody, *South Carolina During Reconstruction* (University of North Carolina Press, Chapel Hill, 1932); James Marten, *Texas: Divided Loyalty and Dissent in the Lone Star State, 1856–1874* (University Press of Kentucky, Lexington, 1990); and Richard O. Curry, "The Abolitionists and Reconstruction: A Critical Appraisal," *Journal of Southern History*, XXXIV (November 1968), 527–545.

The military's active participation in the transition of slaves to freedom is detailed in numerous reports of *The War of the Rebellion*. Other materials can be found in U.S. Grant's *Personal Memoirs*.

The American Slave contains the recollections of many blacks as they experienced "first freedom." Leon F. Litwack's *Been in the Storm So Long: The Aftermath of Slavery* (Vintage Books, New York, 1980), is a detailed history of the transition from slavery to freedom.

Information on the work of the semimilitary Freedman's Bureau may be found in Martin Abbot, *The Freedman's Bureau in South Carolina, 1865–1872* (University of North Carolina Press, Chapel Hill, 1967); report of John A. Staley, captain and inspector of the Freedman's Bureau, November 16, 1865, in Memphis *Daily Appeal*, November 18, 1865; report of General O.O. Howard, commissioner of the Freedmen's Bureau, 1865, in Memphis *Daily Appeal*,

December 28, 1865; and report of Major H. Sweeny of the Freedman's Bureau from Helena, Arkansas, in Memphis *Post*, January 16, 1867.

Herbert Aptheker, "South Carolina Negro Conventions, 1865," *Journal of Negro History*, XXXI, No. 1 (January 1946), 91–97; Edward F. Sweat, "Francis Cardoza: Profile of Integrity in Reconstruction Politics," *Journal of Negro History*, XXVI, No. 4 (October 1961), 217–232; T. Harry Williams, "The Louisiana Unification Movement of 1873," *Journal of Southern History*, XI, No. 3 (August 1945), 349–369; and R.H. Woody, "Jonathan Jasper Wright, Associate Justice of the Supreme Court of South Carolina, 1870–1877," *Journal of Negro History*, XVIII, No. 2 (April 1933), 114–131, all emphasize politics.

House of Representatives, 39th Congress, 1st Session, Report No. 101, *Memphis Riots and Massacres*, Washington, 1866 (Arno Press, New York, 1969), and Otis A. Singletary, *Negro Militia and Reconstruction* (University of Texas Press, Austin, 1957), deal with violent opposition to radical Reconstruction government in the South.

Clarence Bacote reports on the career of a local black politician in "William Finch, Negro Councilman and Political Activist in Atlanta During Early Reconstruction," *Journal of Negro History*, XL, No. 4 (October 1955), 341–364.

The Memphis *Daily Appeal* (1865–1875), the Memphis *Post* (1866–1869) and the *New Orleans Louisianian* (1874–1878) are useful sources of material on politics and society in the lower Mississippi valley. Focused on education are Henry Allen Bullock, *A History of Negro Education in the South from 1619 to the Present* (Harvard University Press, Cambridge, Mass., 1967); Edgar W. Knight, *Public Education in the South* (Ginn, 1922); Loretta Funke, "The Negro in Education," *Journal of Negro History*, V, No. 1 (January 1920), 1–21; L.P.

Jackson, "The Origin of Hampton Institute," *Journal of Negro History*, X, No. 2 (April 1925), 111–126; Alrutheus A. Taylor, "Fisk University and the Nashville Community, 1866–1900," *Journal of Negro History*, XXXIX, No. 2 (April 1954), 111–126; Philip S. Foner, "Address of Frederick Douglass at the Inauguration of Douglas Institute, Baltimore, October 1, 1865," *Journal of Negro History*, LIV, No. 2 (April 1969), 175–177; speech of General Clinton B. Fisk to freedmen of Tennessee, at Nashville, September 1, 1866, in Memphis *Daily Appeal*, September 7, 1866; George Gurtner, "Color Blind in New Orleans," *Our Sunday Visitor*, January 7, 1996; Louis R. Harlan, "Desegregation in New Orleans Public Schools During Reconstruction," *American Historical Review*, LXVII, No. 3 (April 1962), 663–675; James H. O'Donnell III, ed., "A Freedman Thanks His Patrons: Letters of Taylor Thistle, 1872–1873," *Journal of Southern History*, XXXIII, No. 1 (February 1967), 68–84.

Henry J. Cadbury, "Negro Membership in the Society of Friends," *Journal of Southern History*, XXI (April 1936), 151–213, describes the blacks' secession from an integrated church. Individuals have much to say about religion in their interviews recorded in *The American Slave: A Composite Autobiography*.

Roger L. Ransom and Richard Sutch, *One Kind of Freedom: The Economic Consequences of Emancipation* (Cambridge University Press, Cambridge, 1977), is a sophisticated economic analysis including an appraisal of the sharecrop system. See also Forest McDonald and Grady McWhiney, "The South from Self-Sufficiency to Peonage: An Interpretation," *American Historical Review*, Vol. 85, No. 5 (December 1980), 1095–1118. Testimonies of sharecroppers and laborers are found in *The American Slave: A Composite Autobiography*.

Blacks and the labor movement is the subject of Sumner Eliot Matison, "The Labor Movement and the Negro During Reconstruction," *Journal of Negro History*, XXXIII, No. 4 (October 1948), 426–468.

Dan A. Rudd and Theo. Bond, *From Slavery to Wealth: The Life of Scott Bond. The Rewards of Honesty, Industry, Economy and Perseverance* (Journal Print. Co., Madison, Ark., 1917), is a biography of a successful black businessman. Other studies of blacks in business include J.H. Harmon, "The Negro as a Local Businessman," *Journal of Negro History*, XIV, No. 2 (April 1929), 116–155; Arnett G. Lindsay, "The Negro in Banking," *Journal of Negro History*, XIV, No. 2 (April 1929), 156–201; and C.G. Woodson, "Insurance Business Among Negroes," *Journal of Negro History*, XIV, No. 2 (April 1929), 200–226.

John G. Van Deusen, "The Exodus of 1879," *Journal of Negro History*, XXI, No. 2 (April 1936), 111–129, and Roy Garvin, "Benjamin, or 'Pap' Singleton and His Followers," *Journal of Negro History*, XXXIII, No. 1 (January 1948), 1–23, write of the exodus of blacks discouraged by the failure of reconstruction governments in the South. Edwin D. Hoffman, "From Slavery to Self Reliance: The Record of Achievement of the Freedmen of the Sea Island Region," *Journal of Negro History*, XLI, No. 1 (January 1956), 8–42, and R.A. Carter, "What the Negro Had Done," *Journal of Negro History*, XI (January 1926), 1–7, on the other hand, write of the achievements of blacks.

Index

abandoned plantations: regulated by the military and the Treasury Department 113
Abernathy, William S. 50
abolitionists, abolitionist movement: provoked riots 54
Adams, Charles Francis, Jr. 167
Adams, Henry 163
Adams, Will 164
Adams, William 26
African American businessmen: favored businesses of 188; insurance companies of 190; obstacles faced by 188; success of 188 190; varieties of 188
African American military units 88, 90, 94, 104, 106, 109, 119, 120, 123, 126, 127, 129, 131, 132, 133, 135, 151–152, 184
African American politics: achievements 161; black and white coalition, 160; elections 161; political activity 157; political leaders 159; political organization 157–158; state and national 161
African American prisoners of war: abuse of 134–135; Confederate policies of 134; federal protection of 135; killed during "escape" 134; Lincoln threatened retaliation concerning 134; treatment of 133–134
African American religious expression: black churches, separation of 173; conjurers, 26, 27, 30; conversion experience 25; creation of spirituals 24; funerals 20–21; meeting places 24–25; prayer grounds 26; prayer houses 25; prayers for freedom 25; shouting, dancing and singing 24; slave clergy 22, 23; in slave-holder churches 19–23; social services of black churches 174; superstitions and magic 26, 27; visions 26

African American soldiers: in army of occupation 151; agitation for removal from South 151; in battle 131; campaigns and skirmishes 130–133; cries for vengeance of 132; education of 129, 167; garrison duty of 127, 131; hailed by black population 123, 129; joined in destruction 89, 90; numbers and casualties 135; officers of 128; opposition to 121, 122, 151; proved themselves in combat 130; raids for 123; recruitment of 105, 106, 121, 122, 123; schools for 109, 167; served with both armies 116; in state militias 152;
African American working men: artisans 63; variety of skills 63, 65
African American working women: domestic service 12–13, 62, 70, 73, 74, 75; specialization of 74, 75; variations in 65
African Methodist Episcopal Church (Raleigh, North Carolina) 168
Albright, George Washington 129
Alford, Barney 65, 186
Allen, Henry W. 199
Allen, Jim 42
Allen, Martha 42
Allen, Mathew 43
Allen, Sam 165
Allen, Washington 23
American Missionary Association 128, 167, 170

Benjamin, Sarah 144
Berry, Fanny 42
Bess, Jack 184
Best, Nathan 10, 108, 144
Betts, Ellen 32
Bibb, Henry 83
Binns, Arrie 19
Binns, Franklin 154

Bishop, Joshua 106
Bishop College 172
Black, William Edward 152
black clergy: education of 174 175; intellectual and social leaders 74; other occupations of 175–176; preaching of 176
black codes 156
black drivers 29, 70, 82; duties of 82, 83; privileges of 82 83; range of behavior 83; of slave elite 82; whipping boss 83
black military laborers: construction of forts 122; construction units of 126–127; raids to secure 123; railroad construction 126–127
black sailors: prejudice against 125; rating of 124, 125, 126
Blackburn, Jasper 157
Blackshear, Ira 165
Blackshear, Luke 46, 65
Blair, Frank P. 88
Blanchard, Olivier 21
Bland, Henry 143
Blewit, Peter 116, 142
Blount, David 47, 70, 82
Bobbit, Clay 44
Bobbitt, Henry 142
Boggans, Wanda 21, 98, 154
Boggs, Susan 22
Bolton, James 23, 35
Boles, Elvira 42
Bolton, James 142
Bond, Scott 179
Bones, Tom 116
Boone, Andrew 142
Border States: importance to the Union of 100; wooed by Confederates 101
Bost, W. L. 26, 42, 48, 58
Bostwick, Alec 57
Boudreaux, Felice 21, 154
Bowe, Mary Wallace 152
Boyd, Harrison 182
Boyd, James 32, 141
Boyd, Millie 13

215